igort

5

is the perfect number

[1994-2002]

JONATHAN CAPE

Book Design: Igort

Translation: John Cullen

Thanks to Michele Vetri for collusion and invaluable advice.

With the collaboration of: Sabrina Muzi, Omar Martini, Dimitri Moretti.

My gratitude to Simone Romani, who managed the production of this co-edition.

Special thanks to David B, Baru, Loustal.

To my overseas friends, Seth and Adrian Tomine.

Thanks also to Ina Pizzuto, Leila Marzocchi, Lorenzo Mattotti. Thanks. I mean it. Igort

i g o r t

5

dedicated to
georges simenon
george herriman

JONATHAN CAPE

Published by Jonathan Cape 2004

2 4 6 8 10 9 7 5 3 1

Entire contents copyright © Igort (Igor Tuveri) 2003

Translation copyright © John Cullen 2004

First published in Italy in 2002 as 5 è il numero perfetto by Coconino Press

First published in Great Britain in 2004 by
Jonathan Cape
Random House, 20 Vauxhall Bridge Road, London SW1V 2SA

Random House Australia (Pty) Limited
20 Alfred Street, Milsons Point, Sydney,
New South Wales 2061, Australia

Random House New Zealand Limited
18 Poland Road, Glenfield,
Auckland 10, New Zealand

Random House South Africa (Pty) Limited
Endulini, 5A Jubilee Road, Parktown 2193, South Africa

The Random House Group Limited Reg. No. 954009
www.randomhouse.co.uk

A CIP catalogue record for this book is available from the British Library

ISBN 0-224-07387-7

Printed and bound in Italy
by Coconino Press, Bologna

chapter one
Neapolitan tears

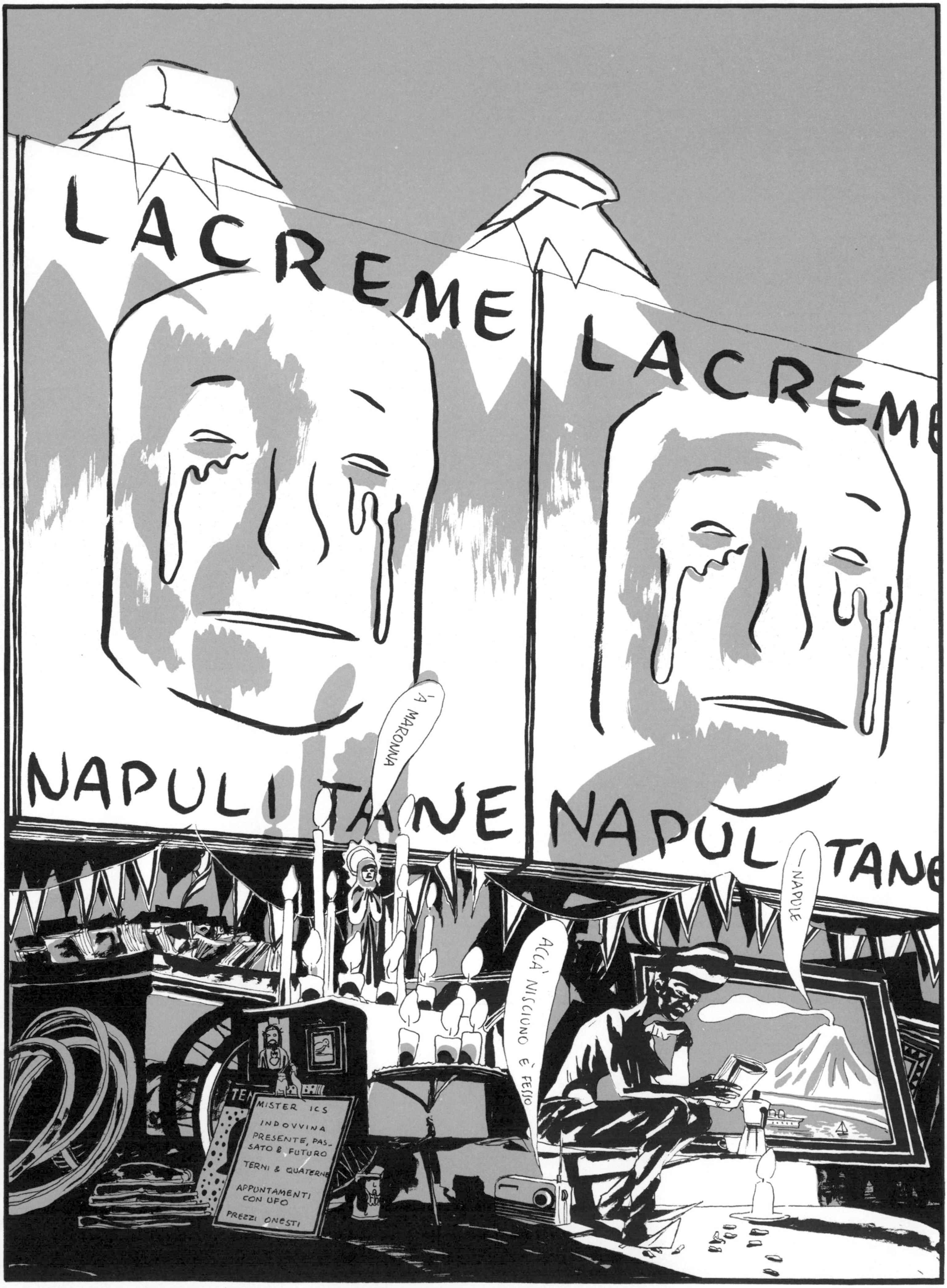
LACREME NAPULITANE
LACREME NAPULITANE
'A MARONNA
ACCÀ NISCIUNO È FESSO
—NAPULE
MISTER ICS
INDOVVINA
PRESENTE, PASSATO & FUTURO
TERNI & QUATERNE
APPUNTAMENTI CON UFO
PREZZI ONESTI

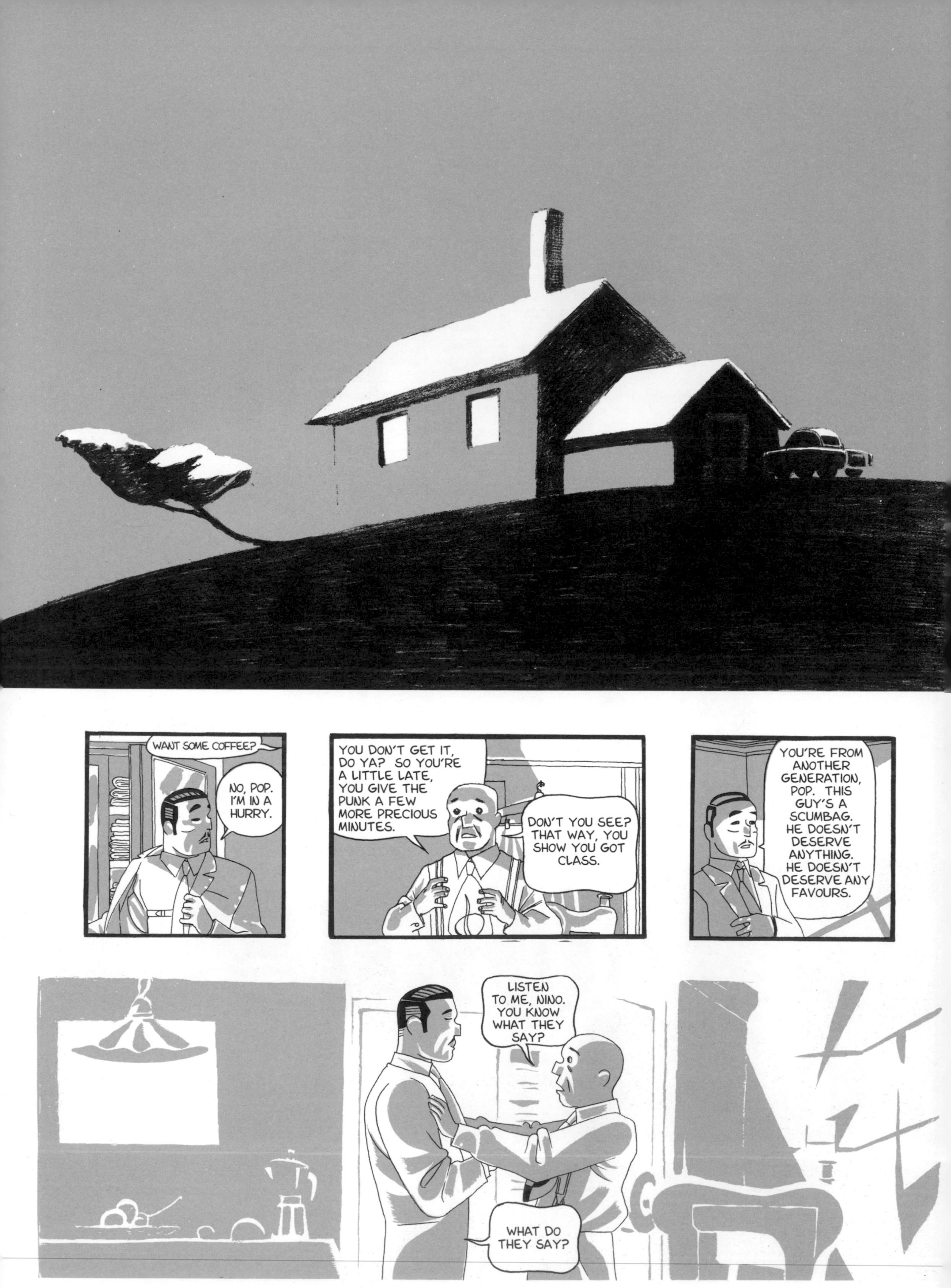
WANT SOME COFFEE?
NO, POP. I'M IN A HURRY.
YOU DON'T GET IT, DO YA? SO YOU'RE A LITTLE LATE, YOU GIVE THE PUNK A FEW MORE PRECIOUS MINUTES.
DON'T YOU SEE? THAT WAY, YOU SHOW YOU GOT CLASS.
YOU'RE FROM ANOTHER GENERATION, POP. THIS GUY'S A SCUMBAG. HE DOESN'T DESERVE ANYTHING. HE DOESN'T DESERVE ANY FAVOURS.
LISTEN TO ME, NINO. YOU KNOW WHAT THEY SAY?
WHAT DO THEY SAY?

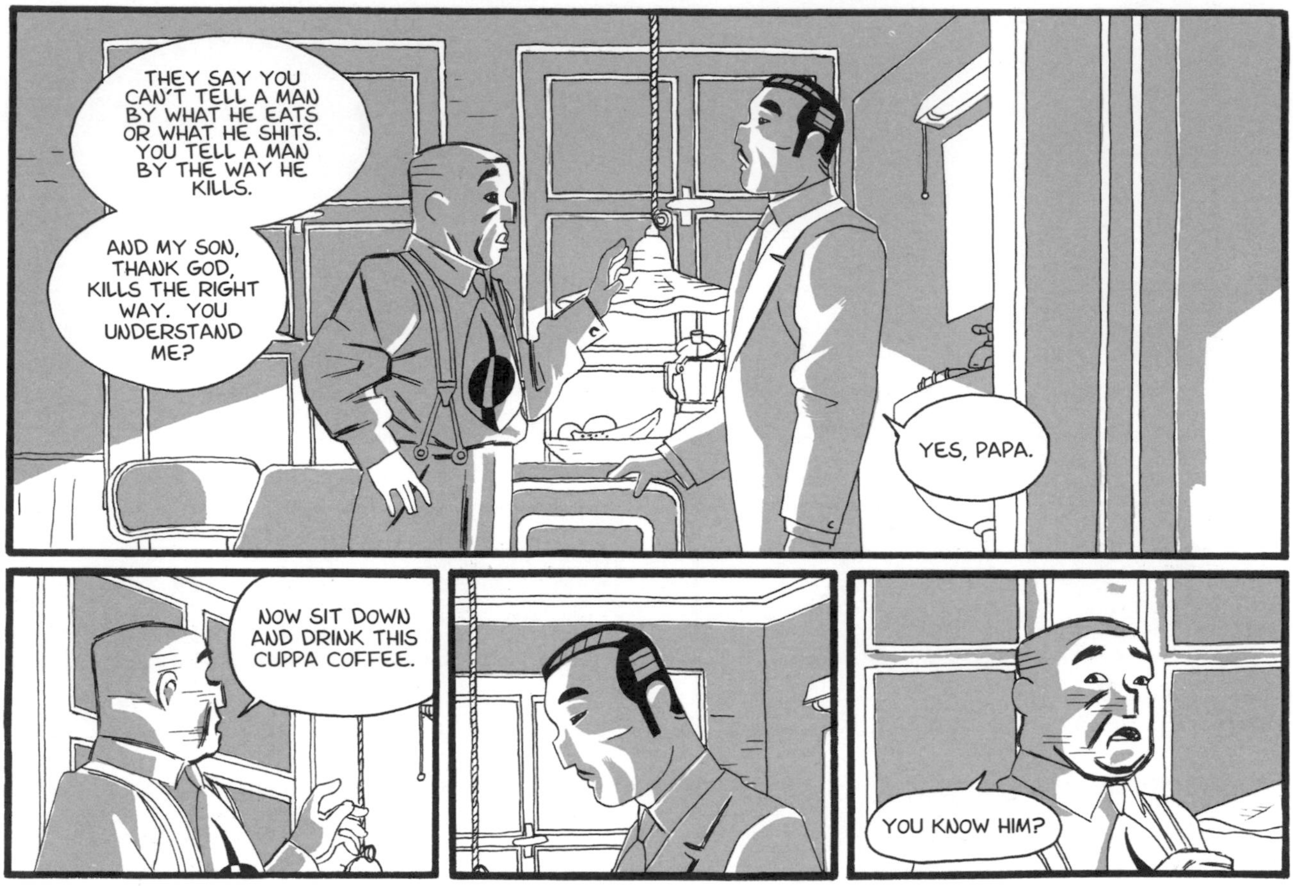
THEY SAY YOU CAN'T TELL A MAN BY WHAT HE EATS OR WHAT HE SHITS. YOU TELL A MAN BY THE WAY HE KILLS.
AND MY SON, THANK GOD, KILLS THE RIGHT WAY. YOU UNDERSTAND ME?
YES, PAPA.
NOW SIT DOWN AND DRINK THIS CUPPA COFFEE.
YOU KNOW HIM?

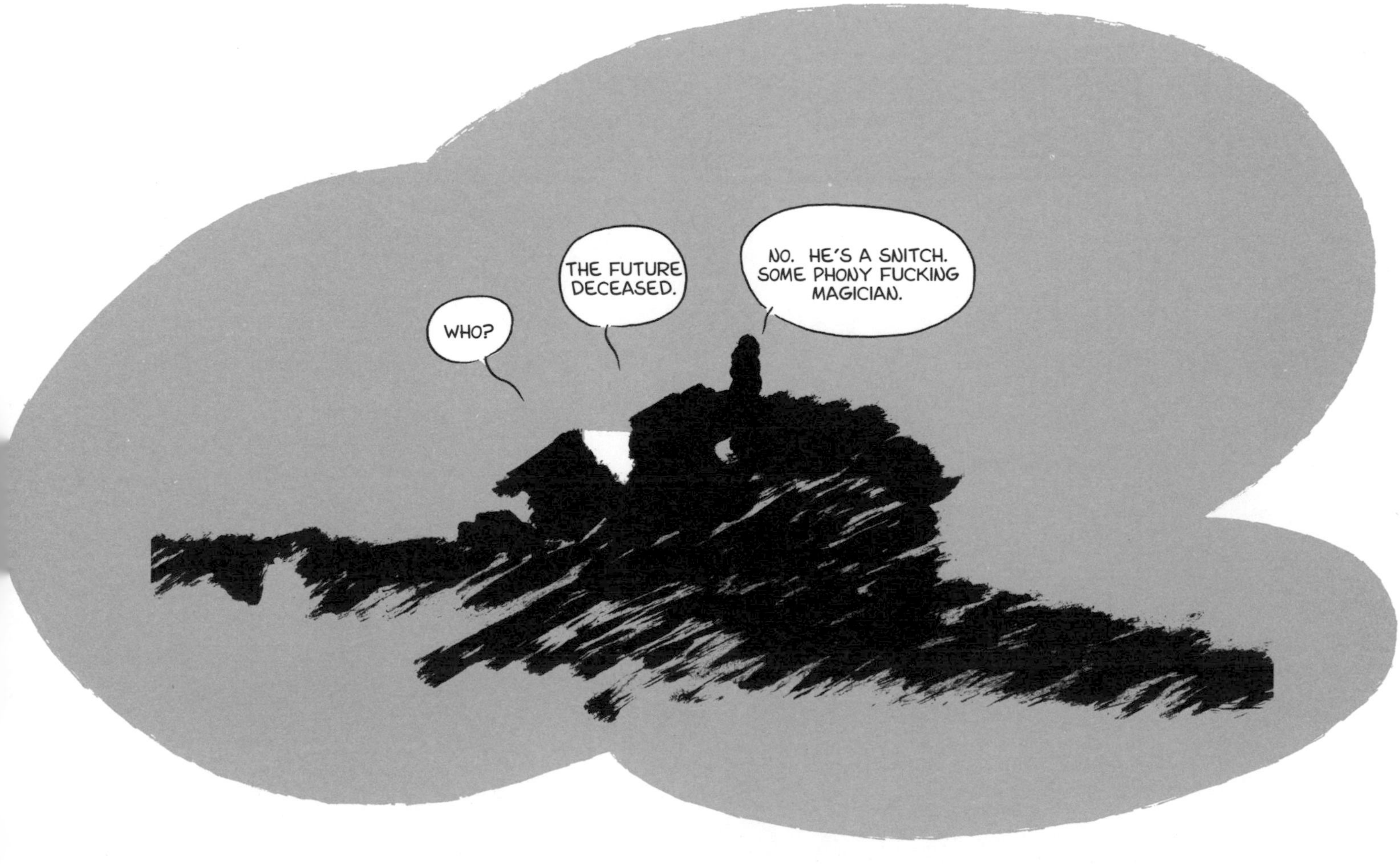
WHO?
THE FUTURE DECEASED.
NO. HE'S A SNITCH. SOME PHONY FUCKING MAGICIAN.

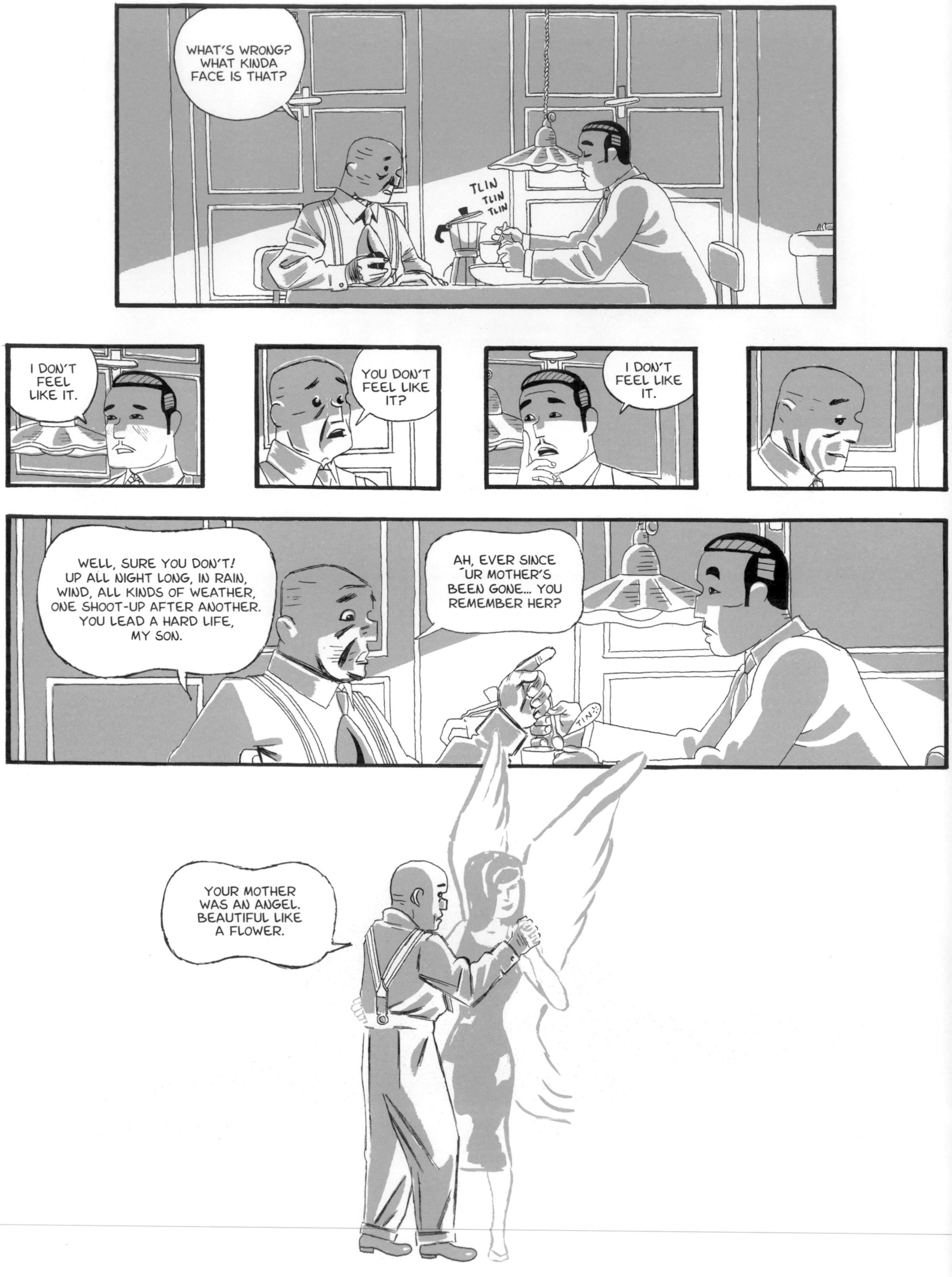
WHAT'S WRONG? WHAT KINDA FACE IS THAT?
TLIN TLIN TLIN
I DON'T FEEL LIKE IT.
YOU DON'T FEEL LIKE IT?
I DON'T FEEL LIKE IT.
WELL, SURE YOU DON'T! UP ALL NIGHT LONG, IN RAIN, WIND, ALL KINDS OF WEATHER, ONE SHOOT-UP AFTER ANOTHER. YOU LEAD A HARD LIFE, MY SON.
AH, EVER SINCE 'UR MOTHER'S BEEN GONE... YOU REMEMBER HER?
TIN
YOUR MOTHER WAS AN ANGEL. BEAUTIFUL LIKE A FLOWER.

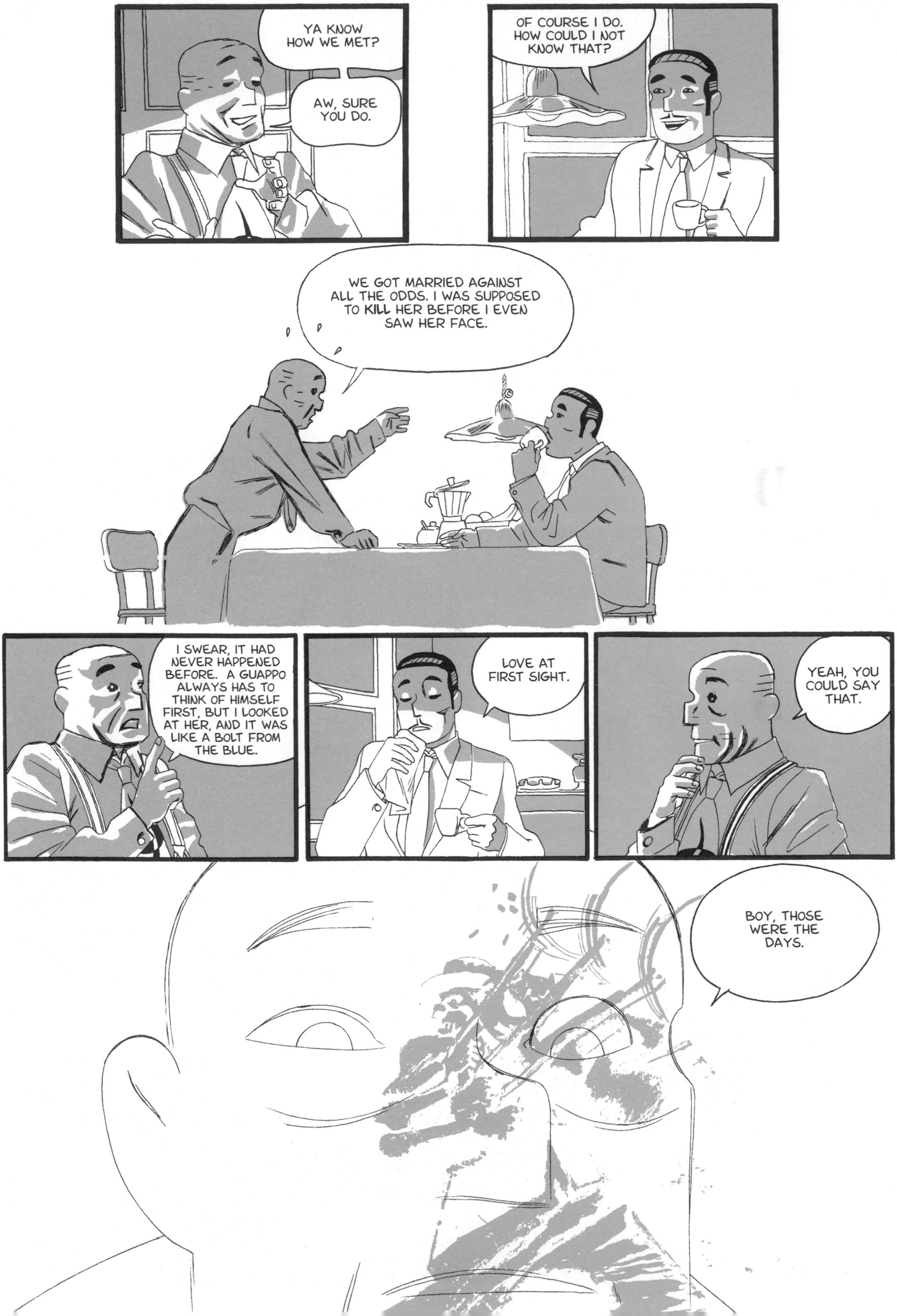
YA KNOW HOW WE MET?
AW, SURE YOU DO.
OF COURSE I DO. HOW COULD I NOT KNOW THAT?
WE GOT MARRIED AGAINST ALL THE ODDS. I WAS SUPPOSED TO **KILL** HER BEFORE I EVEN SAW HER FACE.
I SWEAR, IT HAD NEVER HAPPENED BEFORE. A GUAPPO ALWAYS HAS TO THINK OF HIMSELF FIRST, BUT I LOOKED AT HER, AND IT WAS LIKE A BOLT FROM THE BLUE.
LOVE AT FIRST SIGHT.
YEAH, YOU COULD SAY THAT.
BOY, THOSE WERE THE DAYS.

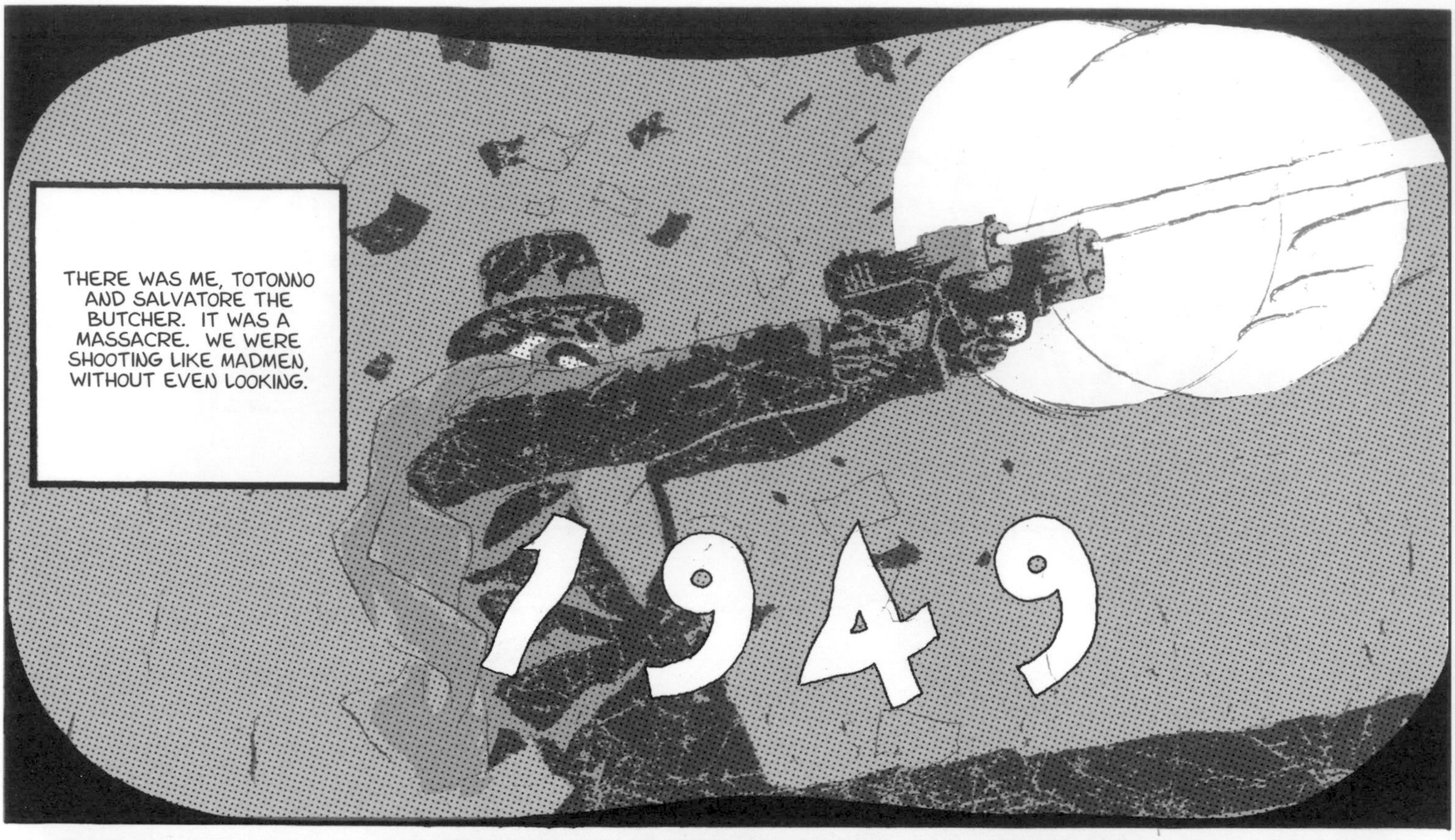
THERE WAS ME, TOTONNO AND SALVATORE THE BUTCHER. IT WAS A MASSACRE. WE WERE SHOOTING LIKE MADMEN, WITHOUT EVEN LOOKING.
1949

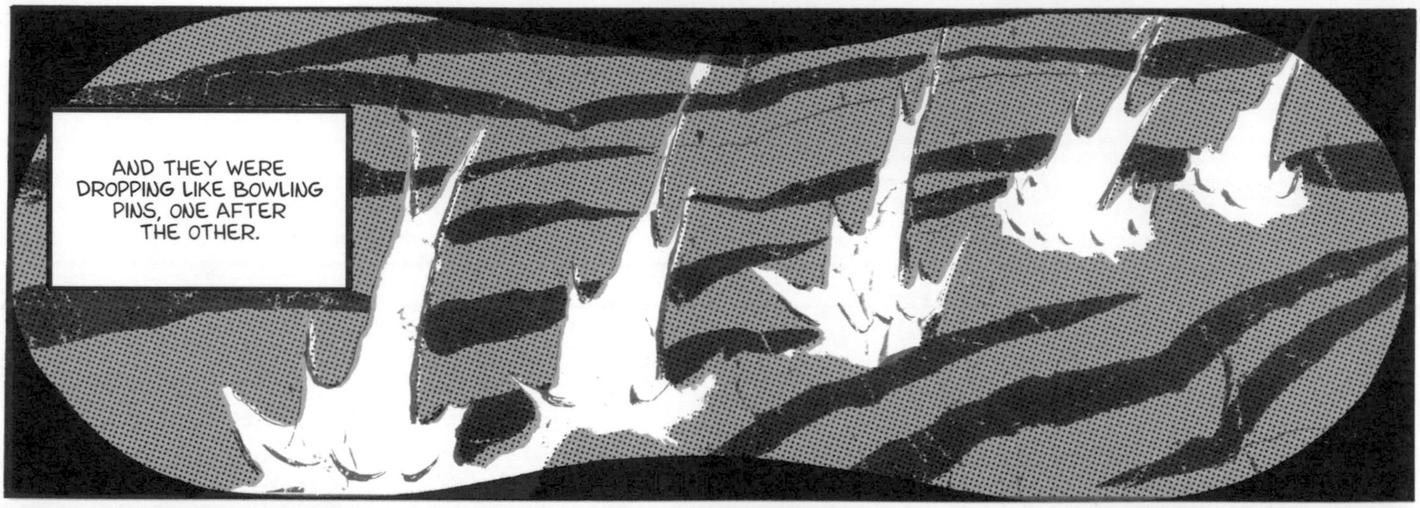
AND THEY WERE DROPPING LIKE BOWLING PINS, ONE AFTER THE OTHER.

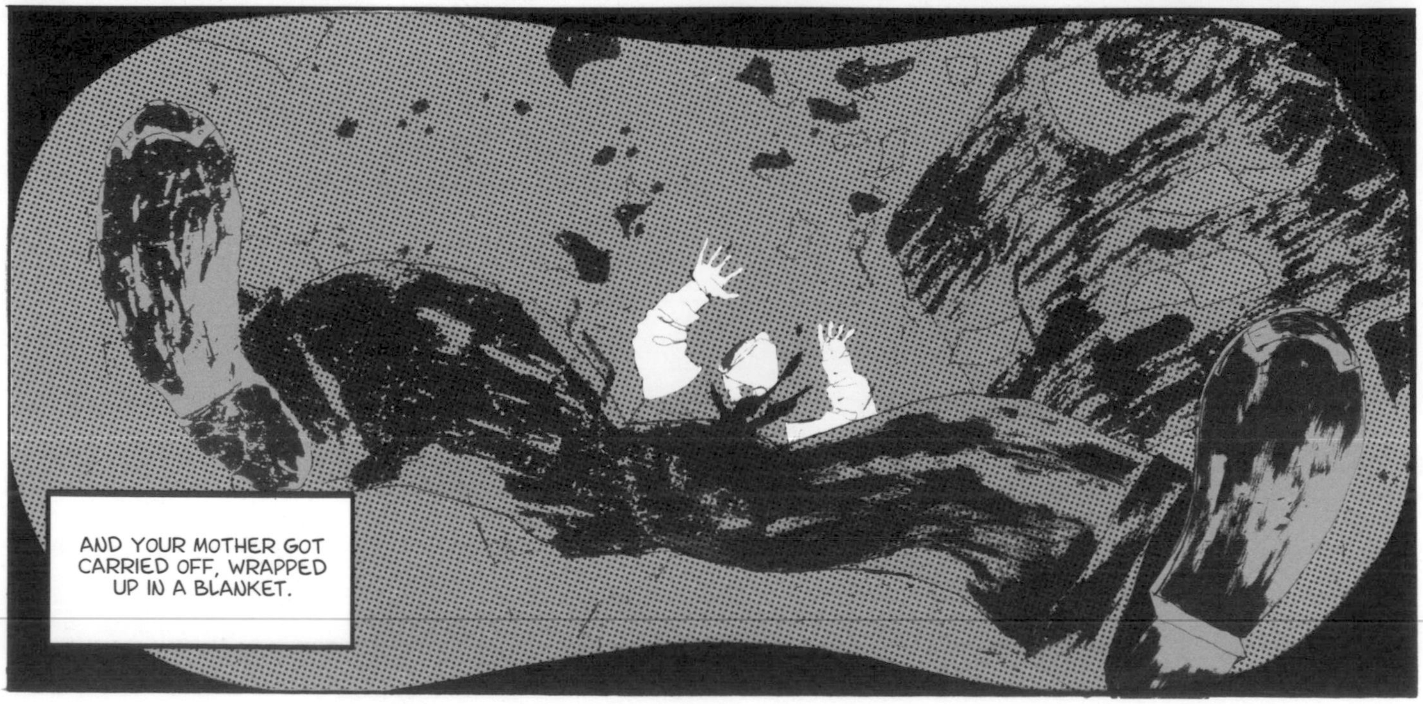
AND YOUR MOTHER GOT CARRIED OFF, WRAPPED UP IN A BLANKET.

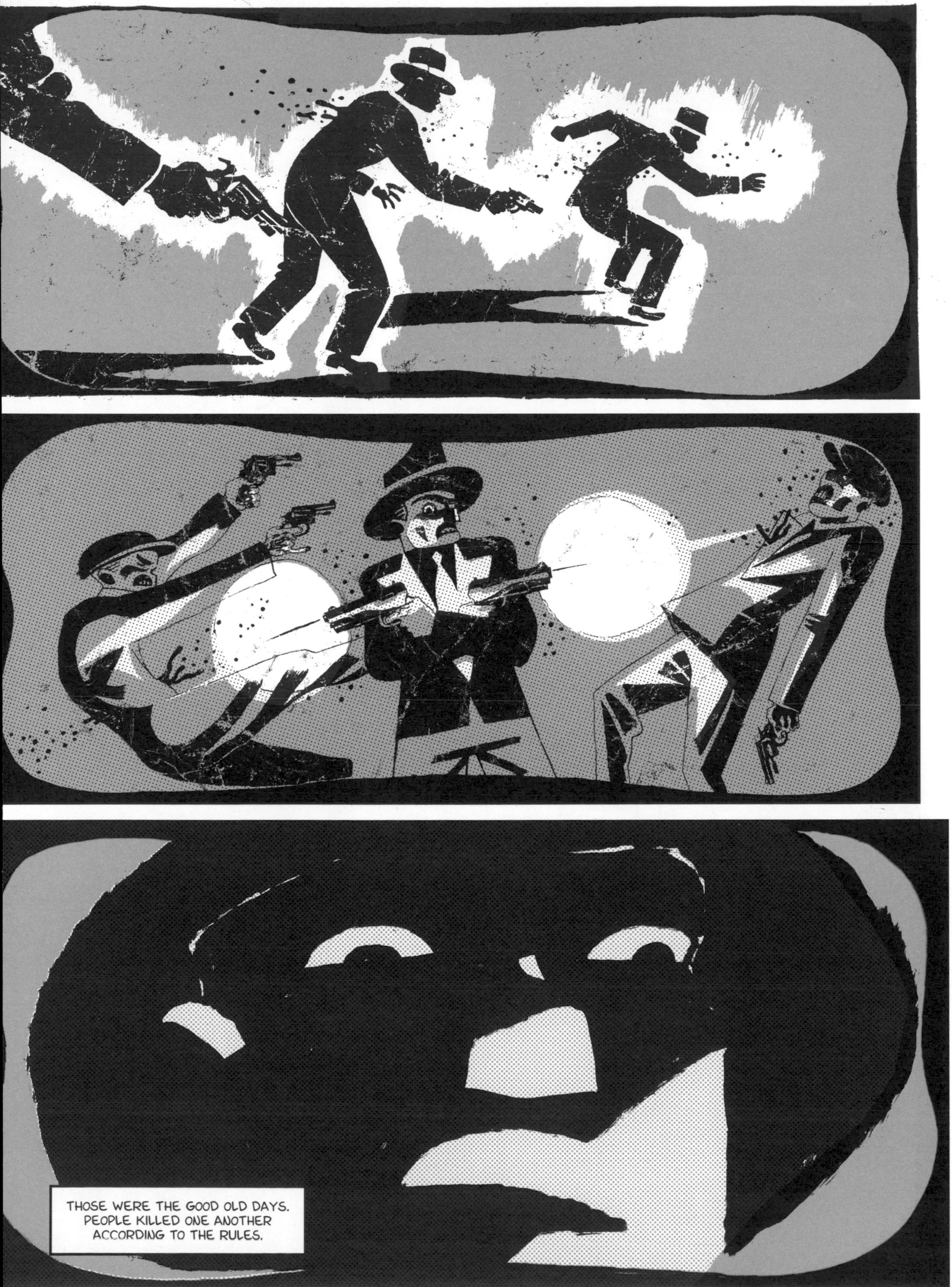
THOSE WERE THE GOOD OLD DAYS. PEOPLE KILLED ONE ANOTHER ACCORDING TO THE RULES.

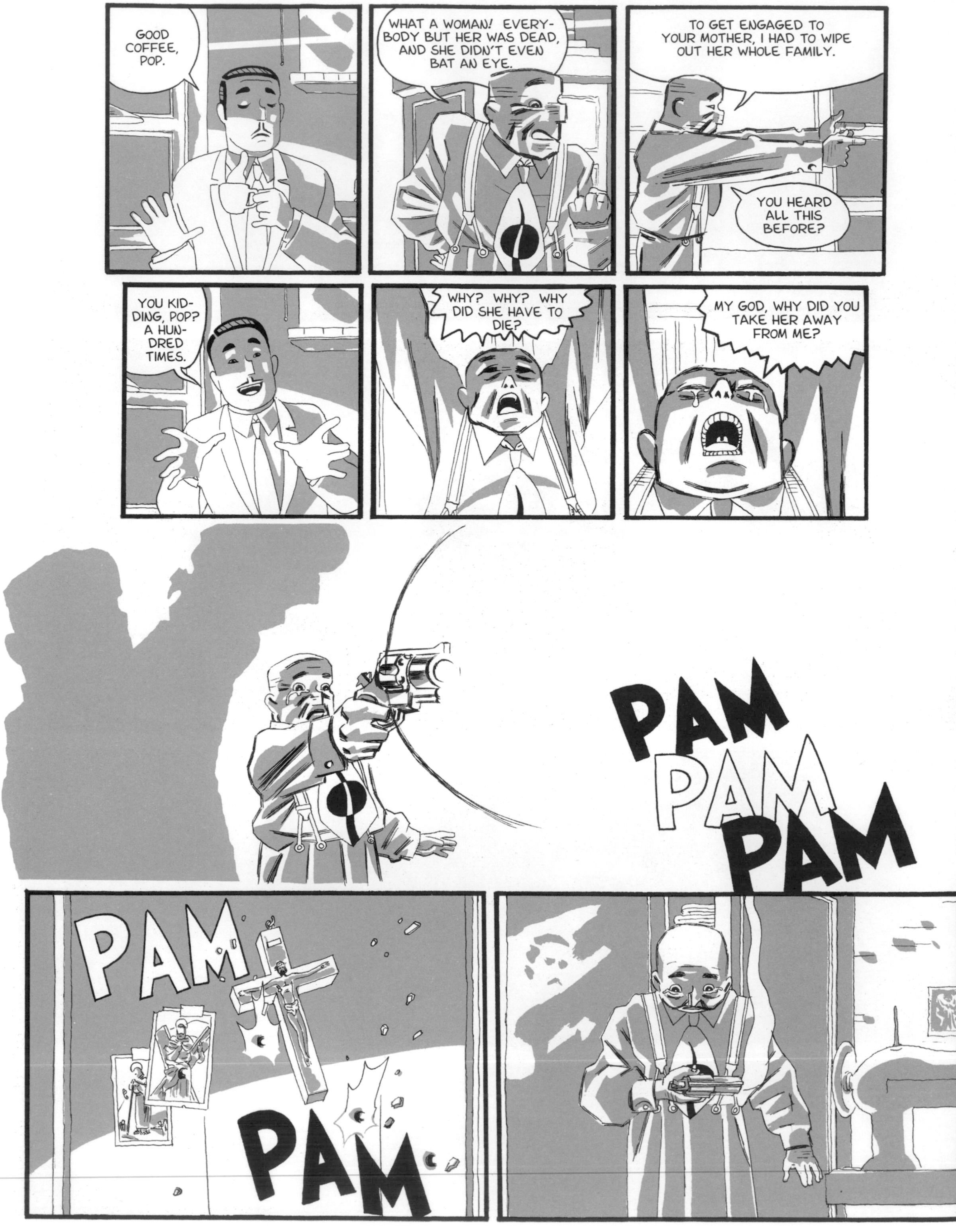
GOOD COFFEE, POP.
WHAT A WOMAN! EVERY-BODY BUT HER WAS DEAD, AND SHE DIDN'T EVEN BAT AN EYE.
TO GET ENGAGED TO YOUR MOTHER, I HAD TO WIPE OUT HER WHOLE FAMILY.
YOU HEARD ALL THIS BEFORE?
YOU KID-DING, POP? A HUN-DRED TIMES.
WHY? WHY? WHY DID SHE HAVE TO DIE?
MY GOD, WHY DID YOU TAKE HER AWAY FROM ME?
PAM
PAM
PAM
PAM
PAM

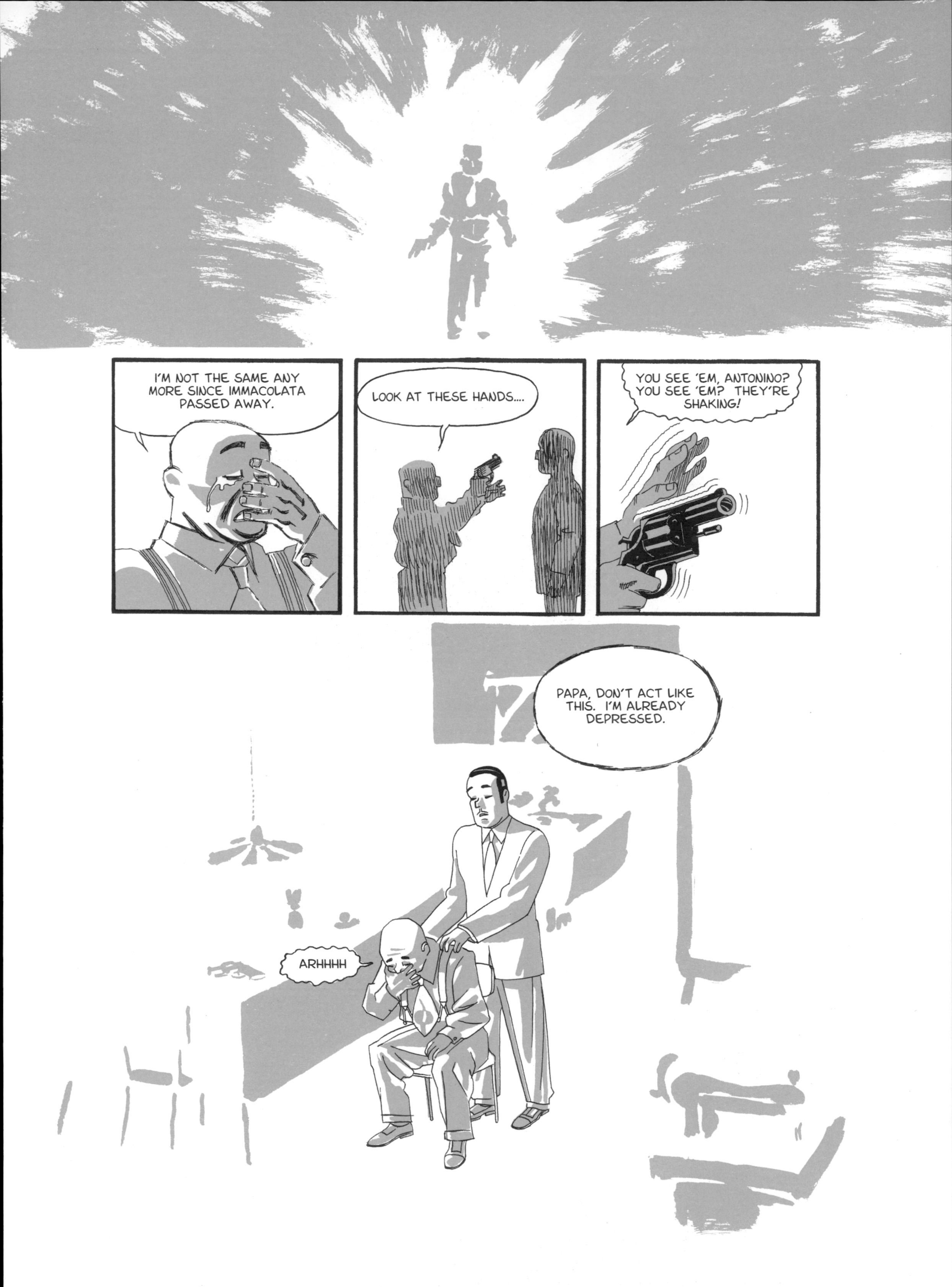
I'M NOT THE SAME ANY MORE SINCE IMMACOLATA PASSED AWAY.
LOOK AT THESE HANDS....
YOU SEE 'EM, ANTONINO? YOU SEE 'EM? THEY'RE SHAKING!
PAPA, DON'T ACT LIKE THIS. I'M ALREADY DEPRESSED.
ARHHHH

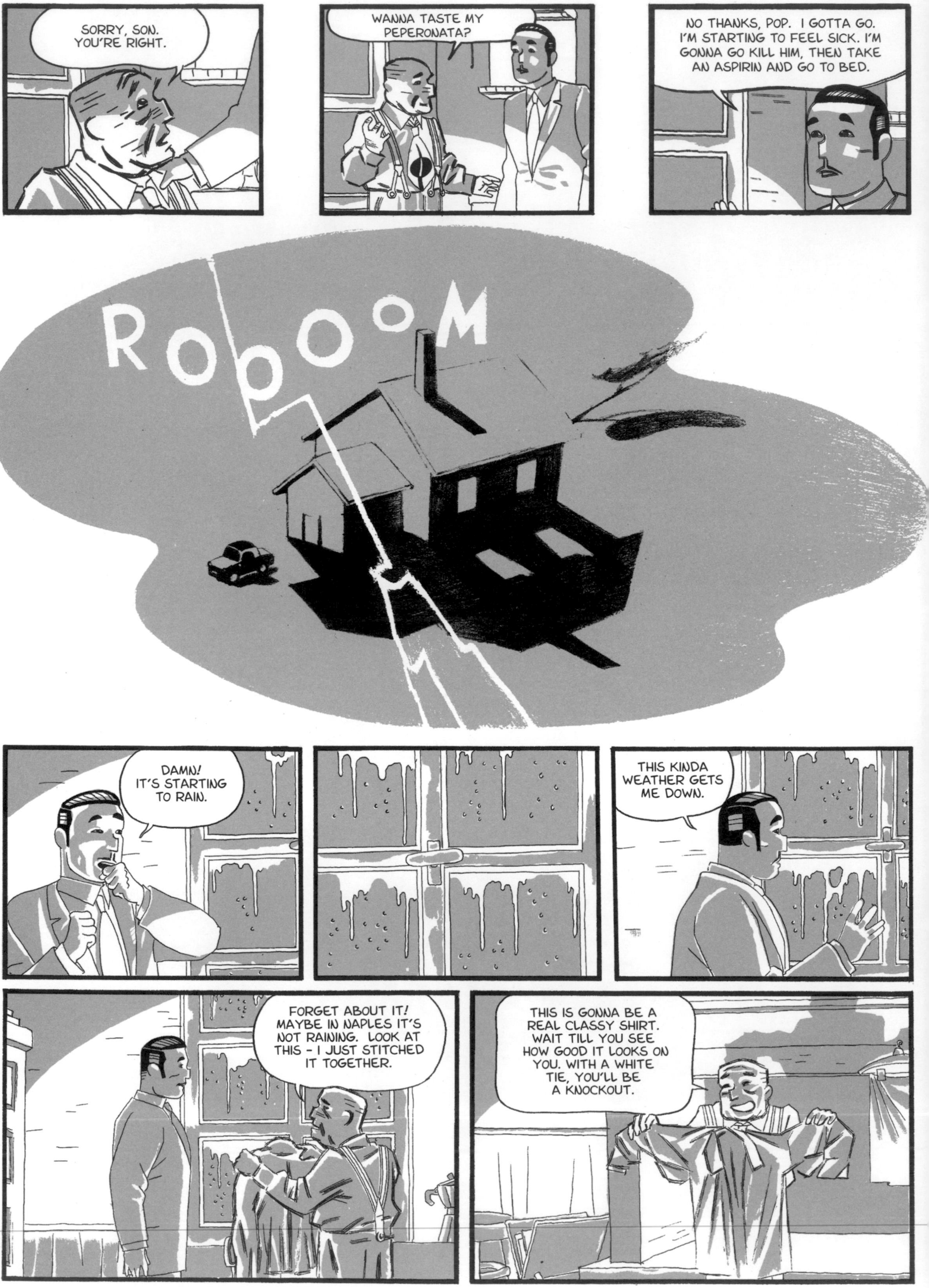
SORRY, SON. YOU'RE RIGHT.
WANNA TASTE MY PEPERONATA?
NO THANKS, POP. I GOTTA GO. I'M STARTING TO FEEL SICK. I'M GONNA GO KILL HIM, THEN TAKE AN ASPIRIN AND GO TO BED.
ROOOOM
DAMN! IT'S STARTING TO RAIN.
THIS KINDA WEATHER GETS ME DOWN.
FORGET ABOUT IT! MAYBE IN NAPLES IT'S NOT RAINING. LOOK AT THIS - I JUST STITCHED IT TOGETHER.
THIS IS GONNA BE A REAL CLASSY SHIRT. WAIT TILL YOU SEE HOW GOOD IT LOOKS ON YOU. WITH A WHITE TIE, YOU'LL BE A KNOCKOUT.

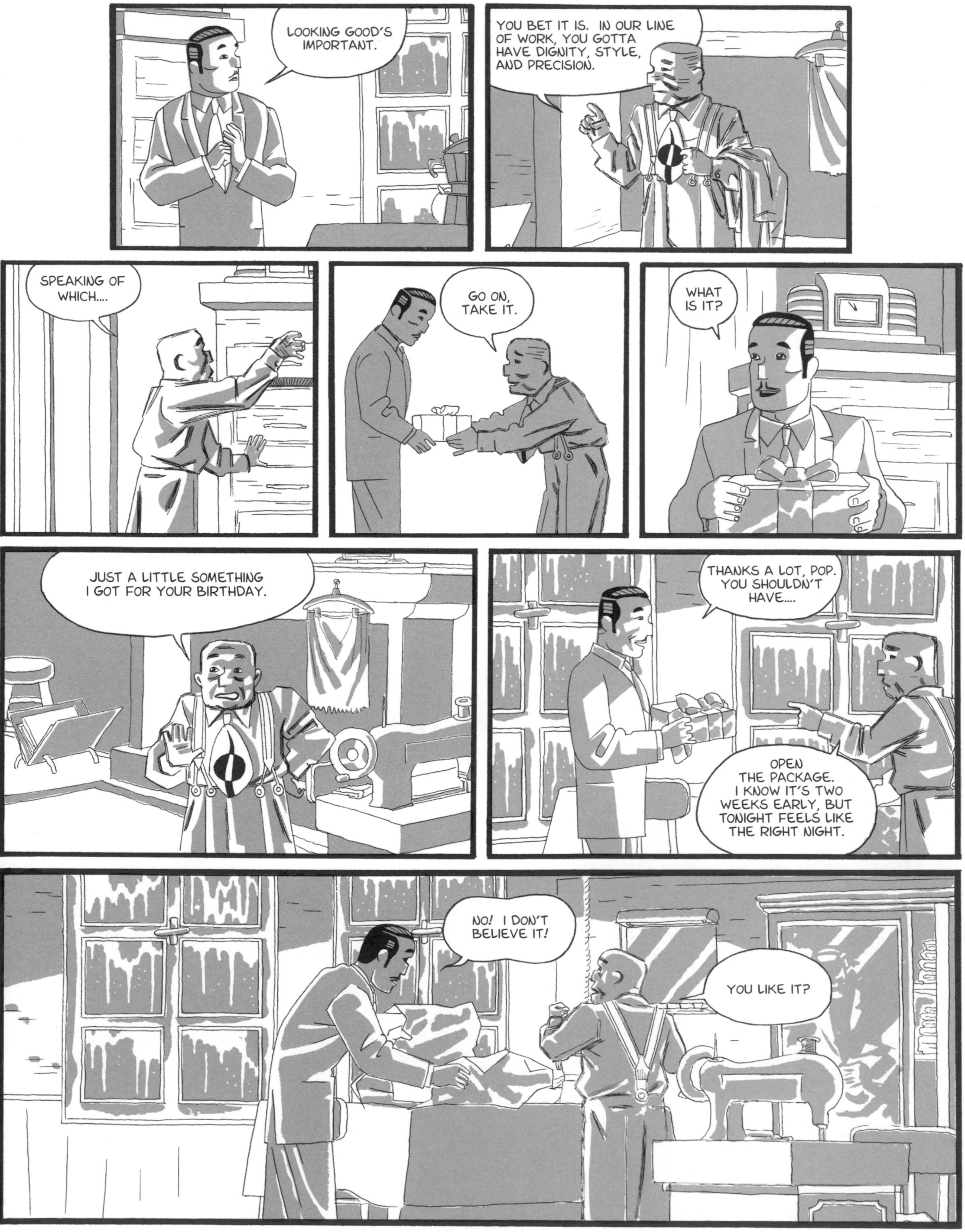
LOOKING GOOD'S IMPORTANT.
YOU BET IT IS. IN OUR LINE OF WORK, YOU GOTTA HAVE DIGNITY, STYLE, AND PRECISION.
SPEAKING OF WHICH....
GO ON, TAKE IT.
WHAT IS IT?
JUST A LITTLE SOMETHING I GOT FOR YOUR BIRTHDAY.
THANKS A LOT, POP. YOU SHOULDN'T HAVE....
OPEN THE PACKAGE. I KNOW IT'S TWO WEEKS EARLY, BUT TONIGHT FEELS LIKE THE RIGHT NIGHT.
NO! I DON'T BELIEVE IT!
YOU LIKE IT?

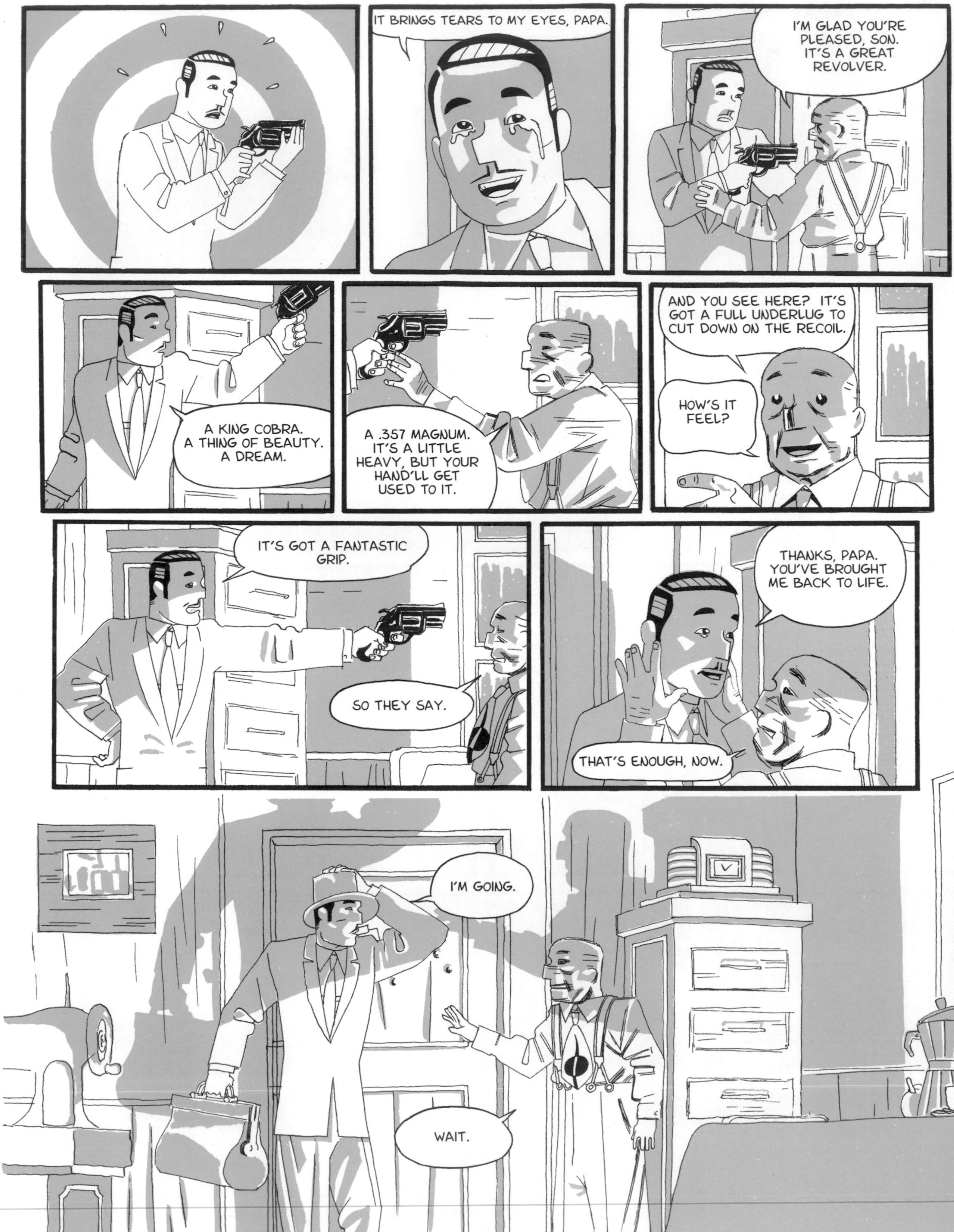
IT BRINGS TEARS TO MY EYES, PAPA.
I'M GLAD YOU'RE PLEASED, SON. IT'S A GREAT REVOLVER.
A KING COBRA. A THING OF BEAUTY. A DREAM.
A .357 MAGNUM. IT'S A LITTLE HEAVY, BUT YOUR HAND'LL GET USED TO IT.
AND YOU SEE HERE? IT'S GOT A FULL UNDERLUG TO CUT DOWN ON THE RECOIL.
HOW'S IT FEEL?
IT'S GOT A FANTASTIC GRIP.
SO THEY SAY.
THANKS, PAPA. YOU'VE BROUGHT ME BACK TO LIFE.
THAT'S ENOUGH, NOW.
I'M GOING.
WAIT.

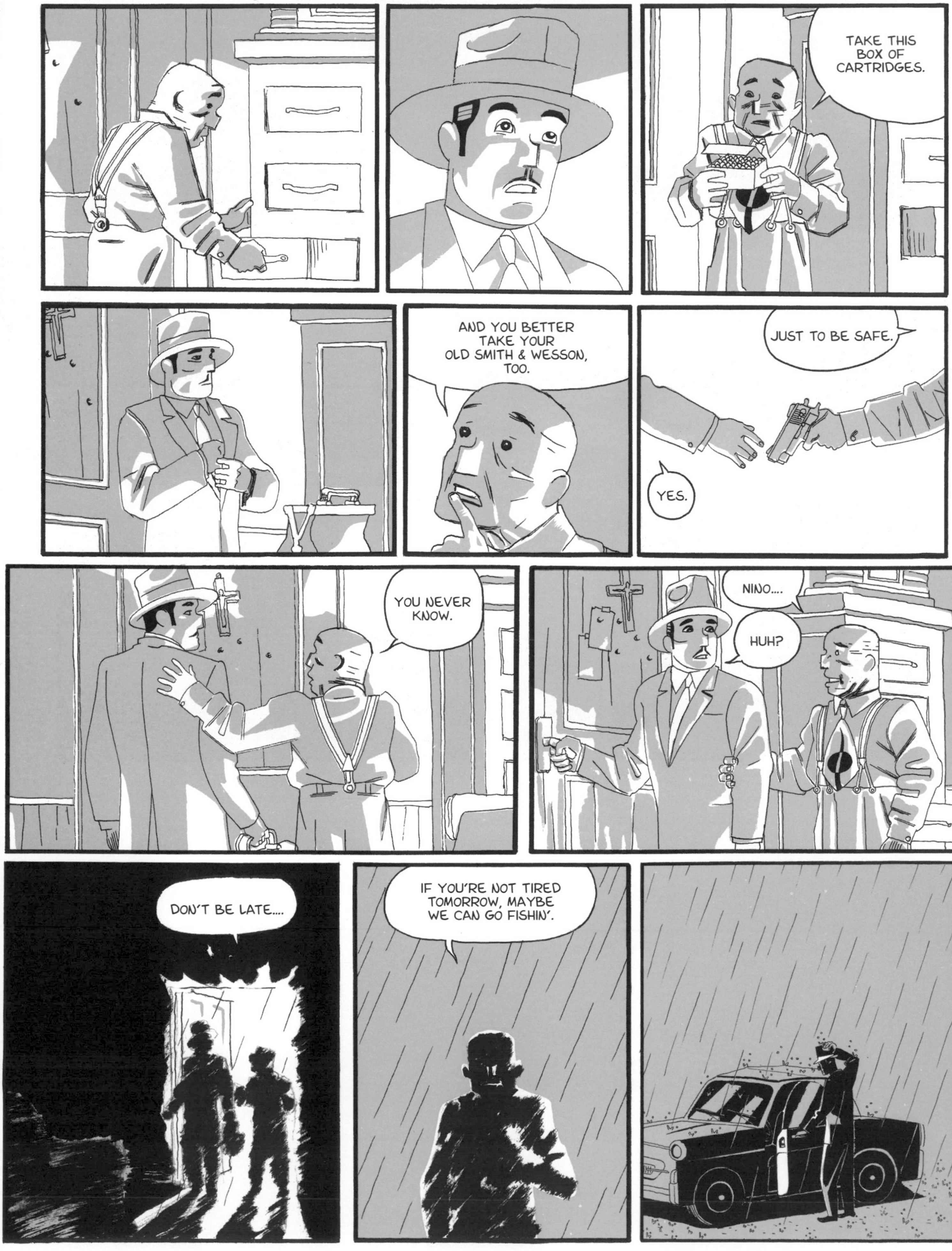
TAKE THIS BOX OF CARTRIDGES.
AND YOU BETTER TAKE YOUR OLD SMITH & WESSON, TOO.
JUST TO BE SAFE.
YES.
YOU NEVER KNOW.
NINO....
HUH?
DON'T BE LATE....
IF YOU'RE NOT TIRED TOMORROW, MAYBE WE CAN GO FISHIN'.

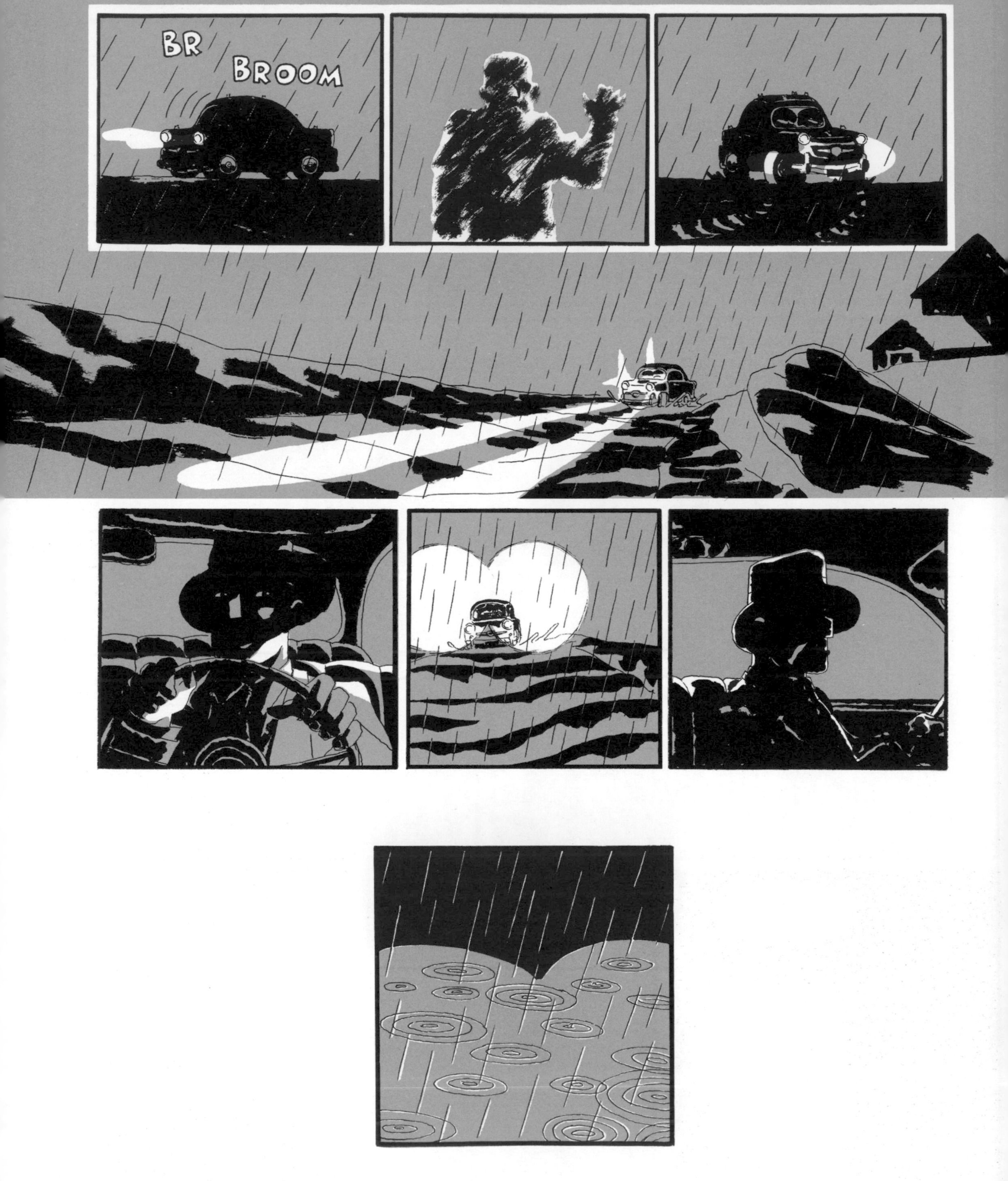
BR
BROOM

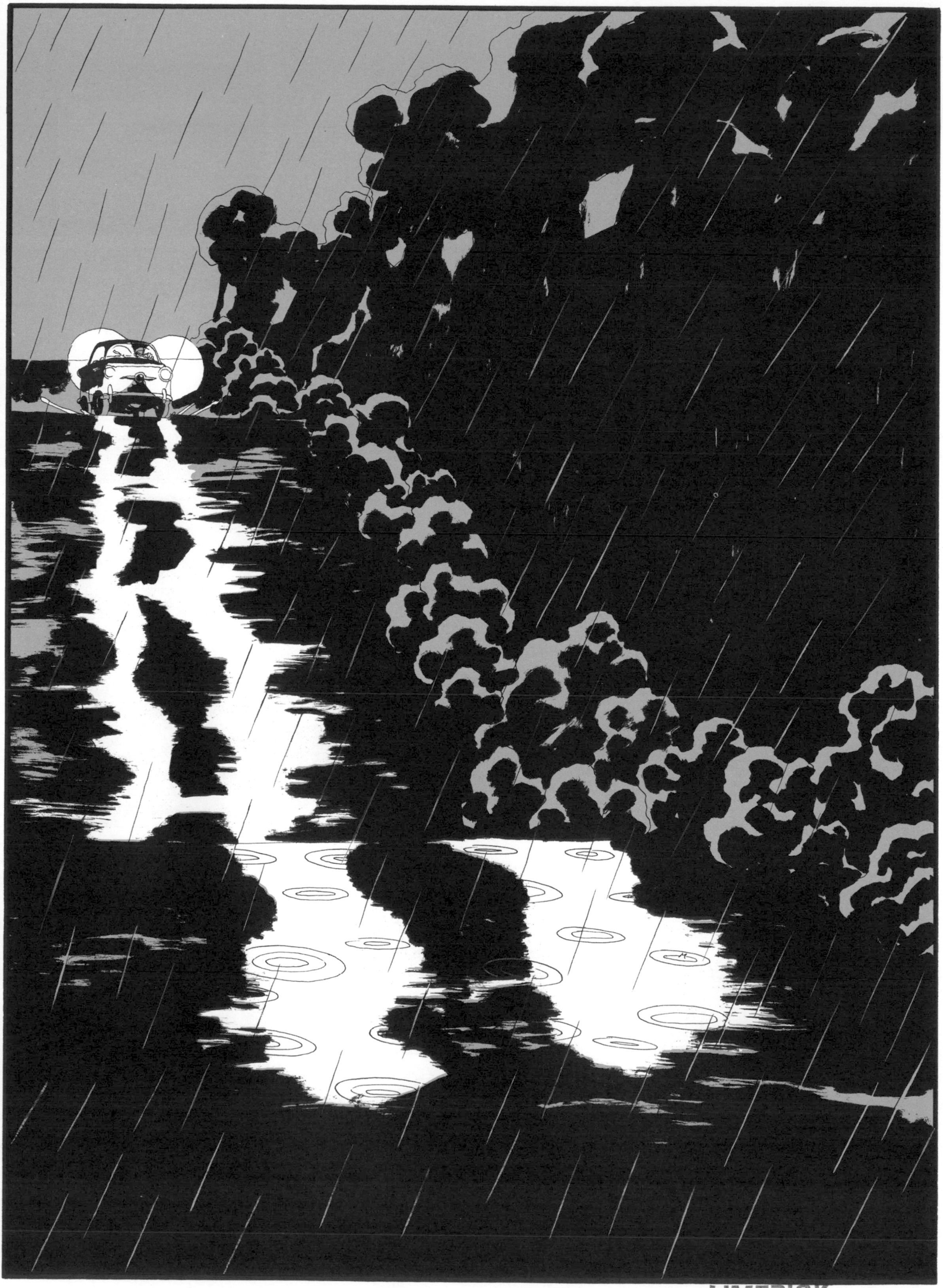

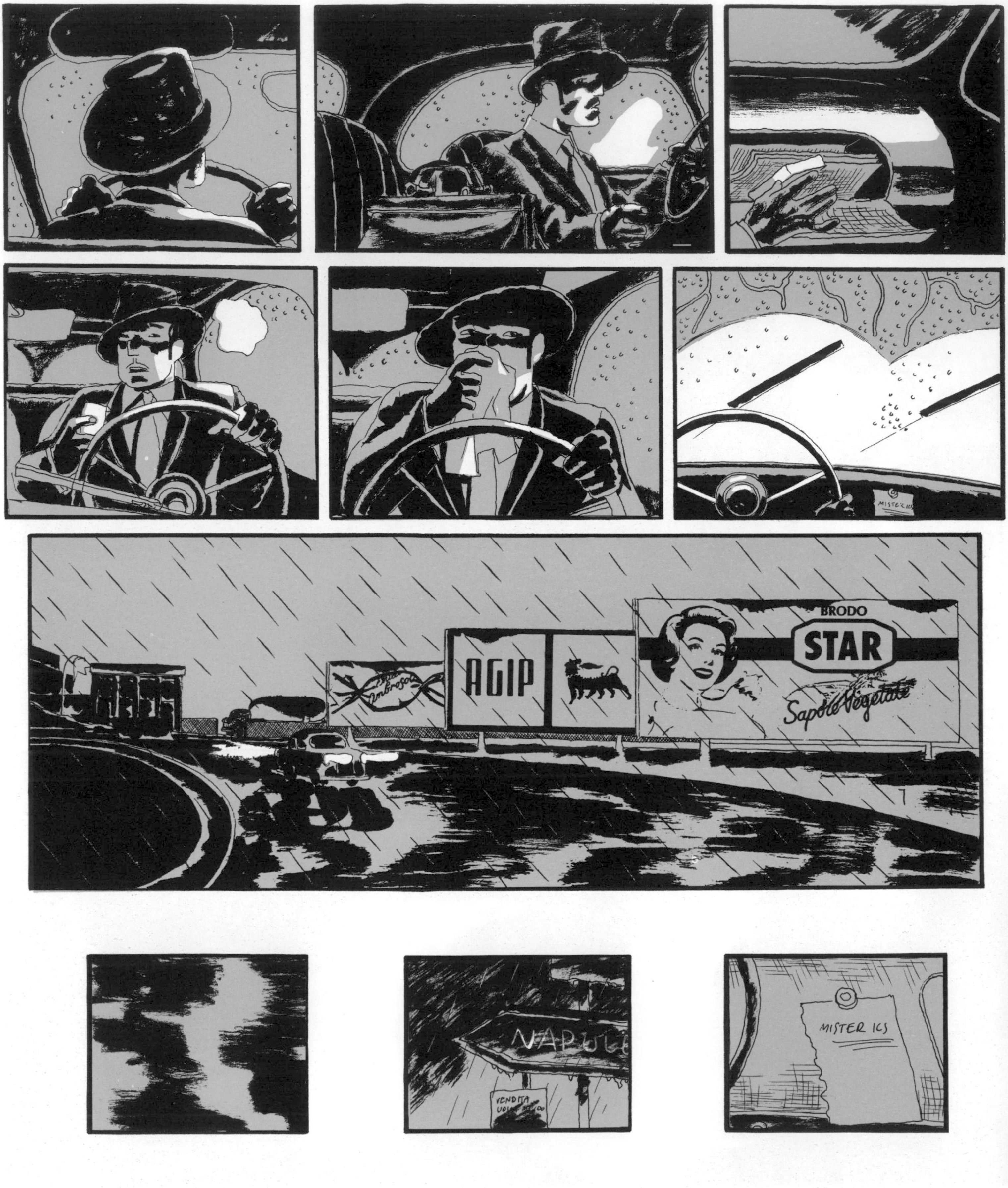
MISTER ICS
BRODO
STAR
AGIP
MISTER ICS

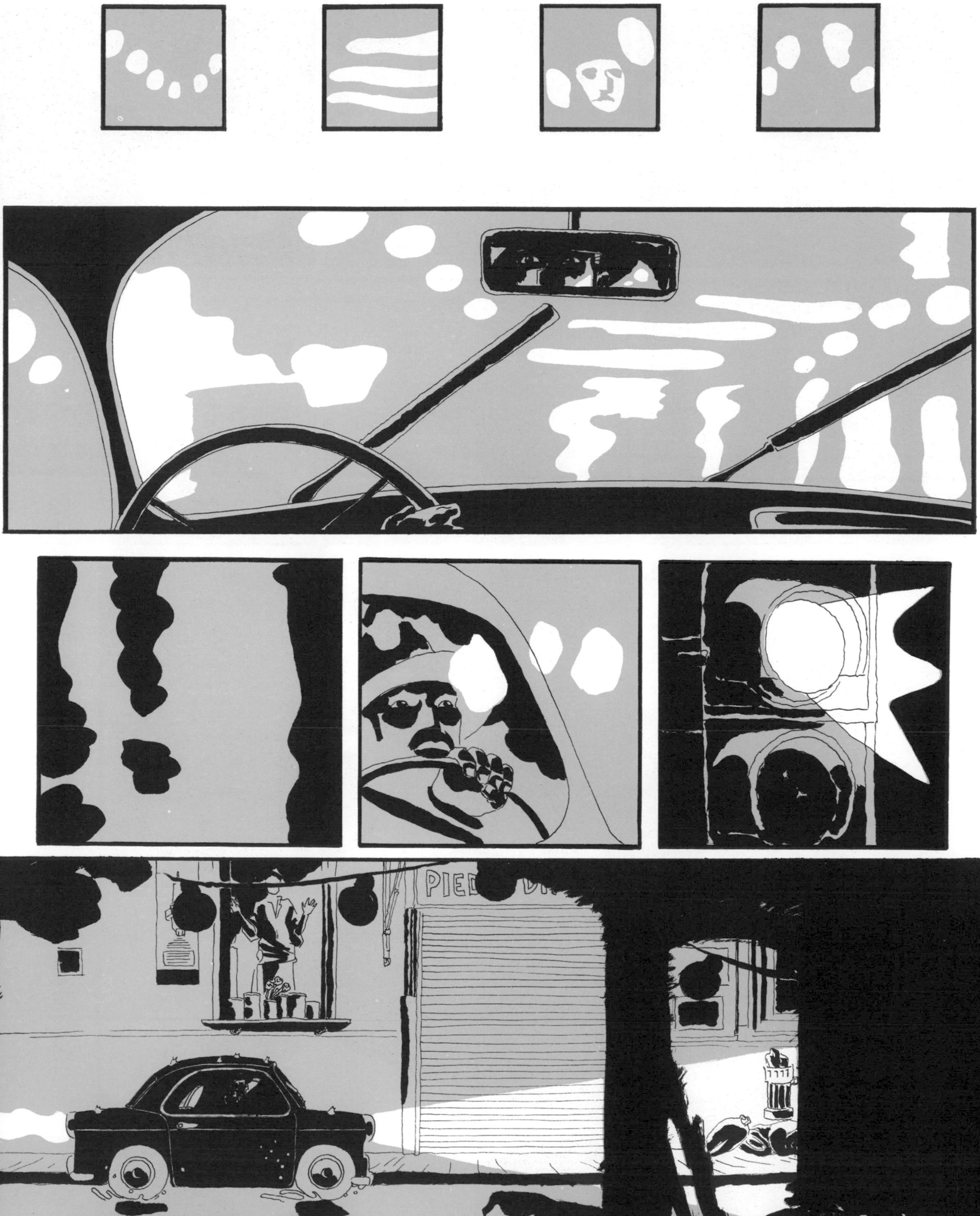

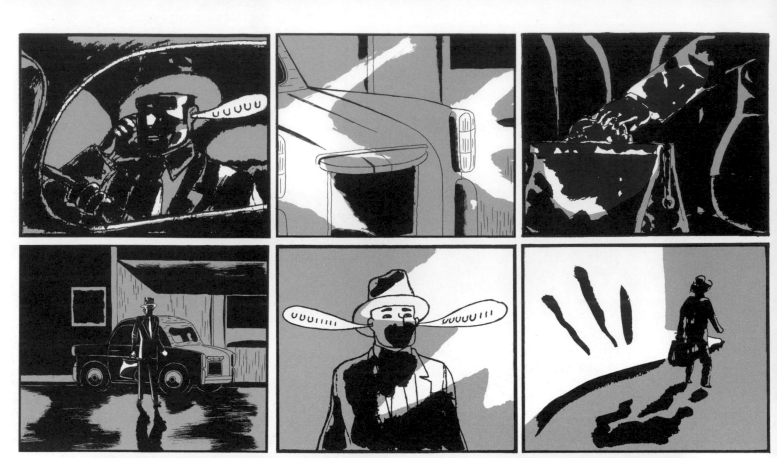

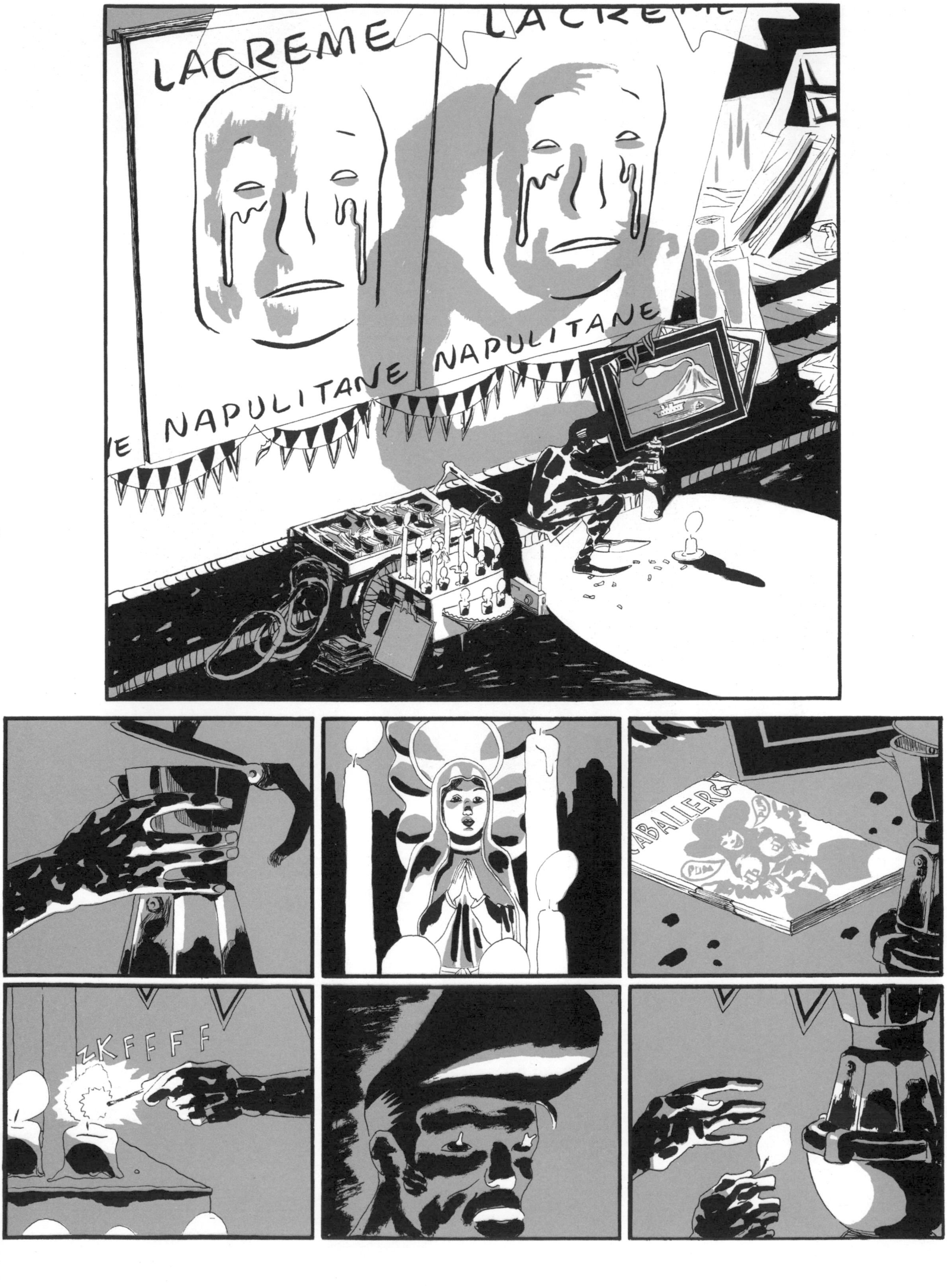
LACREME
NAPULITANE
NAPULITANE
PUM
ZKFFFFF

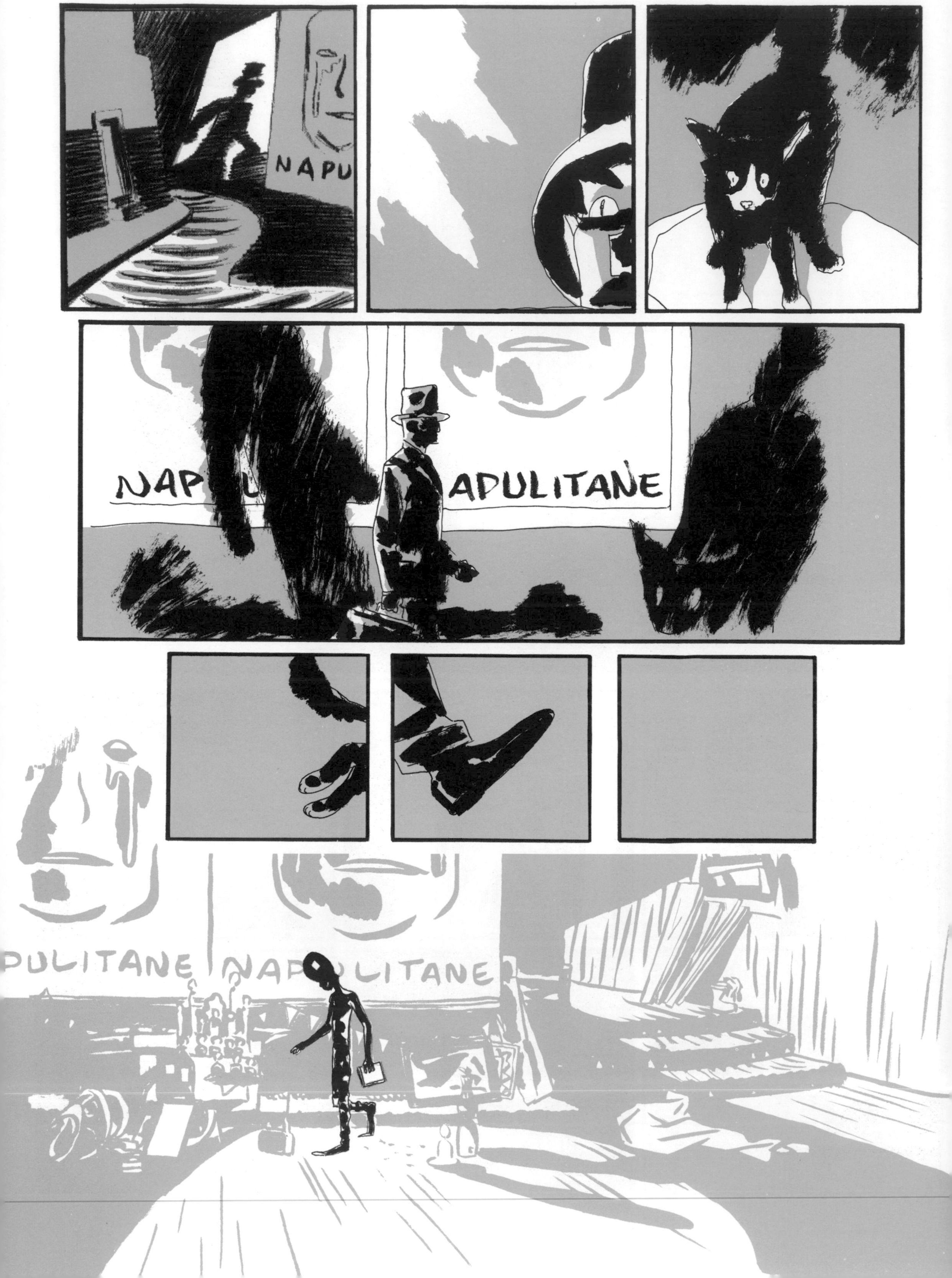
NAPU
NAP
APULITANE
PULITANE
NAPULITANE

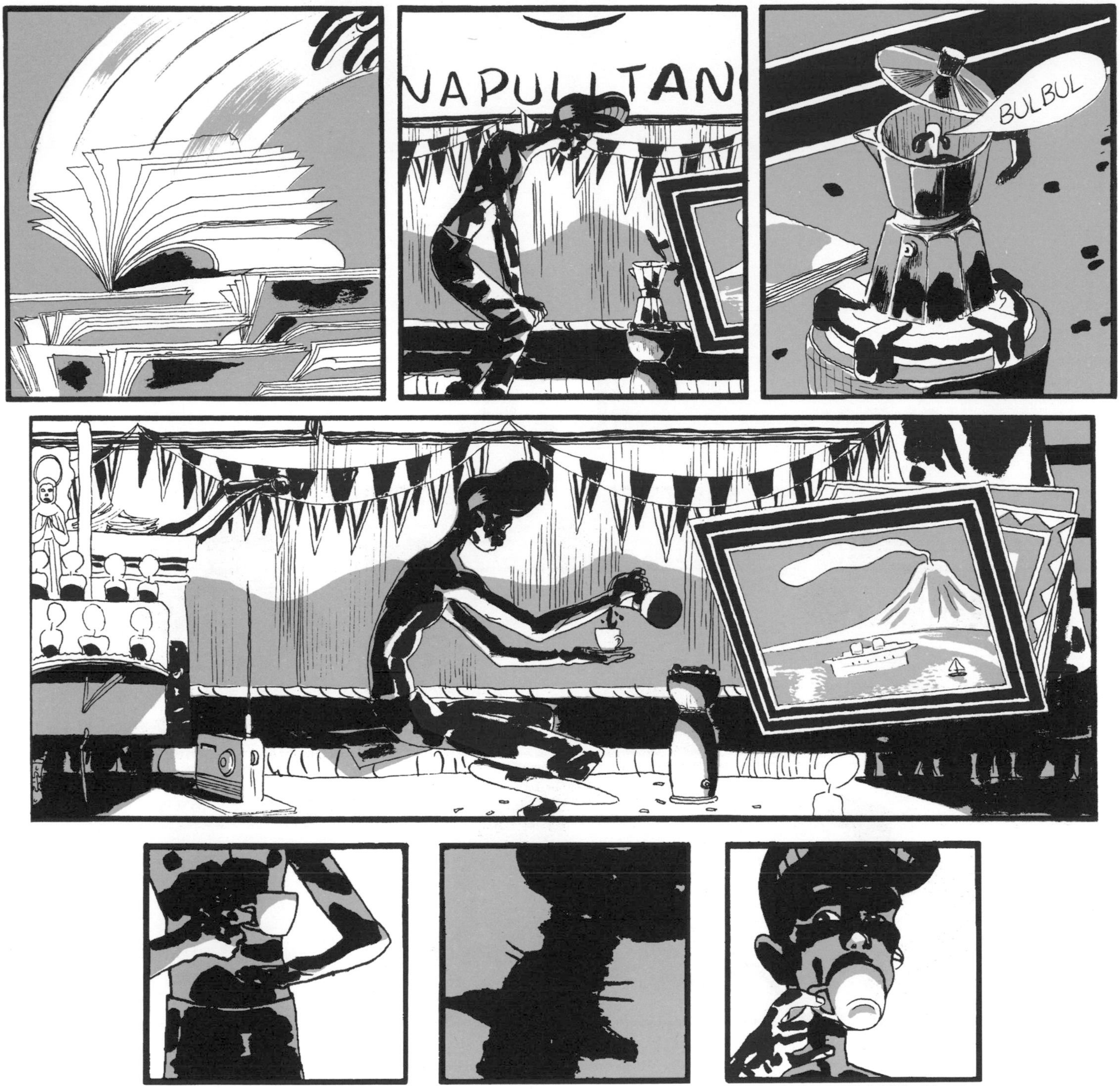
NAPULITAN
BULBUL

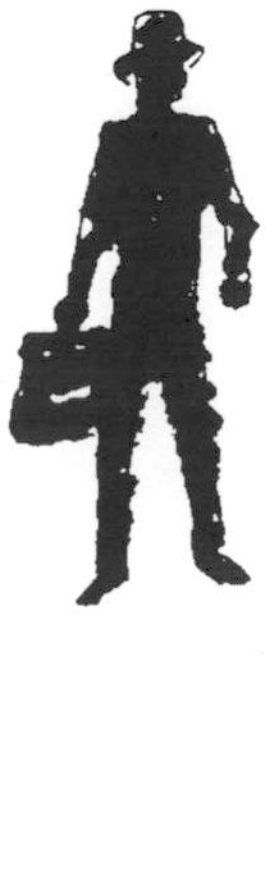

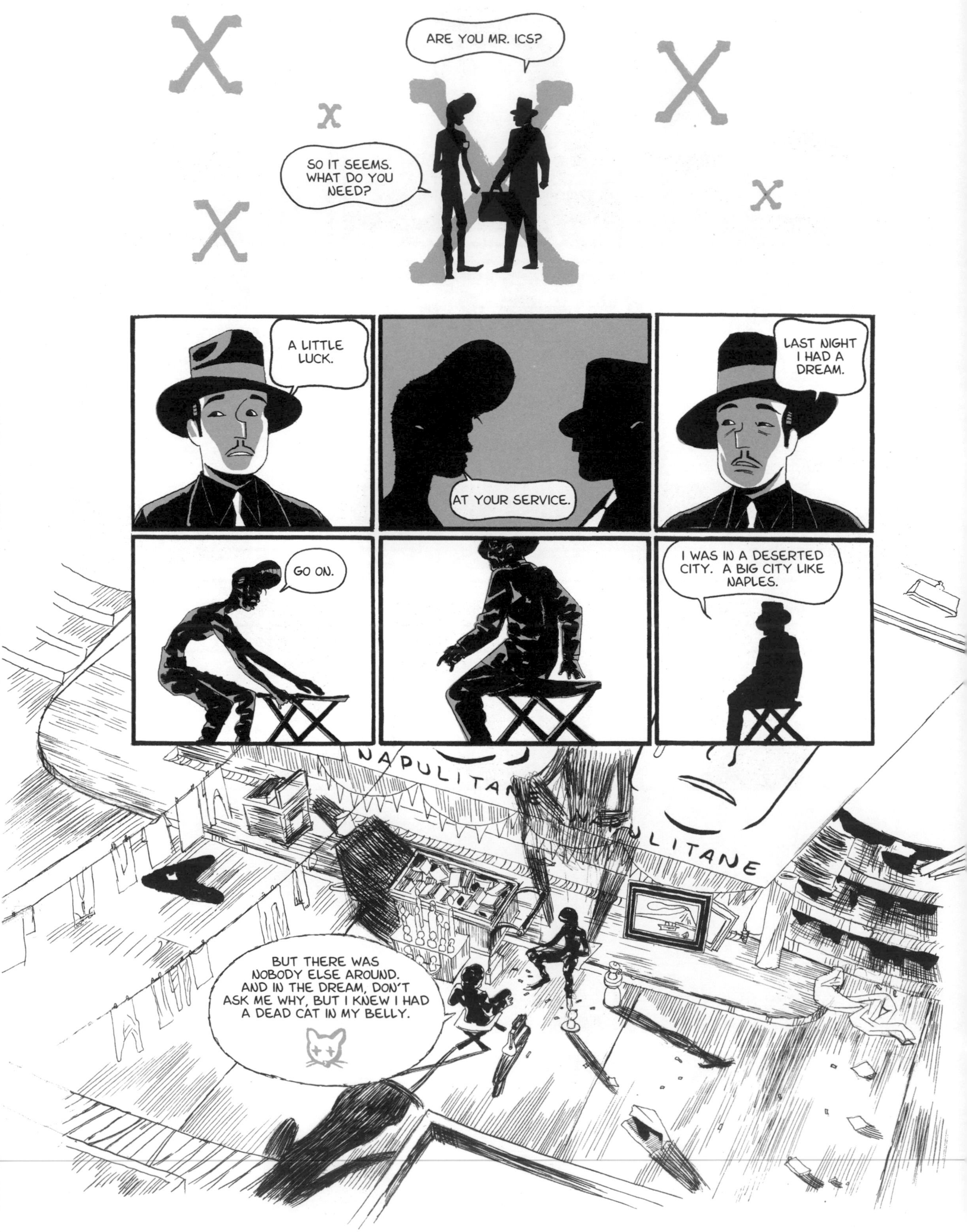
ARE YOU MR. ICS?
SO IT SEEMS. WHAT DO YOU NEED?
A LITTLE LUCK.
AT YOUR SERVICE.
LAST NIGHT I HAD A DREAM.
GO ON.
I WAS IN A DESERTED CITY. A BIG CITY LIKE NAPLES.
NAPULITANE
NAPULITANE
BUT THERE WAS NOBODY ELSE AROUND. AND IN THE DREAM, DON'T ASK ME WHY, BUT I KNEW I HAD A DEAD CAT IN MY BELLY.

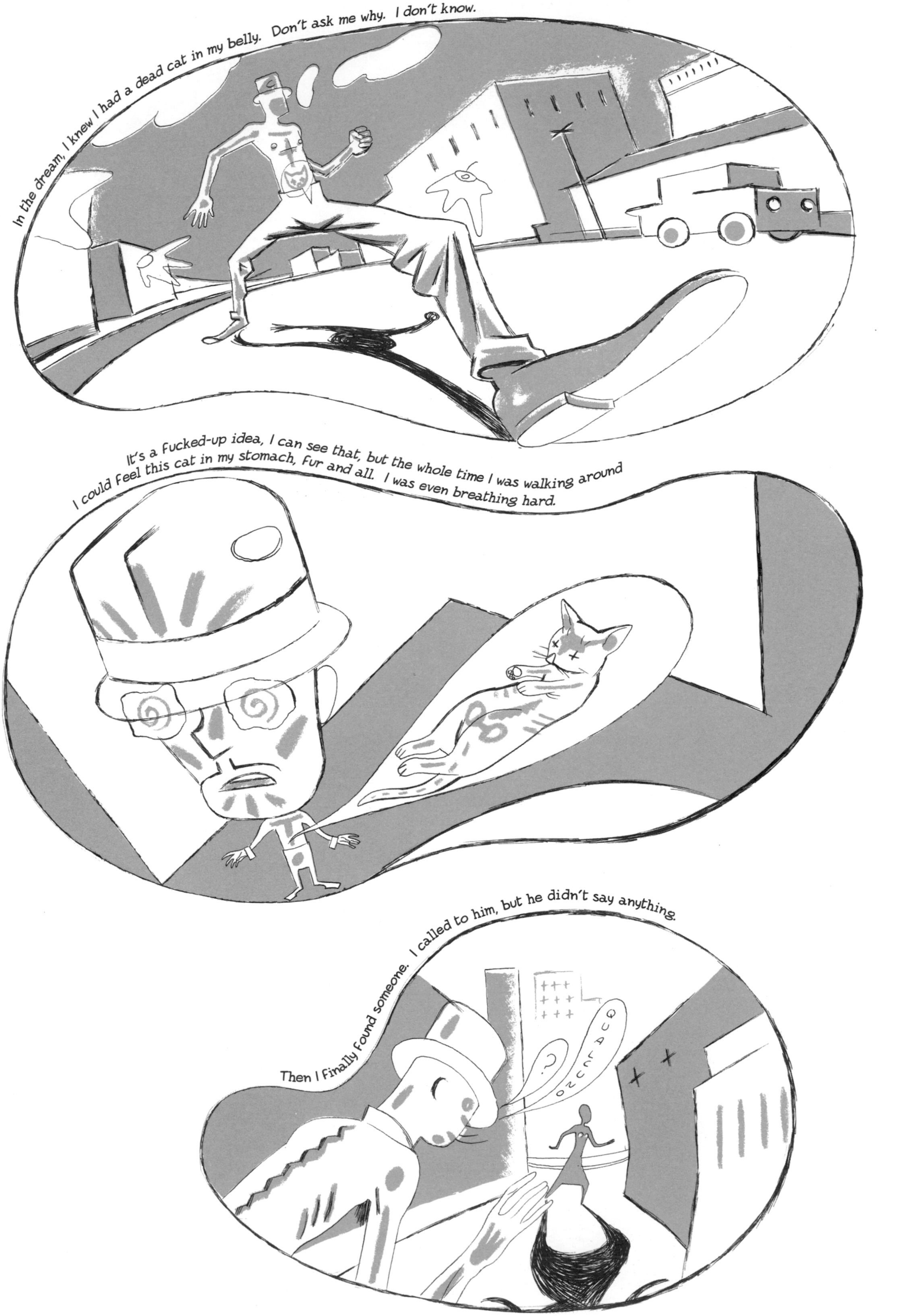
In the dream, I knew I had a dead cat in my belly. Don't ask me why. I don't know.
It's a fucked-up idea, I can see that, but the whole time I was walking around
I could feel this cat in my stomach, fur and all. I was even breathing hard.
Then I finally found someone. I called to him, but he didn't say anything.

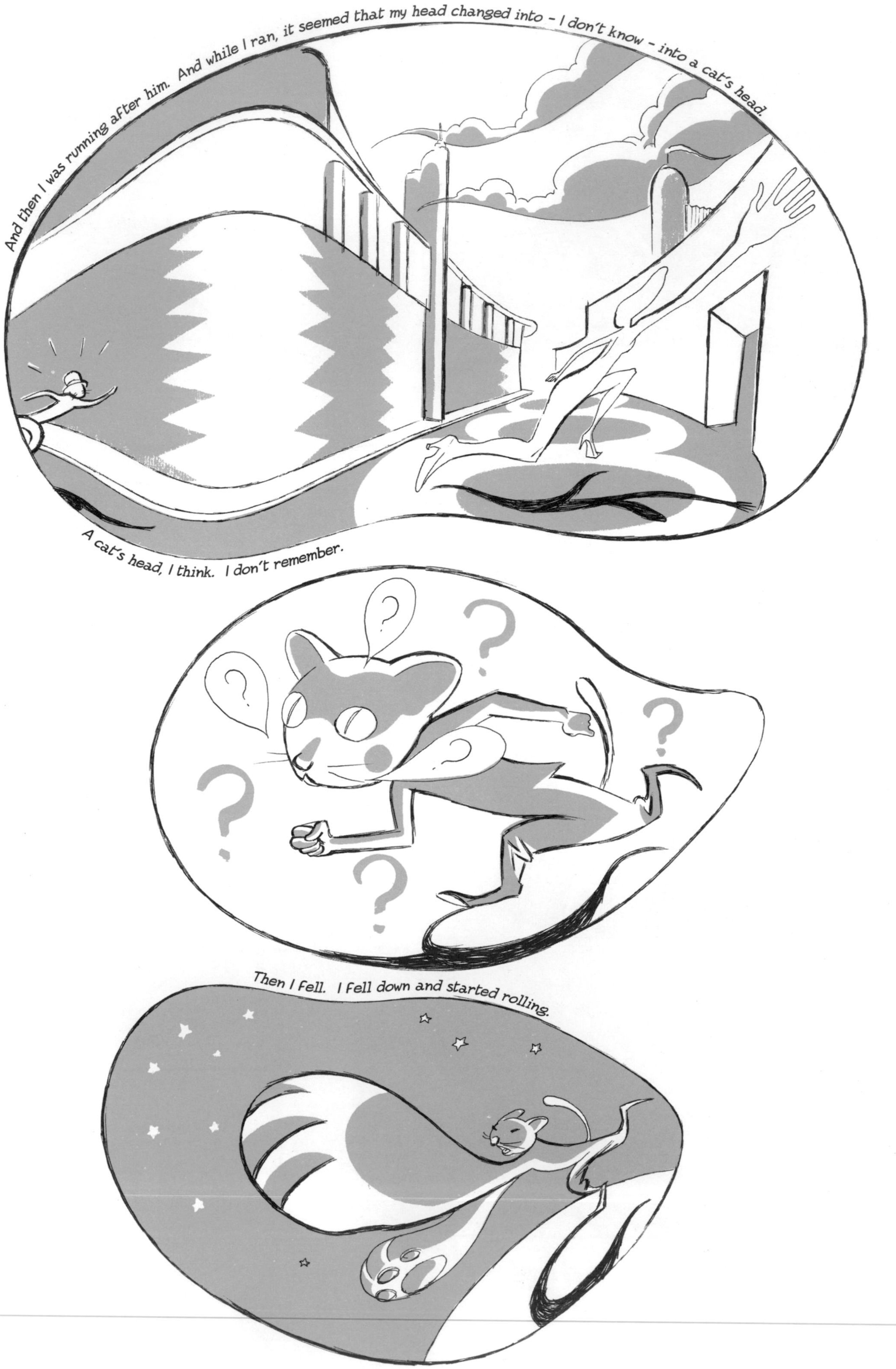
And then I was running after him. And while I ran, it seemed that my head changed into – I don't know – into a cat's head.
A cat's head, I think. I don't remember.
Then I fell. I fell down and started rolling.

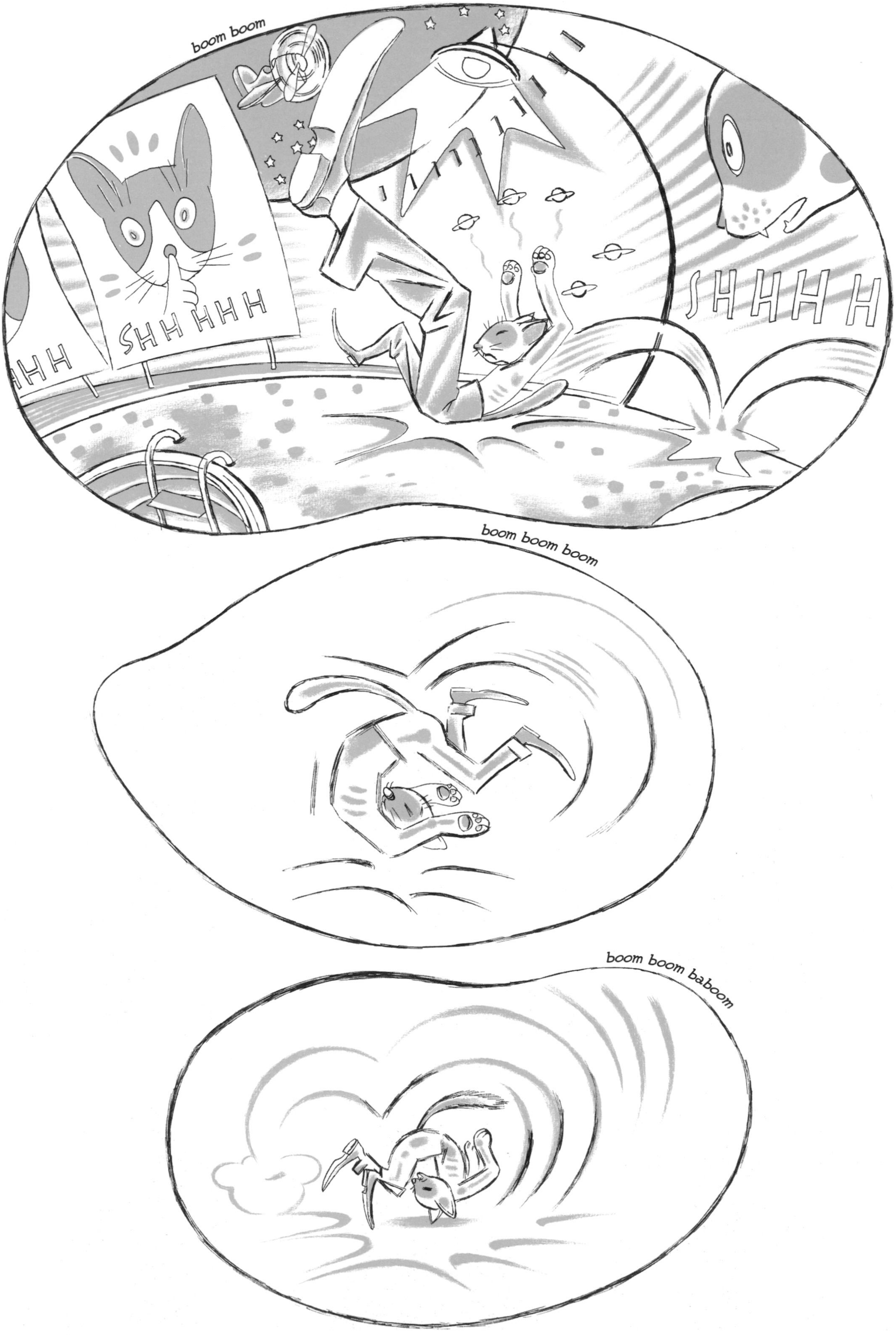
boom boom
SHHHHH
SHHHH
boom boom boom
boom boom baboom

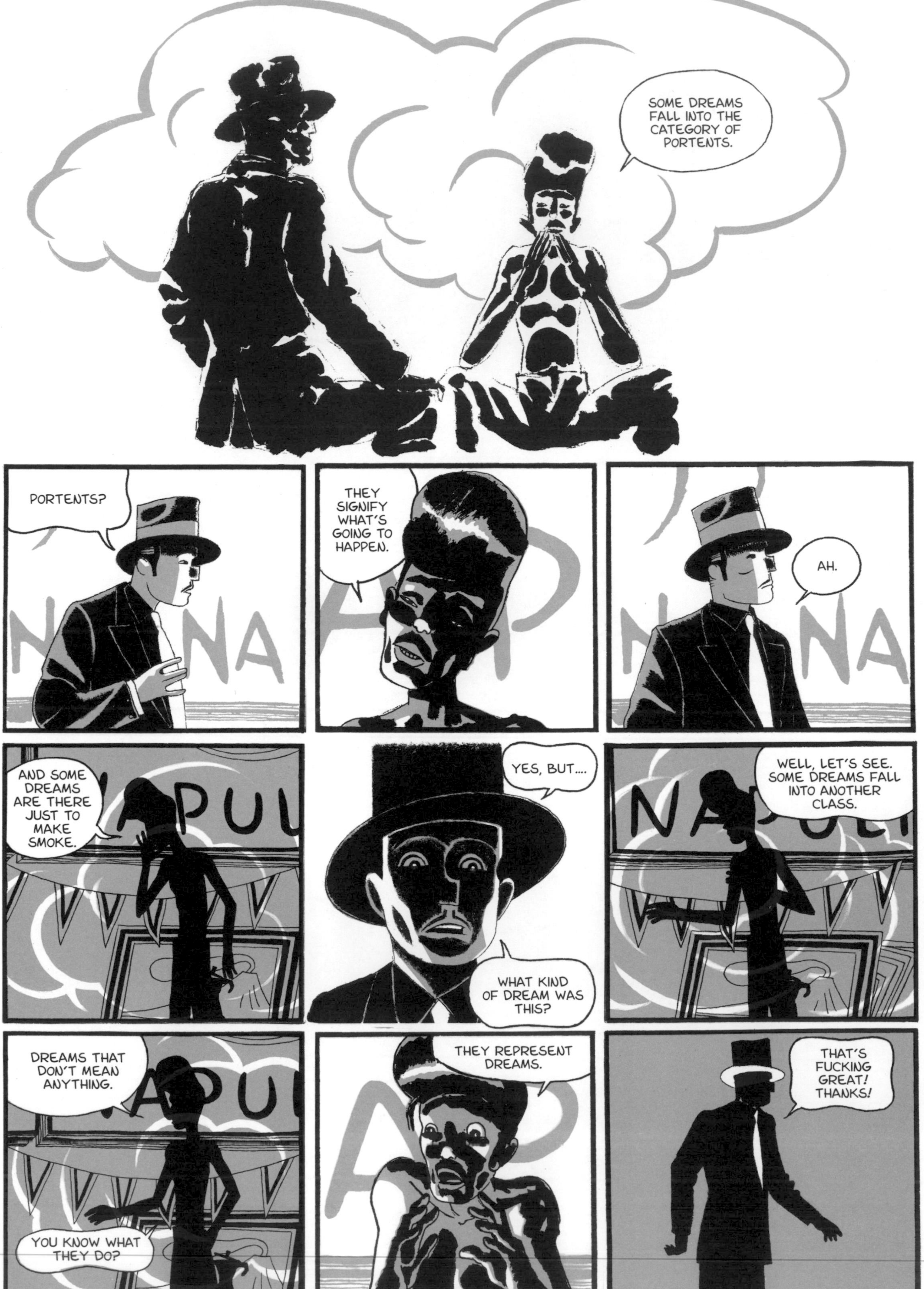
SOME DREAMS FALL INTO THE CATEGORY OF PORTENTS.
PORTENTS?
THEY SIGNIFY WHAT'S GOING TO HAPPEN.
AH.
AND SOME DREAMS ARE THERE JUST TO MAKE SMOKE.
YES, BUT....
WHAT KIND OF DREAM WAS THIS?
WELL, LET'S SEE. SOME DREAMS FALL INTO ANOTHER CLASS.
DREAMS THAT DON'T MEAN ANYTHING.
YOU KNOW WHAT THEY DO?
THEY REPRESENT DREAMS.
THAT'S FUCKING GREAT! THANKS!

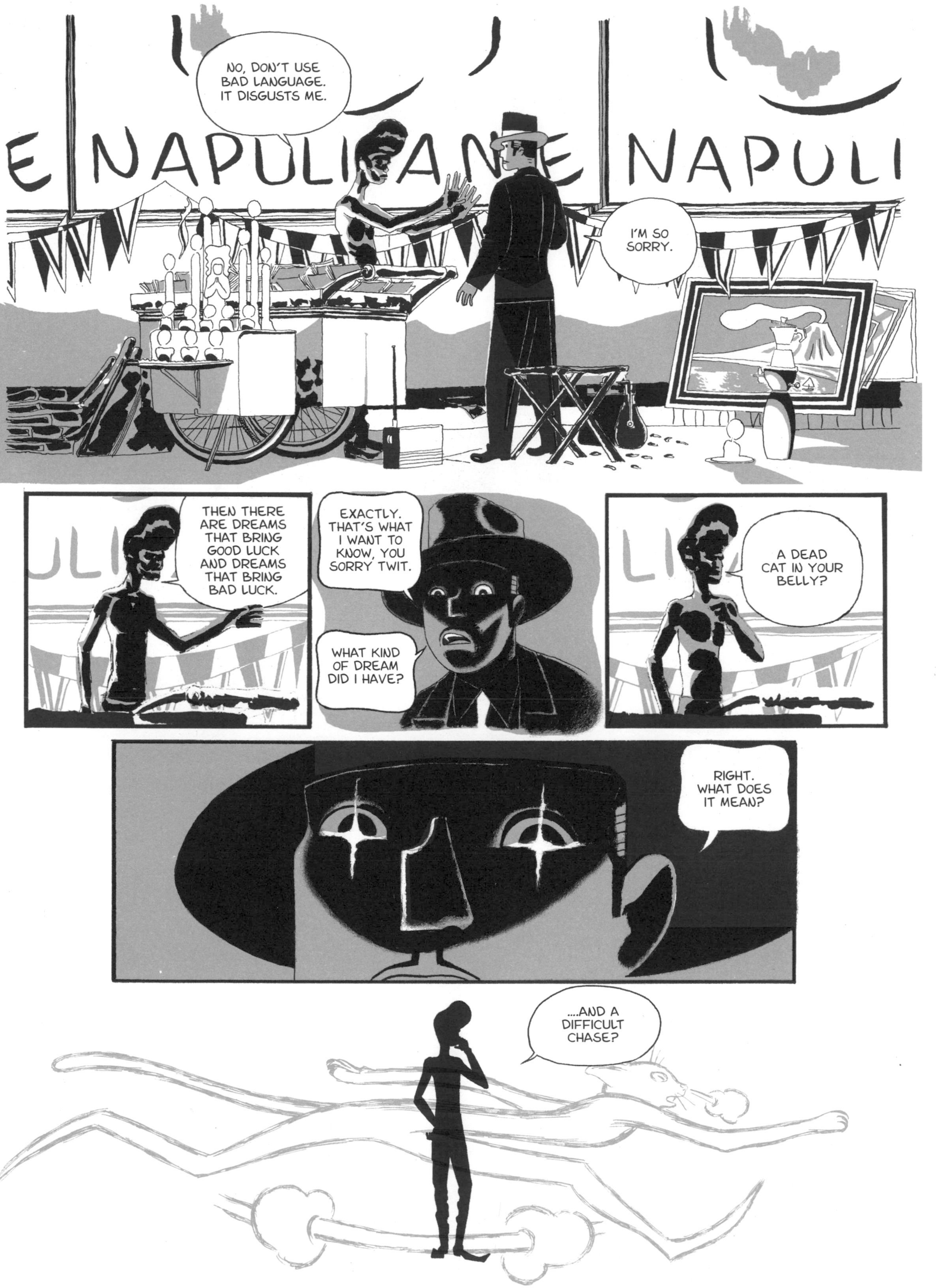
NO, DON'T USE BAD LANGUAGE. IT DISGUSTS ME.
I'M SO SORRY.
THEN THERE ARE DREAMS THAT BRING GOOD LUCK AND DREAMS THAT BRING BAD LUCK.
EXACTLY. THAT'S WHAT I WANT TO KNOW, YOU SORRY TWIT.
WHAT KIND OF DREAM DID I HAVE?
A DEAD CAT IN YOUR BELLY?
RIGHT. WHAT DOES IT MEAN?
....AND A DIFFICULT CHASE?

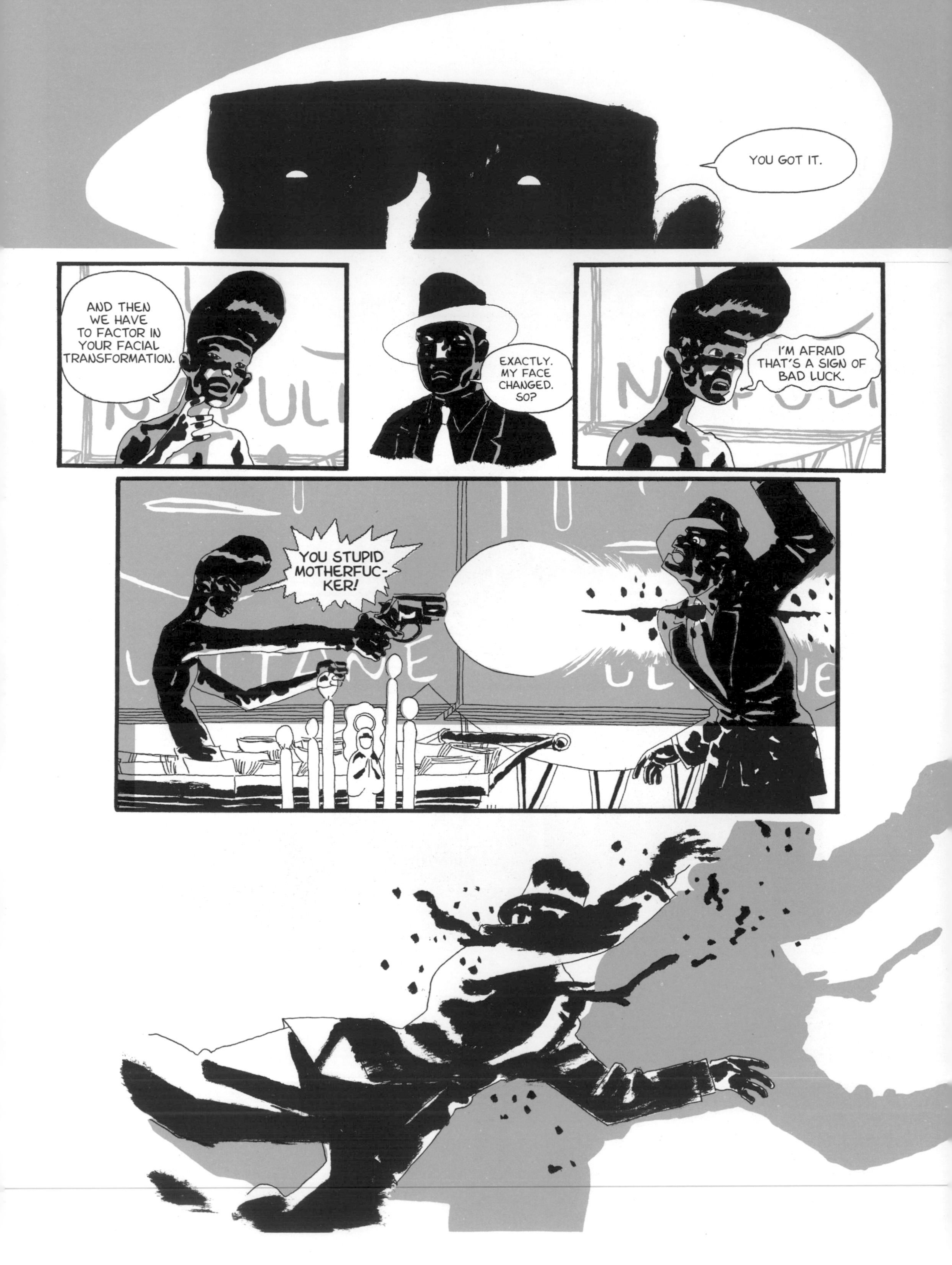
YOU GOT IT.
AND THEN WE HAVE TO FACTOR IN YOUR FACIAL TRANSFORMATION.
EXACTLY. MY FACE CHANGED. SO?
I'M AFRAID THAT'S A SIGN OF BAD LUCK.
YOU STUPID MOTHERFUC-KER!

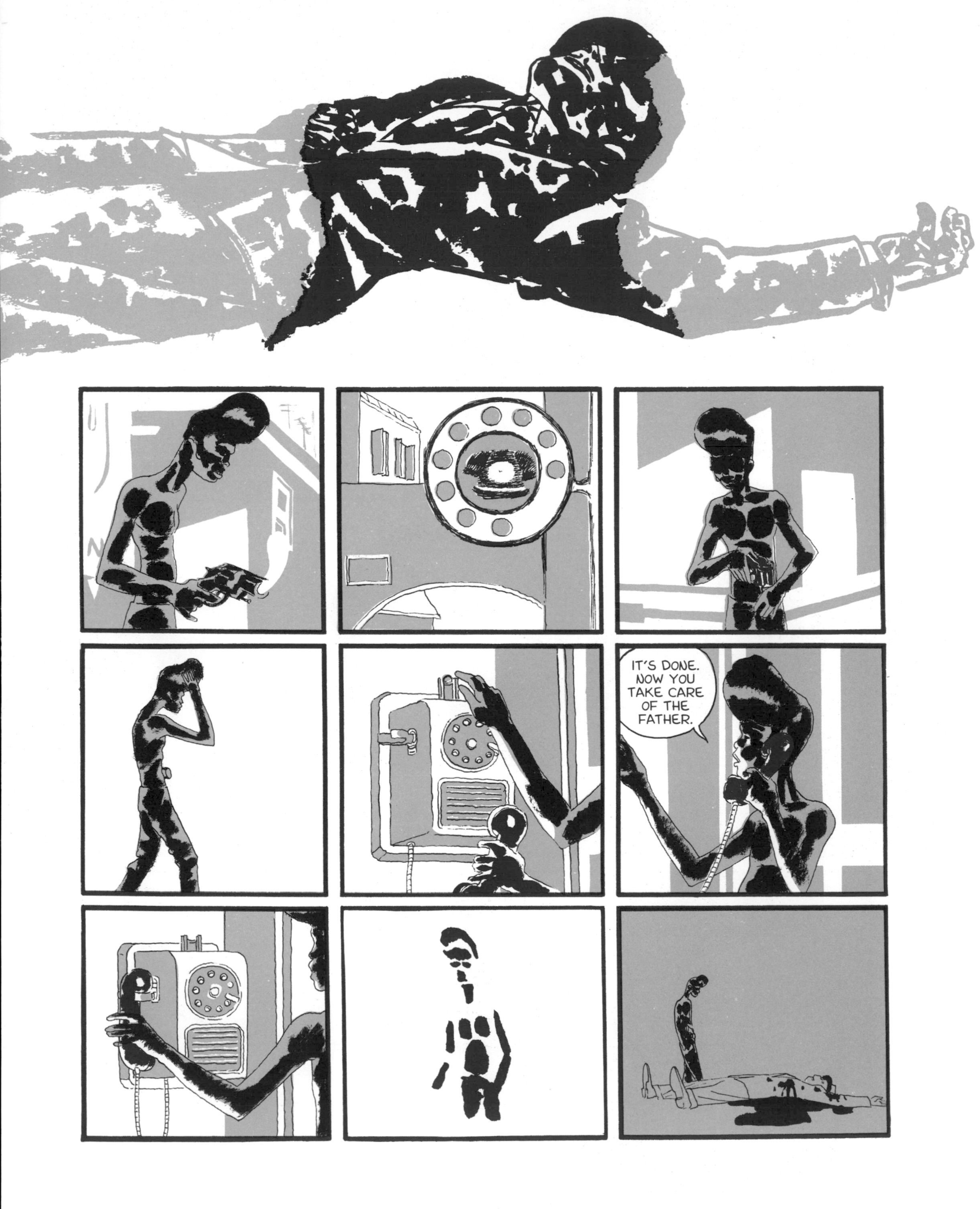
IT'S DONE. NOW YOU TAKE CARE OF THE FATHER.

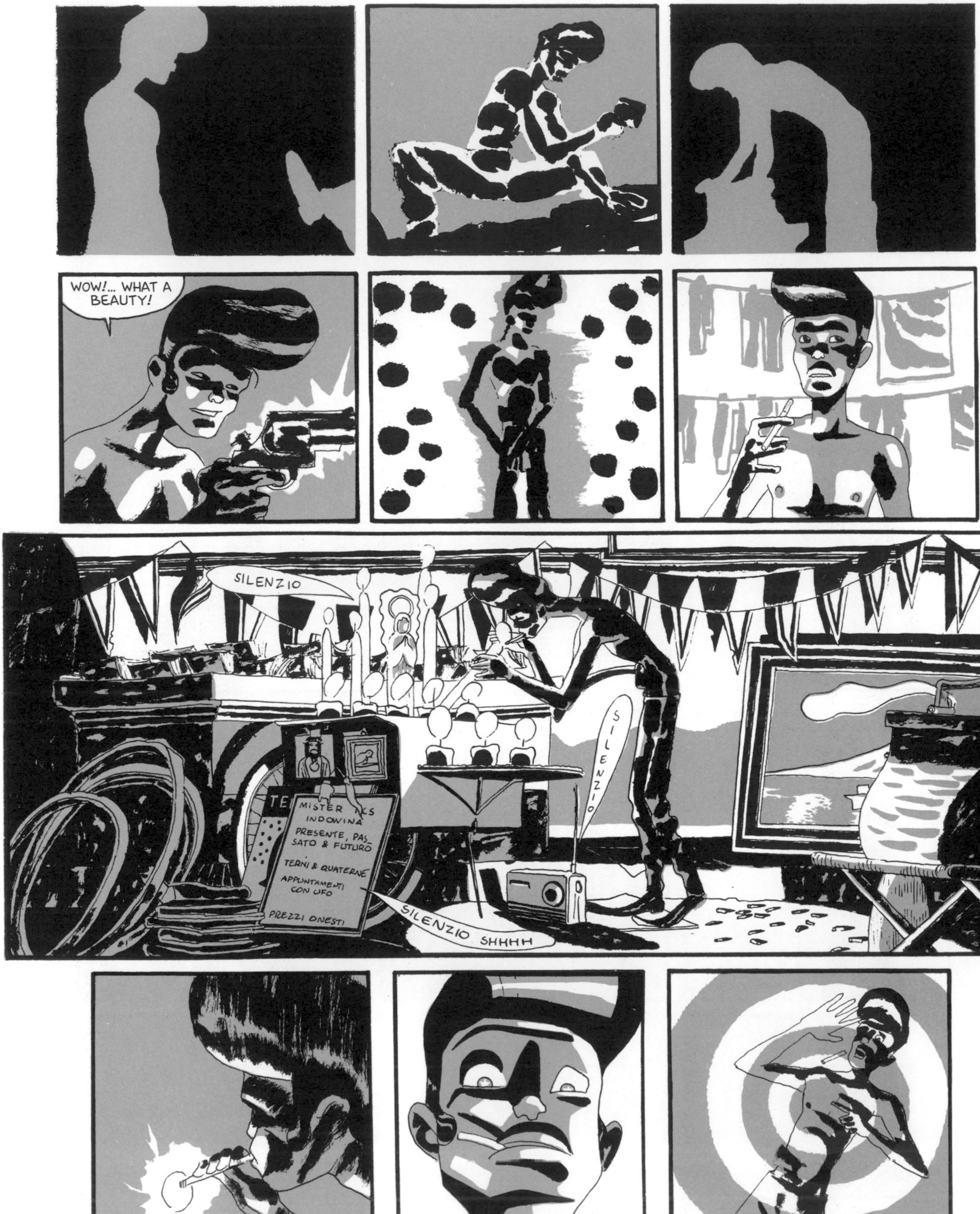
WOW!... WHAT A BEAUTY!
SILENZIO
SILENZIO
MISTER
INDOWINA
PRESENTE, PASSATO & FUTURO
TERNI & QUATERNE
APPUNTAMENTI CON UFO
PREZZI ONESTI
SILENZIO SHHHH

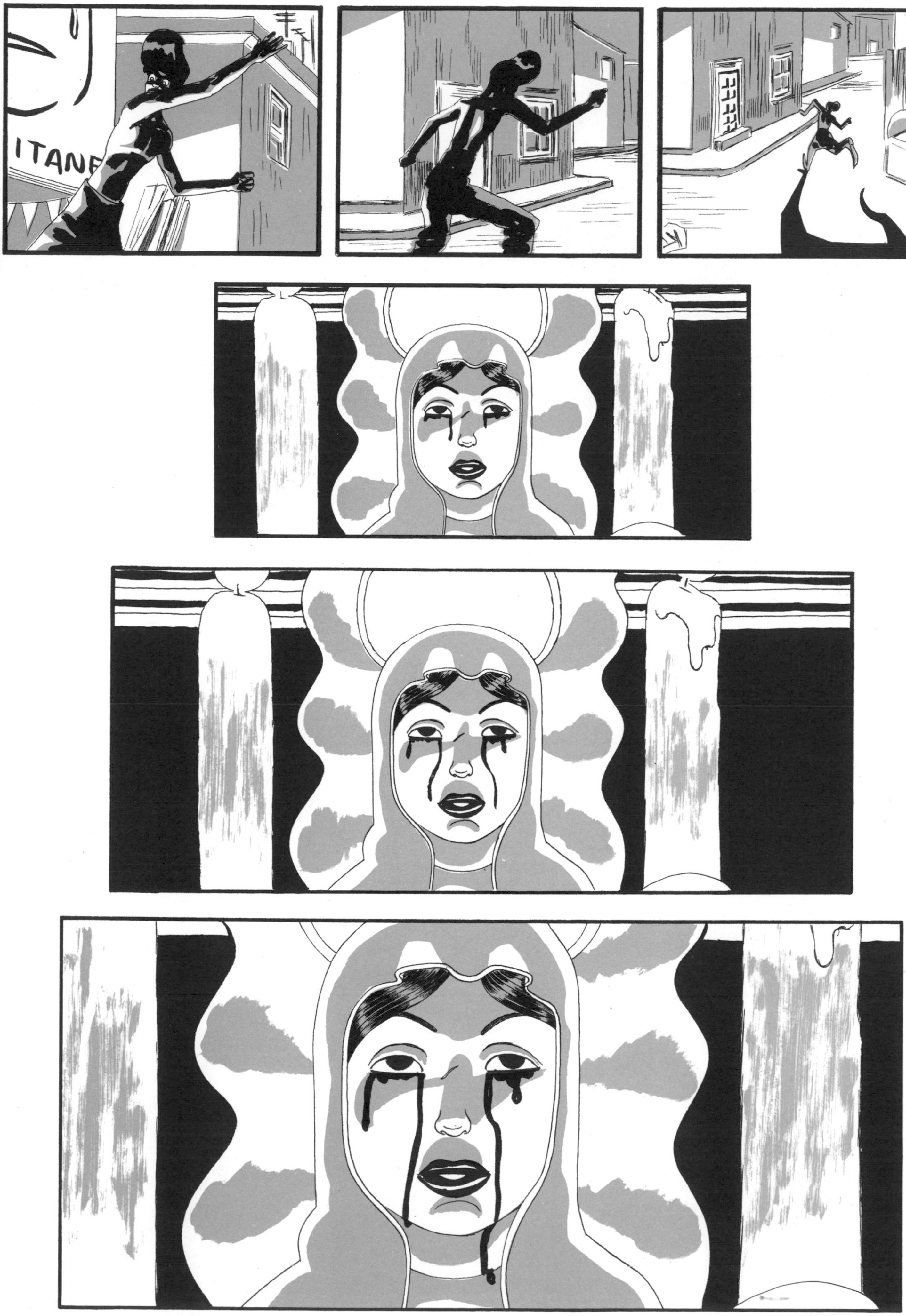
ITANE

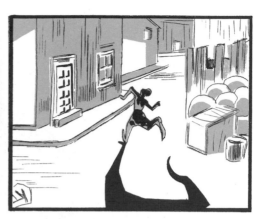

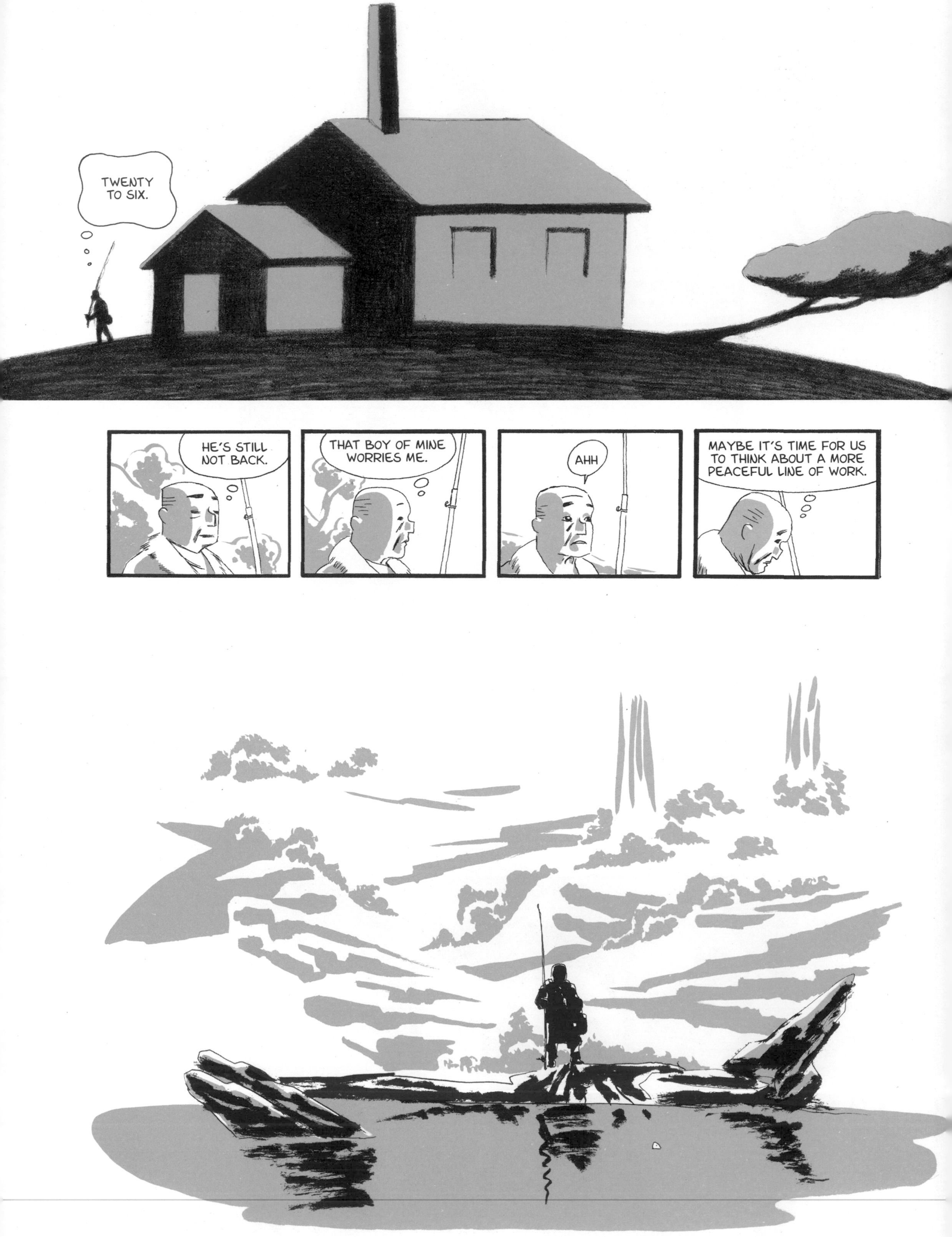
TWENTY TO SIX.
HE'S STILL NOT BACK.
THAT BOY OF MINE WORRIES ME.
AHH
MAYBE IT'S TIME FOR US TO THINK ABOUT A MORE PEACEFUL LINE OF WORK.

chapter two
crossword puzzles

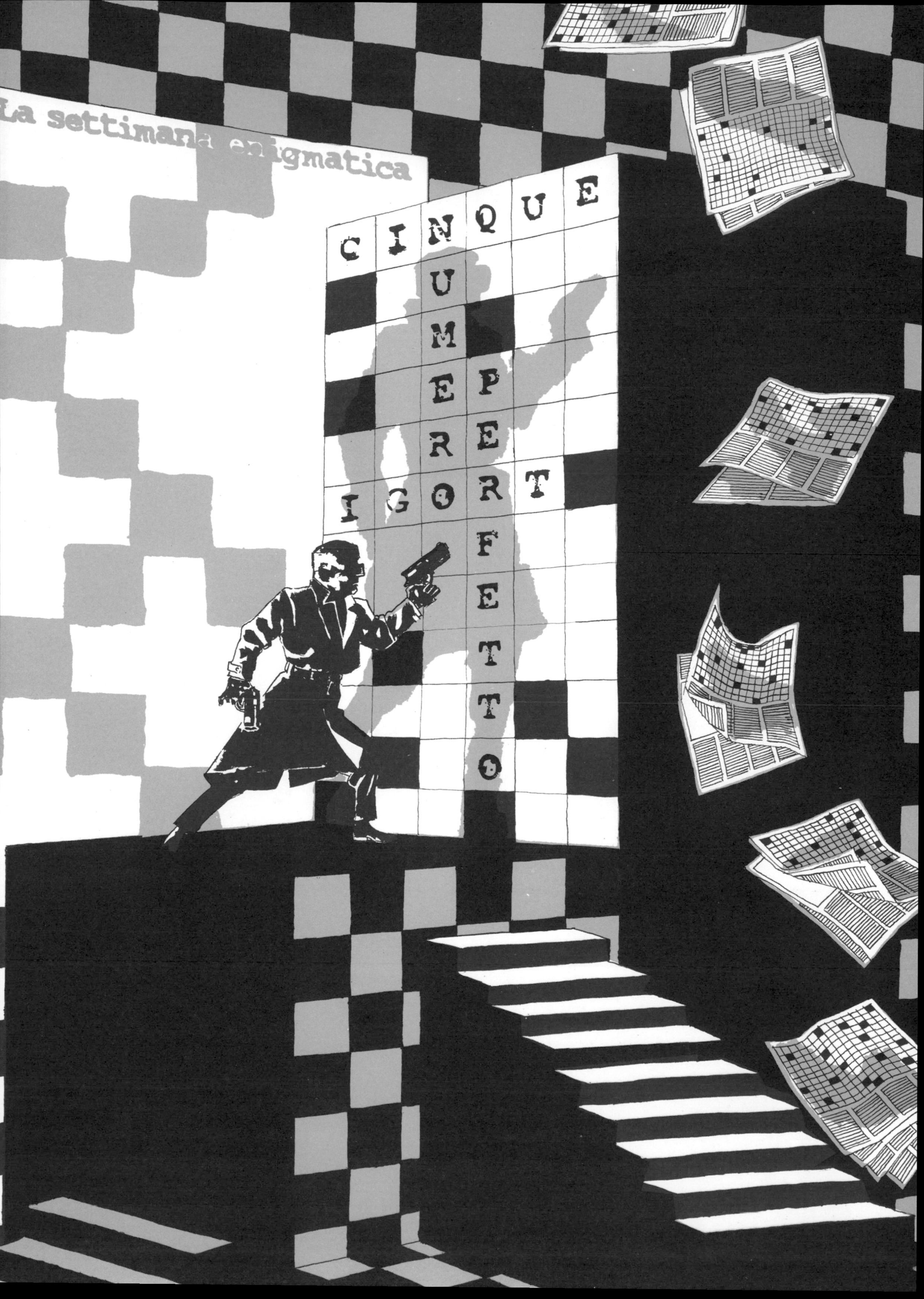
La settimana enigmatica
CINQUE
UMBERTO
PERFETTO
IGORT

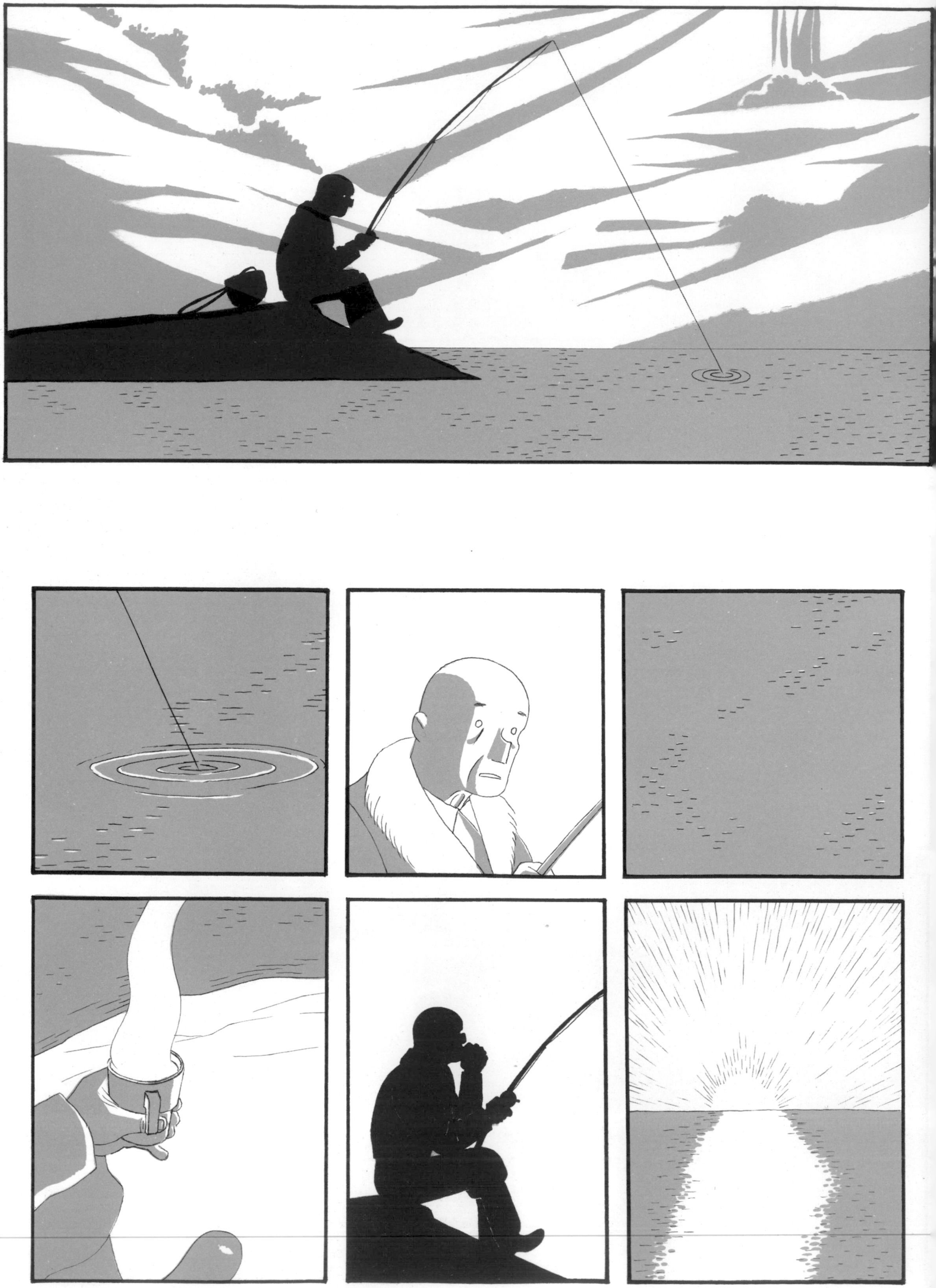

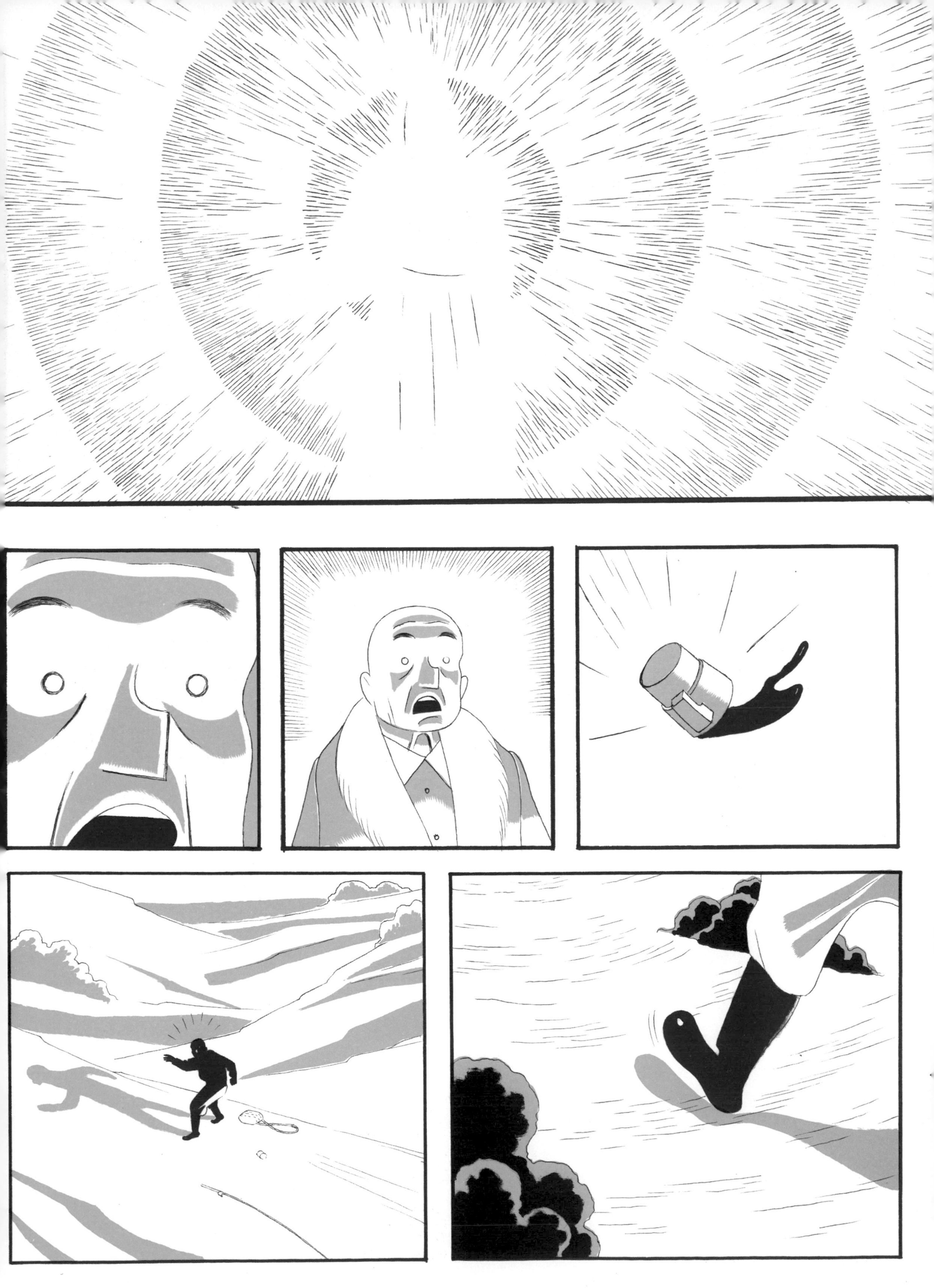

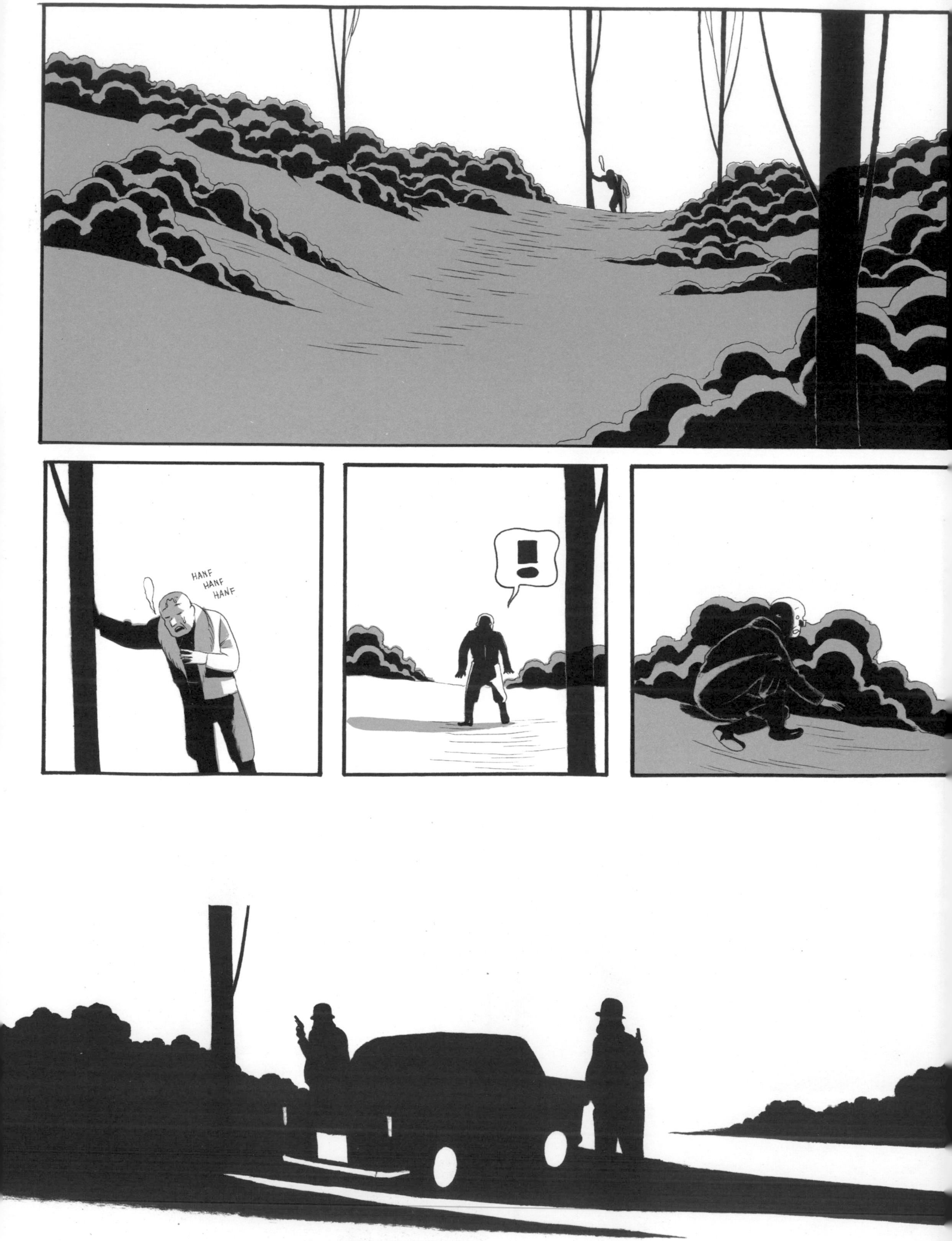
HANF
HANF
HANF

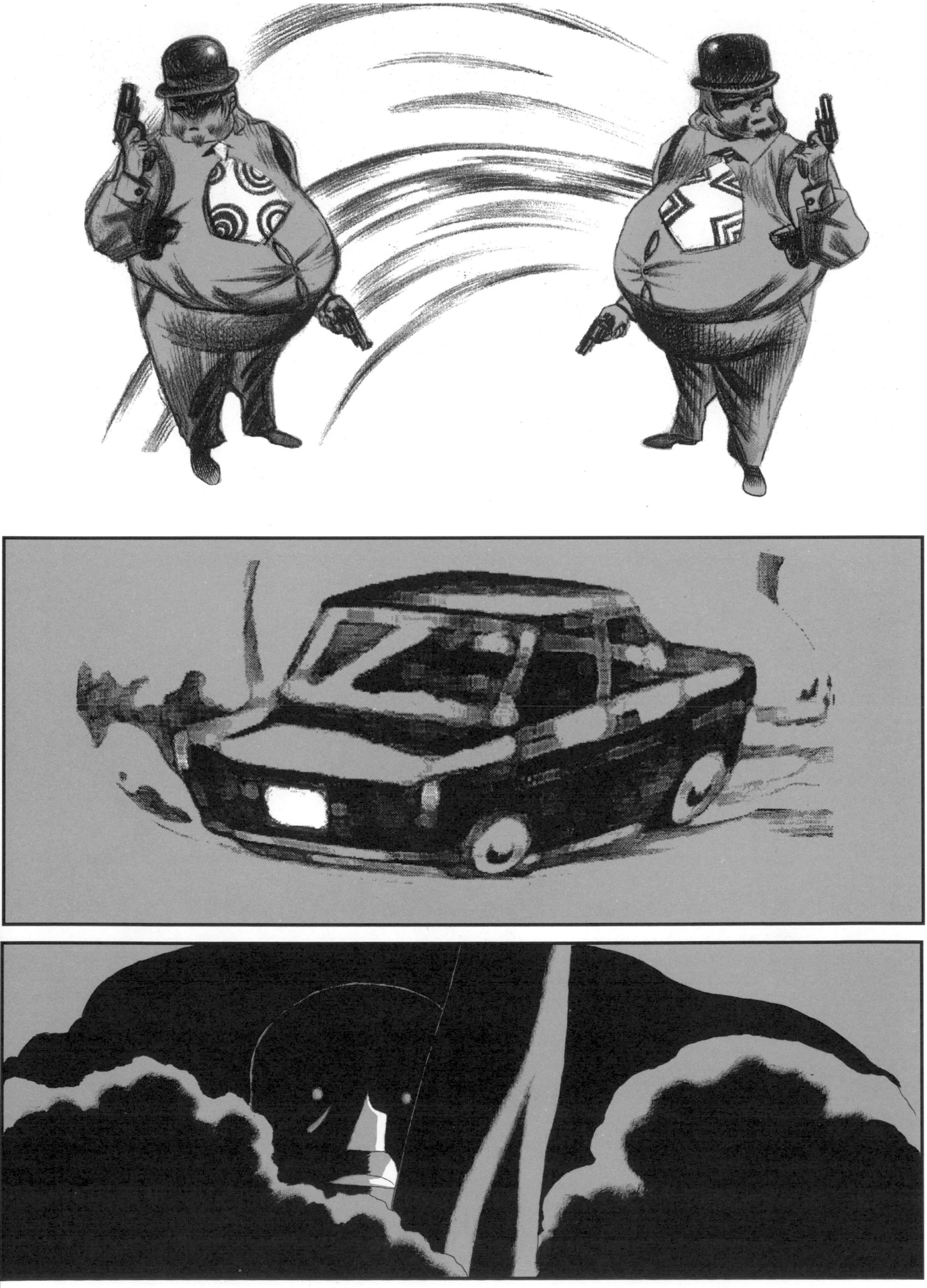

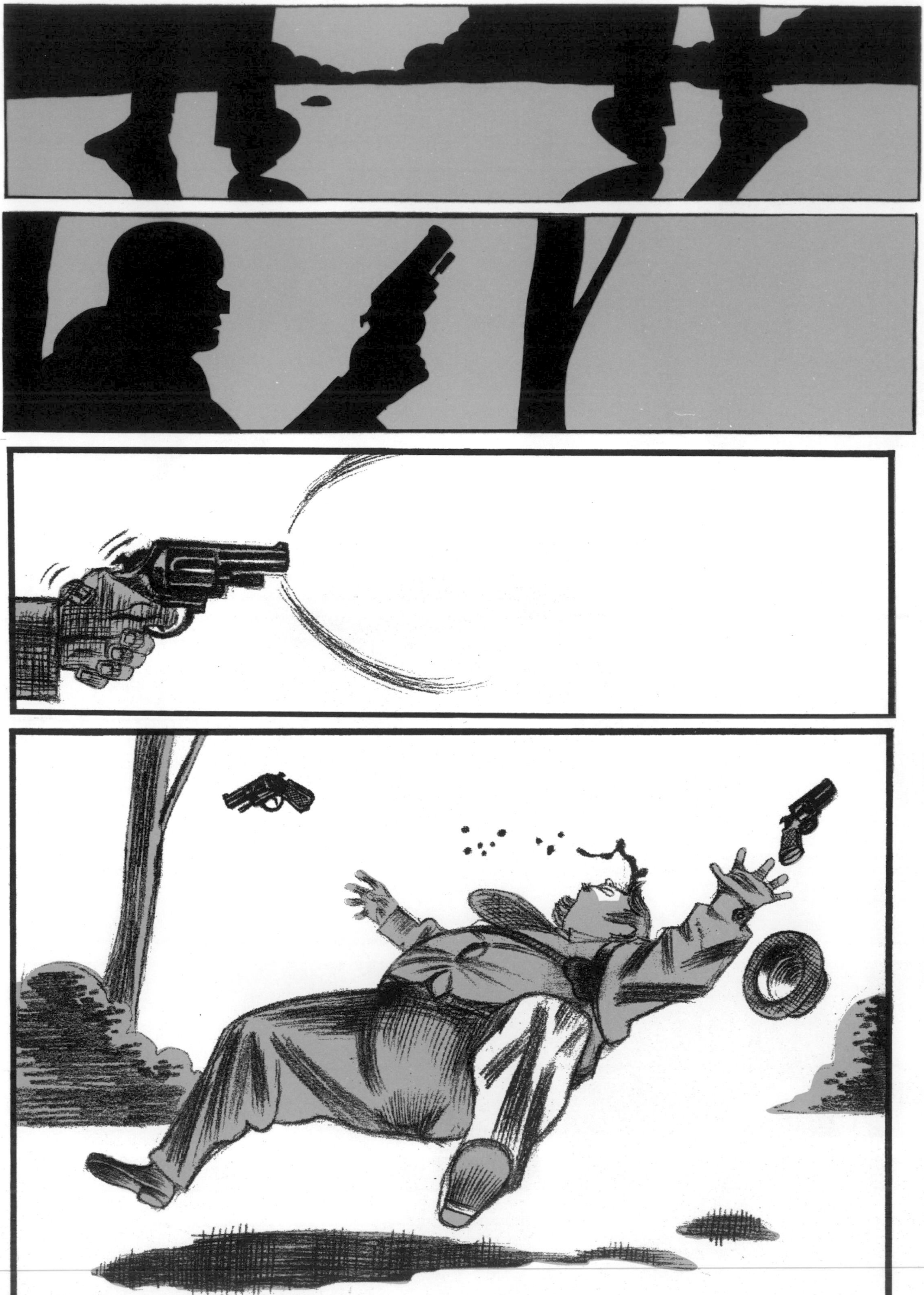

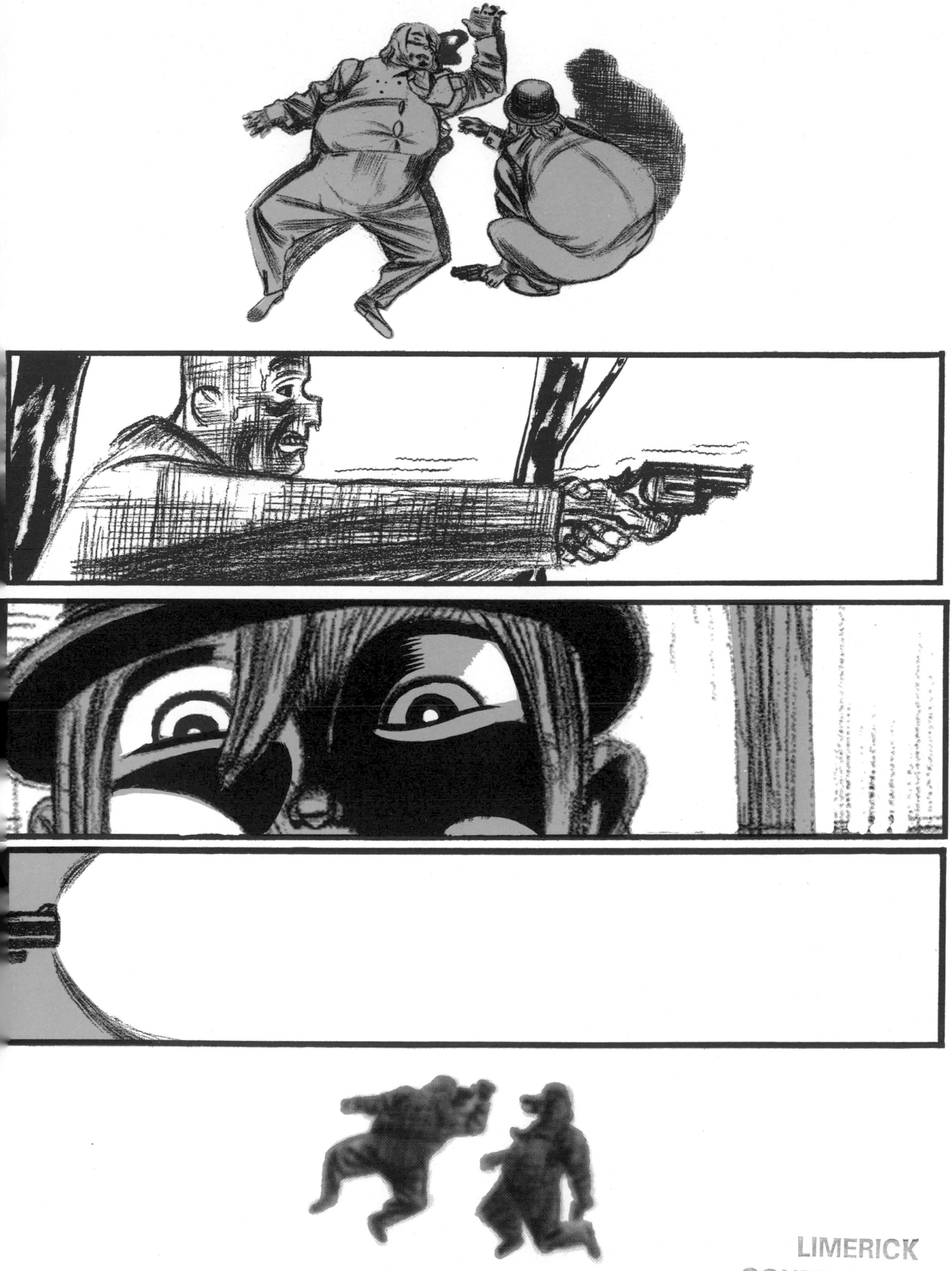

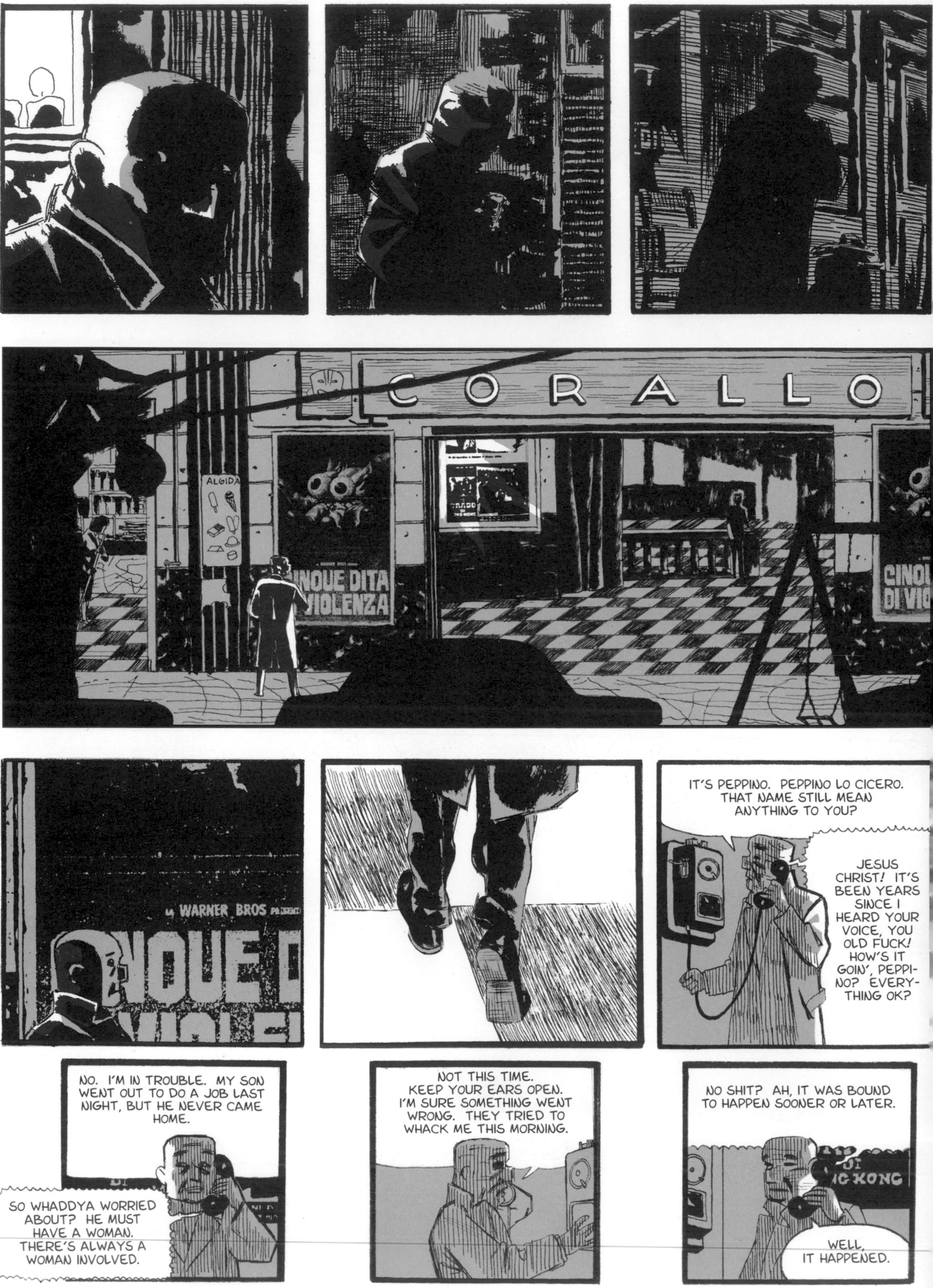

CORALLO
ALGIDA
INQUE DITA
VIOLENZA
WARNER BROS
IT'S PEPPINO. PEPPINO LO CICERO. THAT NAME STILL MEAN ANYTHING TO YOU?
JESUS CHRIST! IT'S BEEN YEARS SINCE I HEARD YOUR VOICE, YOU OLD FUCK! HOW'S IT GOIN', PEPPINO? EVERYTHING OK?
NO. I'M IN TROUBLE. MY SON WENT OUT TO DO A JOB LAST NIGHT, BUT HE NEVER CAME HOME.
SO WHADDYA WORRIED ABOUT? HE MUST HAVE A WOMAN. THERE'S ALWAYS A WOMAN INVOLVED.
NOT THIS TIME. KEEP YOUR EARS OPEN. I'M SURE SOMETHING WENT WRONG. THEY TRIED TO WHACK ME THIS MORNING.
NO SHIT? AH, IT WAS BOUND TO HAPPEN SOONER OR LATER.
WELL, IT HAPPENED.

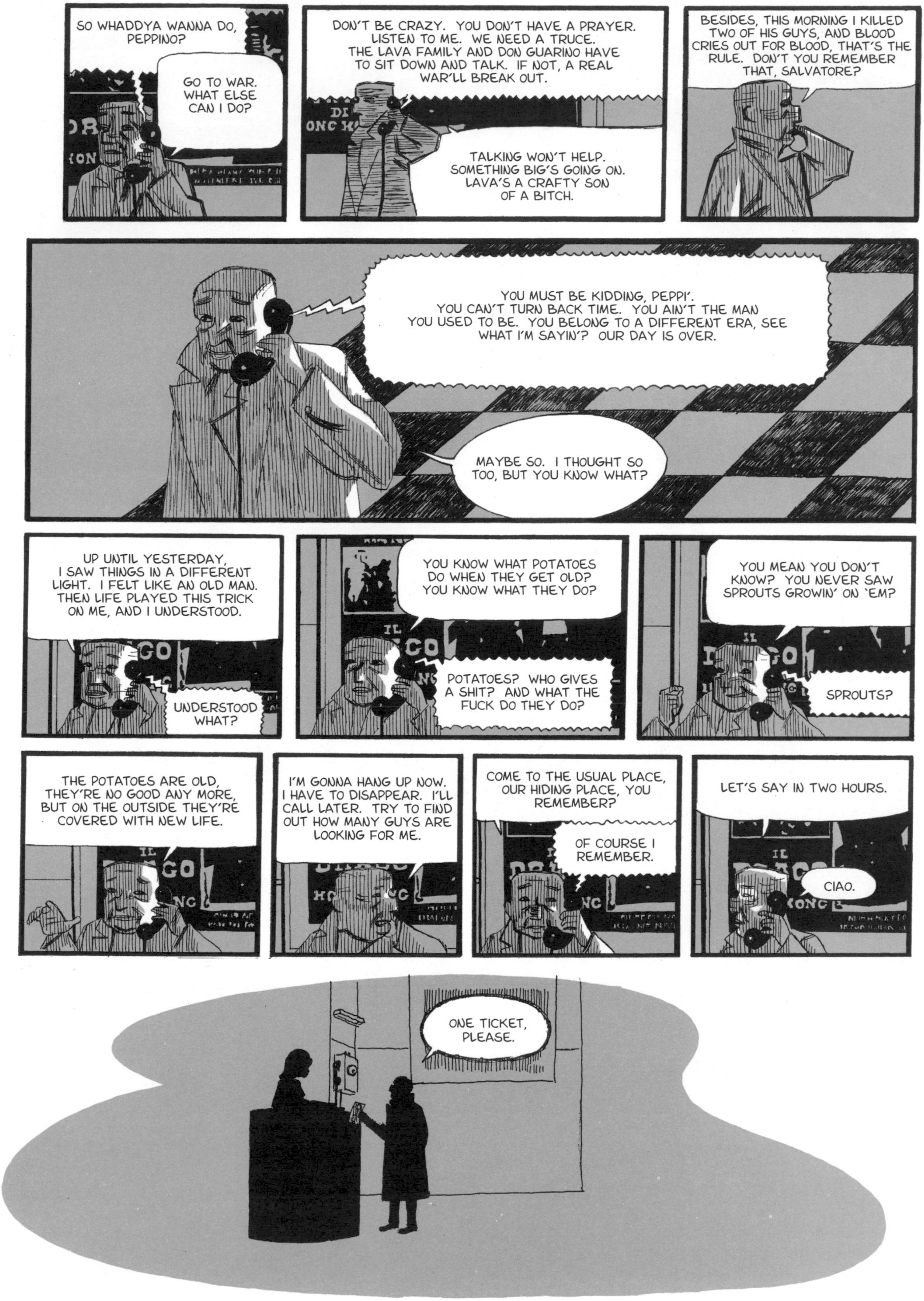
SO WHADDYA WANNA DO, PEPPINO?
GO TO WAR. WHAT ELSE CAN I DO?
DON'T BE CRAZY. YOU DON'T HAVE A PRAYER. LISTEN TO ME. WE NEED A TRUCE. THE LAVA FAMILY AND DON GUARINO HAVE TO SIT DOWN AND TALK. IF NOT, A REAL WAR'LL BREAK OUT.
TALKING WON'T HELP. SOMETHING BIG'S GOING ON. LAVA'S A CRAFTY SON OF A BITCH.
BESIDES, THIS MORNING I KILLED TWO OF HIS GUYS, AND BLOOD CRIES OUT FOR BLOOD, THAT'S THE RULE. DON'T YOU REMEMBER THAT, SALVATORE?
YOU MUST BE KIDDING, PEPPI'. YOU CAN'T TURN BACK TIME. YOU AIN'T THE MAN YOU USED TO BE. YOU BELONG TO A DIFFERENT ERA, SEE WHAT I'M SAYIN'? OUR DAY IS OVER.
MAYBE SO. I THOUGHT SO TOO, BUT YOU KNOW WHAT?
UP UNTIL YESTERDAY, I SAW THINGS IN A DIFFERENT LIGHT. I FELT LIKE AN OLD MAN. THEN LIFE PLAYED THIS TRICK ON ME, AND I UNDERSTOOD.
UNDERSTOOD WHAT?
YOU KNOW WHAT POTATOES DO WHEN THEY GET OLD? YOU KNOW WHAT THEY DO?
POTATOES? WHO GIVES A SHIT? AND WHAT THE FUCK DO THEY DO?
YOU MEAN YOU DON'T KNOW? YOU NEVER SAW SPROUTS GROWIN' ON 'EM?
SPROUTS?
THE POTATOES ARE OLD, THEY'RE NO GOOD ANY MORE, BUT ON THE OUTSIDE THEY'RE COVERED WITH NEW LIFE.
I'M GONNA HANG UP NOW. I HAVE TO DISAPPEAR. I'LL CALL LATER. TRY TO FIND OUT HOW MANY GUYS ARE LOOKING FOR ME.
COME TO THE USUAL PLACE, OUR HIDING PLACE, YOU REMEMBER?
OF COURSE I REMEMBER.
LET'S SAY IN TWO HOURS.
CIAO.
ONE TICKET, PLEASE.

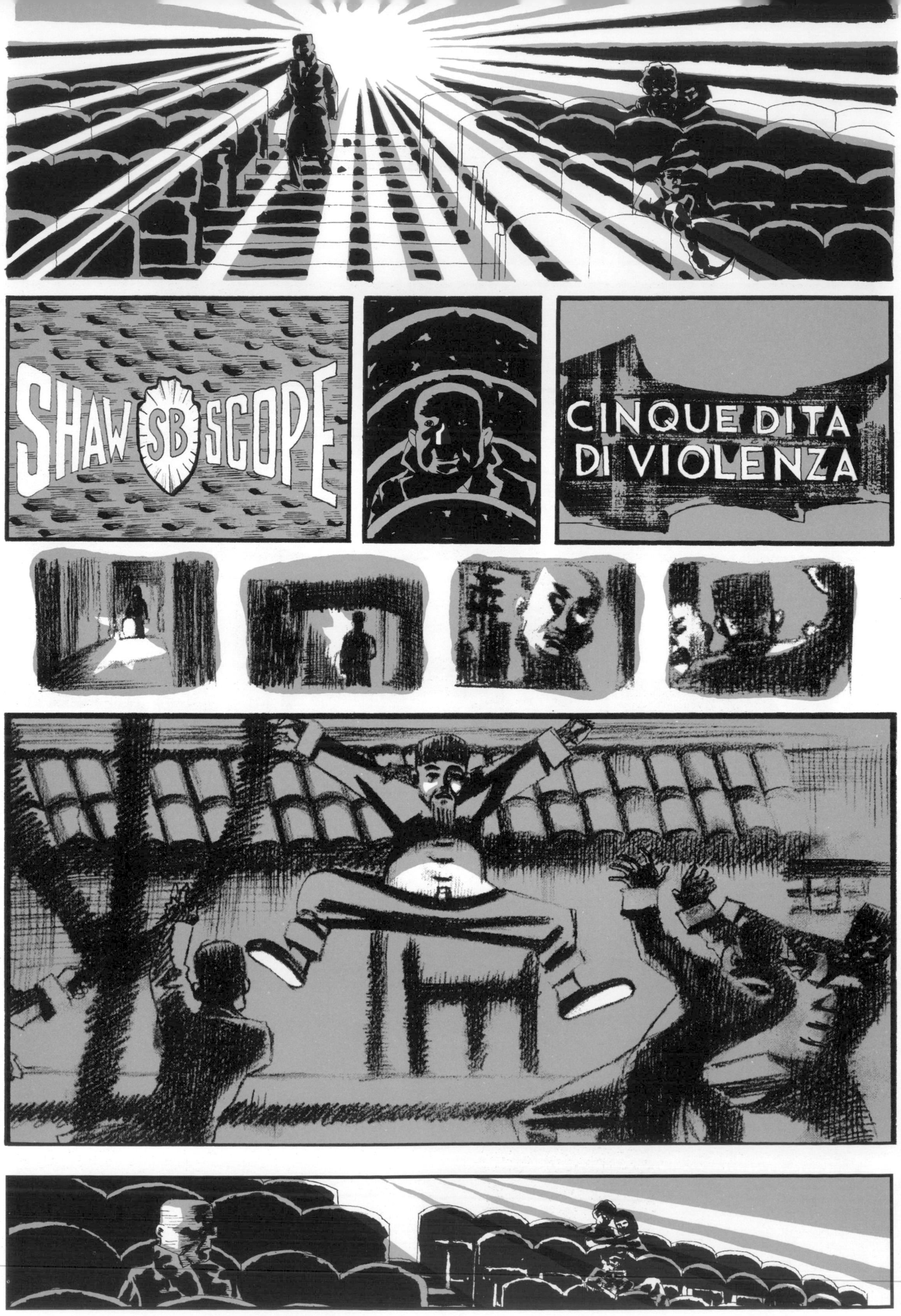
SHAW SB SCOPE
CINQUE DITA DI VIOLENZA

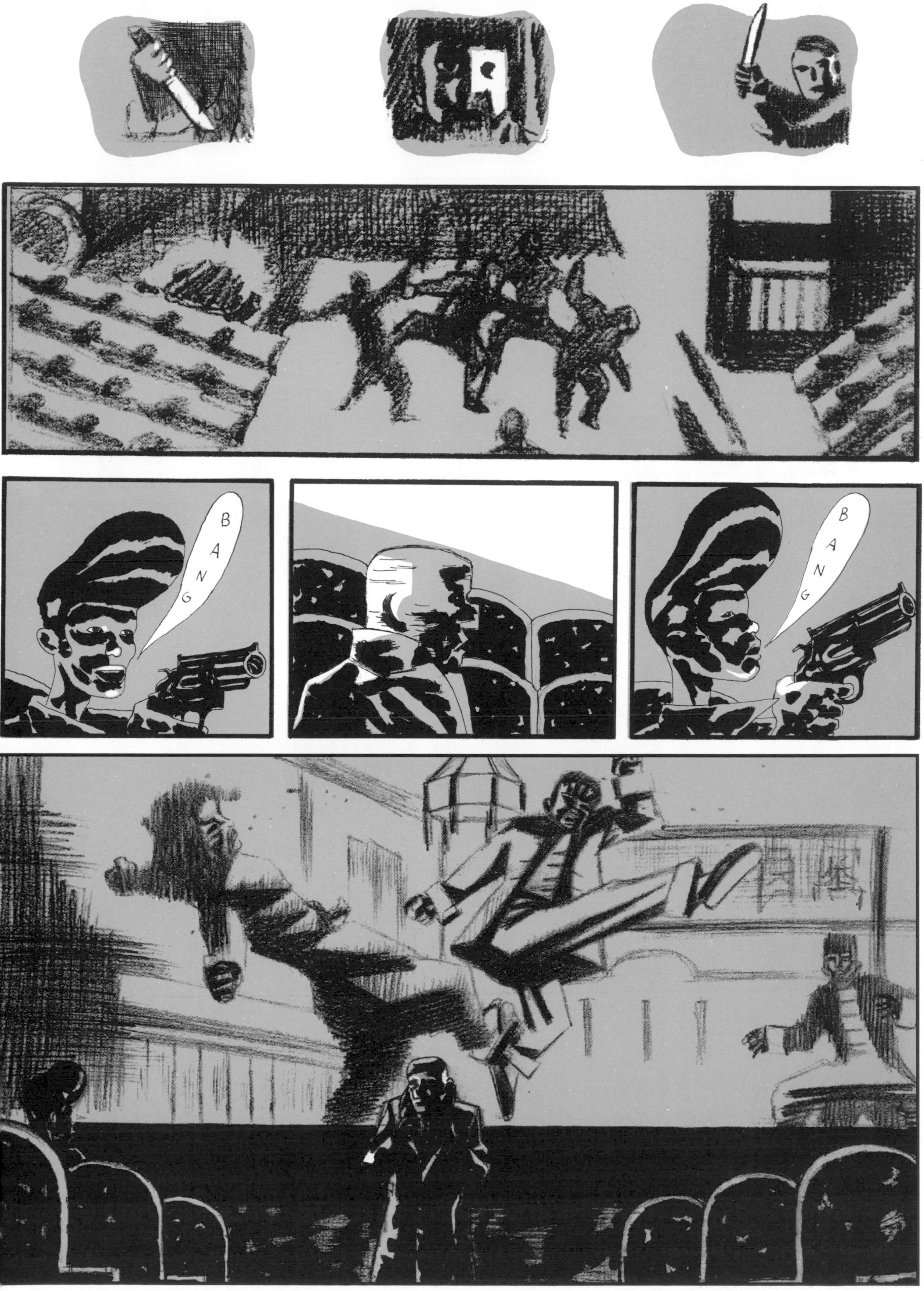
BANG
BANG

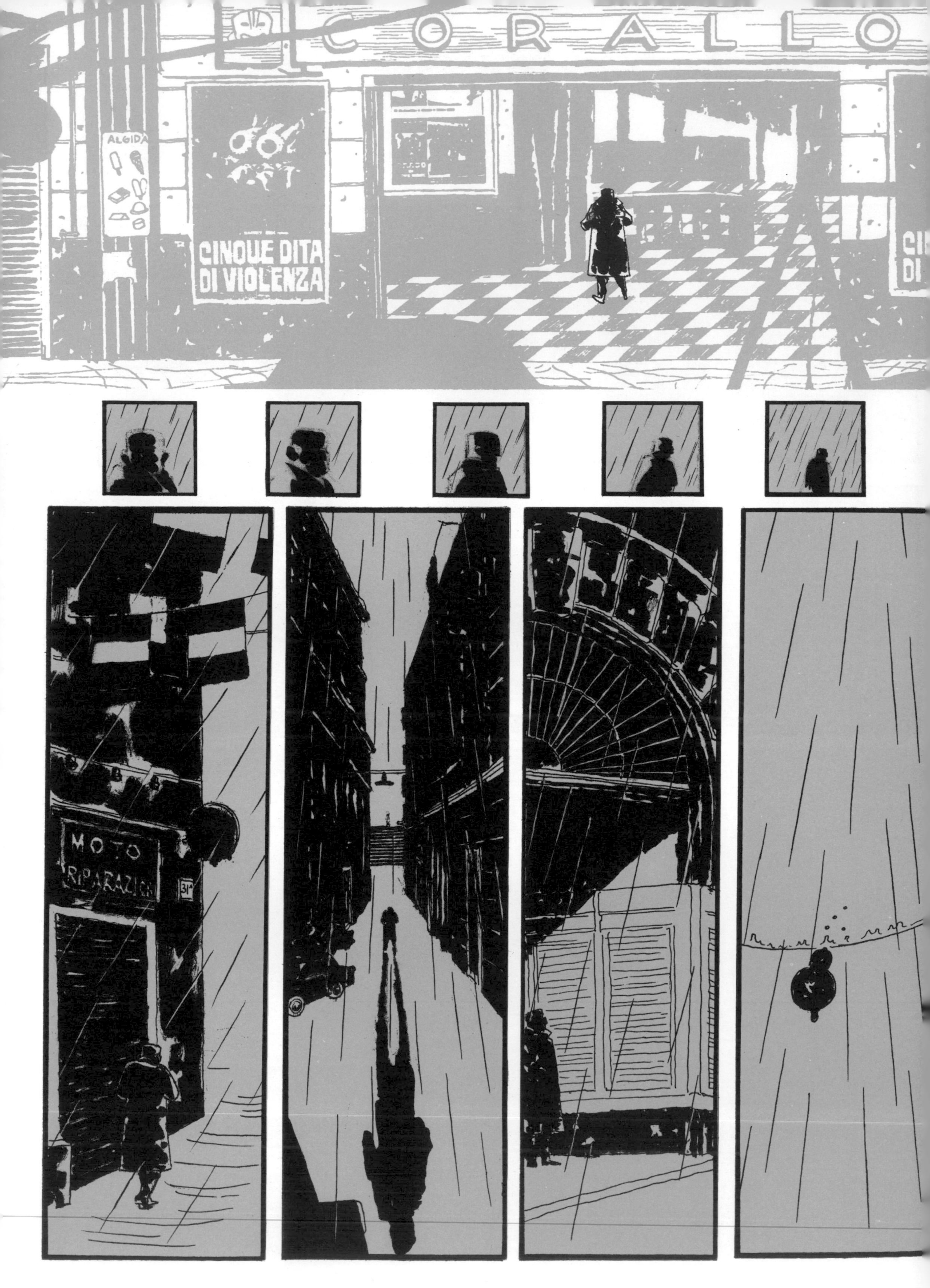
CORALLO
ALGIDA
CINQUE DITA DI VIOLENZA
MOTO
RIPARAZION
31a

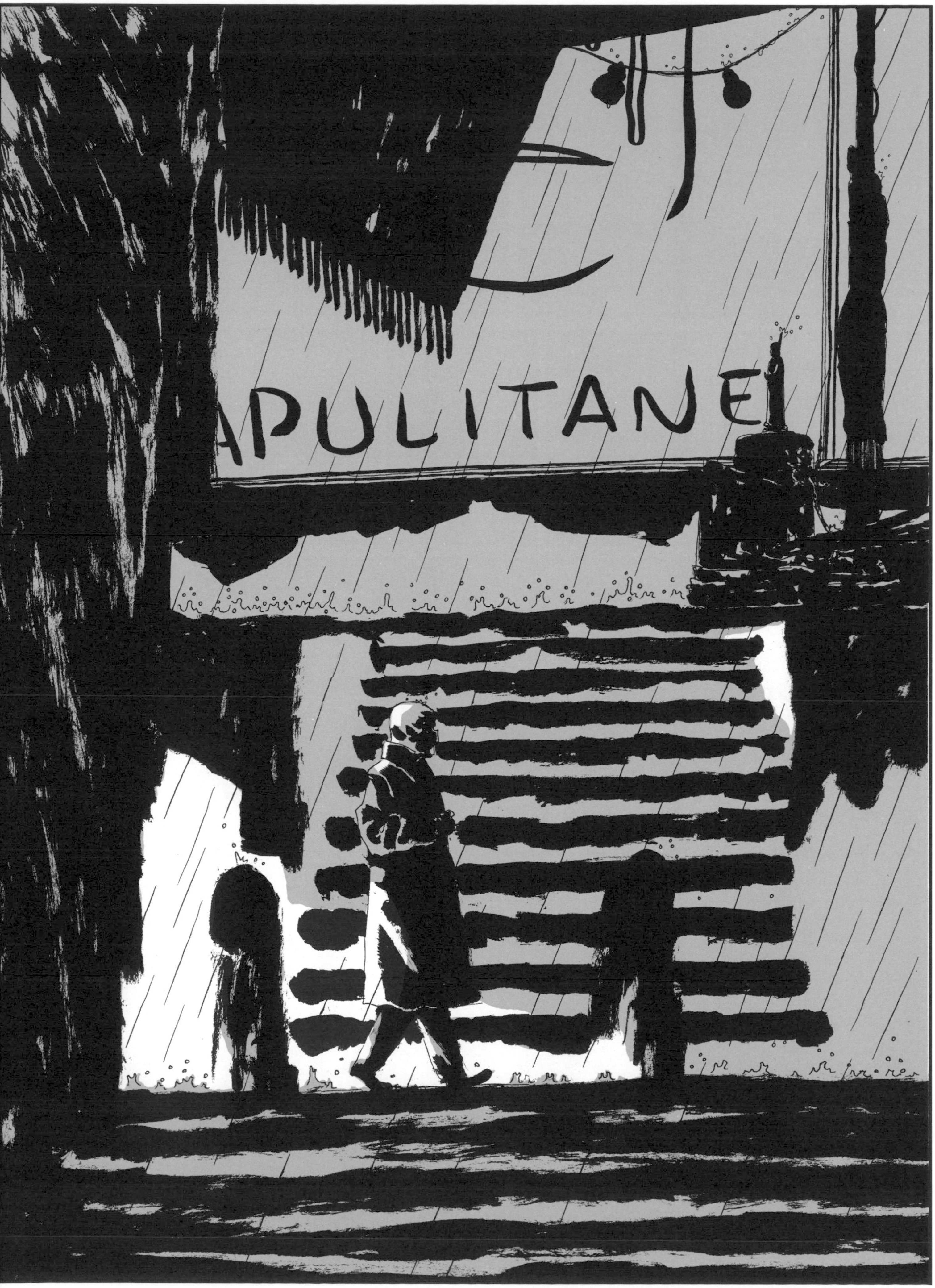
APULITANE

PERICOLO
DI CROLLO
CR..
CROK
WUMP
CROK CROK

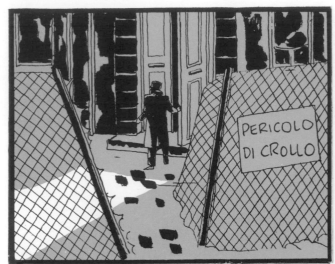

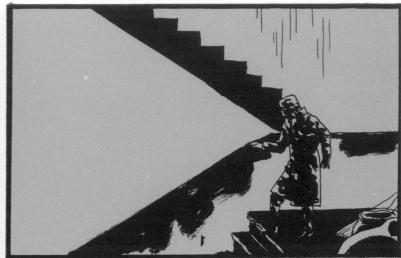

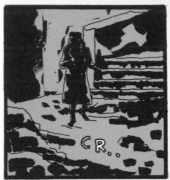

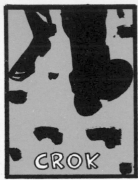

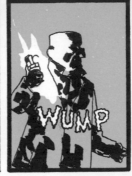

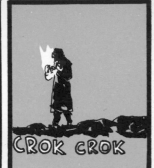

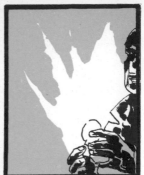

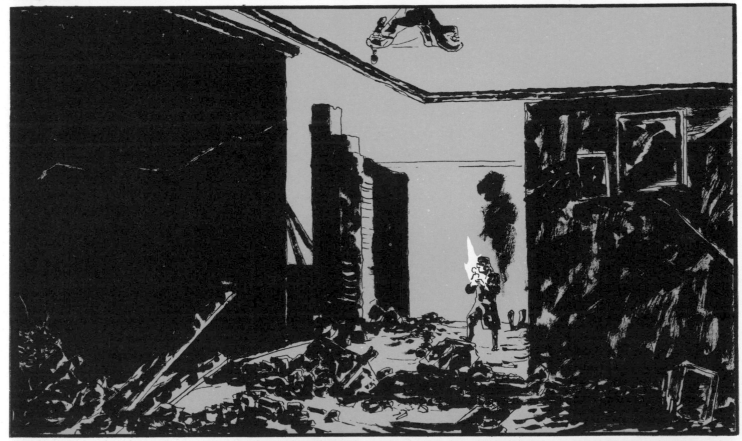

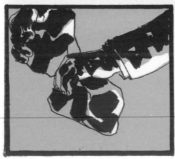

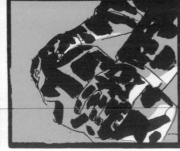

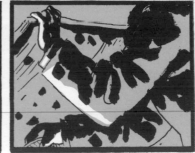

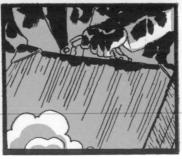

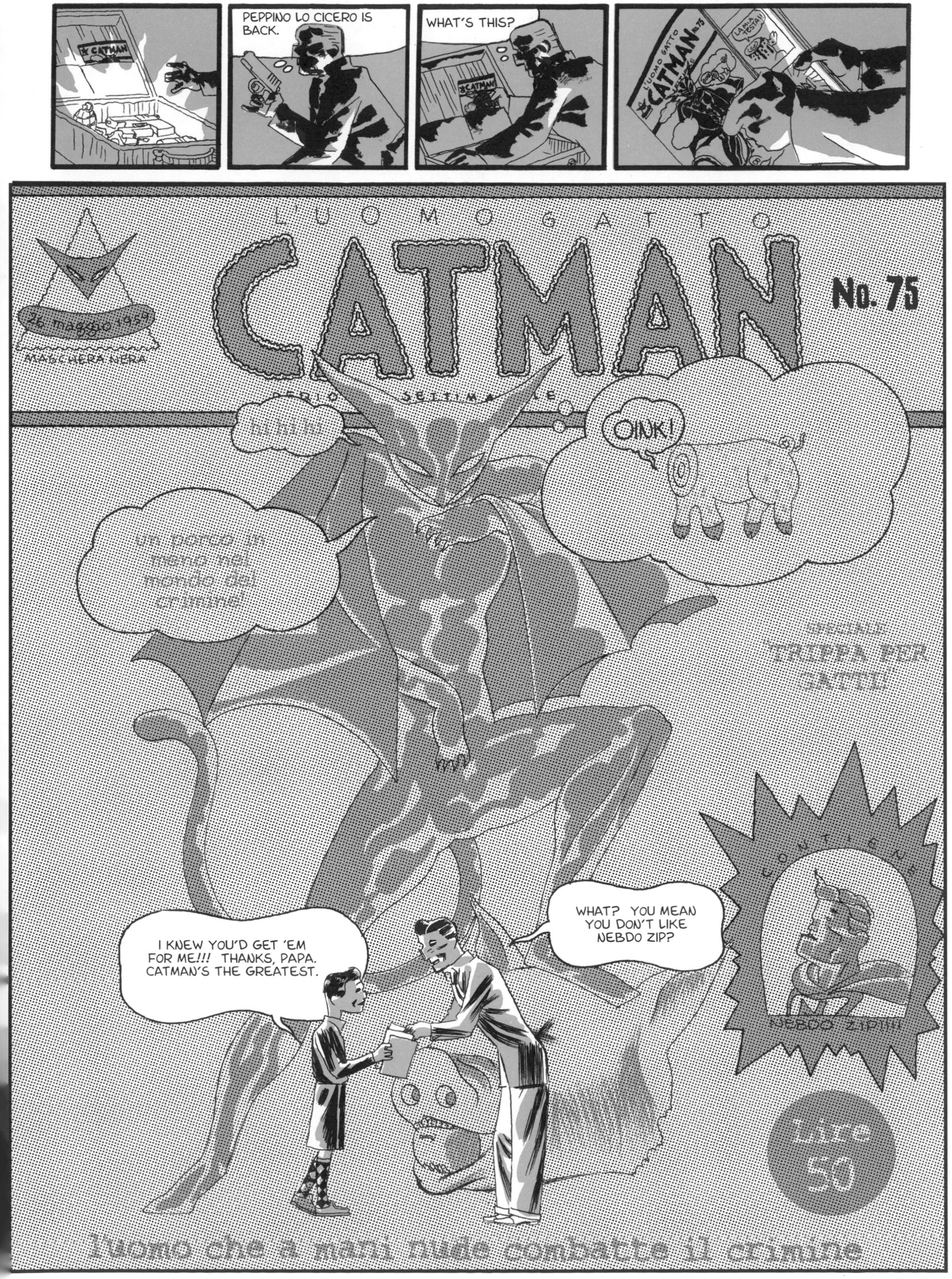
PEPPINO LO CICERO IS BACK.
WHAT'S THIS?
L'UOMO GATTO
CATMAN
No. 75
26 maggio 1959
MASCHERA NERA
OINK!
un porco in meno nel mondo del crimine!
TRIPPA PER GATTI!
CONTIENE
NEBDO ZIP!!!!
Lire 50
WHAT? YOU MEAN YOU DON'T LIKE NEBDO ZIP?
I KNEW YOU'D GET 'EM FOR ME!!! THANKS, PAPA. CATMAN'S THE GREATEST.
l'uomo che a mani nude combatte il crimine

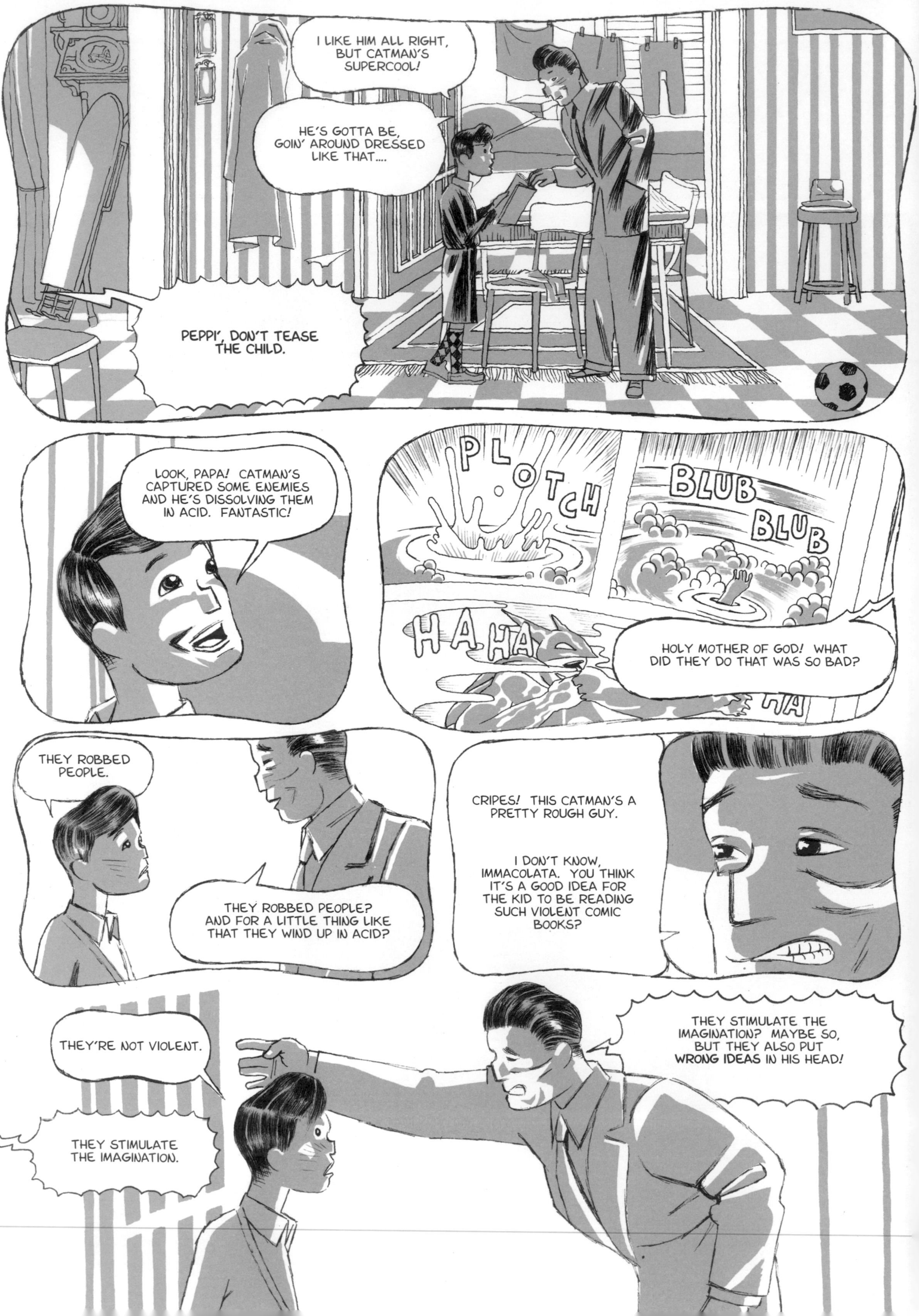
I LIKE HIM ALL RIGHT, BUT CATMAN'S SUPERCOOL!
HE'S GOTTA BE, GOIN' AROUND DRESSED LIKE THAT....
PEPPI', DON'T TEASE THE CHILD.
LOOK, PAPA! CATMAN'S CAPTURED SOME ENEMIES AND HE'S DISSOLVING THEM IN ACID. FANTASTIC!
PLOTCH
BLUB
BLUB
HA HA HA
HA
HOLY MOTHER OF GOD! WHAT DID THEY DO THAT WAS SO BAD?
THEY ROBBED PEOPLE.
THEY ROBBED PEOPLE? AND FOR A LITTLE THING LIKE THAT THEY WIND UP IN ACID?
CRIPES! THIS CATMAN'S A PRETTY ROUGH GUY.
I DON'T KNOW, IMMACOLATA. YOU THINK IT'S A GOOD IDEA FOR THE KID TO BE READING SUCH VIOLENT COMIC BOOKS?
THEY'RE NOT VIOLENT.
THEY STIMULATE THE IMAGINATION.
THEY STIMULATE THE IMAGINATION? MAYBE SO, BUT THEY ALSO PUT WRONG IDEAS IN HIS HEAD!

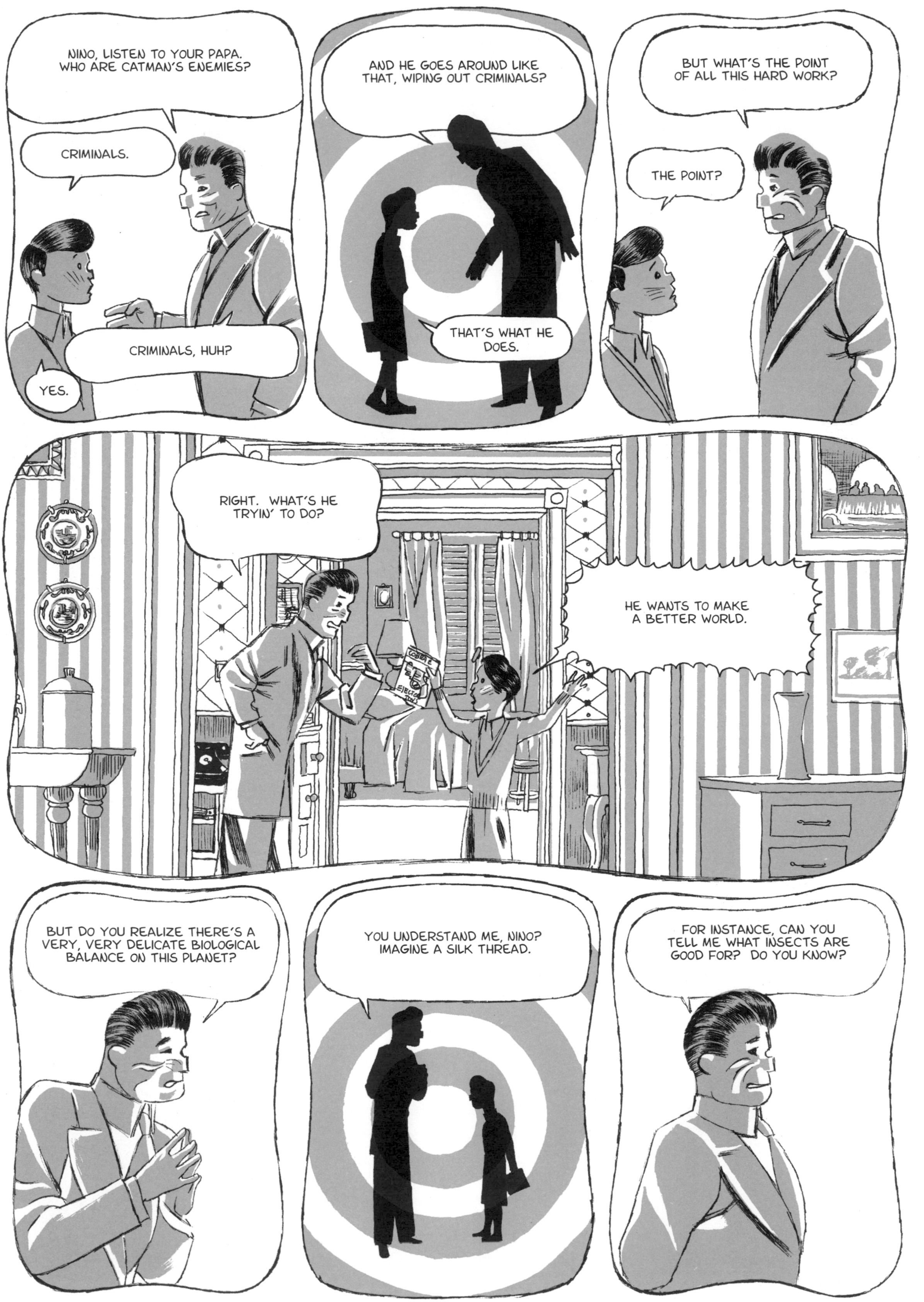
NINO, LISTEN TO YOUR PAPA. WHO ARE CATMAN'S ENEMIES?
CRIMINALS.
CRIMINALS, HUH?
YES.
AND HE GOES AROUND LIKE THAT, WIPING OUT CRIMINALS?
THAT'S WHAT HE DOES.
BUT WHAT'S THE POINT OF ALL THIS HARD WORK?
THE POINT?
RIGHT. WHAT'S HE TRYIN' TO DO?
HE WANTS TO MAKE A BETTER WORLD.
BUT DO YOU REALIZE THERE'S A VERY, VERY DELICATE BIOLOGICAL BALANCE ON THIS PLANET?
YOU UNDERSTAND ME, NINO? IMAGINE A SILK THREAD.
FOR INSTANCE, CAN YOU TELL ME WHAT INSECTS ARE GOOD FOR? DO YOU KNOW?

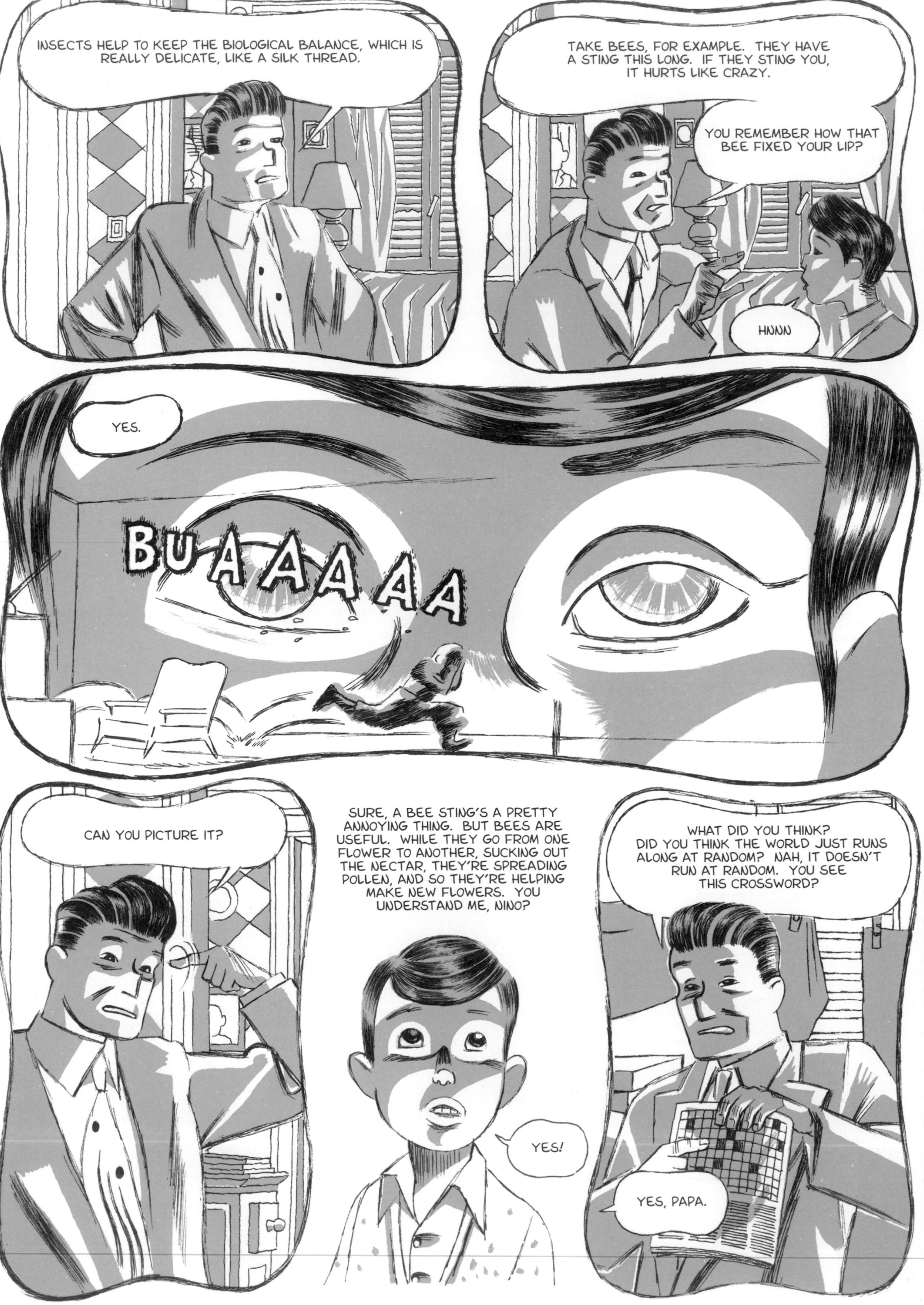
INSECTS HELP TO KEEP THE BIOLOGICAL BALANCE, WHICH IS REALLY DELICATE, LIKE A SILK THREAD.
TAKE BEES, FOR EXAMPLE. THEY HAVE A STING THIS LONG. IF THEY STING YOU, IT HURTS LIKE CRAZY.
YOU REMEMBER HOW THAT BEE FIXED YOUR LIP?
HNNN
YES.
BUAAAAA
CAN YOU PICTURE IT?
SURE, A BEE STING'S A PRETTY ANNOYING THING. BUT BEES ARE USEFUL. WHILE THEY GO FROM ONE FLOWER TO ANOTHER, SUCKING OUT THE NECTAR, THEY'RE SPREADING POLLEN, AND SO THEY'RE HELPING MAKE NEW FLOWERS. YOU UNDERSTAND ME, NINO?
YES!
WHAT DID YOU THINK? DID YOU THINK THE WORLD JUST RUNS ALONG AT RANDOM? NAH, IT DOESN'T RUN AT RANDOM. YOU SEE THIS CROSSWORD?
YES, PAPA.

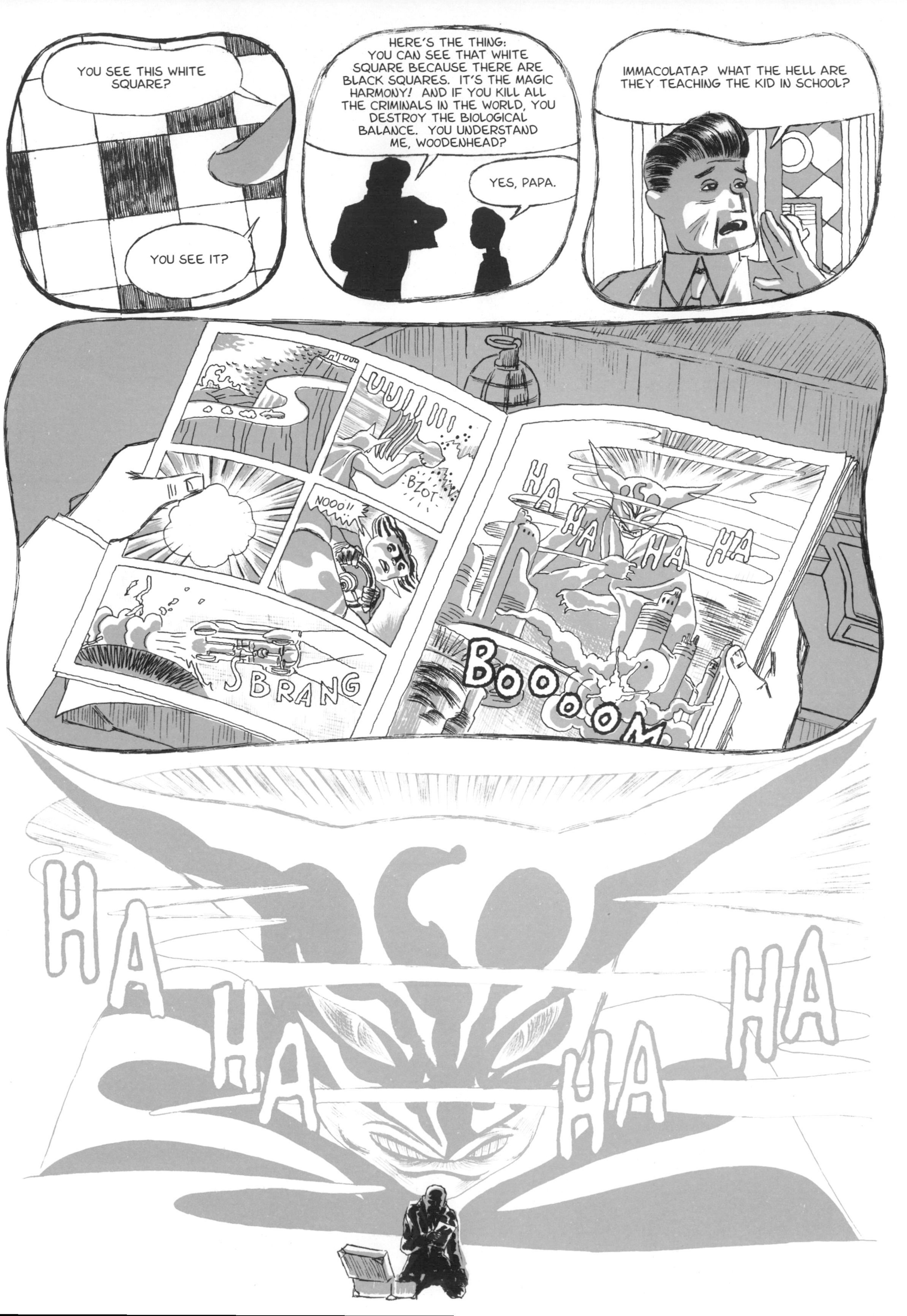
YOU SEE THIS WHITE SQUARE?
YOU SEE IT?
HERE'S THE THING: YOU CAN SEE THAT WHITE SQUARE BECAUSE THERE ARE BLACK SQUARES. IT'S THE MAGIC HARMONY! AND IF YOU KILL ALL THE CRIMINALS IN THE WORLD, YOU DESTROY THE BIOLOGICAL BALANCE. YOU UNDERSTAND ME, WOODENHEAD?
YES, PAPA.
IMMACOLATA? WHAT THE HELL ARE THEY TEACHING THE KID IN SCHOOL?
UUU!!!!!
BZOT
NOOO!!
SBRANG
HA HA HA HA HA
BOOOOOM
HA HA HA HA HA

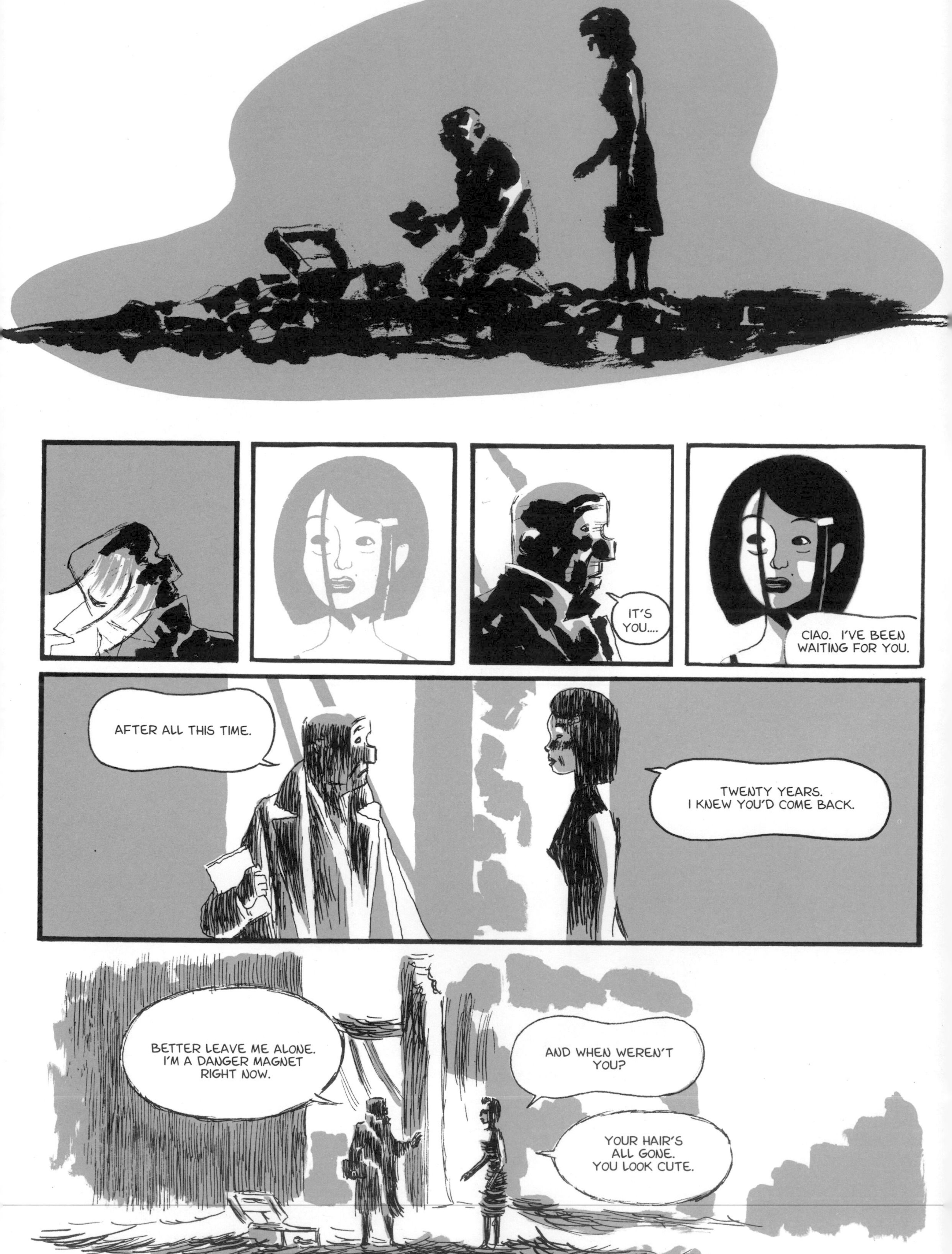
IT'S YOU....
CIAO. I'VE BEEN WAITING FOR YOU.
AFTER ALL THIS TIME.
TWENTY YEARS. I KNEW YOU'D COME BACK.
BETTER LEAVE ME ALONE. I'M A DANGER MAGNET RIGHT NOW.
AND WHEN WEREN'T YOU?
YOUR HAIR'S ALL GONE. YOU LOOK CUTE.

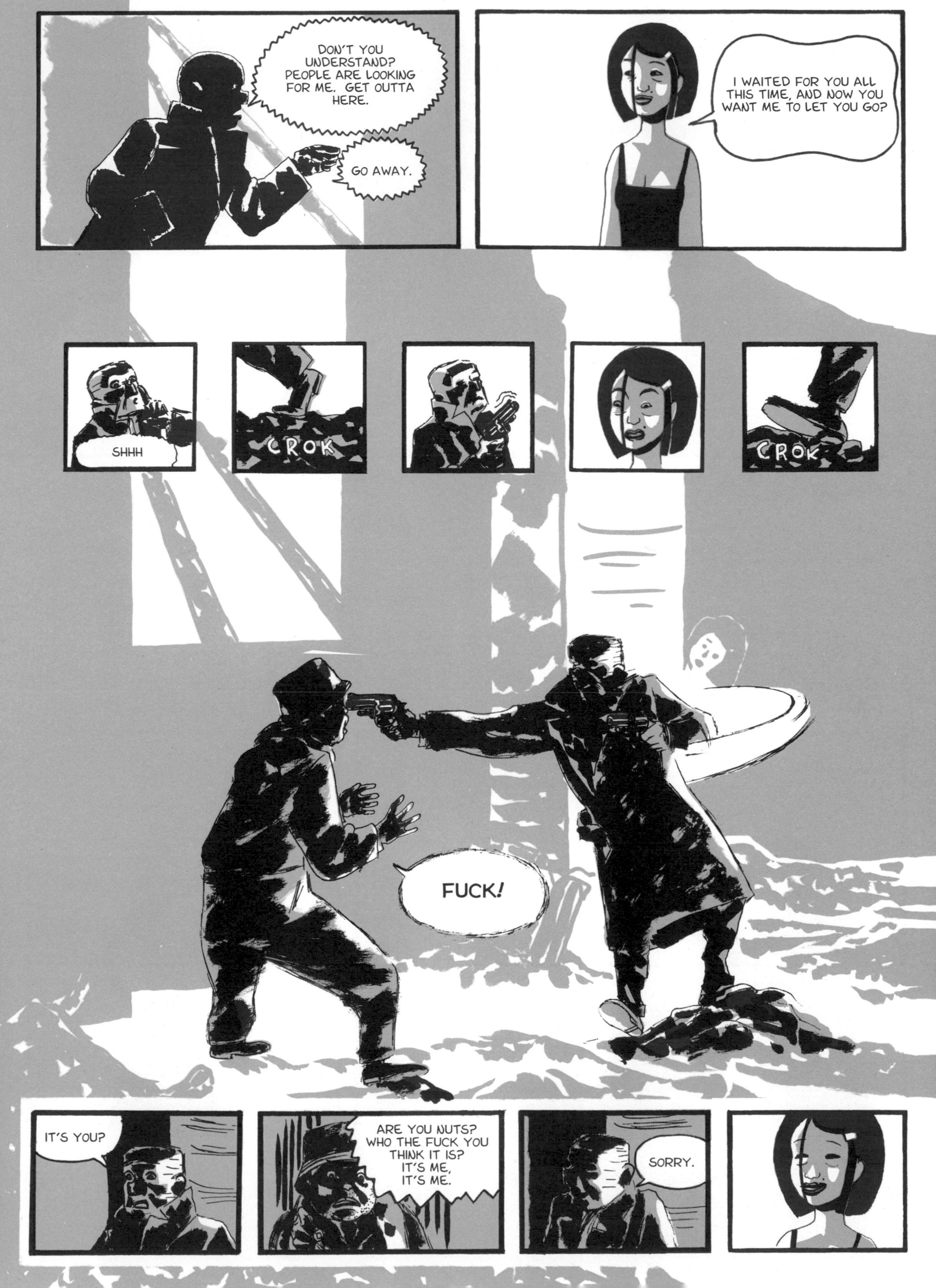

DON'T YOU UNDERSTAND? PEOPLE ARE LOOKING FOR ME. GET OUTTA HERE.
GO AWAY.
I WAITED FOR YOU ALL THIS TIME, AND NOW YOU WANT ME TO LET YOU GO?
SHHH
CROK
CROK
FUCK!
IT'S YOU?
ARE YOU NUTS? WHO THE FUCK YOU THINK IT IS? IT'S ME, IT'S ME.
SORRY.

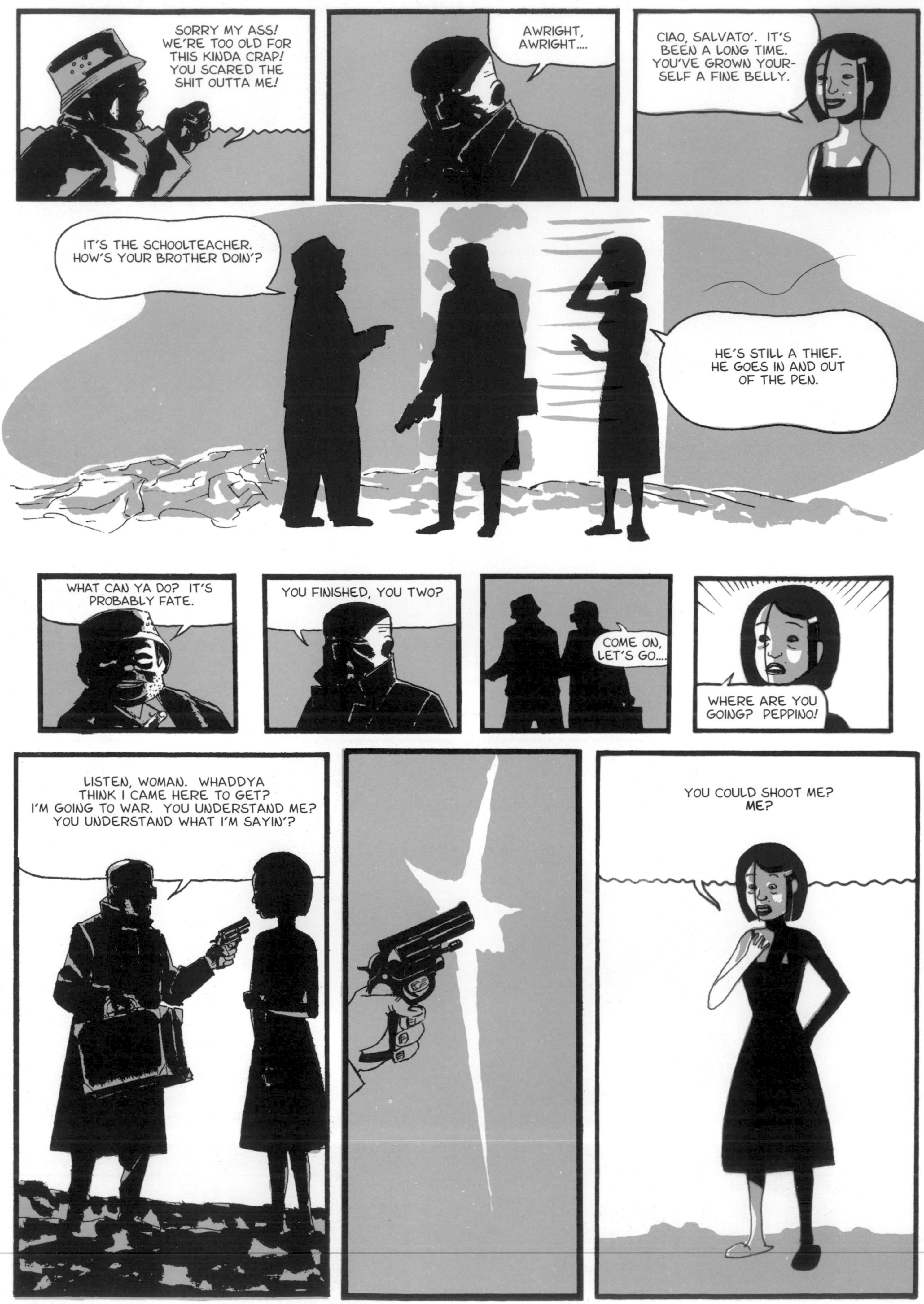
SORRY MY ASS! WE'RE TOO OLD FOR THIS KINDA CRAP! YOU SCARED THE SHIT OUTTA ME!
AWRIGHT, AWRIGHT....
CIAO, SALVATO'. IT'S BEEN A LONG TIME. YOU'VE GROWN YOURSELF A FINE BELLY.
IT'S THE SCHOOLTEACHER. HOW'S YOUR BROTHER DOIN'?
HE'S STILL A THIEF. HE GOES IN AND OUT OF THE PEN.
WHAT CAN YA DO? IT'S PROBABLY FATE.
YOU FINISHED, YOU TWO?
COME ON, LET'S GO....
WHERE ARE YOU GOING? PEPPINO!
LISTEN, WOMAN. WHADDYA THINK I CAME HERE TO GET? I'M GOING TO WAR. YOU UNDERSTAND ME? YOU UNDERSTAND WHAT I'M SAYIN'?
YOU COULD SHOOT ME? **ME?**

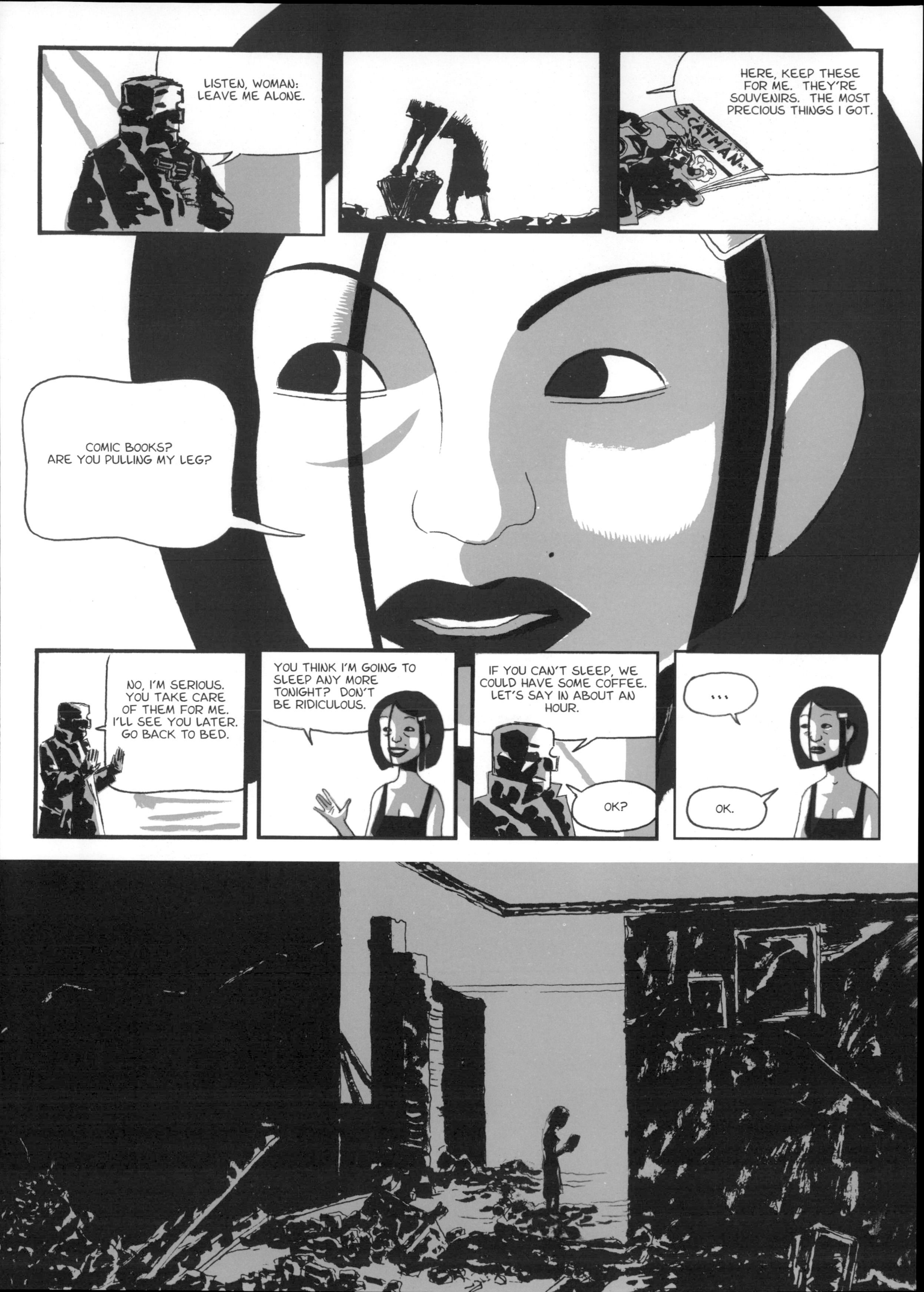
LISTEN, WOMAN: LEAVE ME ALONE.
HERE, KEEP THESE FOR ME. THEY'RE SOUVENIRS. THE MOST PRECIOUS THINGS I GOT.
CATMAN
COMIC BOOKS? ARE YOU PULLING MY LEG?
NO, I'M SERIOUS. YOU TAKE CARE OF THEM FOR ME. I'LL SEE YOU LATER. GO BACK TO BED.
YOU THINK I'M GOING TO SLEEP ANY MORE TONIGHT? DON'T BE RIDICULOUS.
IF YOU CAN'T SLEEP, WE COULD HAVE SOME COFFEE. LET'S SAY IN ABOUT AN HOUR.
OK?
...
OK.

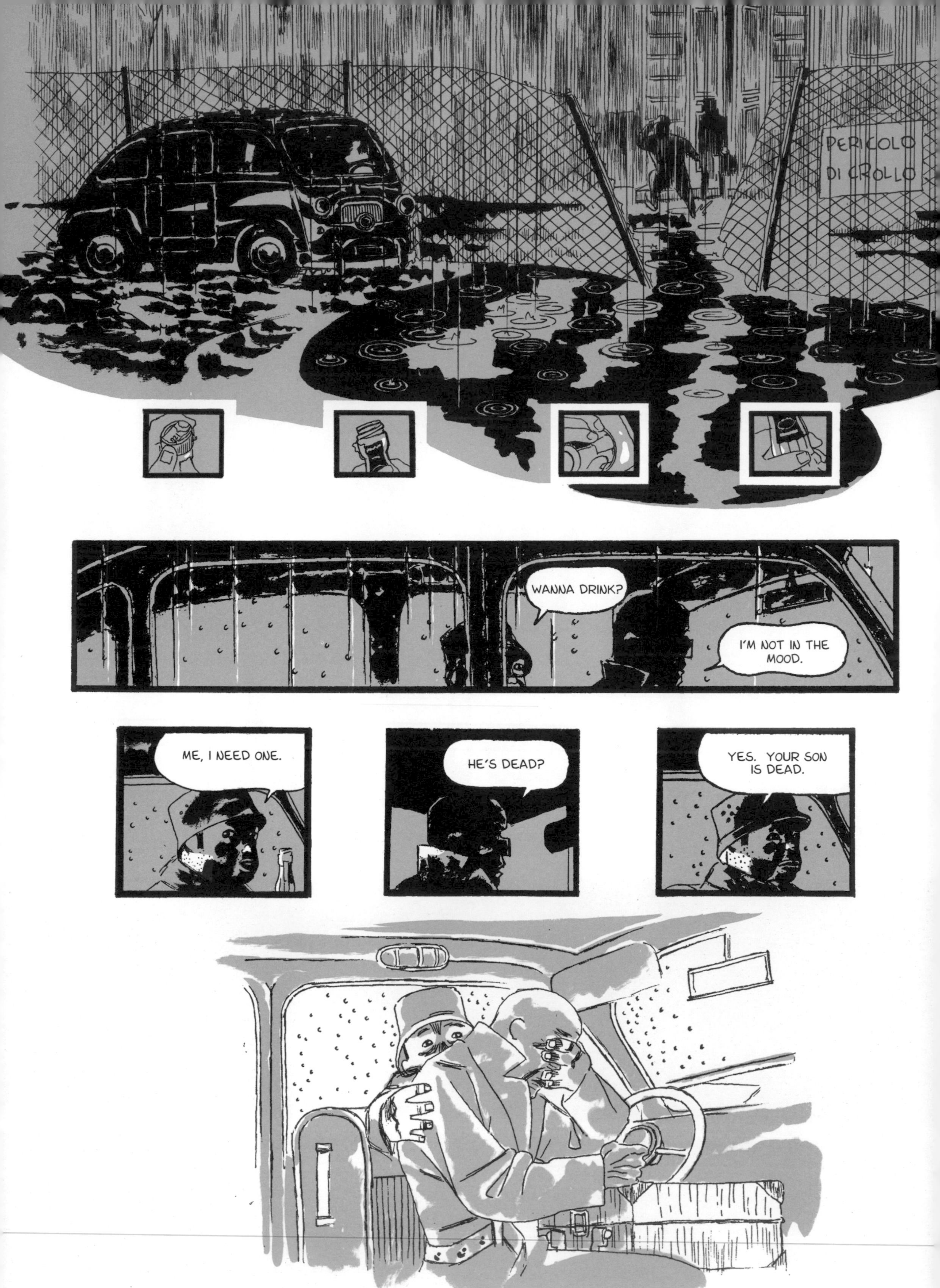
PERICOLO DI CROLLO
WANNA DRINK?
I'M NOT IN THE MOOD.
ME, I NEED ONE.
HE'S DEAD?
YES. YOUR SON IS DEAD.

WHADDYA THINKIN' ABOUT NOW, PEPPINO? HUH? WHADDYA THINK YOU'RE GONNA DO?
ARE YOU WITH ME?
9mm

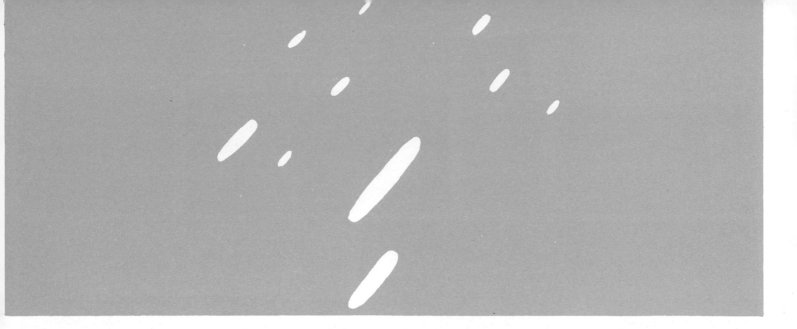

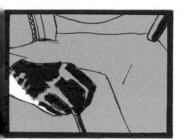

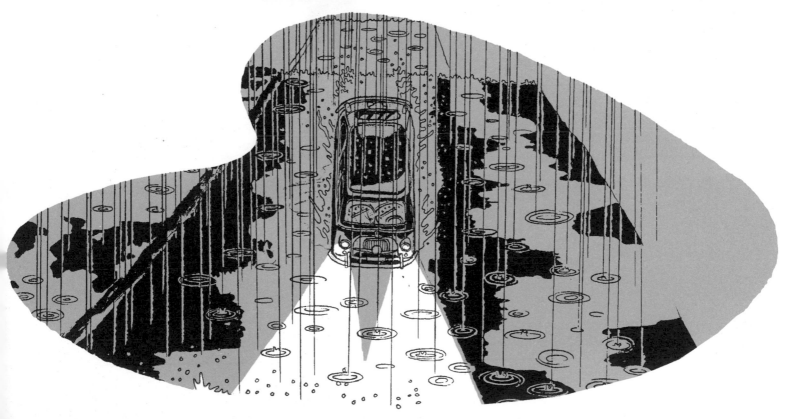

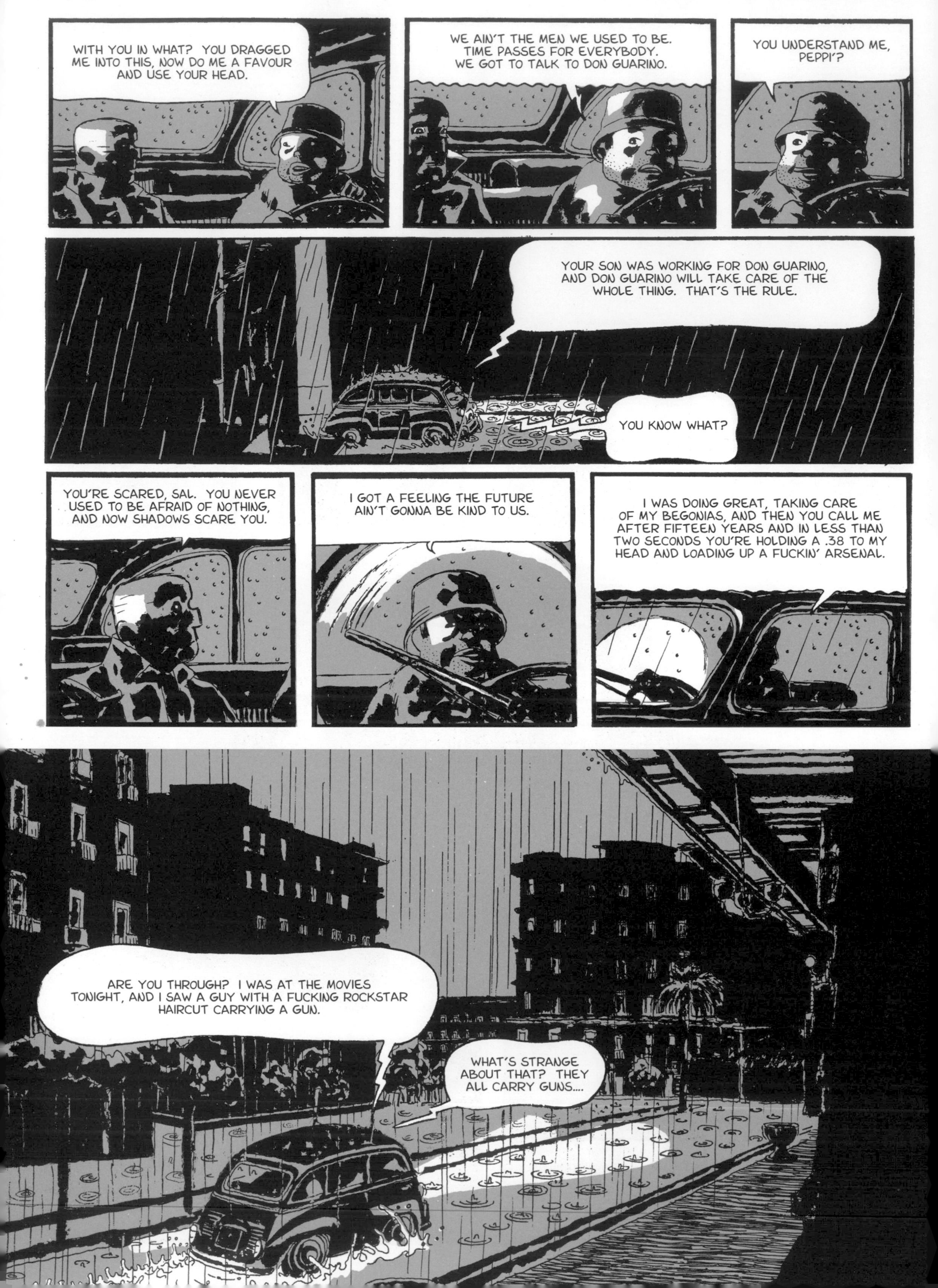
WITH YOU IN WHAT? YOU DRAGGED ME INTO THIS, NOW DO ME A FAVOUR AND USE YOUR HEAD.
WE AIN'T THE MEN WE USED TO BE. TIME PASSES FOR EVERYBODY. WE GOT TO TALK TO DON GUARINO.
YOU UNDERSTAND ME, PEPPI'?
YOUR SON WAS WORKING FOR DON GUARINO, AND DON GUARINO WILL TAKE CARE OF THE WHOLE THING. THAT'S THE RULE.
YOU KNOW WHAT?
YOU'RE SCARED, SAL. YOU NEVER USED TO BE AFRAID OF NOTHING, AND NOW SHADOWS SCARE YOU.
I GOT A FEELING THE FUTURE AIN'T GONNA BE KIND TO US.
I WAS DOING GREAT, TAKING CARE OF MY BEGONIAS, AND THEN YOU CALL ME AFTER FIFTEEN YEARS AND IN LESS THAN TWO SECONDS YOU'RE HOLDING A .38 TO MY HEAD AND LOADING UP A FUCKIN' ARSENAL.
ARE YOU THROUGH? I WAS AT THE MOVIES TONIGHT, AND I SAW A GUY WITH A FUCKING ROCKSTAR HAIRCUT CARRYING A GUN.
WHAT'S STRANGE ABOUT THAT? THEY ALL CARRY GUNS....

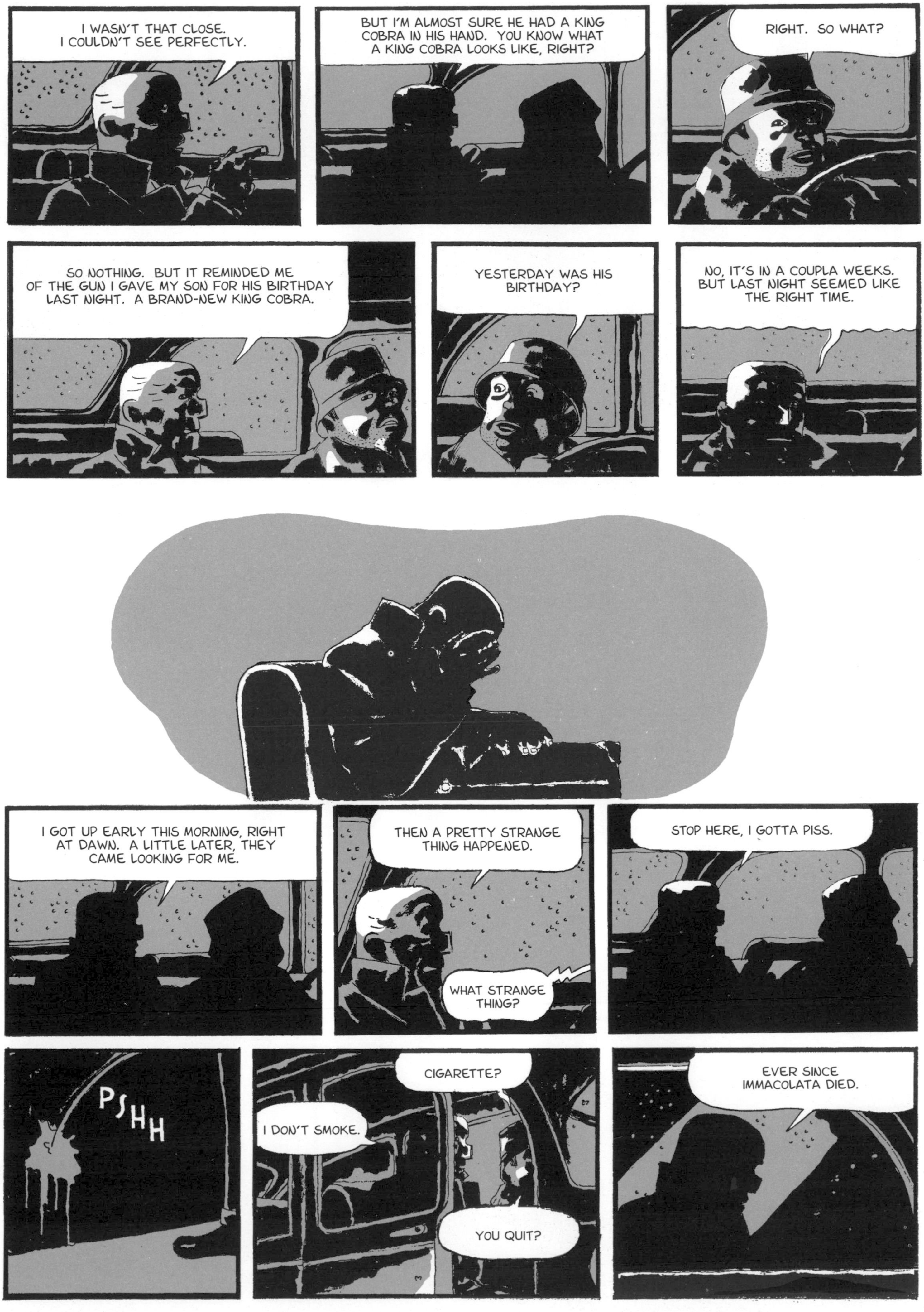
I WASN'T THAT CLOSE. I COULDN'T SEE PERFECTLY.
BUT I'M ALMOST SURE HE HAD A KING COBRA IN HIS HAND. YOU KNOW WHAT A KING COBRA LOOKS LIKE, RIGHT?
RIGHT. SO WHAT?
SO NOTHING. BUT IT REMINDED ME OF THE GUN I GAVE MY SON FOR HIS BIRTHDAY LAST NIGHT. A BRAND-NEW KING COBRA.
YESTERDAY WAS HIS BIRTHDAY?
NO, IT'S IN A COUPLA WEEKS. BUT LAST NIGHT SEEMED LIKE THE RIGHT TIME.
I GOT UP EARLY THIS MORNING, RIGHT AT DAWN. A LITTLE LATER, THEY CAME LOOKING FOR ME.
THEN A PRETTY STRANGE THING HAPPENED.
WHAT STRANGE THING?
STOP HERE, I GOTTA PISS.
PSHH
CIGARETTE?
I DON'T SMOKE.
YOU QUIT?
EVER SINCE IMMACOLATA DIED.

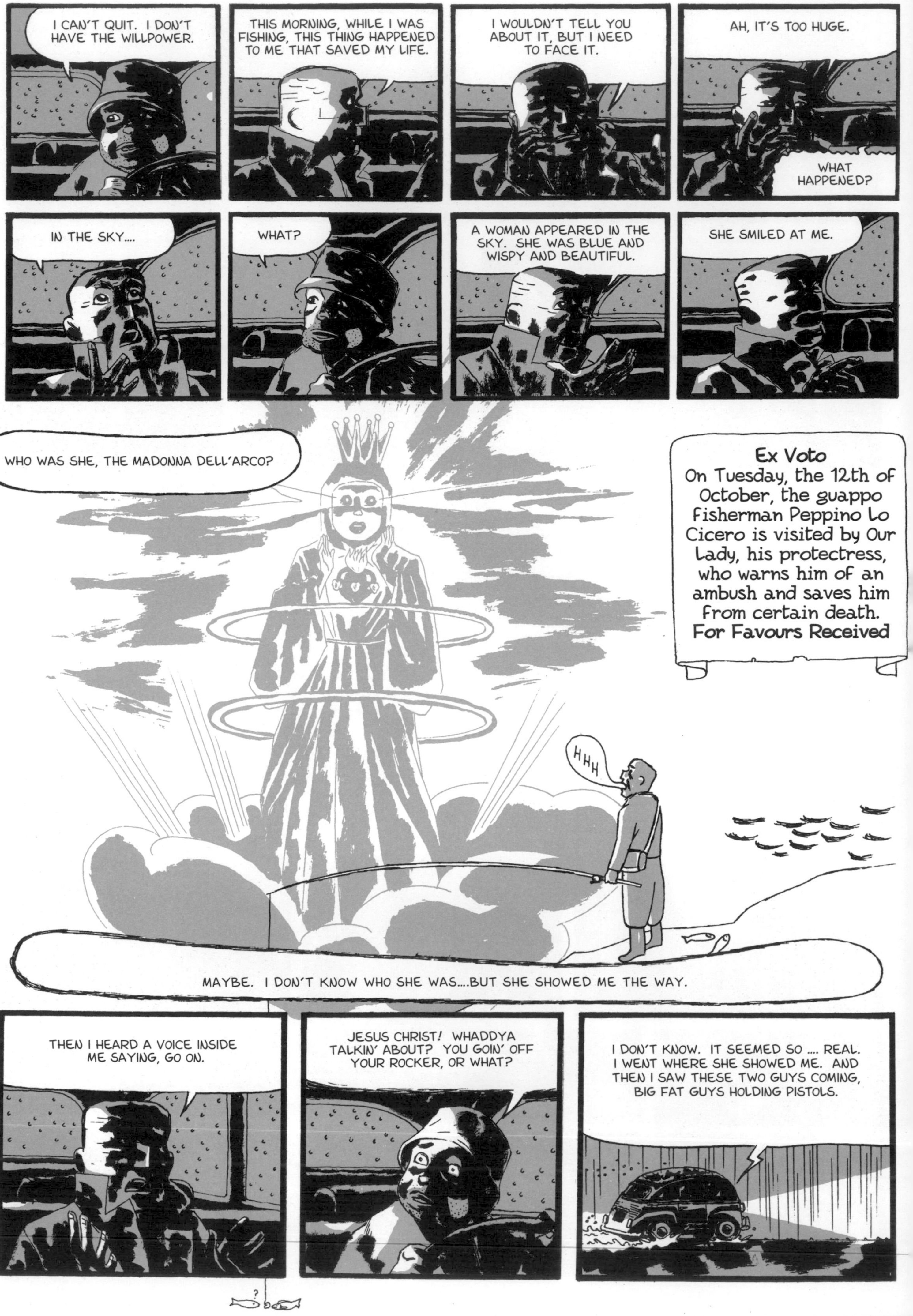
I CAN'T QUIT. I DON'T HAVE THE WILLPOWER.
THIS MORNING, WHILE I WAS FISHING, THIS THING HAPPENED TO ME THAT SAVED MY LIFE.
I WOULDN'T TELL YOU ABOUT IT, BUT I NEED TO FACE IT.
AH, IT'S TOO HUGE.
WHAT HAPPENED?
IN THE SKY....
WHAT?
A WOMAN APPEARED IN THE SKY. SHE WAS BLUE AND WISPY AND BEAUTIFUL.
SHE SMILED AT ME.
WHO WAS SHE, THE MADONNA DELL'ARCO?
Ex Voto
On Tuesday, the 12th of October, the guappo fisherman Peppino Lo Cicero is visited by Our Lady, his protectress, who warns him of an ambush and saves him from certain death.
For Favours Received
HHH
MAYBE. I DON'T KNOW WHO SHE WAS....BUT SHE SHOWED ME THE WAY.
THEN I HEARD A VOICE INSIDE ME SAYING, GO ON.
JESUS CHRIST! WHADDYA TALKIN' ABOUT? YOU GOIN' OFF YOUR ROCKER, OR WHAT?
I DON'T KNOW. IT SEEMED SO .... REAL. I WENT WHERE SHE SHOWED ME. AND THEN I SAW THESE TWO GUYS COMING, BIG FAT GUYS HOLDING PISTOLS.
?

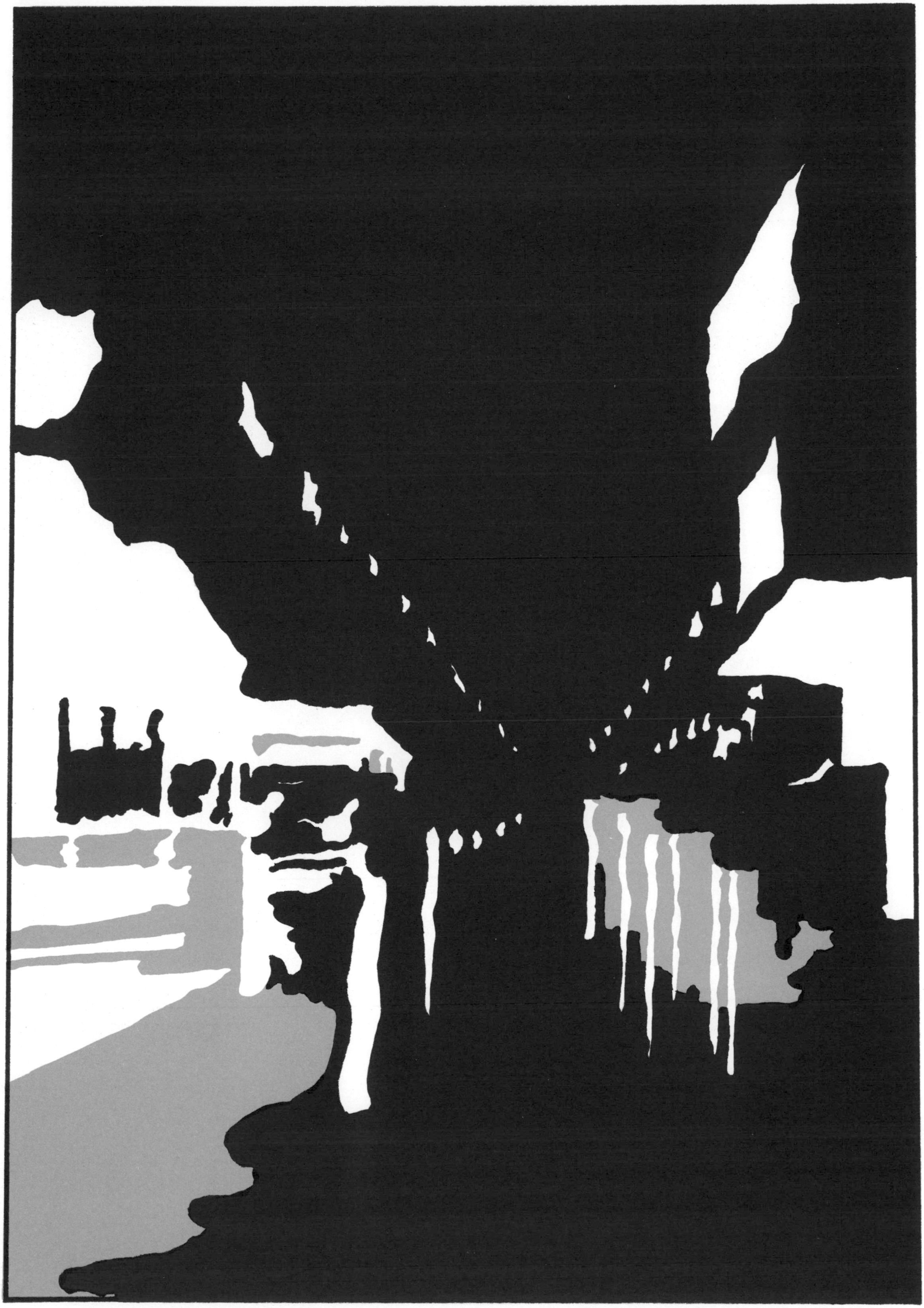

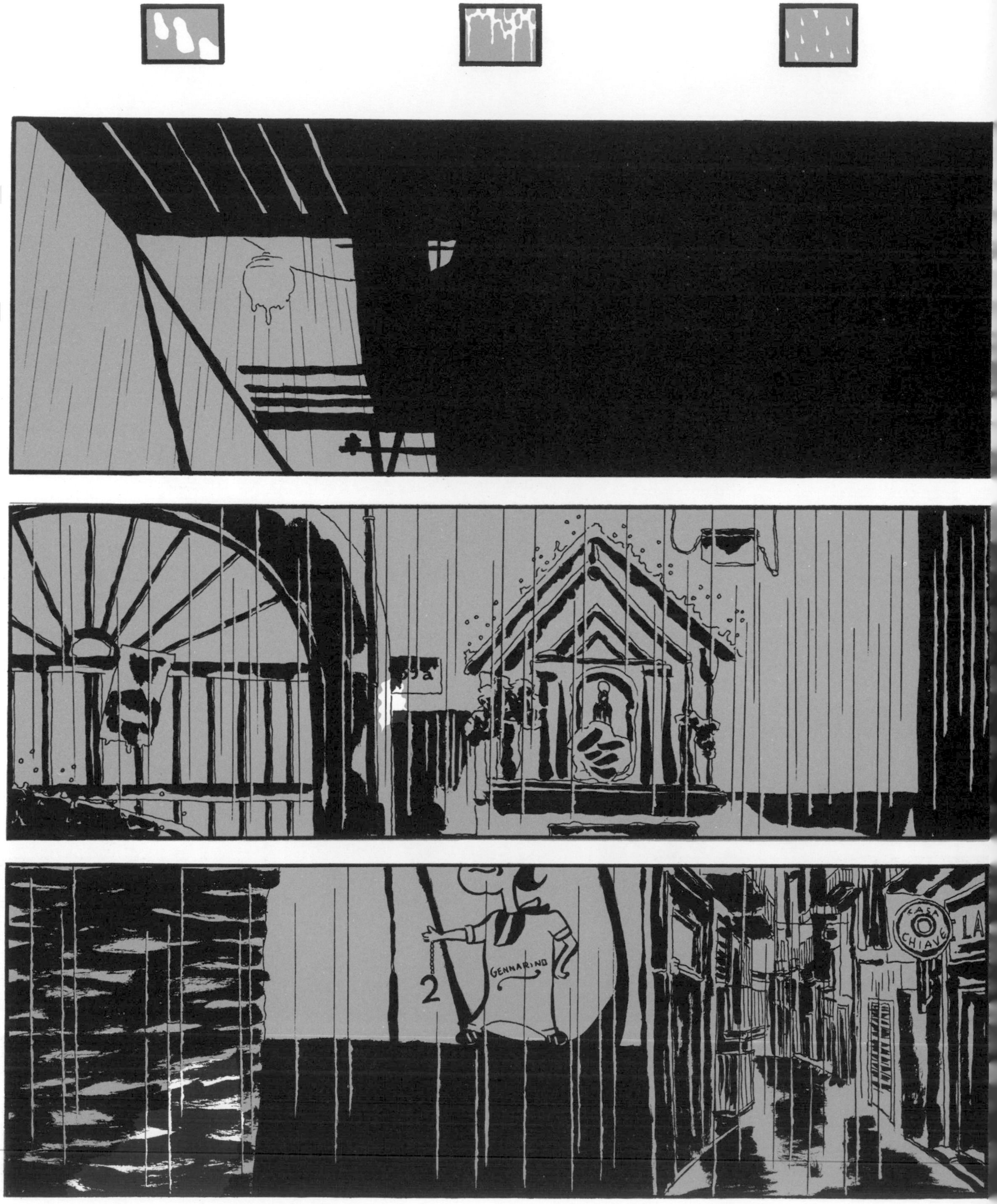
2
GENNARINO
CASA CHIAVE
LA

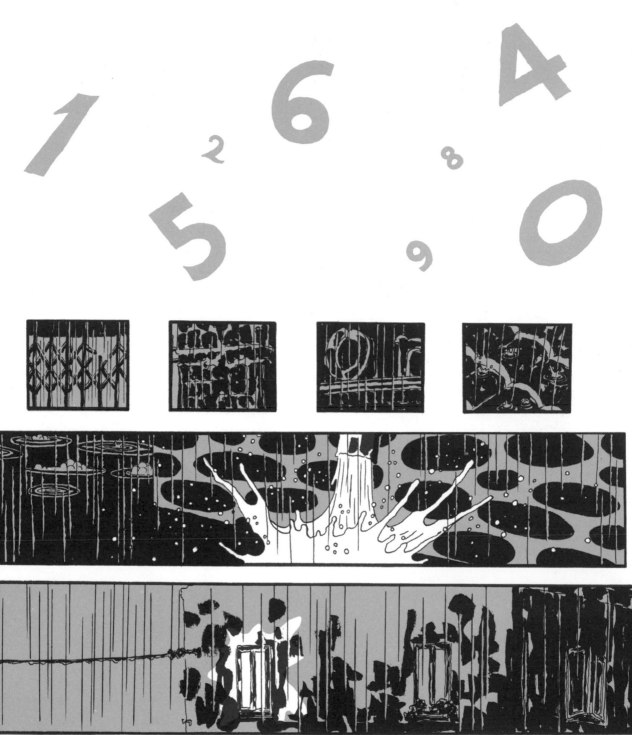

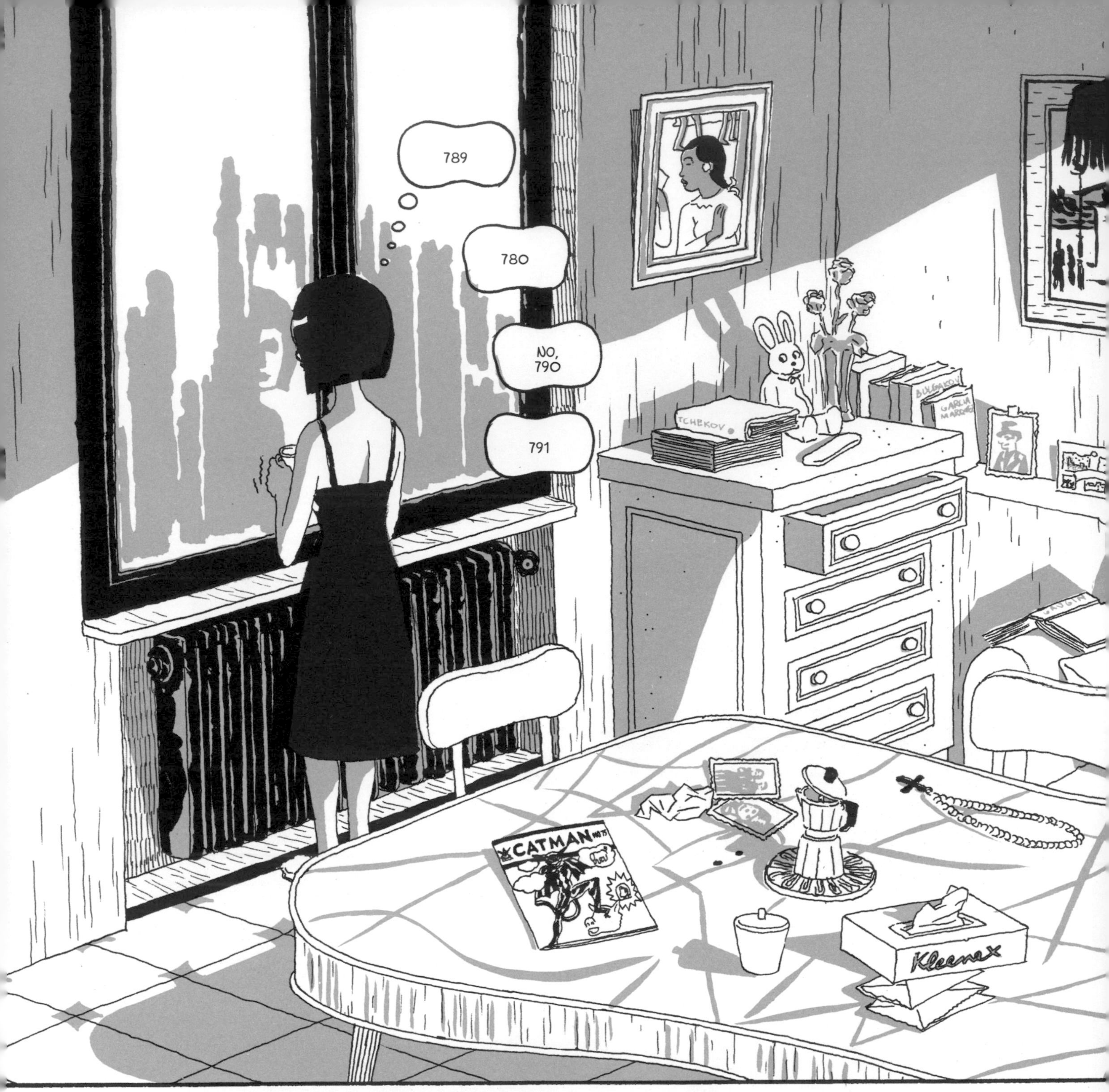
789
780
NO, 790
791
TCHEKOV
CATMAN
Kleenex

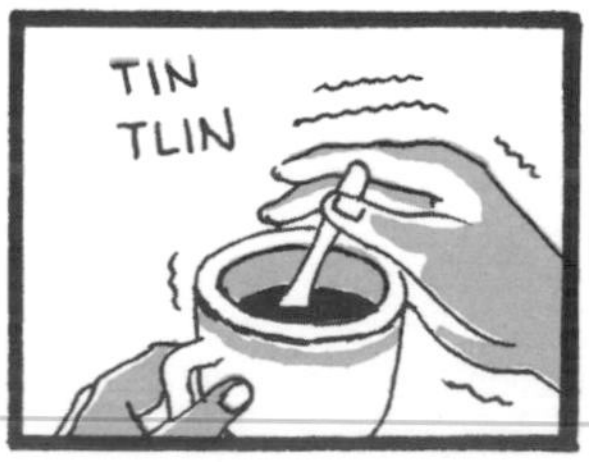
TIN TLIN

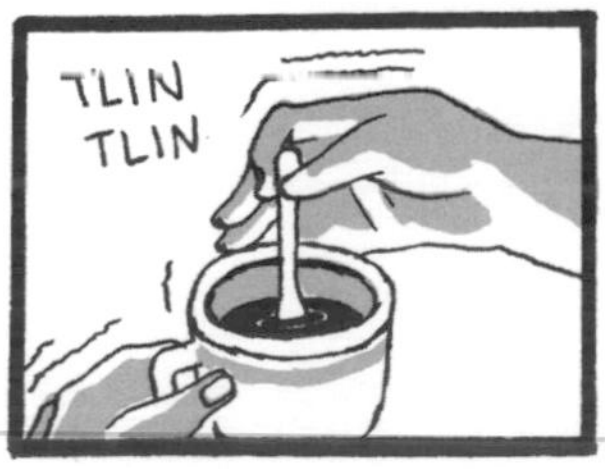
TLIN TLIN

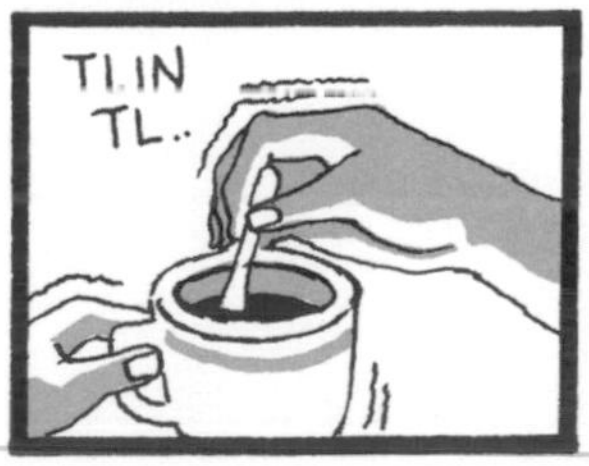
TLIN TL..

chapter three
the guappo life

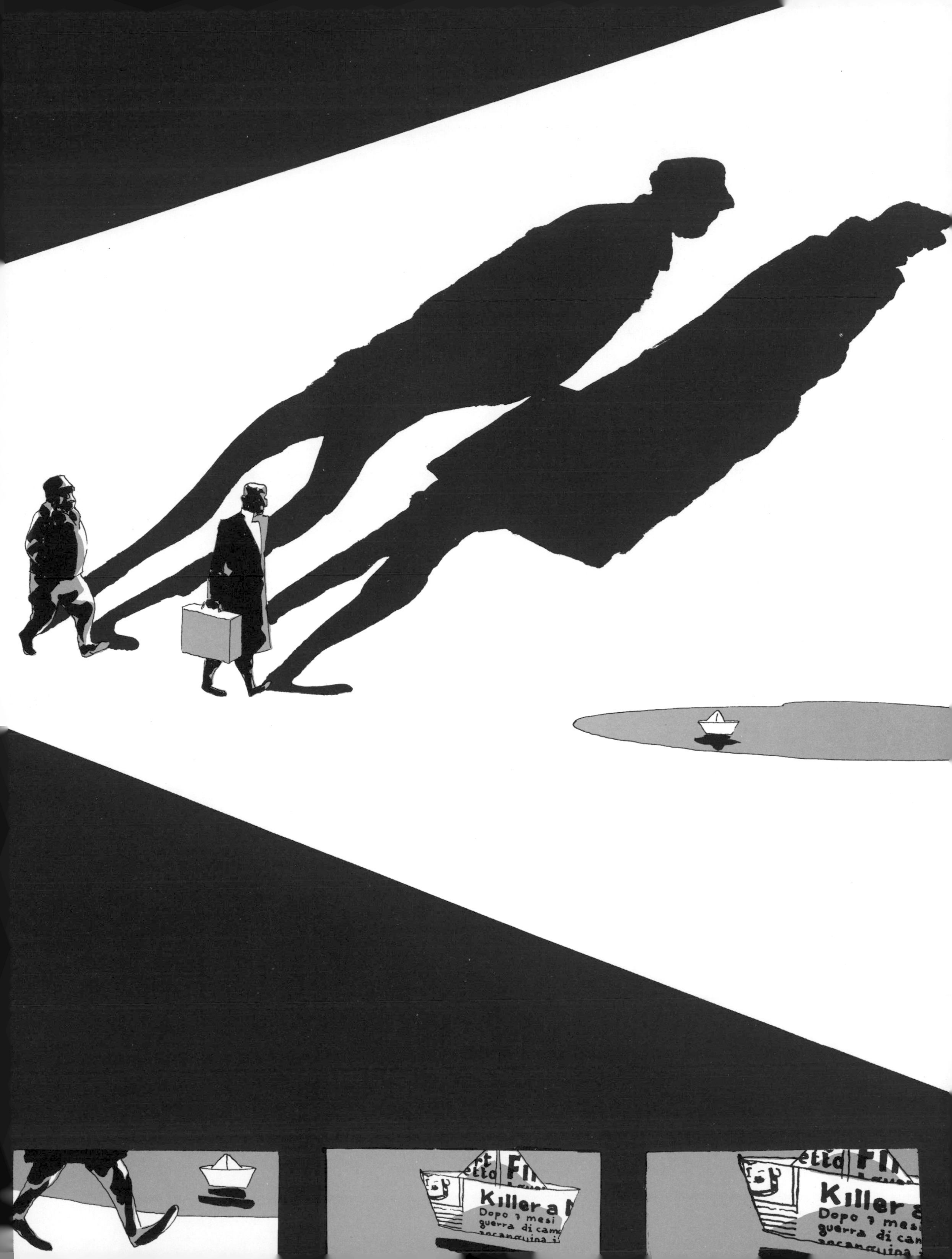
Killer a
Dopo 7 mesi
guerra di cam
Killer a
Dopo 7 mesi
guerra di cam

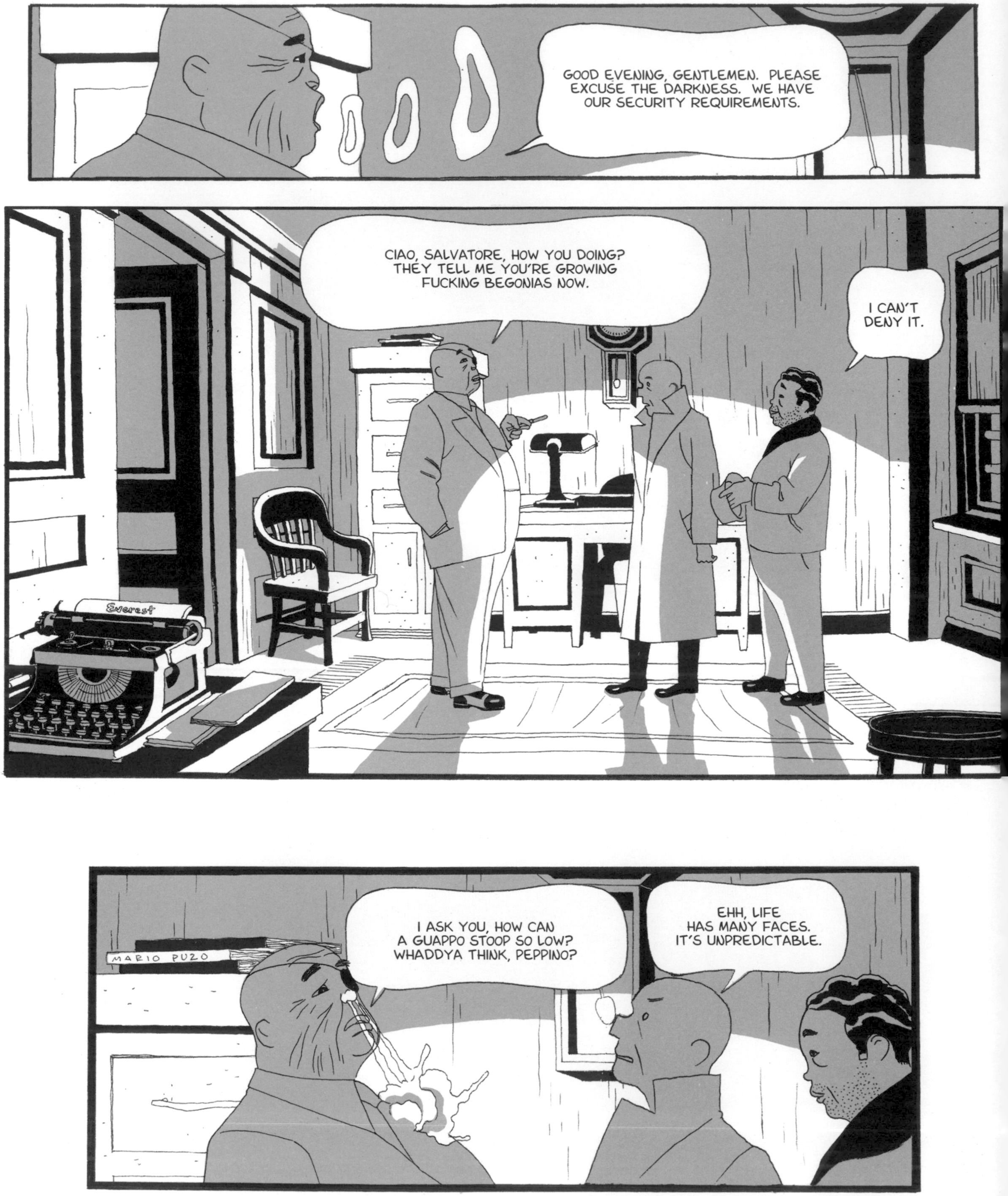
GOOD EVENING, GENTLEMEN. PLEASE EXCUSE THE DARKNESS. WE HAVE OUR SECURITY REQUIREMENTS.
CIAO, SALVATORE, HOW YOU DOING? THEY TELL ME YOU'RE GROWING FUCKING BEGONIAS NOW.
I CAN'T DENY IT.
Everest
MARIO PUZO
I ASK YOU, HOW CAN A GUAPPO STOOP SO LOW? WHADDYA THINK, PEPPINO?
EHH, LIFE HAS MANY FACES. IT'S UNPREDICTABLE.

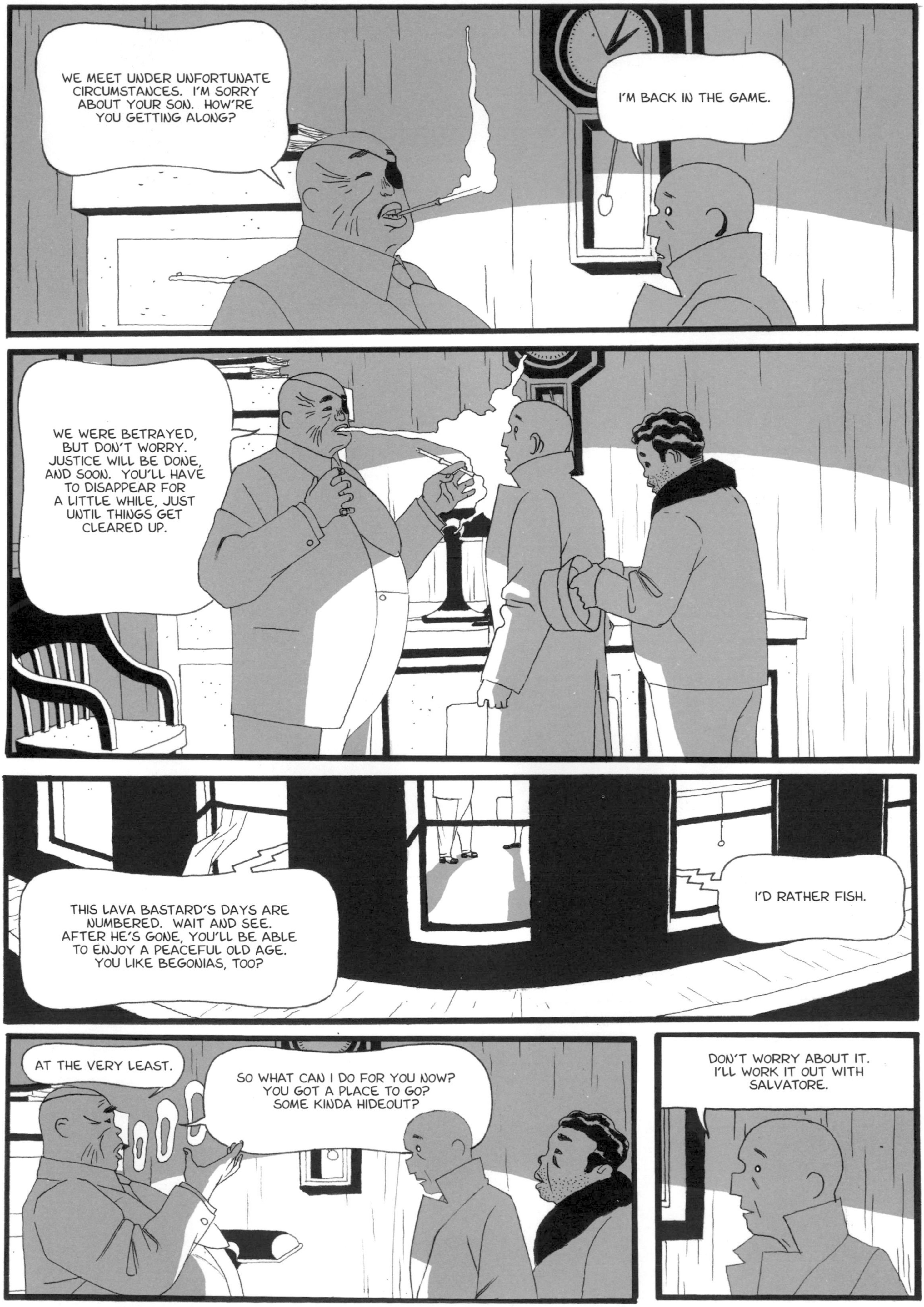
WE MEET UNDER UNFORTUNATE CIRCUMSTANCES. I'M SORRY ABOUT YOUR SON. HOW'RE YOU GETTING ALONG?
I'M BACK IN THE GAME.
WE WERE BETRAYED, BUT DON'T WORRY. JUSTICE WILL BE DONE, AND SOON. YOU'LL HAVE TO DISAPPEAR FOR A LITTLE WHILE, JUST UNTIL THINGS GET CLEARED UP.
THIS LAVA BASTARD'S DAYS ARE NUMBERED. WAIT AND SEE. AFTER HE'S GONE, YOU'LL BE ABLE TO ENJOY A PEACEFUL OLD AGE. YOU LIKE BEGONIAS, TOO?
I'D RATHER FISH.
AT THE VERY LEAST.
SO WHAT CAN I DO FOR YOU NOW? YOU GOT A PLACE TO GO? SOME KINDA HIDEOUT?
DON'T WORRY ABOUT IT. I'LL WORK IT OUT WITH SALVATORE.

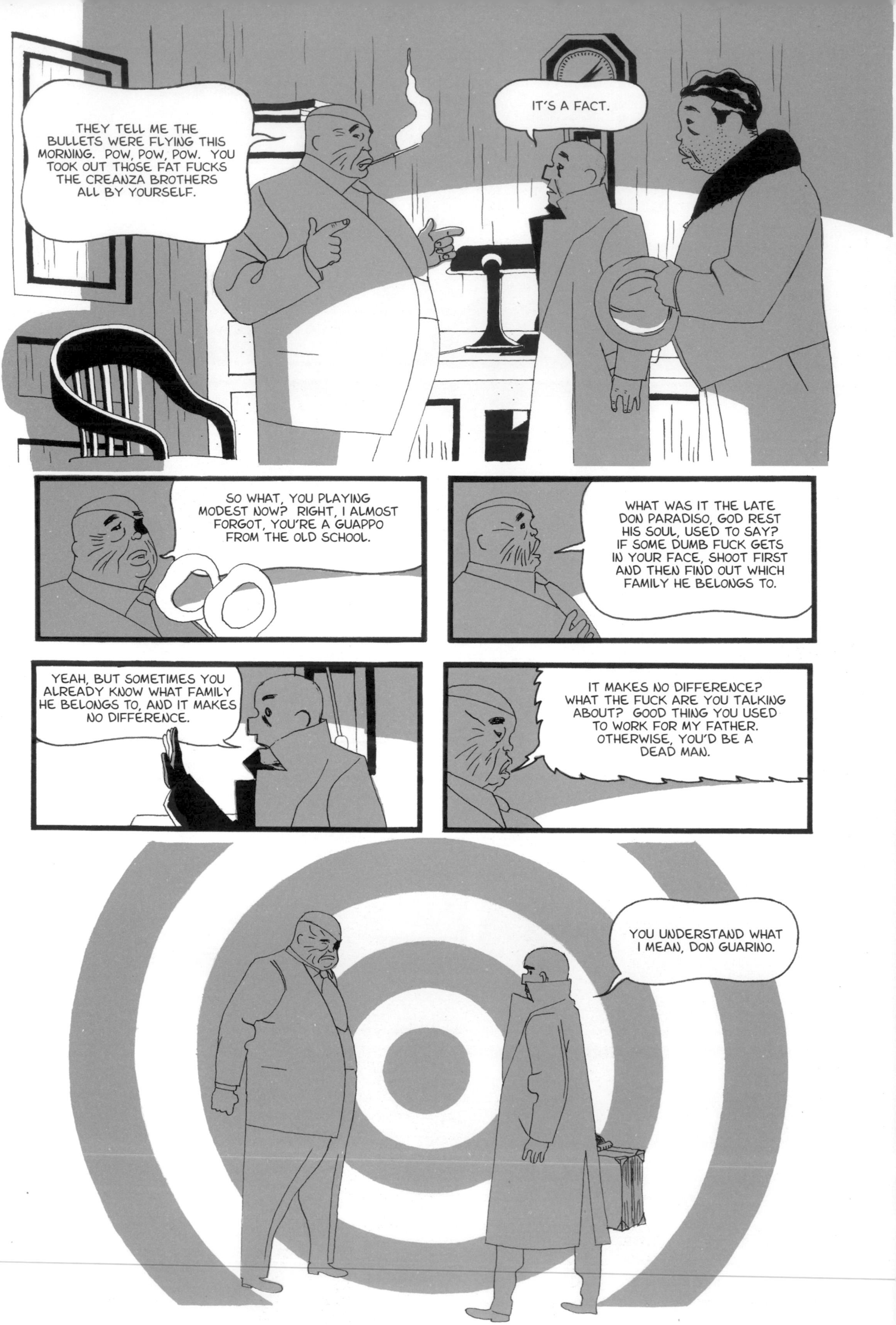
THEY TELL ME THE BULLETS WERE FLYING THIS MORNING. POW, POW, POW. YOU TOOK OUT THOSE FAT FUCKS THE CREANZA BROTHERS ALL BY YOURSELF.
IT'S A FACT.
SO WHAT, YOU PLAYING MODEST NOW? RIGHT, I ALMOST FORGOT, YOU'RE A GUAPPO FROM THE OLD SCHOOL.
WHAT WAS IT THE LATE DON PARADISO, GOD REST HIS SOUL, USED TO SAY? IF SOME DUMB FUCK GETS IN YOUR FACE, SHOOT FIRST AND THEN FIND OUT WHICH FAMILY HE BELONGS TO.
YEAH, BUT SOMETIMES YOU ALREADY KNOW WHAT FAMILY HE BELONGS TO, AND IT MAKES NO DIFFERENCE.
IT MAKES NO DIFFERENCE? WHAT THE FUCK ARE YOU TALKING ABOUT? GOOD THING YOU USED TO WORK FOR MY FATHER. OTHERWISE, YOU'D BE A DEAD MAN.
YOU UNDERSTAND WHAT I MEAN, DON GUARINO.

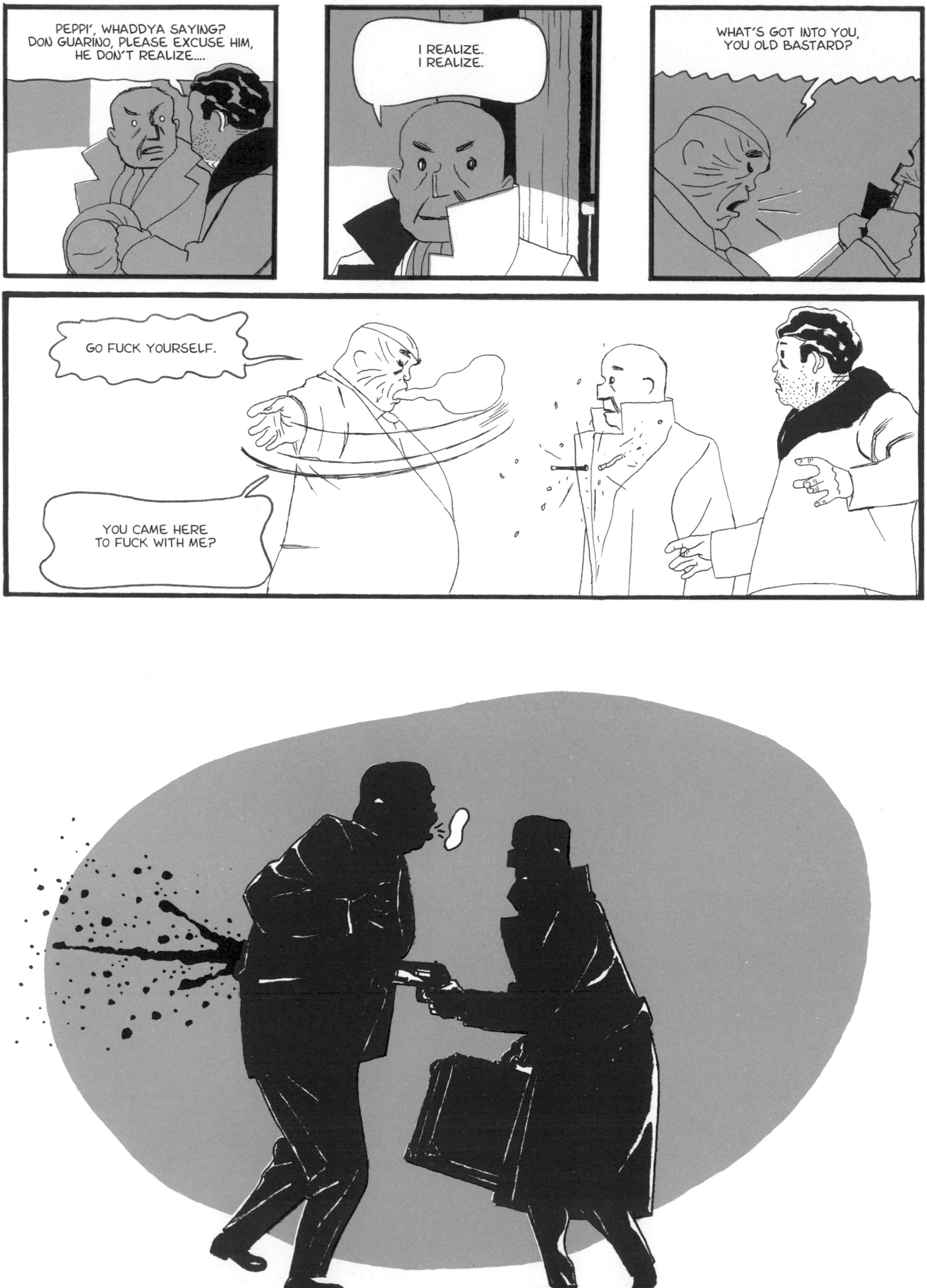
PEPPI', WHADDYA SAYING? DON GUARINO, PLEASE EXCUSE HIM, HE DON'T REALIZE....
I REALIZE. I REALIZE.
WHAT'S GOT INTO YOU, YOU OLD BASTARD?
GO FUCK YOURSELF.
YOU CAME HERE TO FUCK WITH ME?

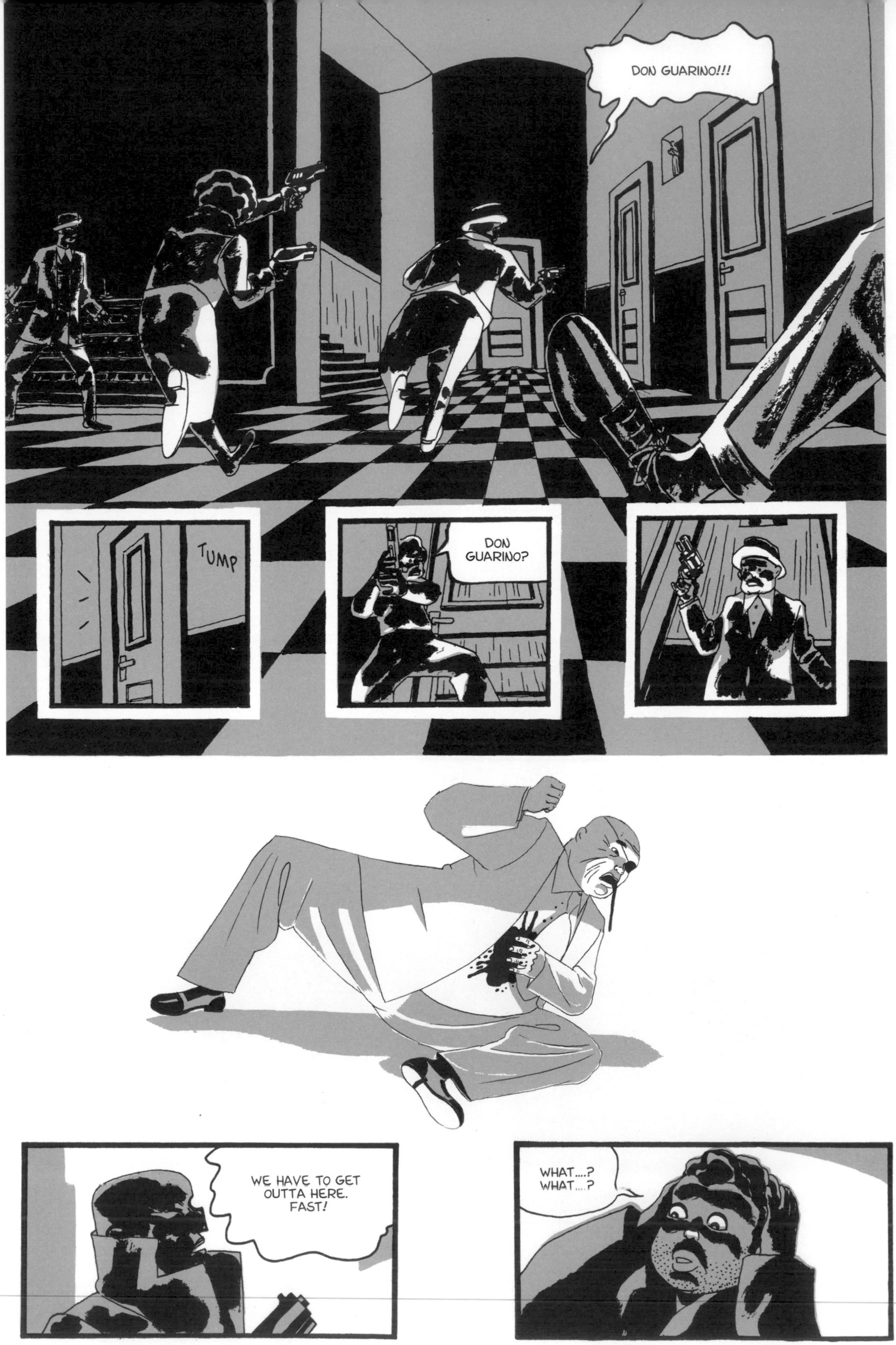
DON GUARINO!!!
TUMP
DON GUARINO?
WE HAVE TO GET OUTTA HERE. FAST!
WHAT....? WHAT....?

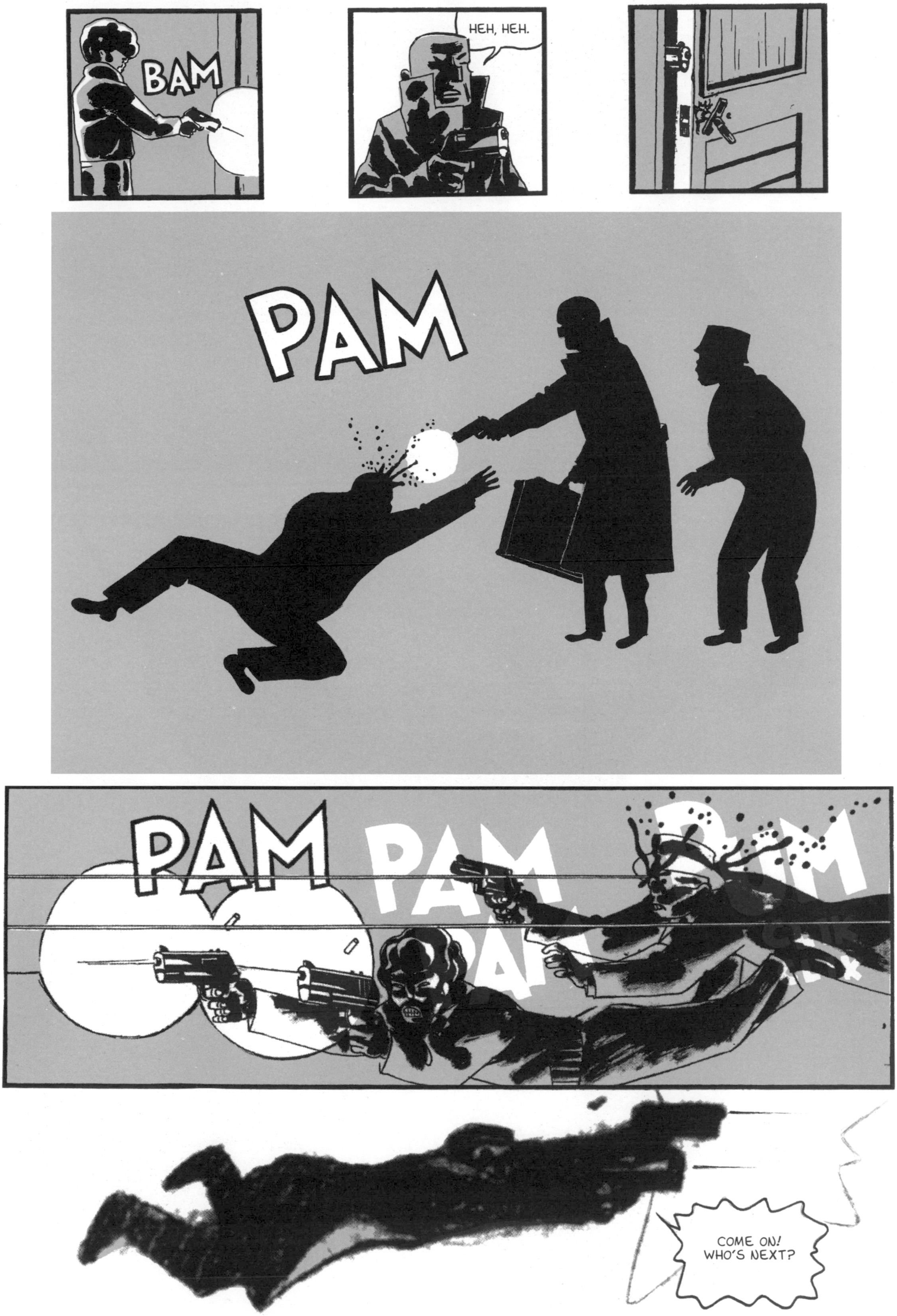
BAM
HEH, HEH.
PAM
PAM
PAM
COME ON! WHO'S NEXT?

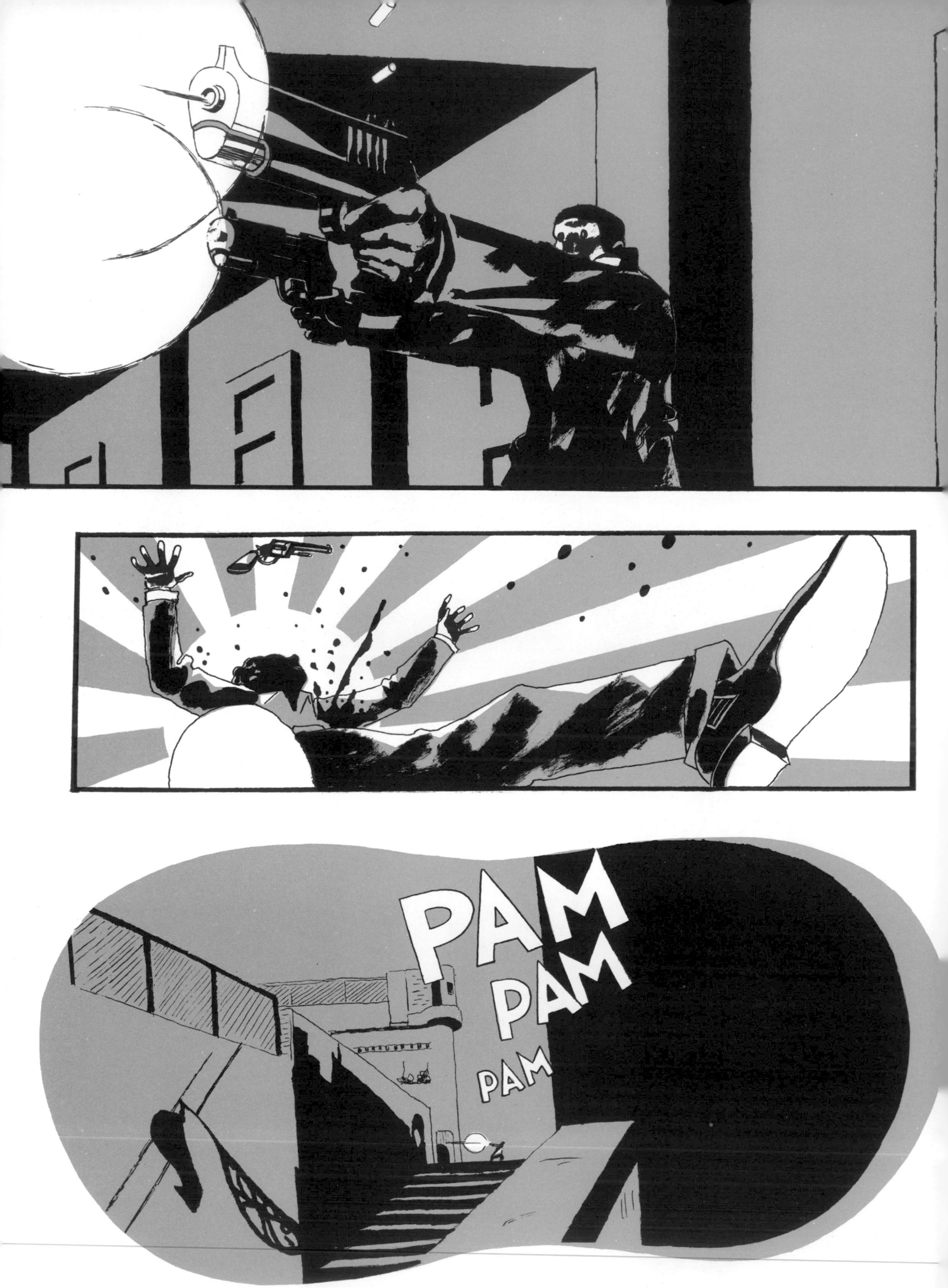
PAM
PAM
PAM

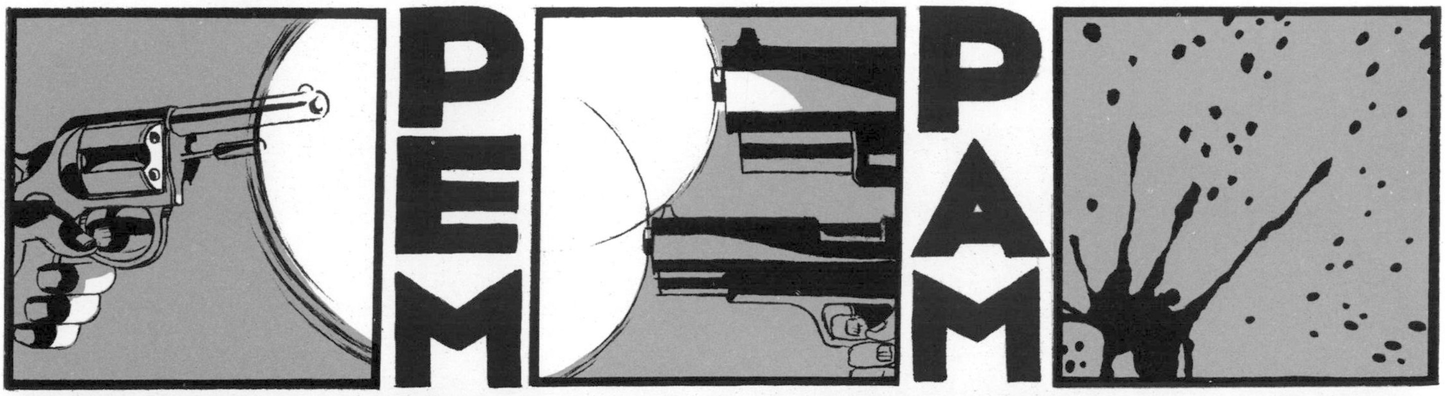
PEM
PAM

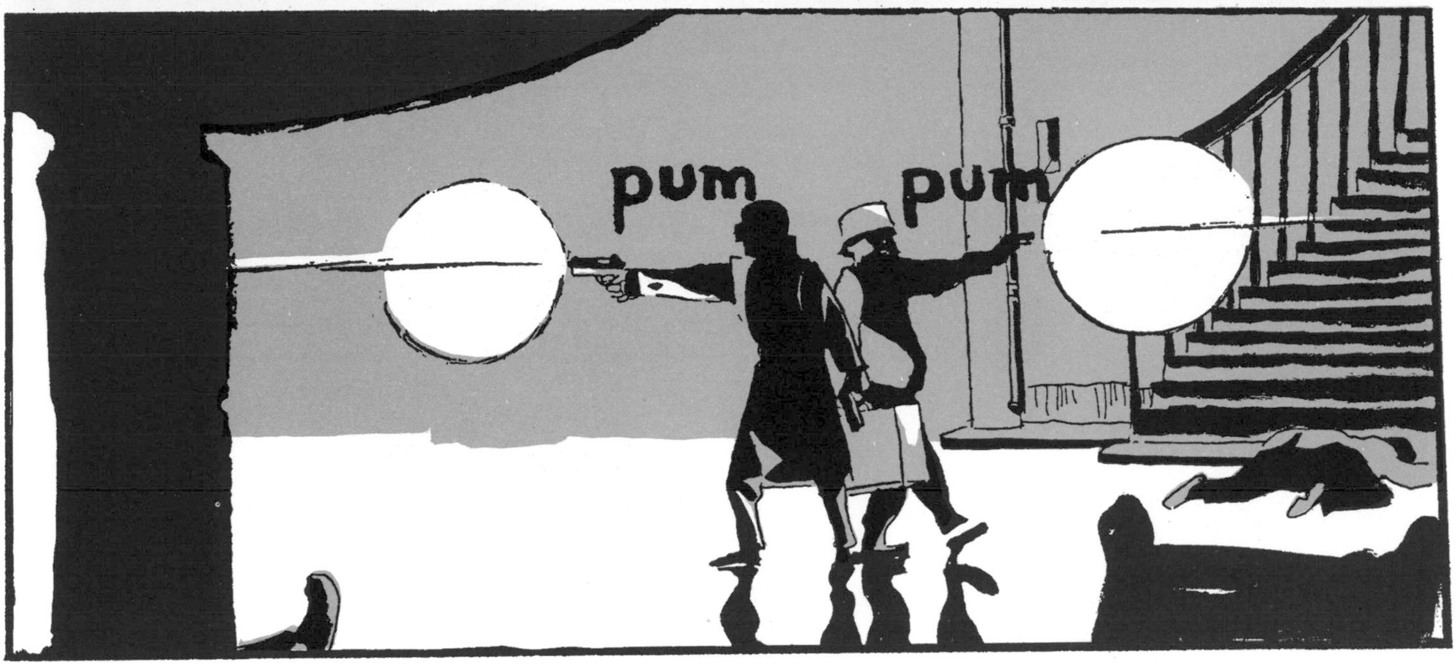
pum
pum

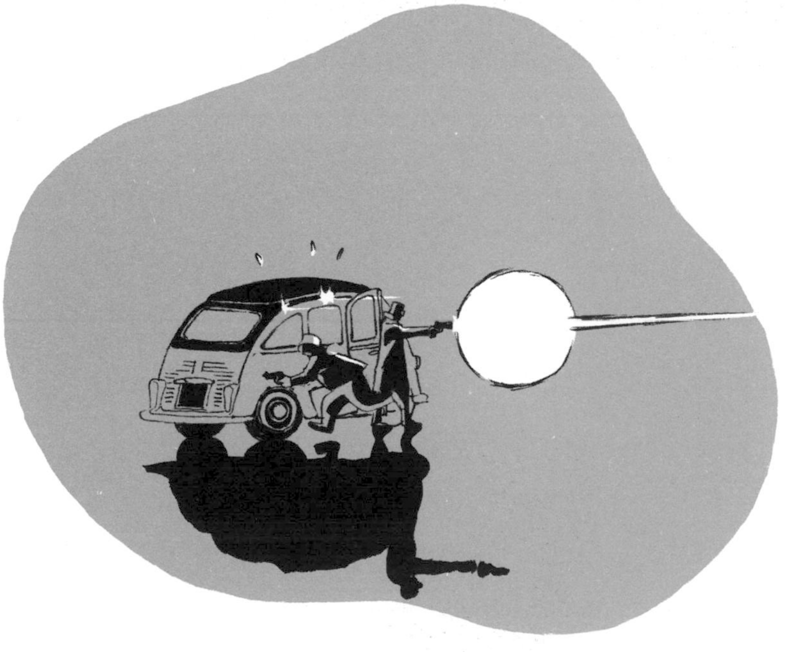

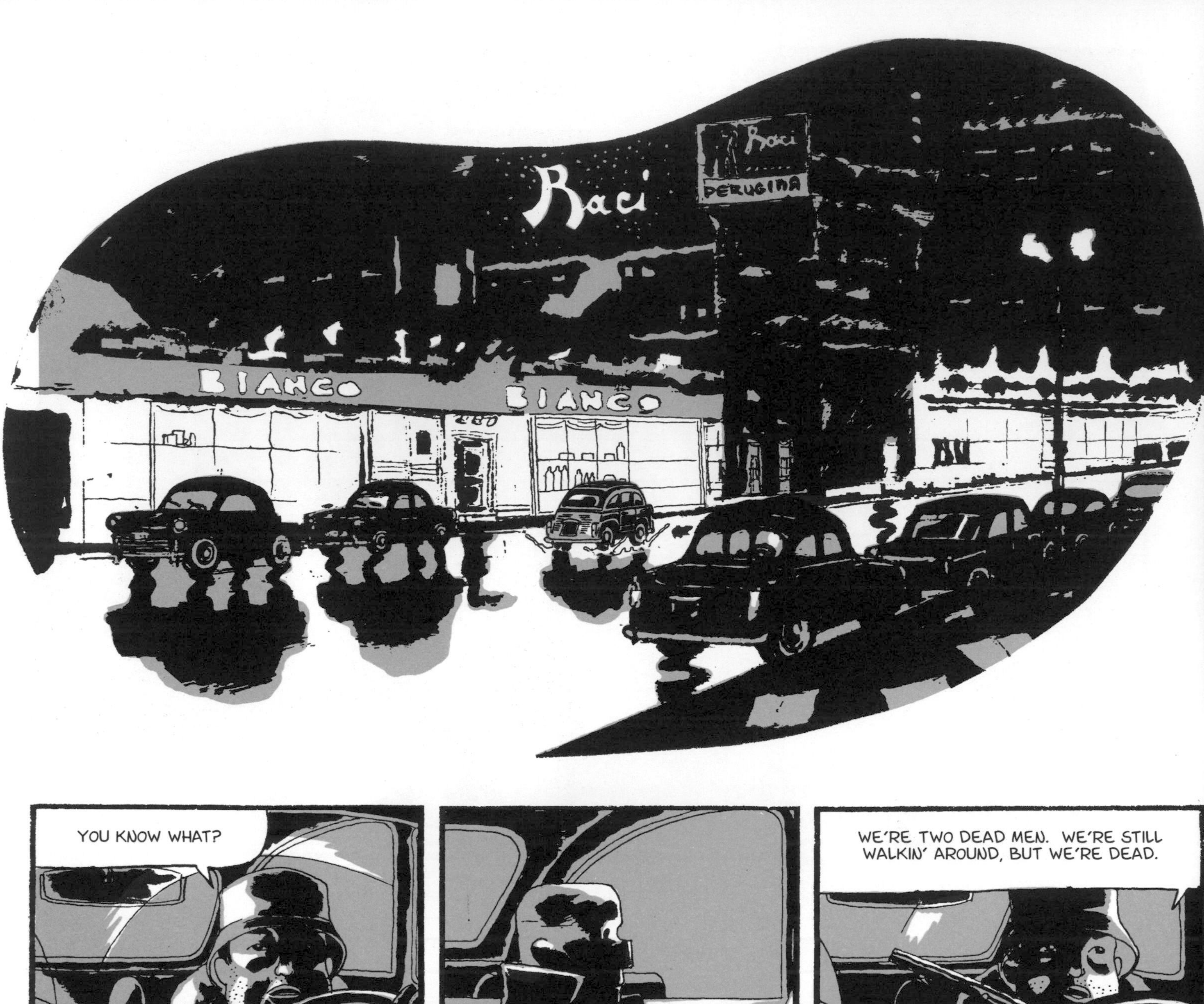
PERUGINA
BIANCO
BIANCO
YOU KNOW WHAT?
WE'RE TWO DEAD MEN. WE'RE STILL WALKIN' AROUND, BUT WE'RE DEAD.
I'M NEVER GONNA FORGIVE YOU. ANOTHER FAMILY IS LOOKIN' TO CLIP US, AND YOU GO AND KILL YOUR BOSS.

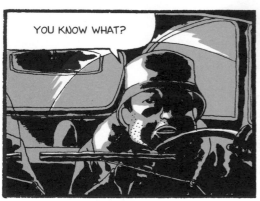

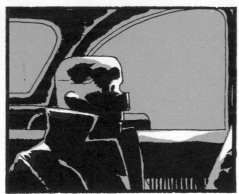

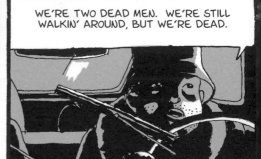

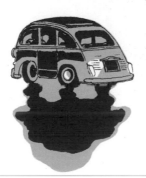

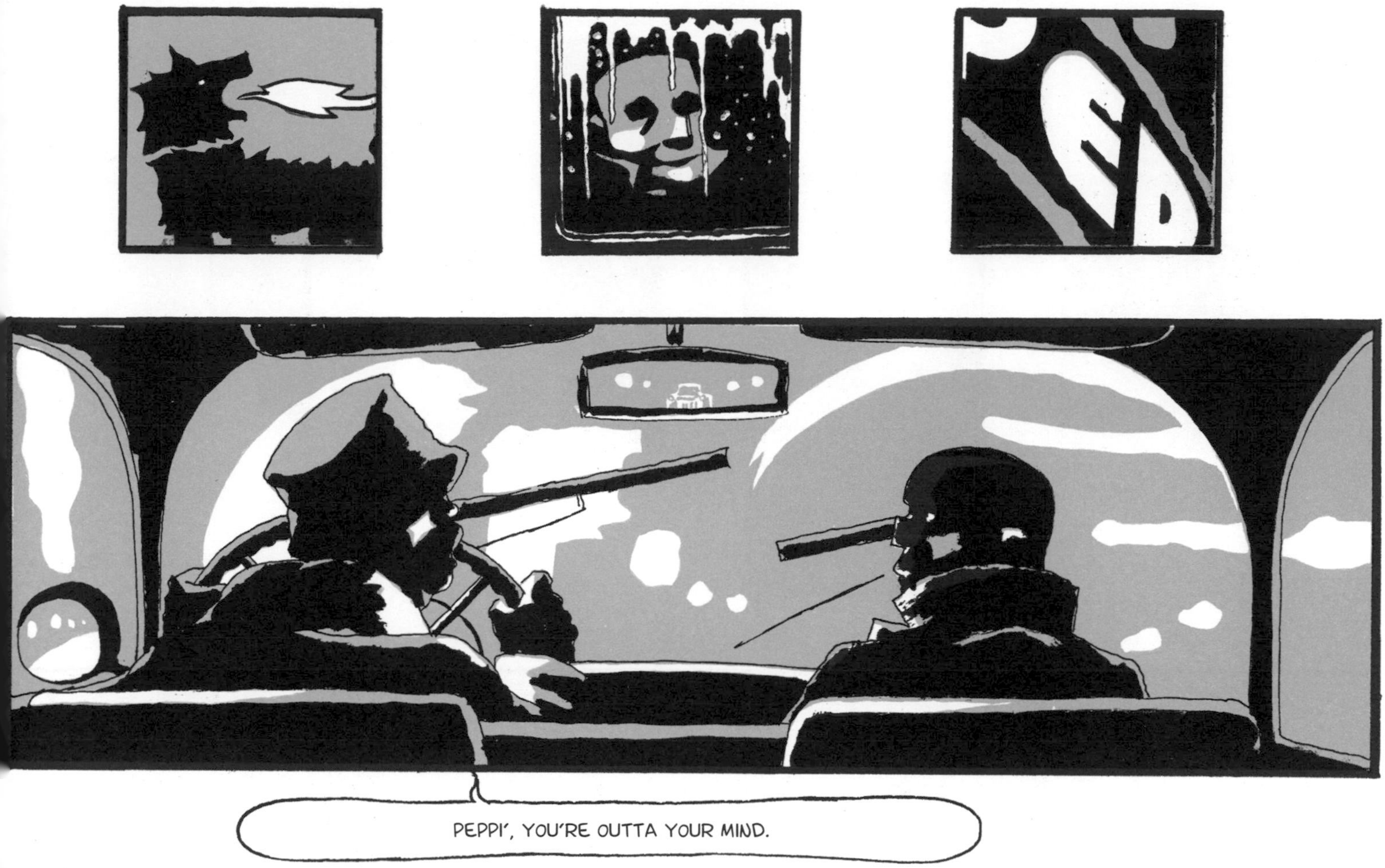
PEPPI', YOU'RE OUTTA YOUR MIND.

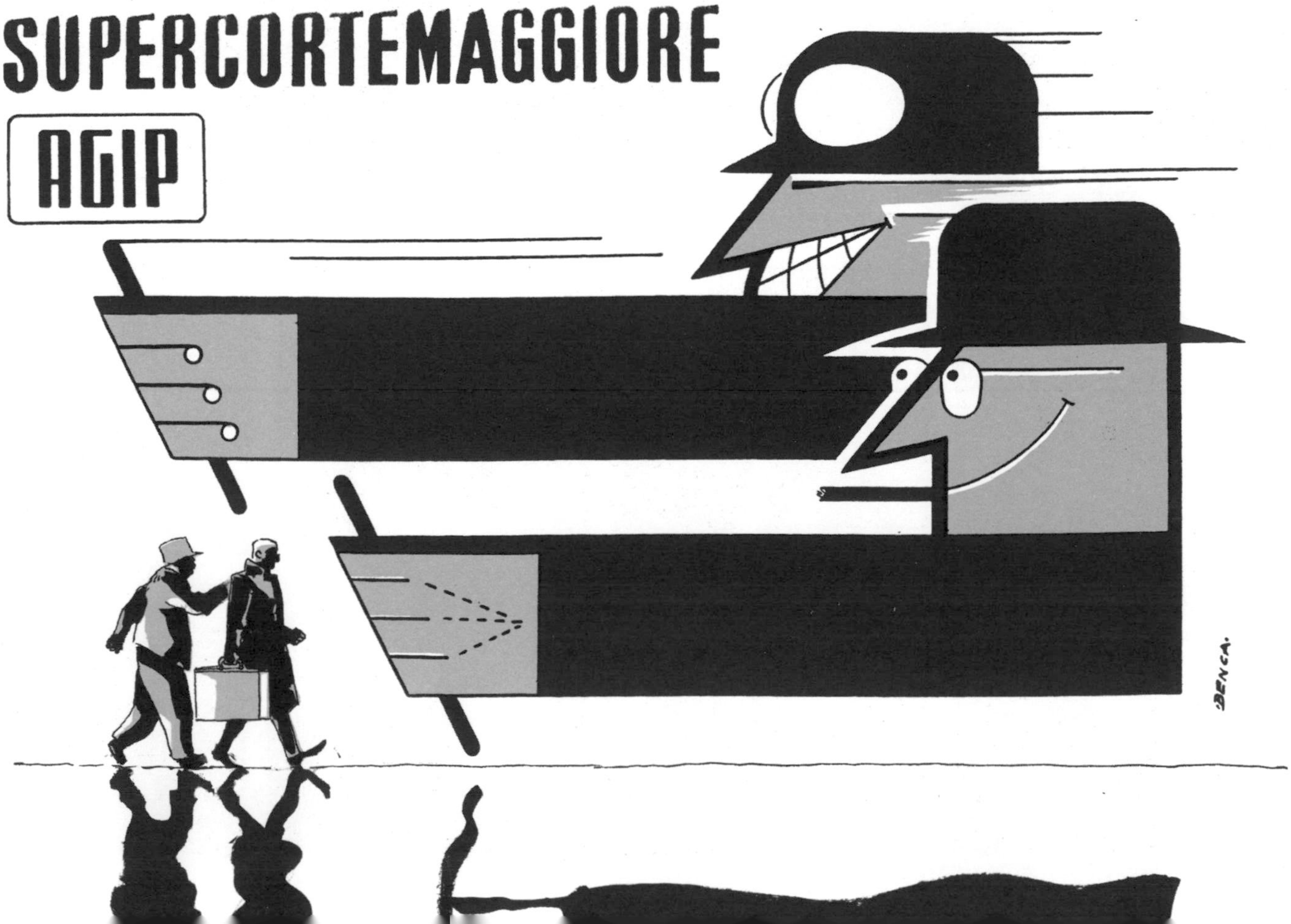
SUPERCORTEMAGGIORE
AGIP

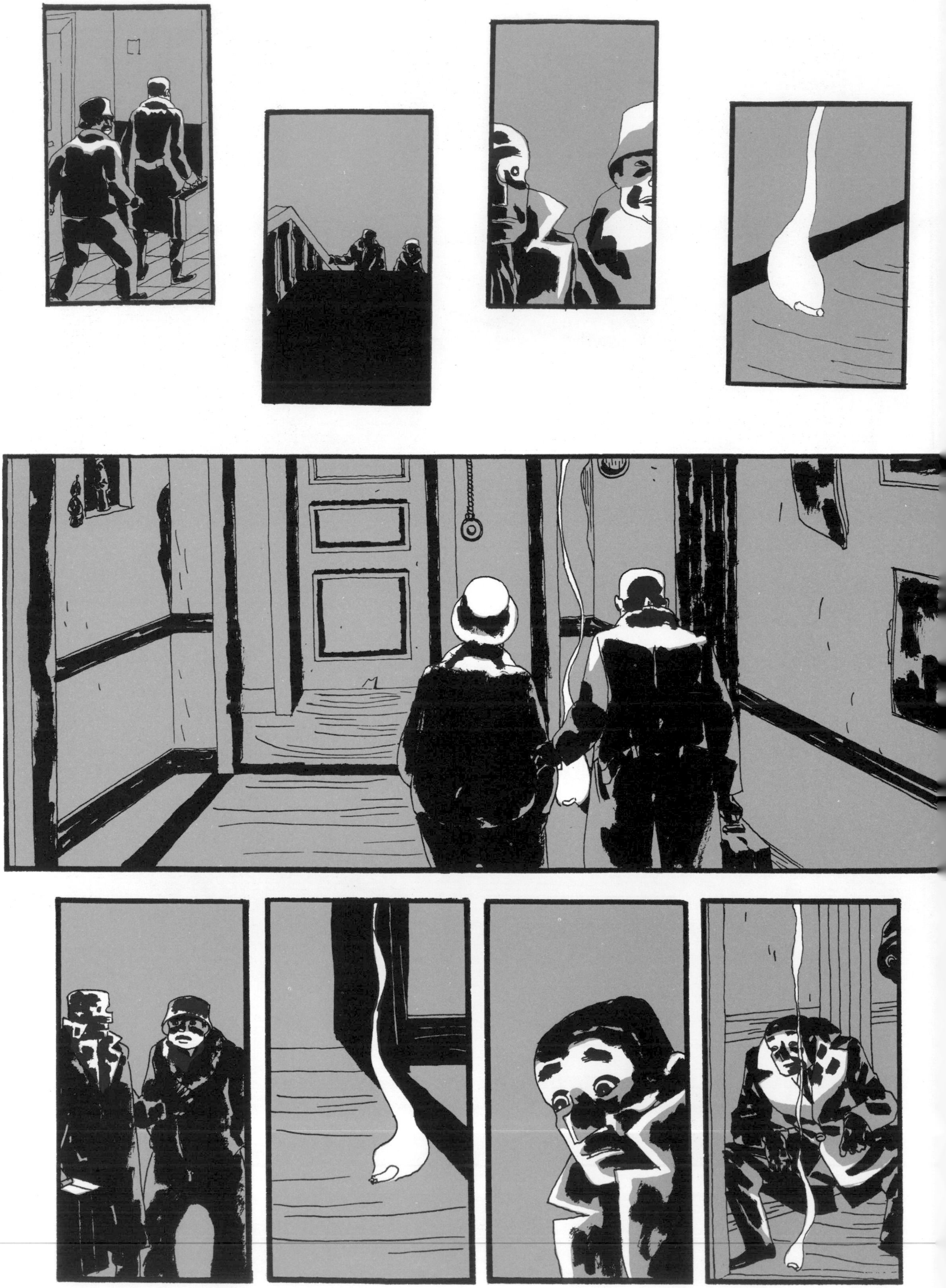

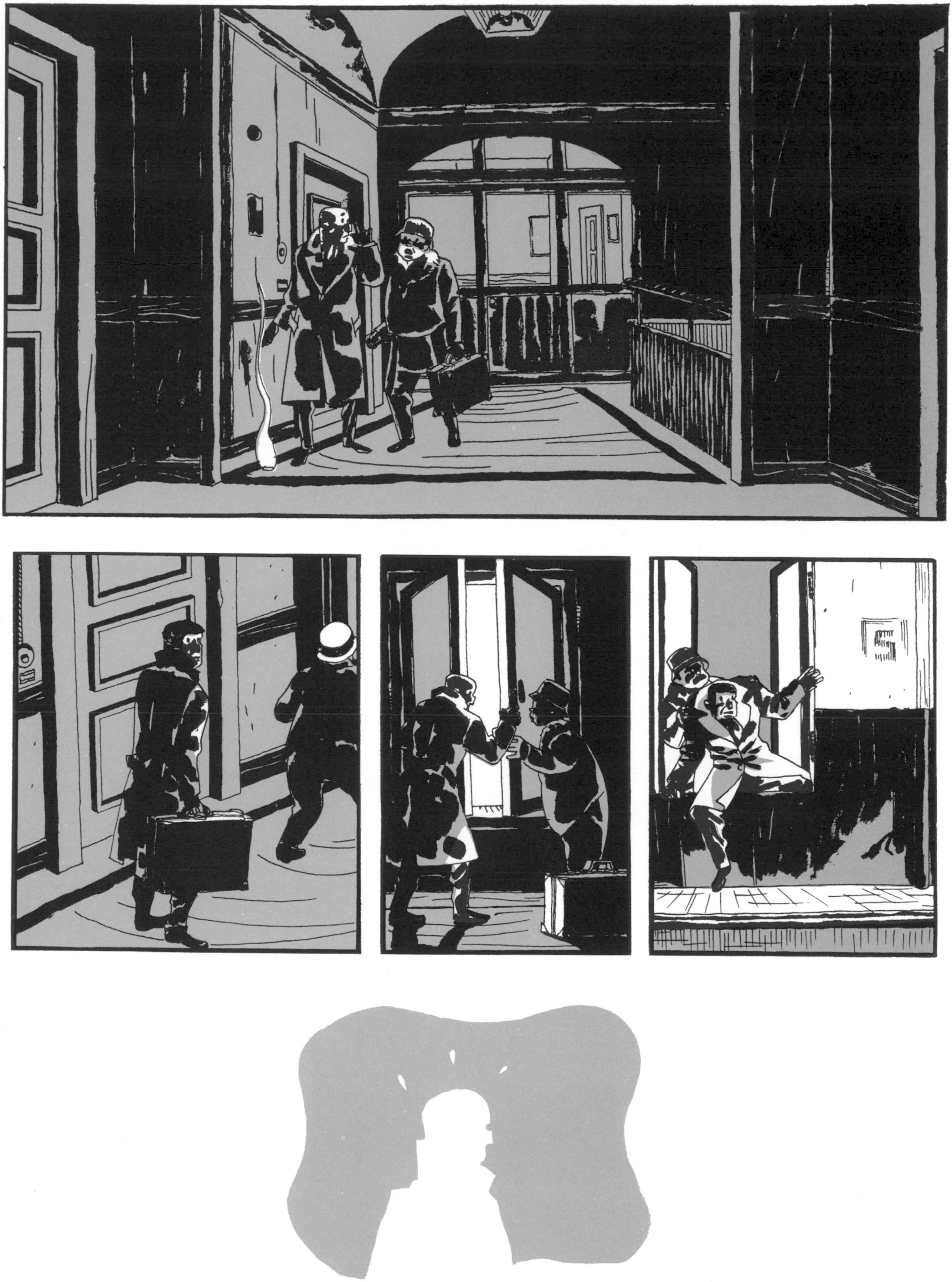

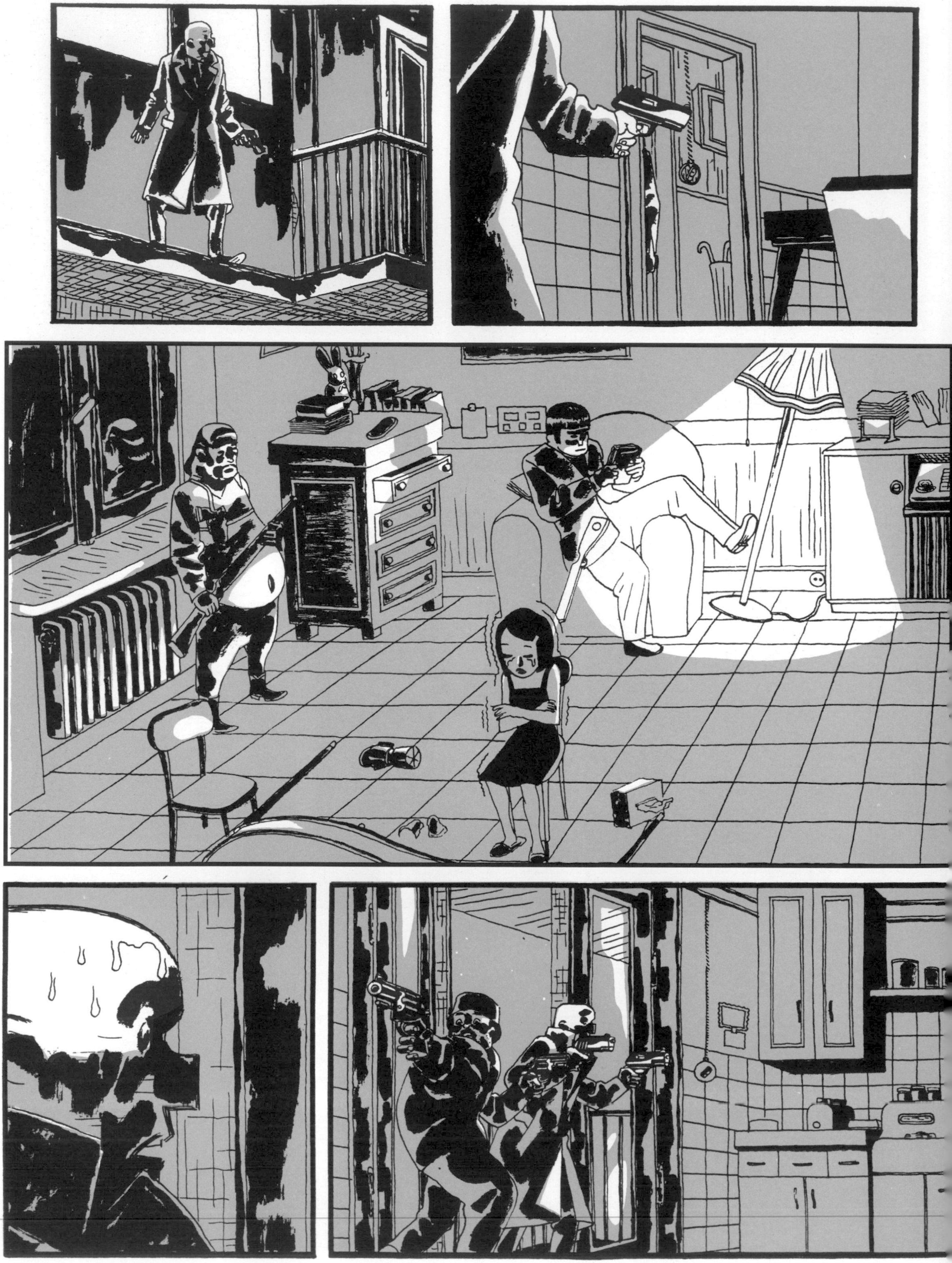

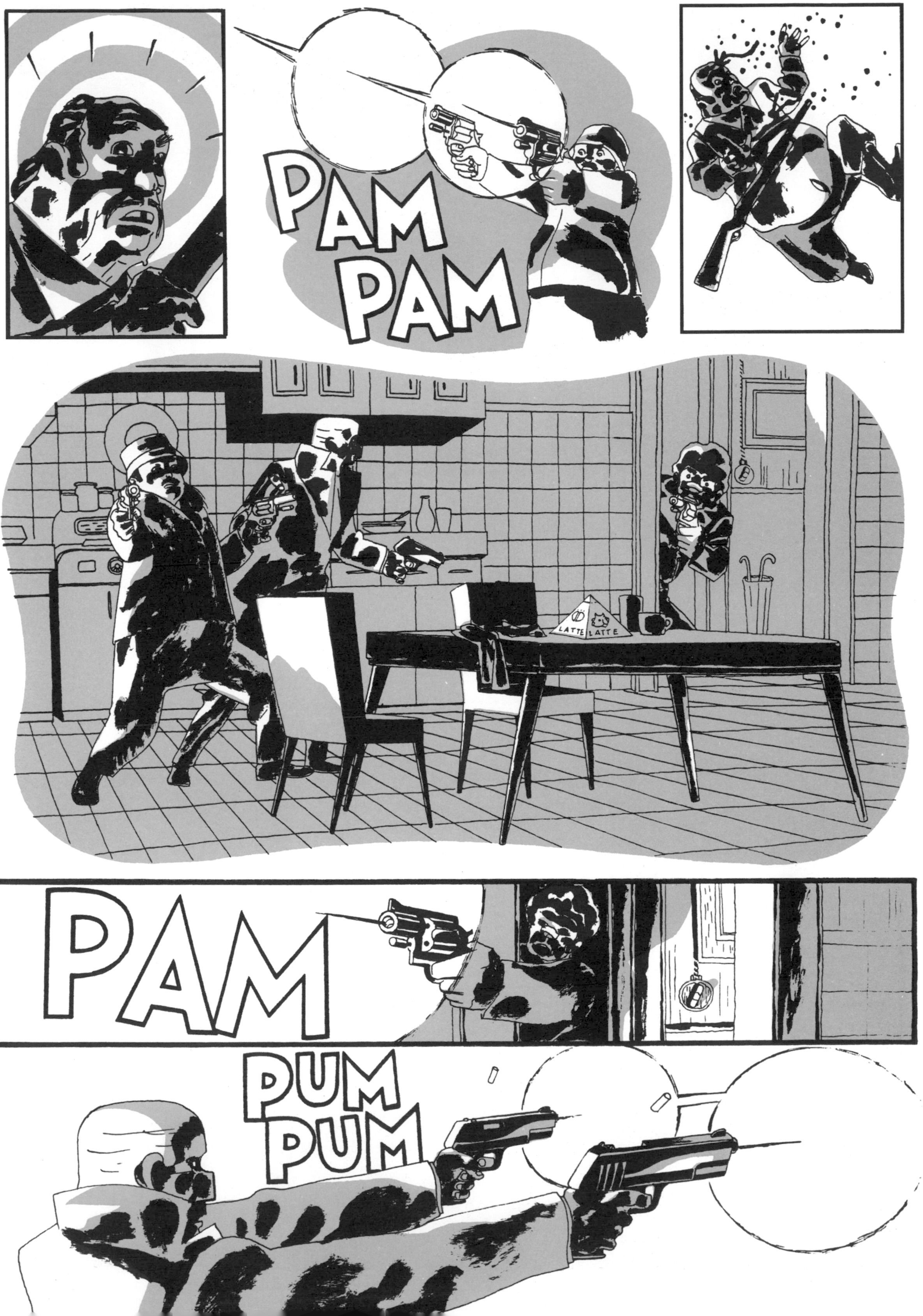
PAM
PAM
LATTE
LATTE
PAM
PUM
PUM

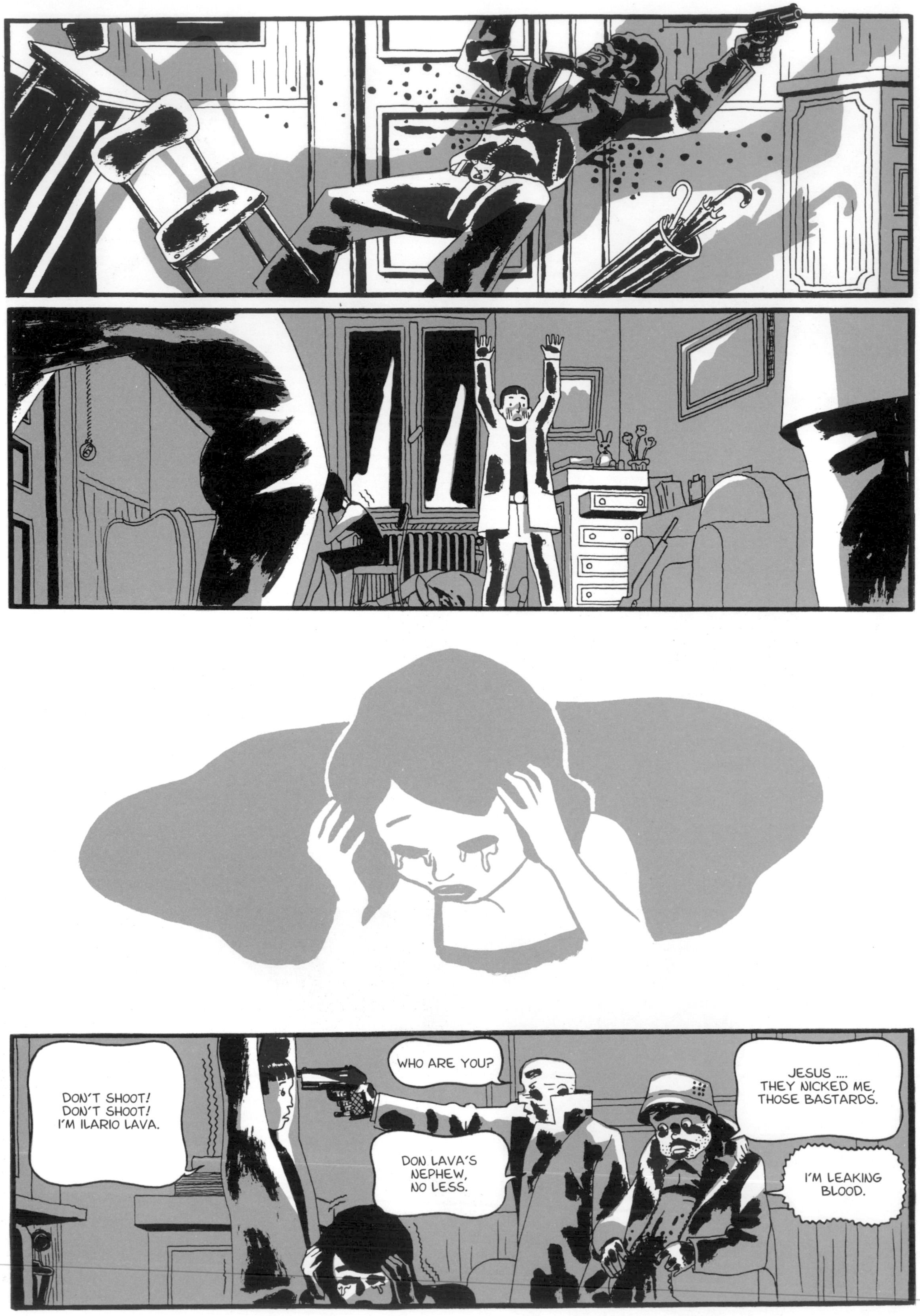
DON'T SHOOT! DON'T SHOOT! I'M ILARIO LAVA.
WHO ARE YOU?
DON LAVA'S NEPHEW, NO LESS.
JESUS .... THEY NICKED ME, THOSE BASTARDS.
I'M LEAKING BLOOD.

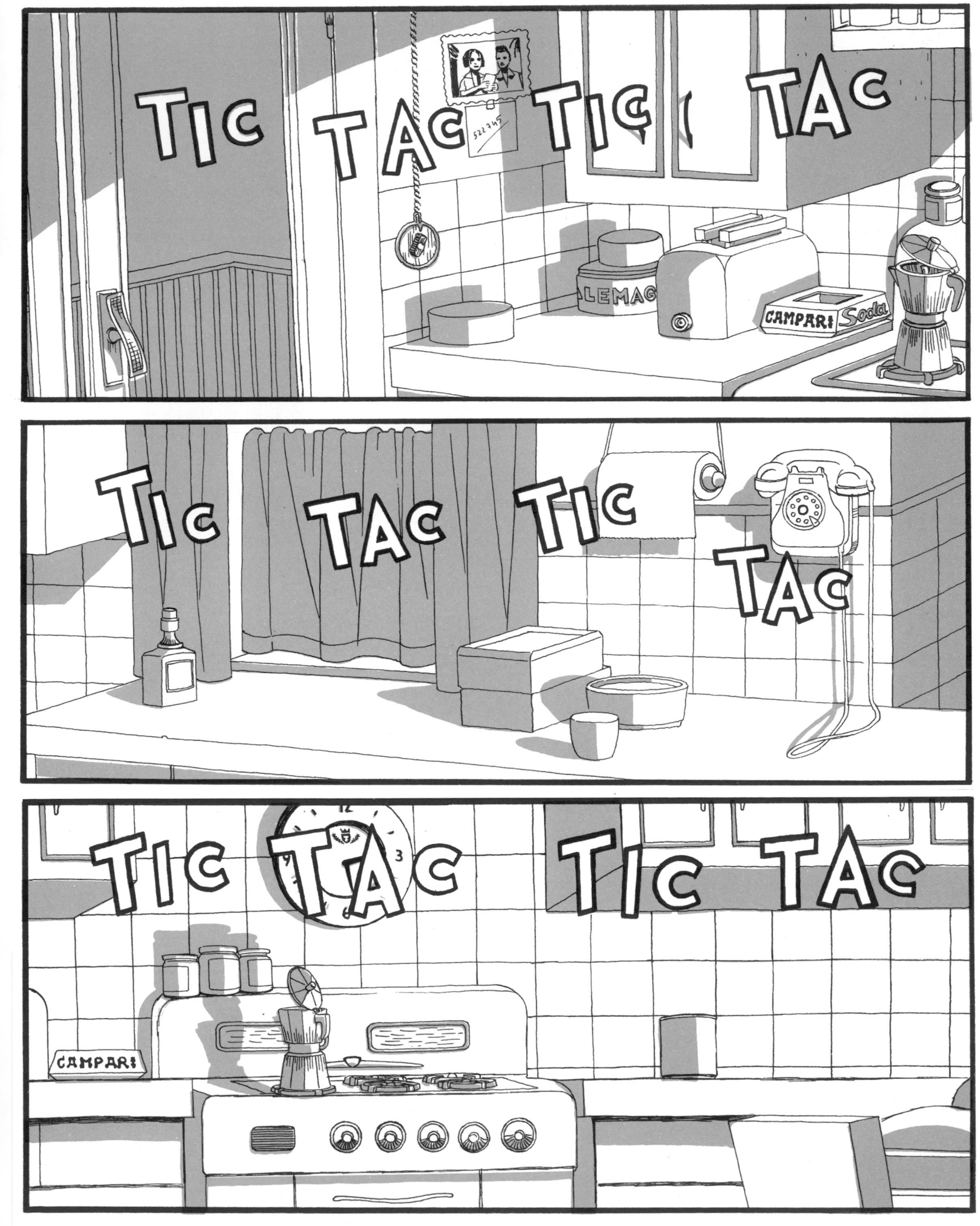

TIC TAC TIC TAC
LEMAG
CAMPARI Soda
TIC TAC TIC TAC
TIC TAC TIC TAC
CAMPARI

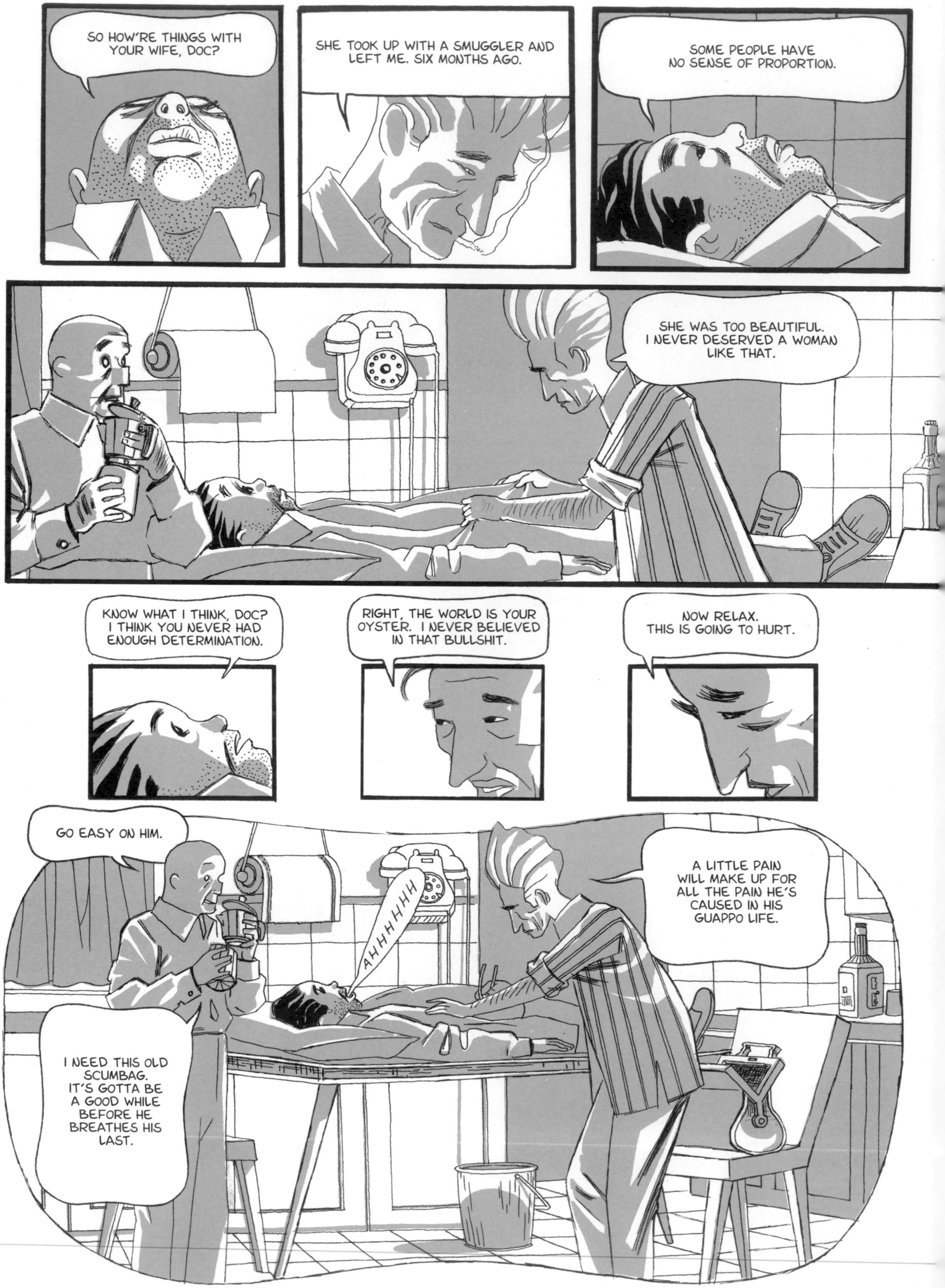
SO HOW'RE THINGS WITH YOUR WIFE, DOC?
SHE TOOK UP WITH A SMUGGLER AND LEFT ME. SIX MONTHS AGO.
SOME PEOPLE HAVE NO SENSE OF PROPORTION.
SHE WAS TOO BEAUTIFUL. I NEVER DESERVED A WOMAN LIKE THAT.
KNOW WHAT I THINK, DOC? I THINK YOU NEVER HAD ENOUGH DETERMINATION.
RIGHT, THE WORLD IS YOUR OYSTER. I NEVER BELIEVED IN THAT BULLSHIT.
NOW RELAX. THIS IS GOING TO HURT.
GO EASY ON HIM.
AHHHHHH
A LITTLE PAIN WILL MAKE UP FOR ALL THE PAIN HE'S CAUSED IN HIS GUAPPO LIFE.
I NEED THIS OLD SCUMBAG. IT'S GOTTA BE A GOOD WHILE BEFORE HE BREATHES HIS LAST.

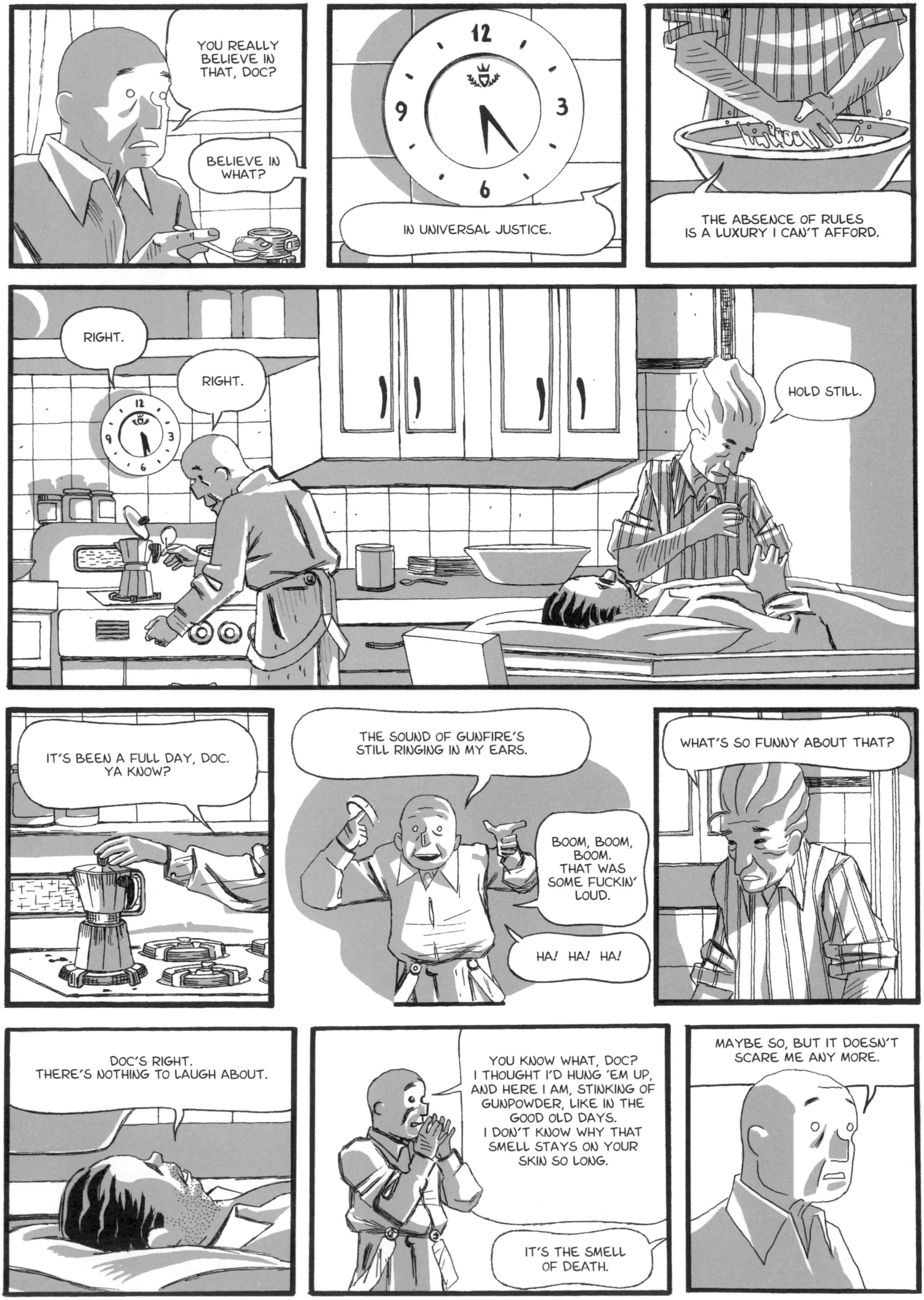
YOU REALLY BELIEVE IN THAT, DOC?
BELIEVE IN WHAT?
IN UNIVERSAL JUSTICE.
THE ABSENCE OF RULES IS A LUXURY I CAN'T AFFORD.
RIGHT.
RIGHT.
HOLD STILL.
IT'S BEEN A FULL DAY, DOC. YA KNOW?
THE SOUND OF GUNFIRE'S STILL RINGING IN MY EARS.
BOOM, BOOM, BOOM. THAT WAS SOME FUCKIN' LOUD.
HA! HA! HA!
WHAT'S SO FUNNY ABOUT THAT?
DOC'S RIGHT. THERE'S NOTHING TO LAUGH ABOUT.
YOU KNOW WHAT, DOC? I THOUGHT I'D HUNG 'EM UP, AND HERE I AM, STINKING OF GUNPOWDER, LIKE IN THE GOOD OLD DAYS. I DON'T KNOW WHY THAT SMELL STAYS ON YOUR SKIN SO LONG.
IT'S THE SMELL OF DEATH.
MAYBE SO, BUT IT DOESN'T SCARE ME ANY MORE.

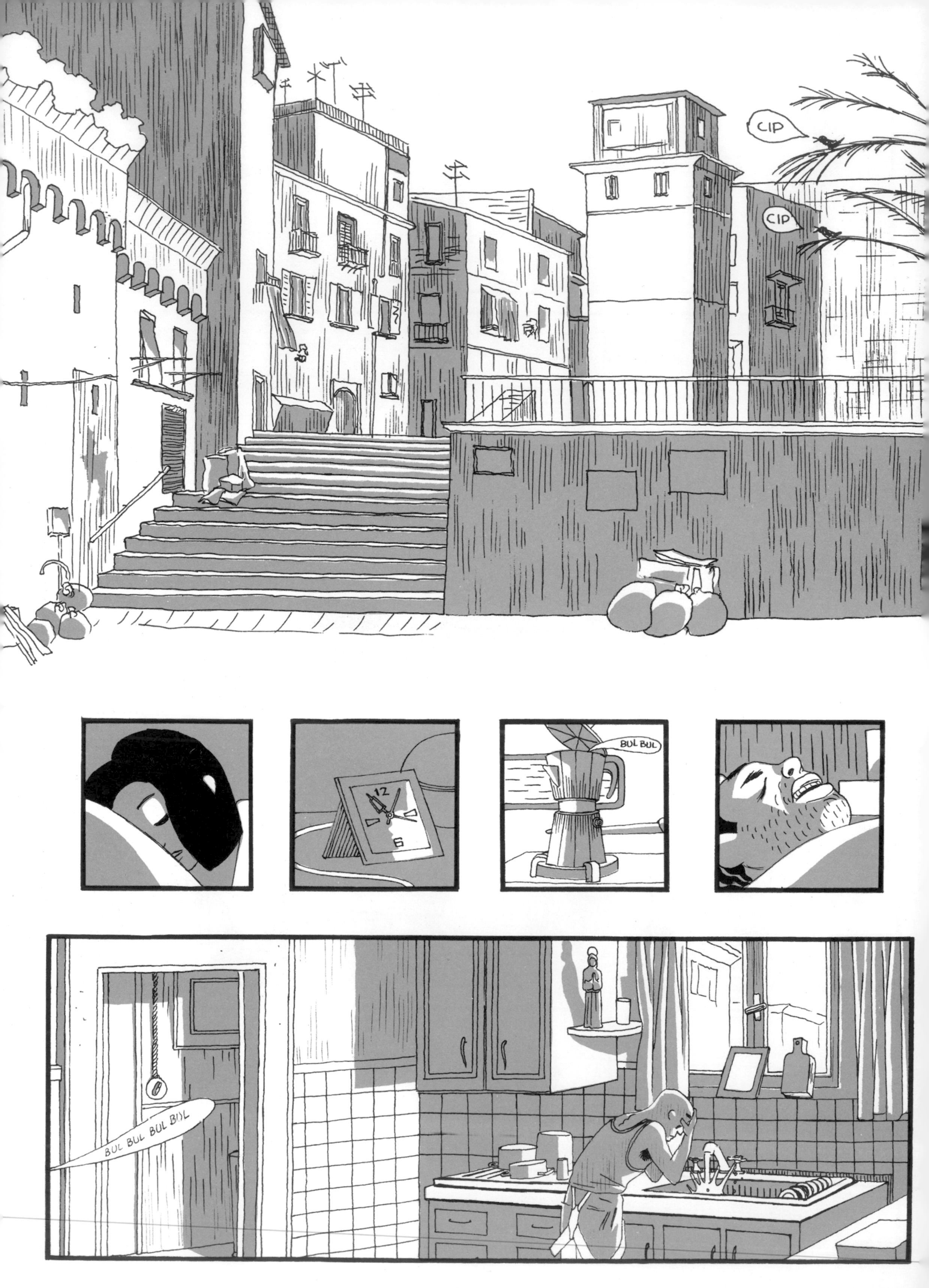
CIP
CIP
BUL BUL
BUL BUL BUL BUL

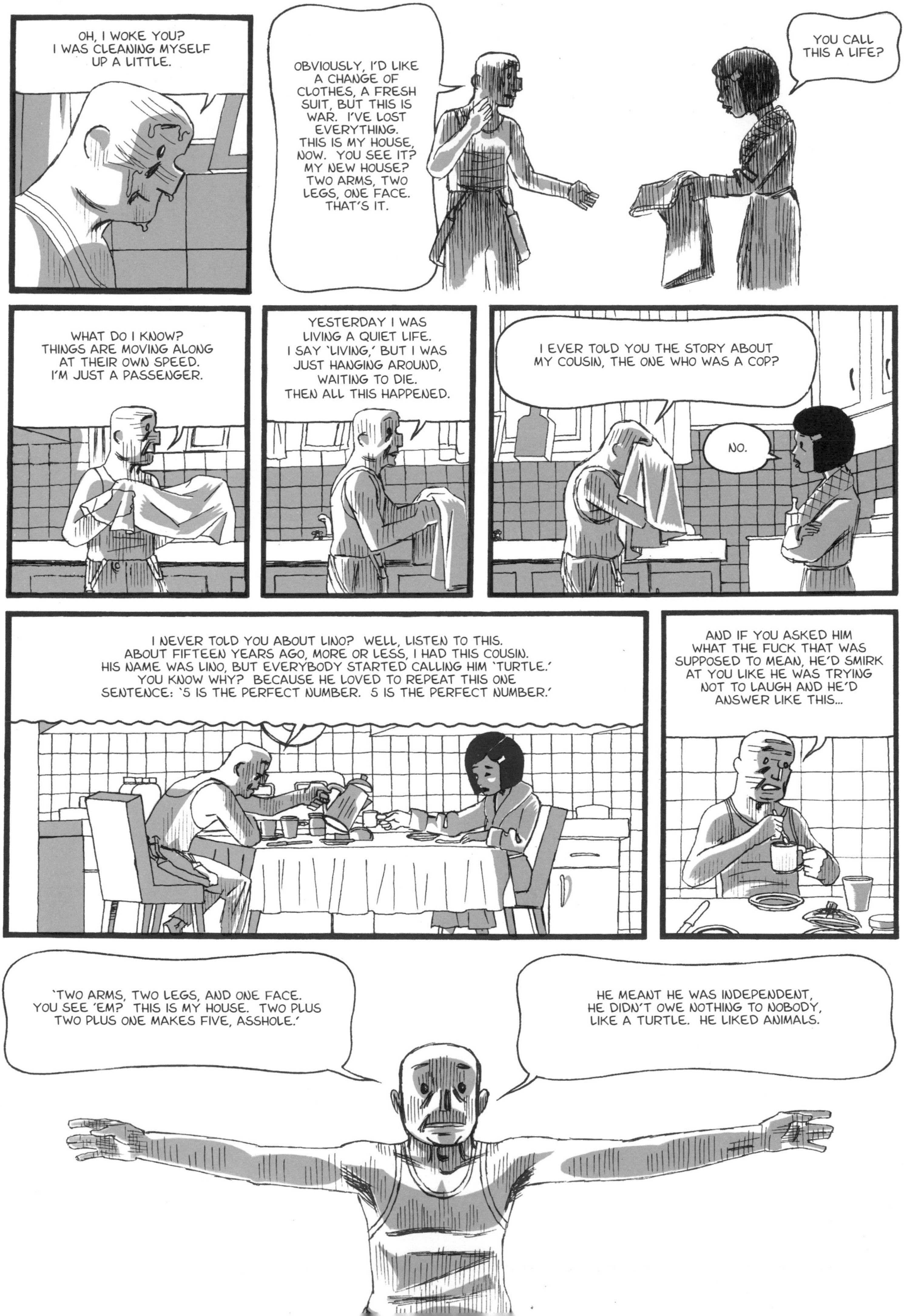
OH, I WOKE YOU? I WAS CLEANING MYSELF UP A LITTLE.
OBVIOUSLY, I'D LIKE A CHANGE OF CLOTHES, A FRESH SUIT, BUT THIS IS WAR. I'VE LOST EVERYTHING. THIS IS MY HOUSE, NOW. YOU SEE IT? MY NEW HOUSE? TWO ARMS, TWO LEGS, ONE FACE. THAT'S IT.
YOU CALL THIS A LIFE?
WHAT DO I KNOW? THINGS ARE MOVING ALONG AT THEIR OWN SPEED. I'M JUST A PASSENGER.
YESTERDAY I WAS LIVING A QUIET LIFE. I SAY 'LIVING,' BUT I WAS JUST HANGING AROUND, WAITING TO DIE. THEN ALL THIS HAPPENED.
I EVER TOLD YOU THE STORY ABOUT MY COUSIN, THE ONE WHO WAS A COP?
NO.
I NEVER TOLD YOU ABOUT LINO? WELL, LISTEN TO THIS. ABOUT FIFTEEN YEARS AGO, MORE OR LESS, I HAD THIS COUSIN. HIS NAME WAS LINO, BUT EVERYBODY STARTED CALLING HIM 'TURTLE.' YOU KNOW WHY? BECAUSE HE LOVED TO REPEAT THIS ONE SENTENCE: '5 IS THE PERFECT NUMBER. 5 IS THE PERFECT NUMBER.'
AND IF YOU ASKED HIM WHAT THE FUCK THAT WAS SUPPOSED TO MEAN, HE'D SMIRK AT YOU LIKE HE WAS TRYING NOT TO LAUGH AND HE'D ANSWER LIKE THIS...
'TWO ARMS, TWO LEGS, AND ONE FACE. YOU SEE 'EM? THIS IS MY HOUSE. TWO PLUS TWO PLUS ONE MAKES FIVE, ASSHOLE.'
HE MEANT HE WAS INDEPENDENT, HE DIDN'T OWE NOTHING TO NOBODY, LIKE A TURTLE. HE LIKED ANIMALS.

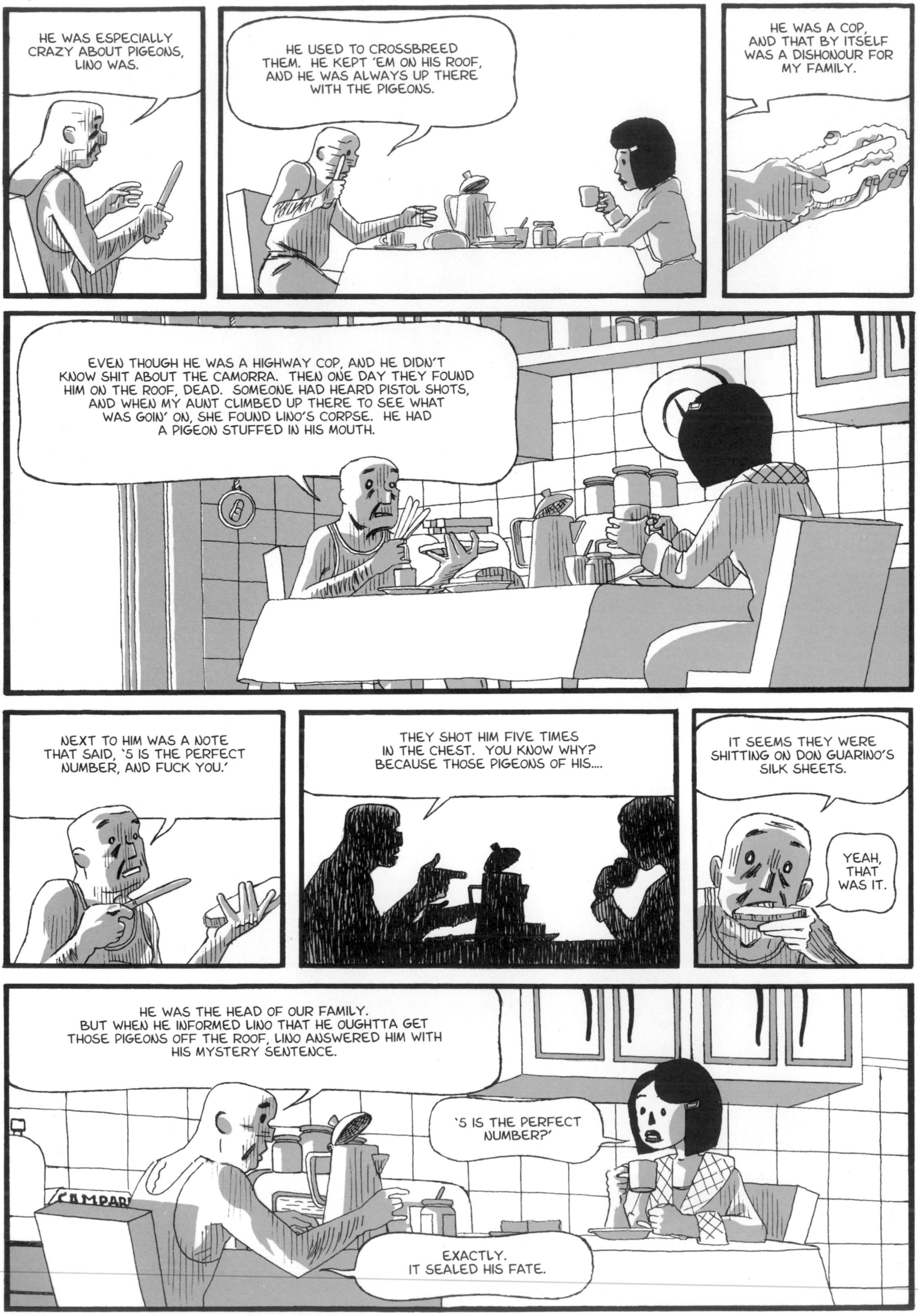
HE WAS ESPECIALLY CRAZY ABOUT PIGEONS, LINO WAS.
HE USED TO CROSSBREED THEM. HE KEPT 'EM ON HIS ROOF, AND HE WAS ALWAYS UP THERE WITH THE PIGEONS.
HE WAS A COP, AND THAT BY ITSELF WAS A DISHONOUR FOR MY FAMILY.
EVEN THOUGH HE WAS A HIGHWAY COP, AND HE DIDN'T KNOW SHIT ABOUT THE CAMORRA. THEN ONE DAY THEY FOUND HIM ON THE ROOF, DEAD. SOMEONE HAD HEARD PISTOL SHOTS, AND WHEN MY AUNT CLIMBED UP THERE TO SEE WHAT WAS GOIN' ON, SHE FOUND LINO'S CORPSE. HE HAD A PIGEON STUFFED IN HIS MOUTH.
NEXT TO HIM WAS A NOTE THAT SAID, '5 IS THE PERFECT NUMBER, AND FUCK YOU.'
THEY SHOT HIM FIVE TIMES IN THE CHEST. YOU KNOW WHY? BECAUSE THOSE PIGEONS OF HIS....
IT SEEMS THEY WERE SHITTING ON DON GUARINO'S SILK SHEETS.
YEAH, THAT WAS IT.
HE WAS THE HEAD OF OUR FAMILY. BUT WHEN HE INFORMED LINO THAT HE OUGHTTA GET THOSE PIGEONS OFF THE ROOF, LINO ANSWERED HIM WITH HIS MYSTERY SENTENCE.
'5 IS THE PERFECT NUMBER?'
CAMPARI
EXACTLY. IT SEALED HIS FATE.

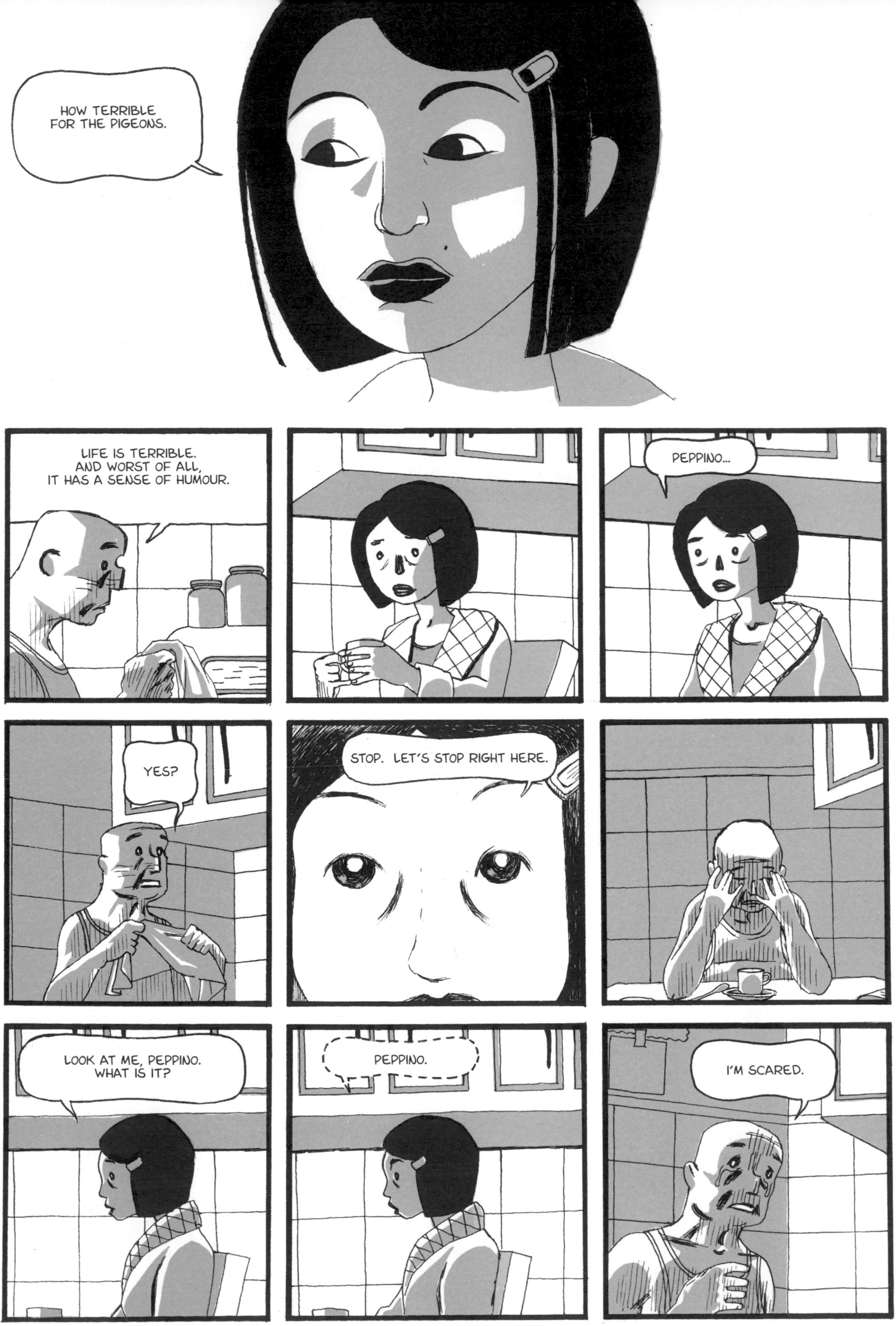
HOW TERRIBLE FOR THE PIGEONS.
LIFE IS TERRIBLE. AND WORST OF ALL, IT HAS A SENSE OF HUMOUR.
PEPPINO...
YES?
STOP. LET'S STOP RIGHT HERE.
LOOK AT ME, PEPPINO. WHAT IS IT?
PEPPINO.
I'M SCARED.

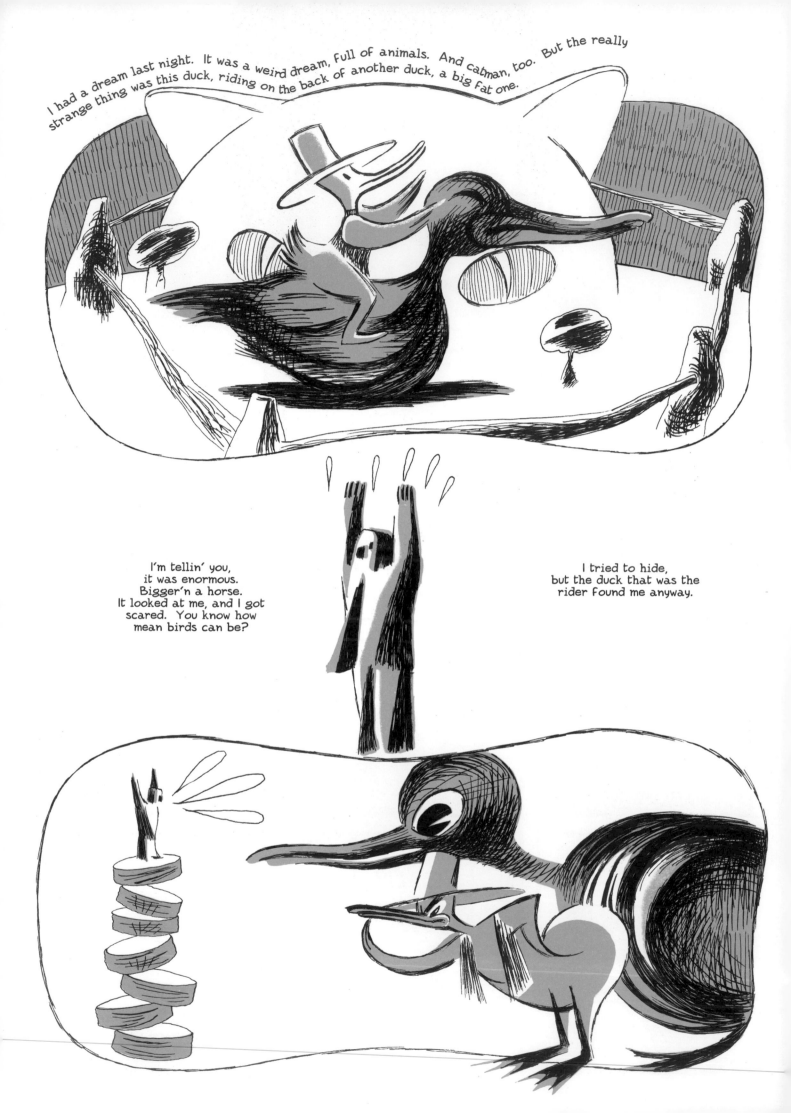

I had a dream last night. It was a weird dream, full of animals. And catman, too. But the really strange thing was this duck, riding on the back of another duck, a big fat one.

I'm tellin' you, it was enormous. Bigger'n a horse. It looked at me, and I got scared. You know how mean birds can be?

I tried to hide, but the duck that was the rider found me anyway.

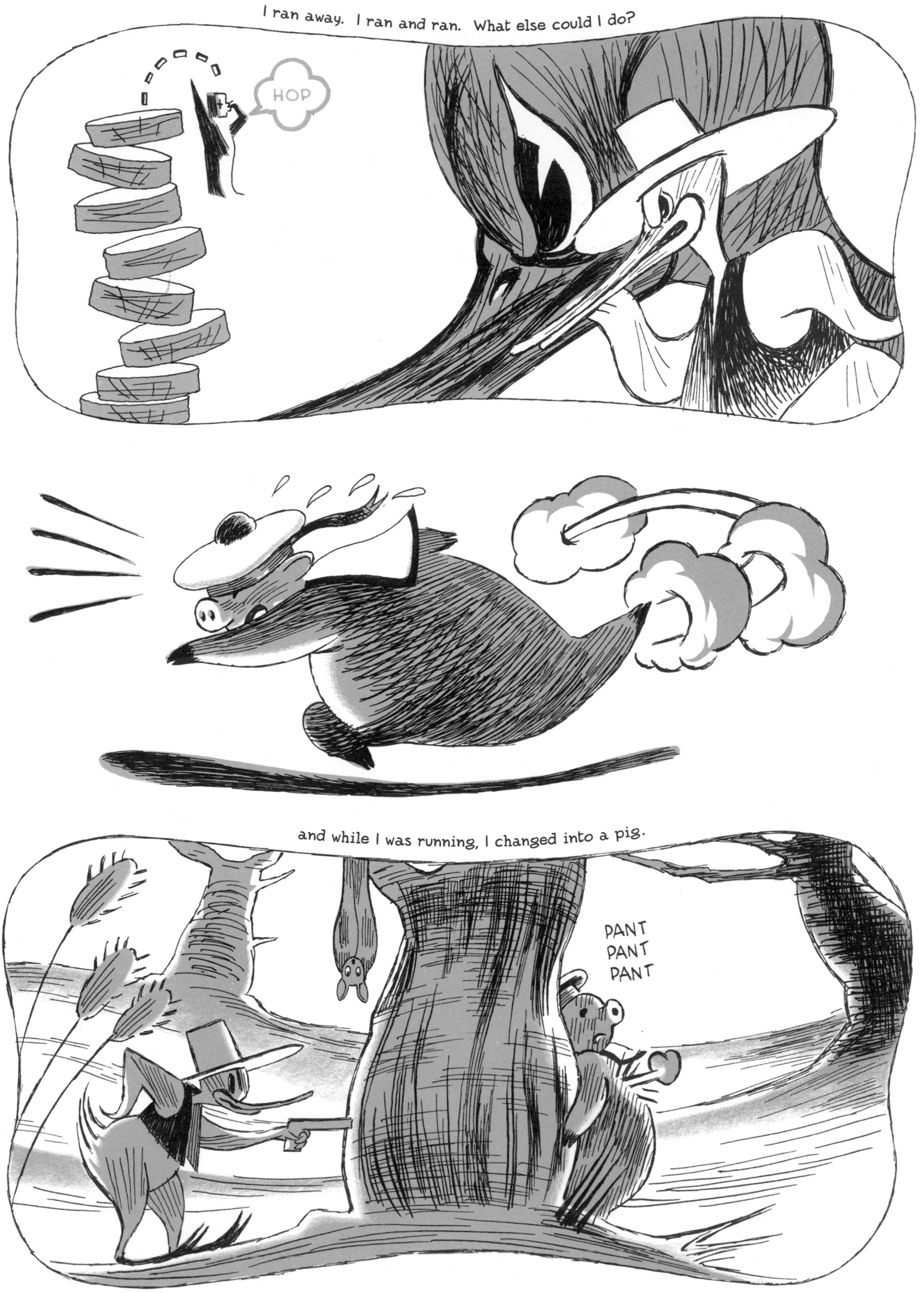
I ran away. I ran and ran. What else could I do?
HOP
and while I was running, I changed into a pig.
PANT
PANT
PANT

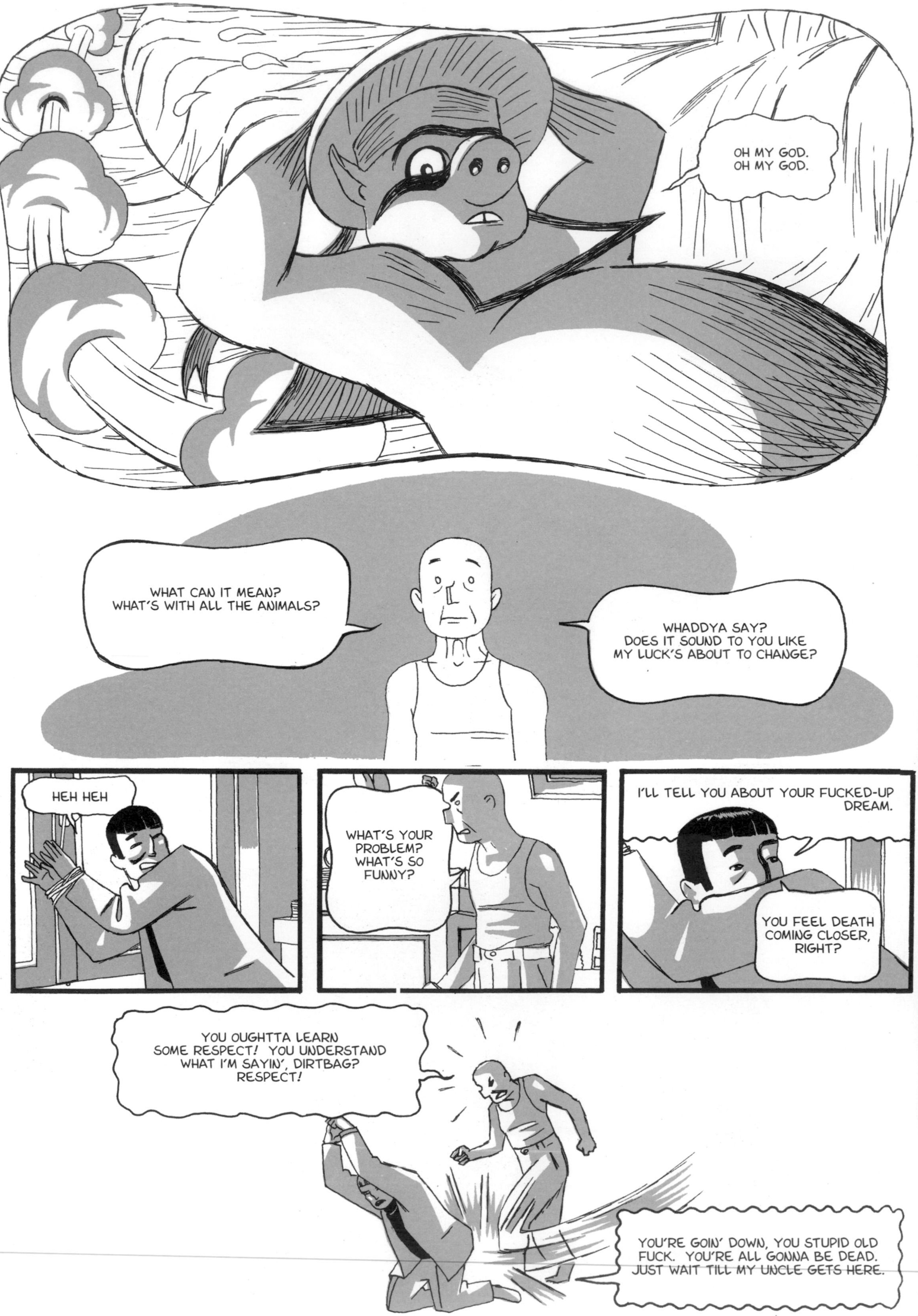
OH MY GOD. OH MY GOD.
WHAT CAN IT MEAN? WHAT'S WITH ALL THE ANIMALS?
WHADDYA SAY? DOES IT SOUND TO YOU LIKE MY LUCK'S ABOUT TO CHANGE?
HEH HEH
WHAT'S YOUR PROBLEM? WHAT'S SO FUNNY?
I'LL TELL YOU ABOUT YOUR FUCKED-UP DREAM.
YOU FEEL DEATH COMING CLOSER, RIGHT?
YOU OUGHTTA LEARN SOME RESPECT! YOU UNDERSTAND WHAT I'M SAYIN', DIRTBAG? RESPECT!
YOU'RE GOIN' DOWN, YOU STUPID OLD FUCK. YOU'RE ALL GONNA BE DEAD. JUST WAIT TILL MY UNCLE GETS HERE.

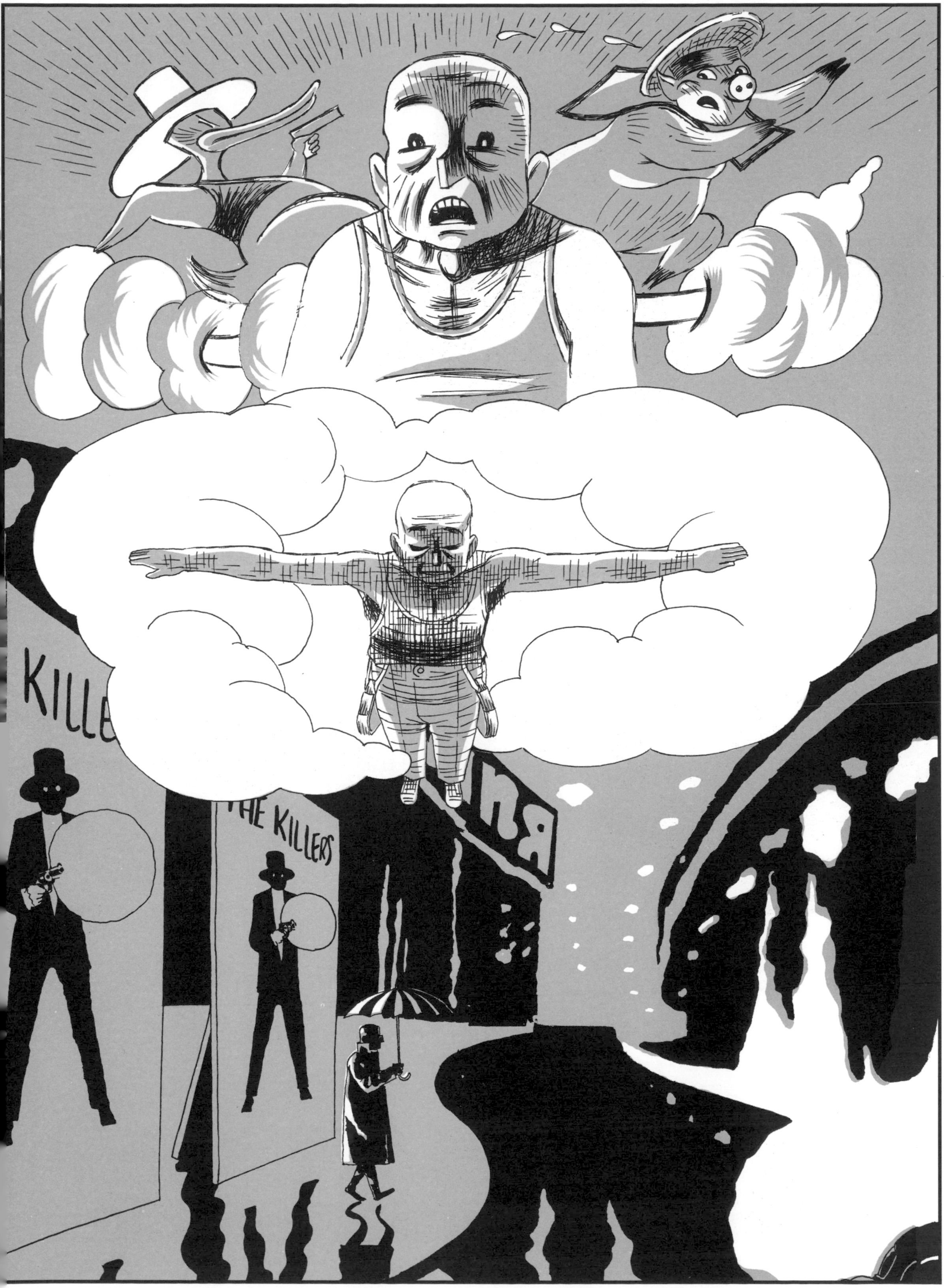
THE KILLERS

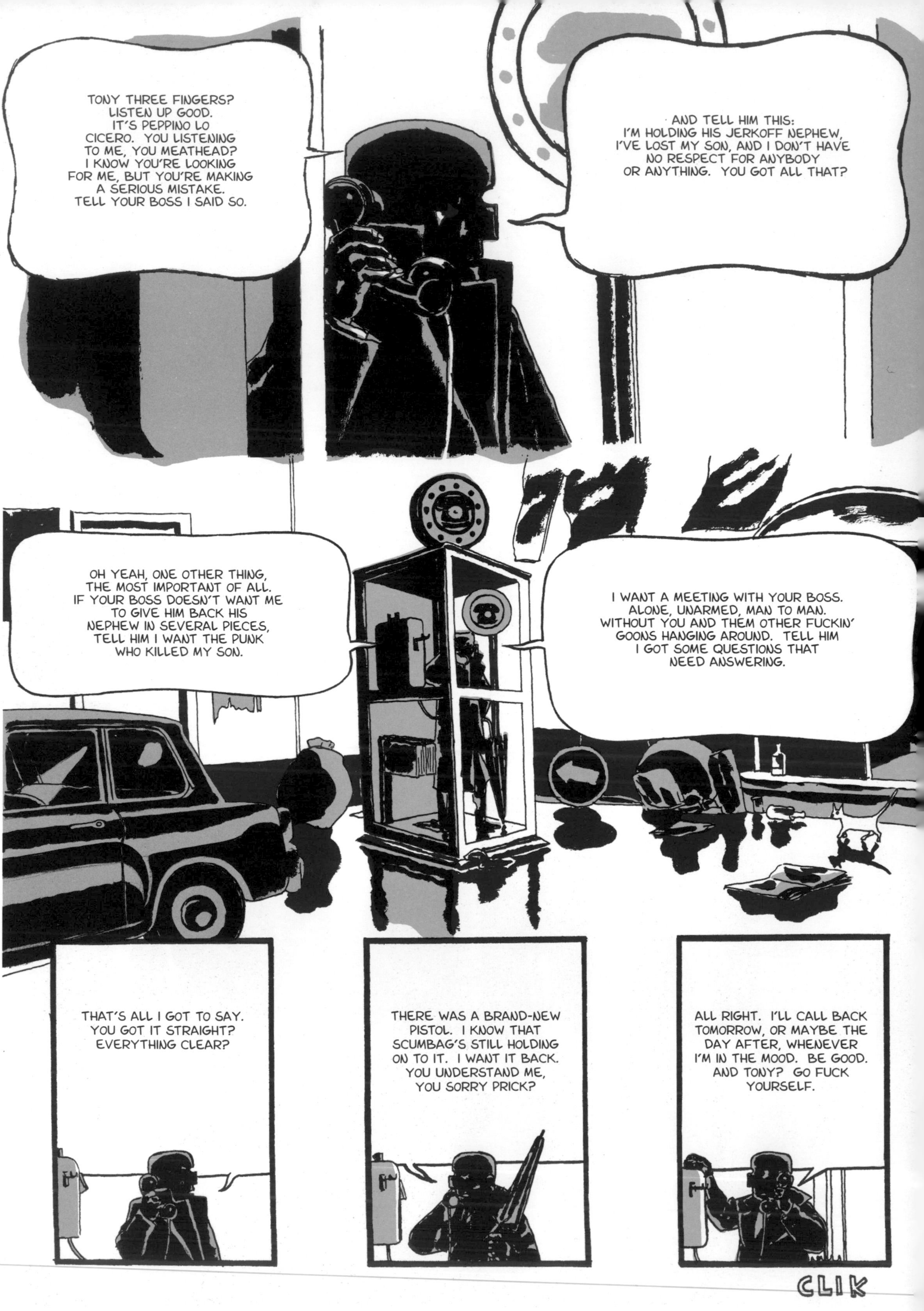
TONY THREE FINGERS? LISTEN UP GOOD. IT'S PEPPINO LO CICERO. YOU LISTENING TO ME, YOU MEATHEAD? I KNOW YOU'RE LOOKING FOR ME, BUT YOU'RE MAKING A SERIOUS MISTAKE. TELL YOUR BOSS I SAID SO.
AND TELL HIM THIS: I'M HOLDING HIS JERKOFF NEPHEW, I'VE LOST MY SON, AND I DON'T HAVE NO RESPECT FOR ANYBODY OR ANYTHING. YOU GOT ALL THAT?
OH YEAH, ONE OTHER THING, THE MOST IMPORTANT OF ALL. IF YOUR BOSS DOESN'T WANT ME TO GIVE HIM BACK HIS NEPHEW IN SEVERAL PIECES, TELL HIM I WANT THE PUNK WHO KILLED MY SON.
I WANT A MEETING WITH YOUR BOSS. ALONE, UNARMED, MAN TO MAN. WITHOUT YOU AND THEM OTHER FUCKIN' GOONS HANGING AROUND. TELL HIM I GOT SOME QUESTIONS THAT NEED ANSWERING.
THAT'S ALL I GOT TO SAY. YOU GOT IT STRAIGHT? EVERYTHING CLEAR?
THERE WAS A BRAND-NEW PISTOL. I KNOW THAT SCUMBAG'S STILL HOLDING ON TO IT. I WANT IT BACK. YOU UNDERSTAND ME, YOU SORRY PRICK?
ALL RIGHT. I'LL CALL BACK TOMORROW, OR MAYBE THE DAY AFTER, WHENEVER I'M IN THE MOOD. BE GOOD. AND TONY? GO FUCK YOURSELF.
CLIK

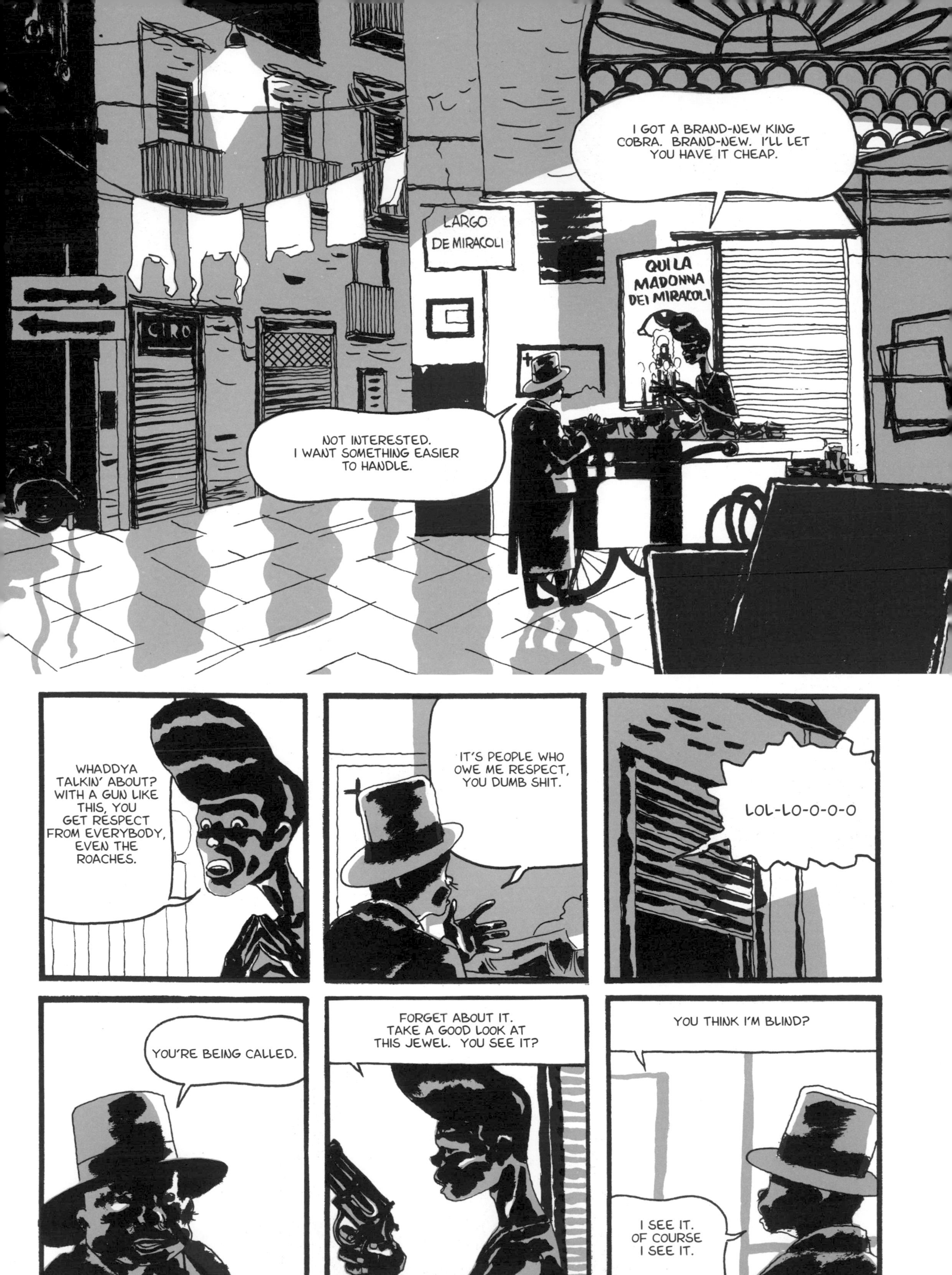
LARGO
DE MIRACOLI
CIRO
QUI LA
MADONNA
DEI MIRACOLI
I GOT A BRAND-NEW KING COBRA. BRAND-NEW. I'LL LET YOU HAVE IT CHEAP.
NOT INTERESTED. I WANT SOMETHING EASIER TO HANDLE.
WHADDYA TALKIN' ABOUT? WITH A GUN LIKE THIS, YOU GET RESPECT FROM EVERYBODY, EVEN THE ROACHES.
IT'S PEOPLE WHO OWE ME RESPECT, YOU DUMB SHIT.
LOL-LO-O-O-O
YOU'RE BEING CALLED.
FORGET ABOUT IT. TAKE A GOOD LOOK AT THIS JEWEL. YOU SEE IT?
YOU THINK I'M BLIND?
I SEE IT. OF COURSE I SEE IT.

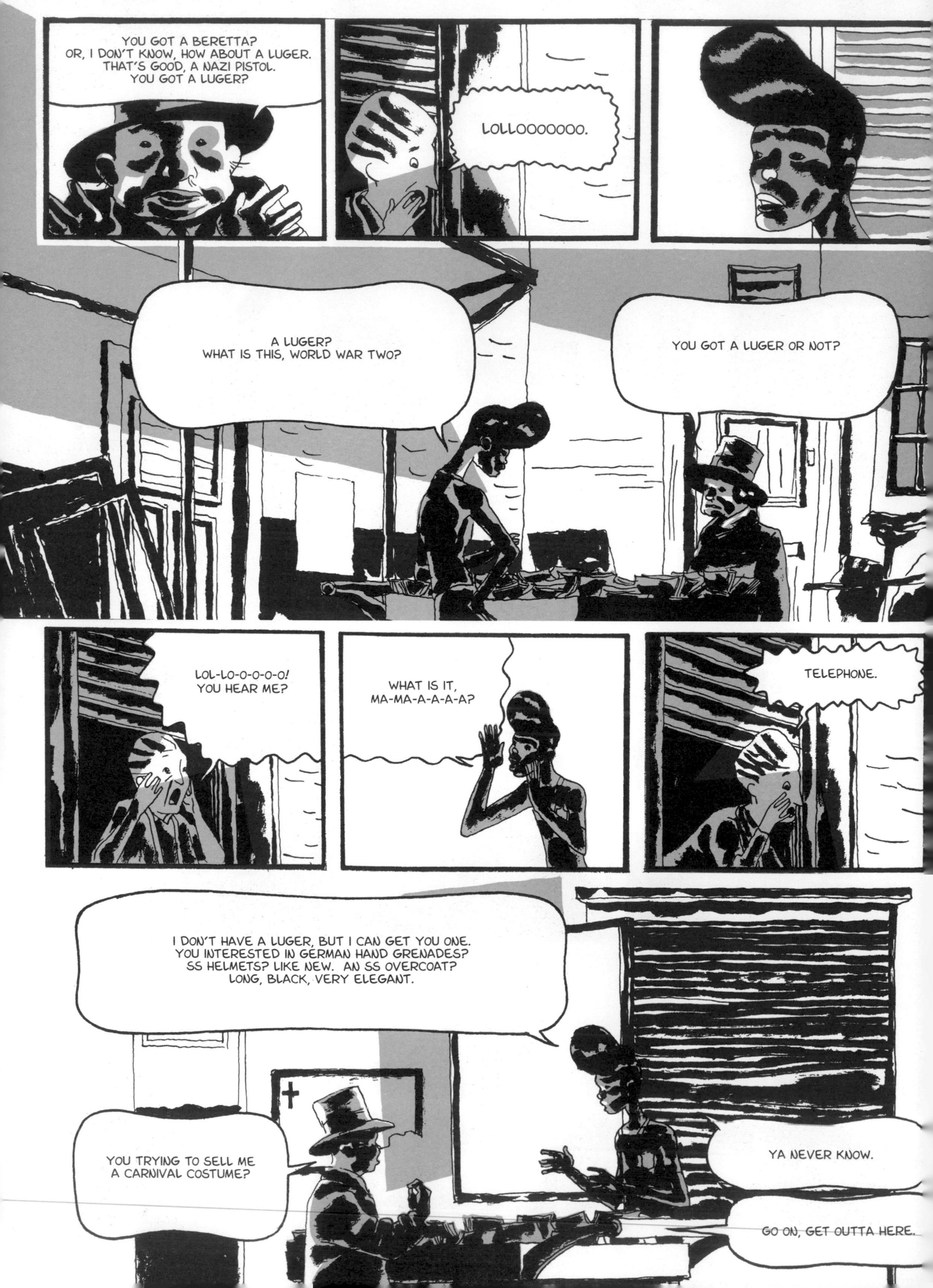
YOU GOT A BERETTA? OR, I DON'T KNOW, HOW ABOUT A LUGER. THAT'S GOOD, A NAZI PISTOL. YOU GOT A LUGER?
LOLLOOOOOOO.
A LUGER? WHAT IS THIS, WORLD WAR TWO?
YOU GOT A LUGER OR NOT?
LOL-LO-O-O-O-O! YOU HEAR ME?
WHAT IS IT, MA-MA-A-A-A-A?
TELEPHONE.
I DON'T HAVE A LUGER, BUT I CAN GET YOU ONE. YOU INTERESTED IN GERMAN HAND GRENADES? SS HELMETS? LIKE NEW. AN SS OVERCOAT? LONG, BLACK, VERY ELEGANT.
YOU TRYING TO SELL ME A CARNIVAL COSTUME?
YA NEVER KNOW.
GO ON, GET OUTTA HERE.

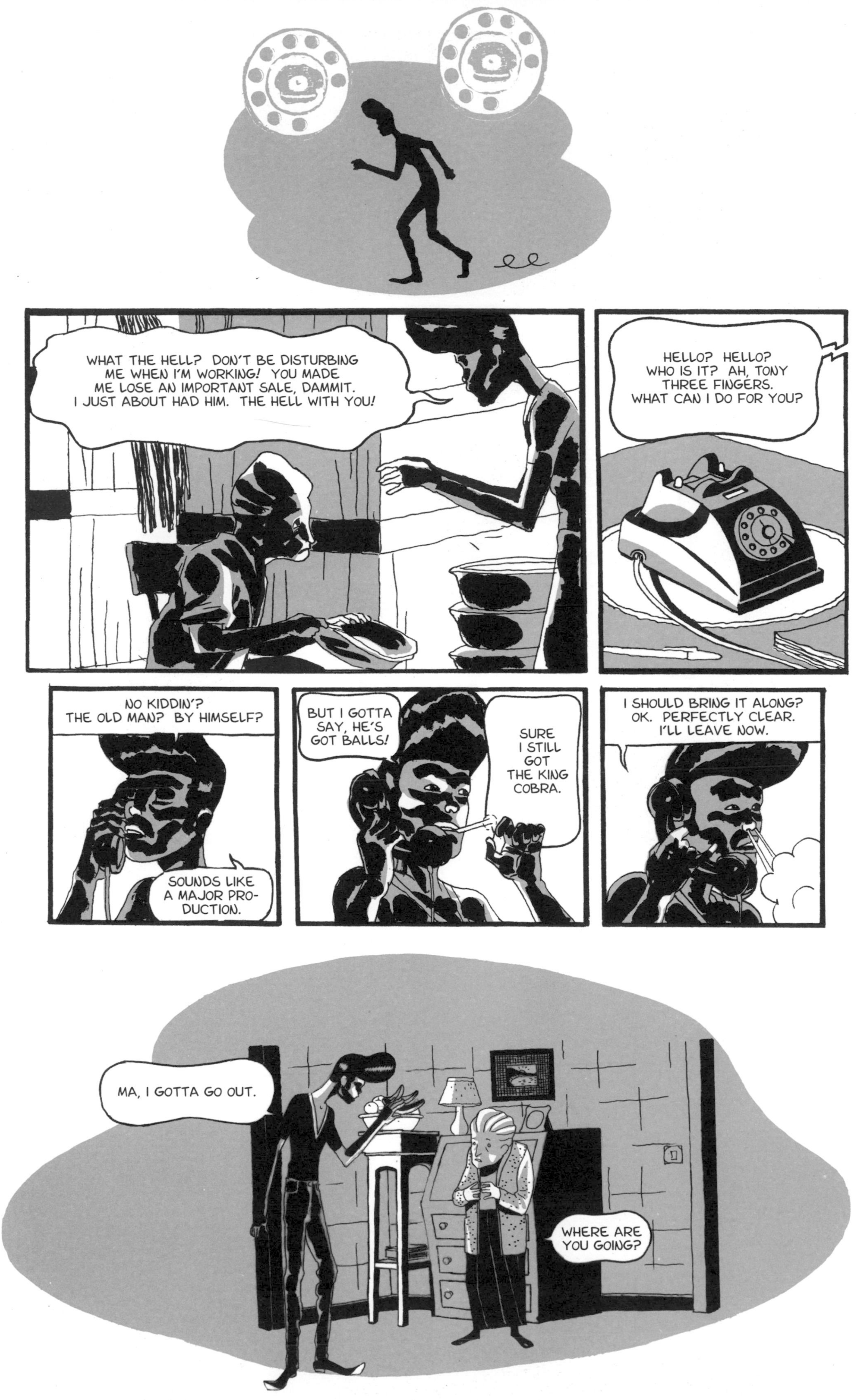
WHAT THE HELL? DON'T BE DISTURBING ME WHEN I'M WORKING! YOU MADE ME LOSE AN IMPORTANT SALE, DAMMIT. I JUST ABOUT HAD HIM. THE HELL WITH YOU!
HELLO? HELLO? WHO IS IT? AH, TONY THREE FINGERS. WHAT CAN I DO FOR YOU?
NO KIDDIN'? THE OLD MAN? BY HIMSELF?
SOUNDS LIKE A MAJOR PRODUCTION.
BUT I GOTTA SAY, HE'S GOT BALLS!
SURE I STILL GOT THE KING COBRA.
I SHOULD BRING IT ALONG? OK. PERFECTLY CLEAR. I'LL LEAVE NOW.
MA, I GOTTA GO OUT.
WHERE ARE YOU GOING?

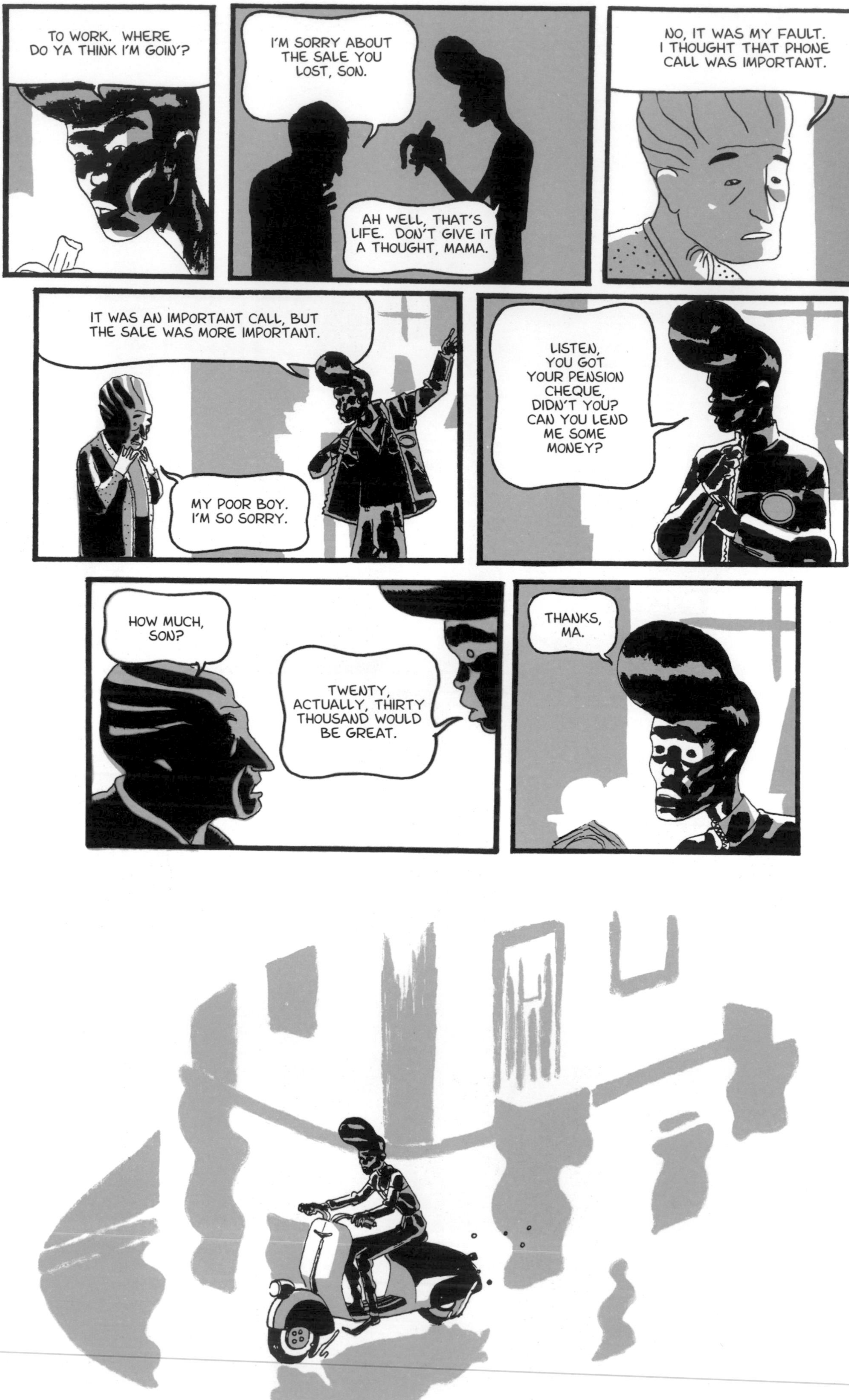
TO WORK. WHERE DO YA THINK I'M GOIN'?
I'M SORRY ABOUT THE SALE YOU LOST, SON.
AH WELL, THAT'S LIFE. DON'T GIVE IT A THOUGHT, MAMA.
NO, IT WAS MY FAULT. I THOUGHT THAT PHONE CALL WAS IMPORTANT.
IT WAS AN IMPORTANT CALL, BUT THE SALE WAS MORE IMPORTANT.
MY POOR BOY. I'M SO SORRY.
LISTEN, YOU GOT YOUR PENSION CHEQUE, DIDN'T YOU? CAN YOU LEND ME SOME MONEY?
HOW MUCH, SON?
TWENTY, ACTUALLY, THIRTY THOUSAND WOULD BE GREAT.
THANKS, MA.

chapter four
the smile of death

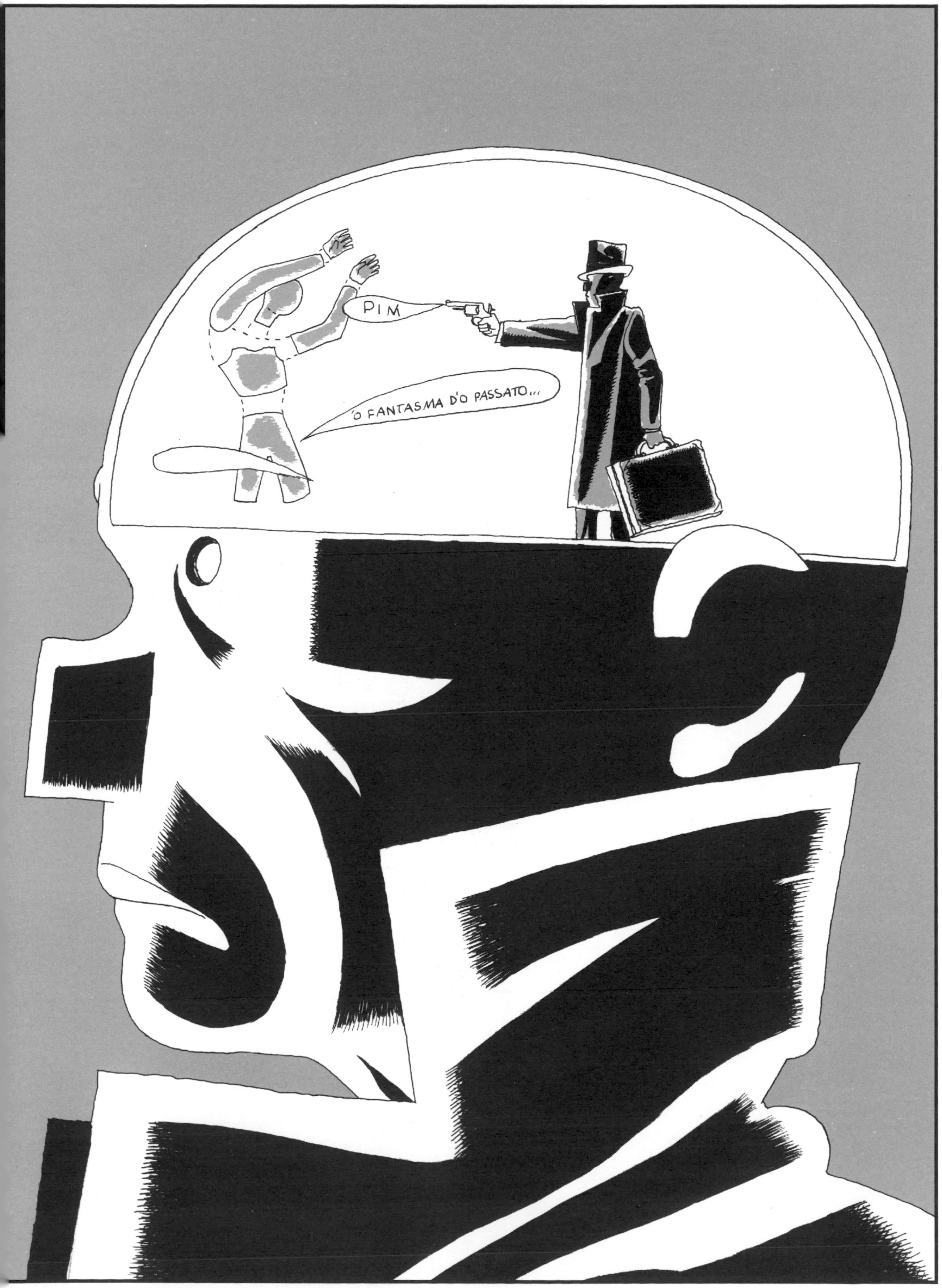
PIM
'O FANTASMA D'O PASSATO...

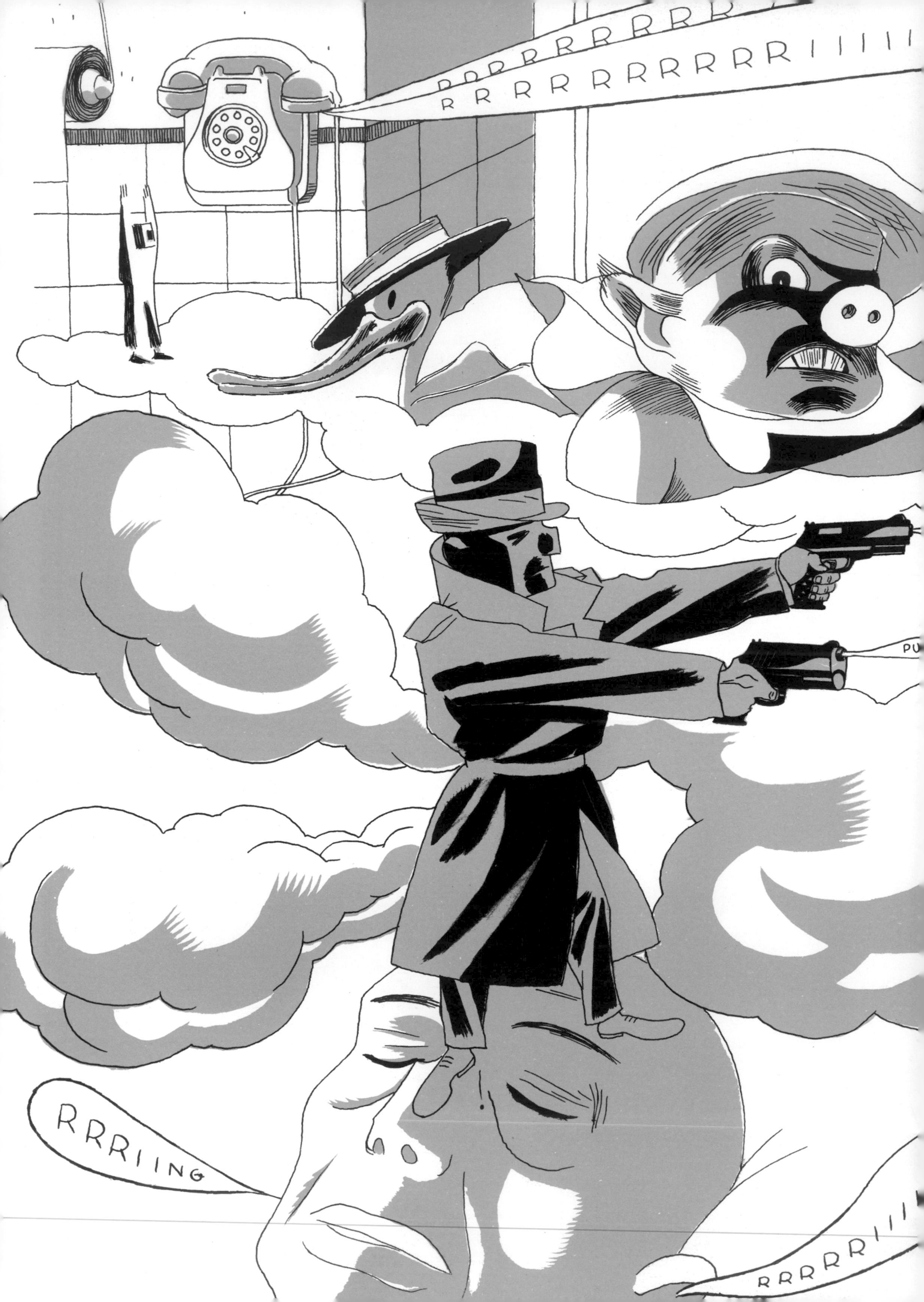

RRRRRRRR
RRRRRRRRRRRIIIIII
RRRIING
PU
RRRRRIII

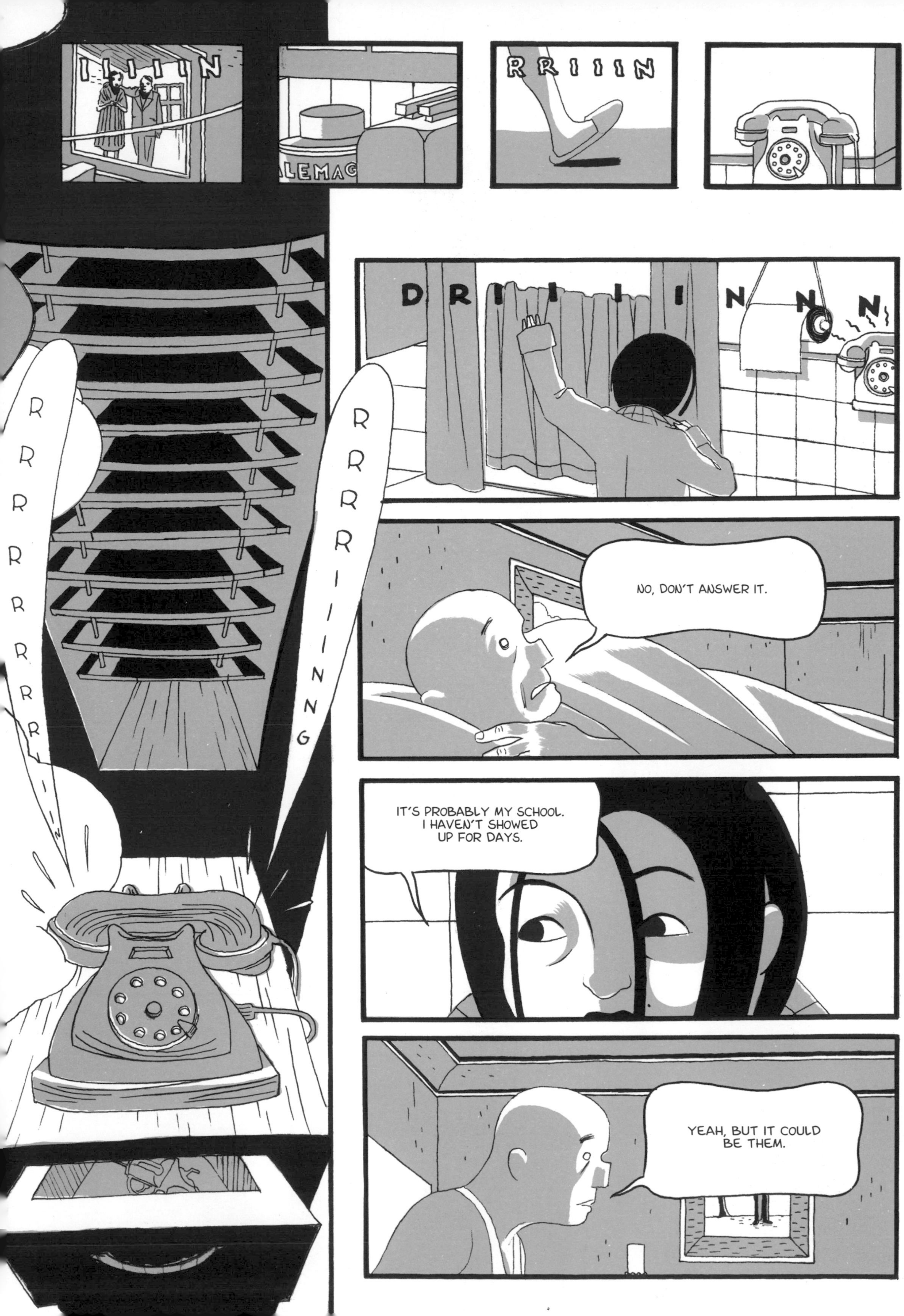
IIIIN
ALEMAG
RRIIIN
DRIIIIINNN
RRRRRRRRRIIN
RRRRIIINNG
NO, DON'T ANSWER IT.
IT'S PROBABLY MY SCHOOL. I HAVEN'T SHOWED UP FOR DAYS.
YEAH, BUT IT COULD BE THEM.

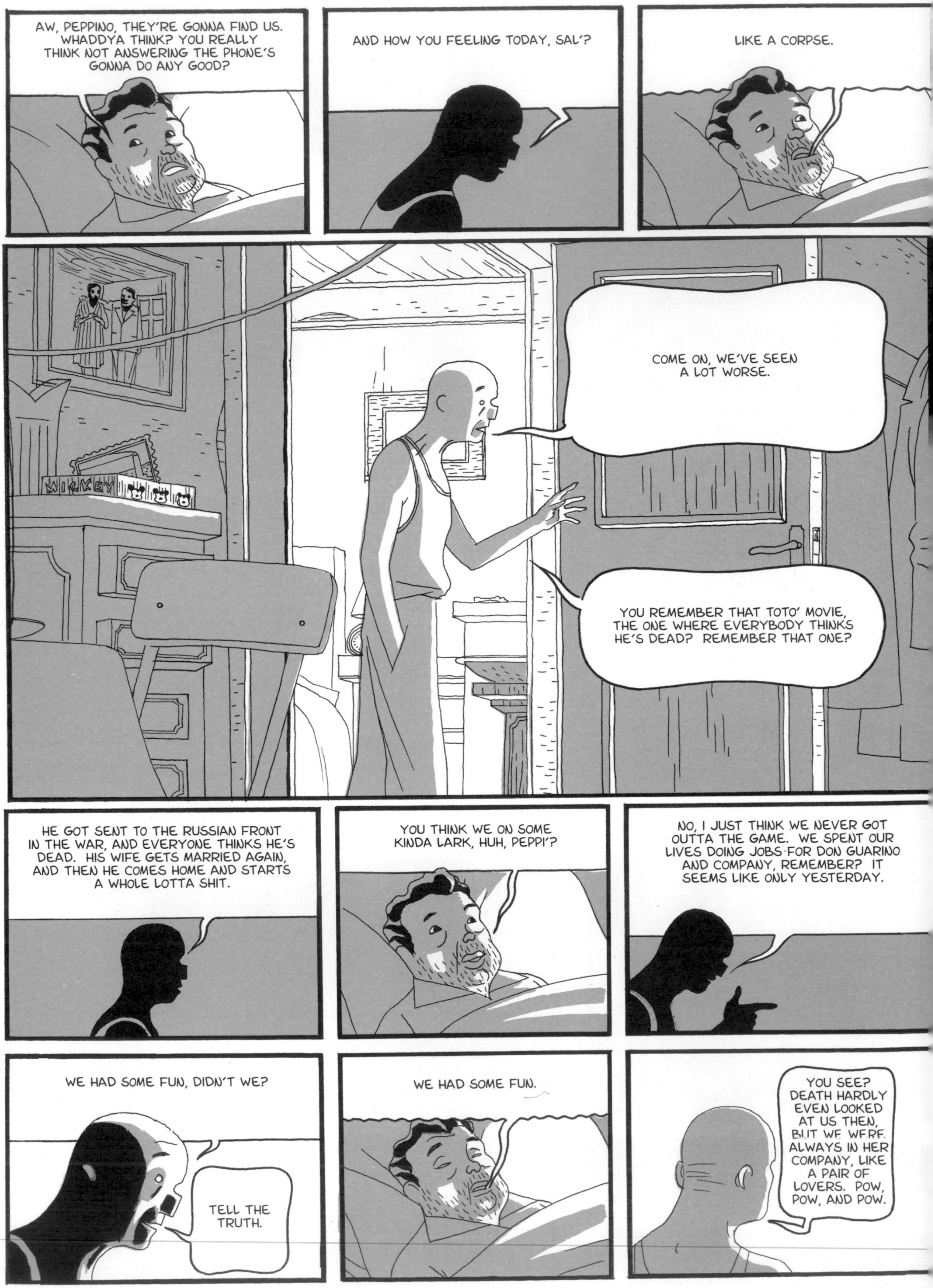
AW, PEPPINO, THEY'RE GONNA FIND US. WHADDYA THINK? YOU REALLY THINK NOT ANSWERING THE PHONE'S GONNA DO ANY GOOD?
AND HOW YOU FEELING TODAY, SAL'?
LIKE A CORPSE.
COME ON, WE'VE SEEN A LOT WORSE.
YOU REMEMBER THAT TOTO' MOVIE, THE ONE WHERE EVERYBODY THINKS HE'S DEAD? REMEMBER THAT ONE?
HE GOT SENT TO THE RUSSIAN FRONT IN THE WAR, AND EVERYONE THINKS HE'S DEAD. HIS WIFE GETS MARRIED AGAIN, AND THEN HE COMES HOME AND STARTS A WHOLE LOTTA SHIT.
YOU THINK WE ON SOME KINDA LARK, HUH, PEPPI'?
NO, I JUST THINK WE NEVER GOT OUTTA THE GAME. WE SPENT OUR LIVES DOING JOBS FOR DON GUARINO AND COMPANY, REMEMBER? IT SEEMS LIKE ONLY YESTERDAY.
WE HAD SOME FUN, DIDN'T WE?
TELL THE TRUTH.
WE HAD SOME FUN.
YOU SEE? DEATH HARDLY EVEN LOOKED AT US THEN, BUT WE WERE ALWAYS IN HER COMPANY, LIKE A PAIR OF LOVERS. POW, POW, AND POW.

YOU KNOW SOMETHIN', SALVATO'? OUR LIVES HAVE REACHED A CERTAIN SPEED. IF YOU STOP OR HESITATE, THAT'S WHEN DEATH HAS A GOOD CHANCE TO SNATCH YOU.

THAT'S WHAT YOU THINK?

THAT'S WHAT I THINK, TOTO'.

TAKE ME, FOR EXAMPLE. I WAS PRACTICALLY DEAD, AND I DIDN'T EVEN NOTICE. WHAT I DID WAS, I WENT FISHING, AND I MADE SHIRTS FOR NINO.

I'M STILL HERE, BUT BY PURE LUCK. DEATH WASN'T INTERESTED IN ME YET. THE BELL WASN'T TOLLING FOR ME.

HELL, IT WASN'T EVEN IN THE BELL TOWER YET. WHAT DO I KNOW? I KNOW ONE THING: THE WORLD GOES AT ITS OWN SPEED. AND YOU CAN'T CHEAT IT, NO YOU CAN'T.

BECAUSE THIS IS ONE OF THE LAWS OF CREATION.

PEPPI', I GOT NO FUCKIN' IDEA WHAT YOU'RE TALKING ABOUT. ALL I KNOW IS, THERE'S A HOLE IN MY GUT, AND THIS TIME I GOT A FEELING I'M SITTING IN THE WAITING ROOM.

WHAT WAITING ROOM, WOODENHEAD?

THE WAITING ROOM FOR DEATH.

OH YEAH? THEN SPIT IN ITS FACE AND FIGHT. YOU STILL GOT YOUR BALLS, OR WHAT?

I GOT 'EM, I GOT 'EM....

THEN DON'T ACT LIKE THE DOCTOR. BAD LUCK ONLY COMES WHEN YOU CALL IT. BELIEVE WHAT I'M TELLING YOU.

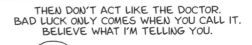

THAT'S WHAT I'M WORRIED ABOUT, YOU SHITHEAD.

YOU'VE BEEN CALLING AND CALLING, AND YOU STILL DON'T REALIZE IT! I DON'T UNDERSTAND YOU ANY MORE.

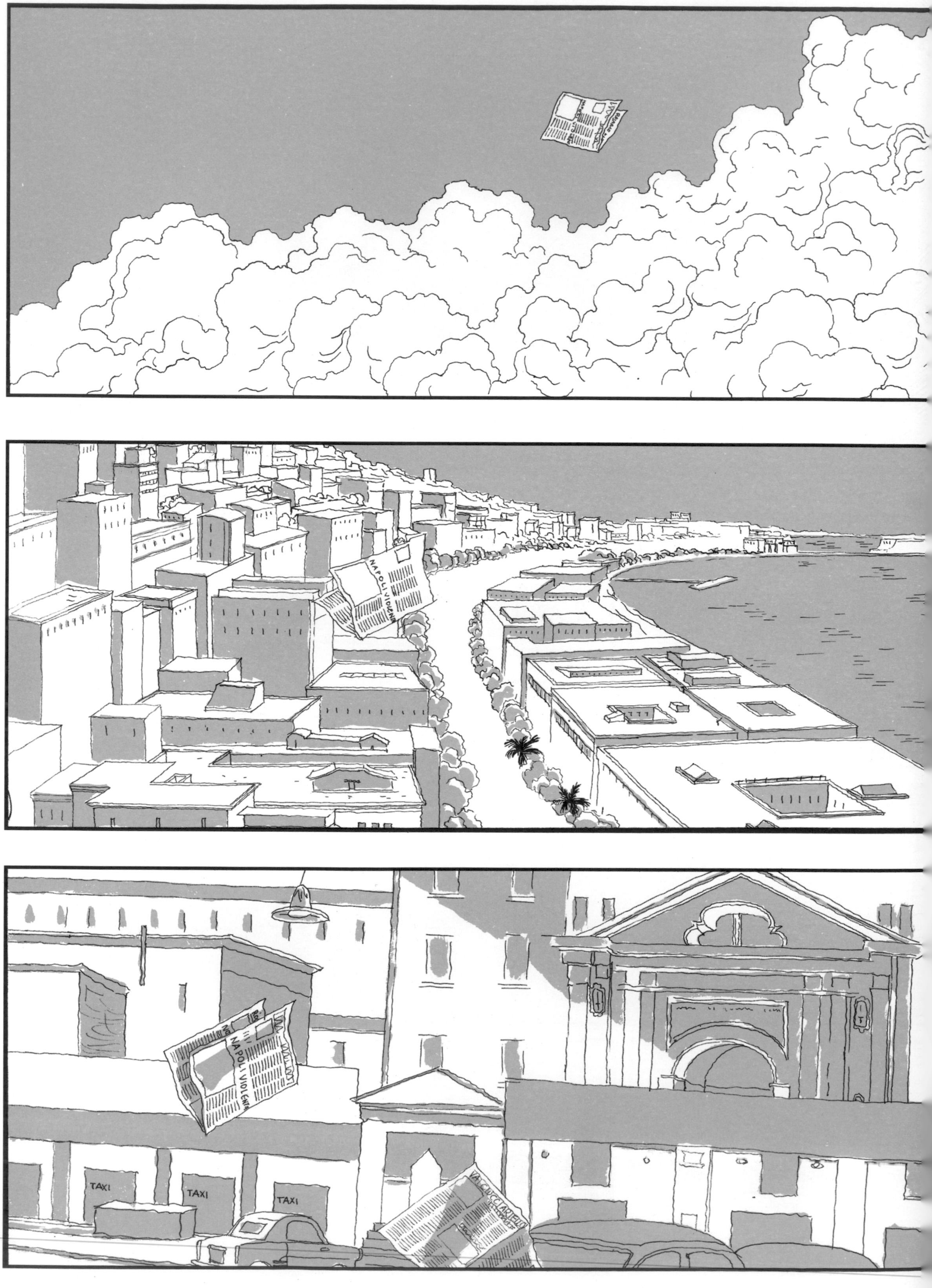
NAPOLI VIOLENTA
NAPOLI VIOLENTA
TAXI
TAXI
TAXI
VA CIUCCIARIELLO

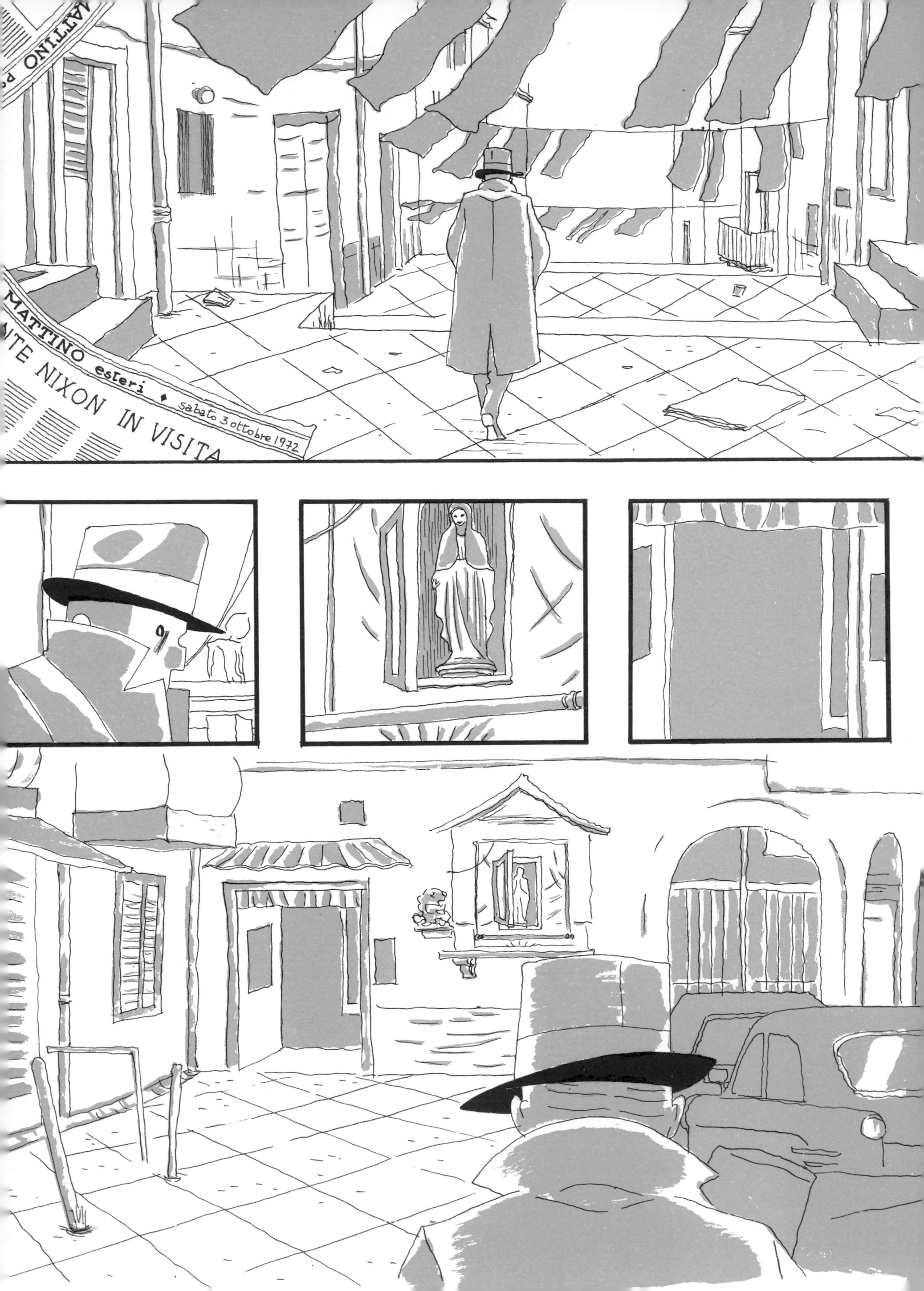
ATTINO
MATTINO esteri ♦ sabato 3 ottobre 1972
NTE NIXON IN VISITA

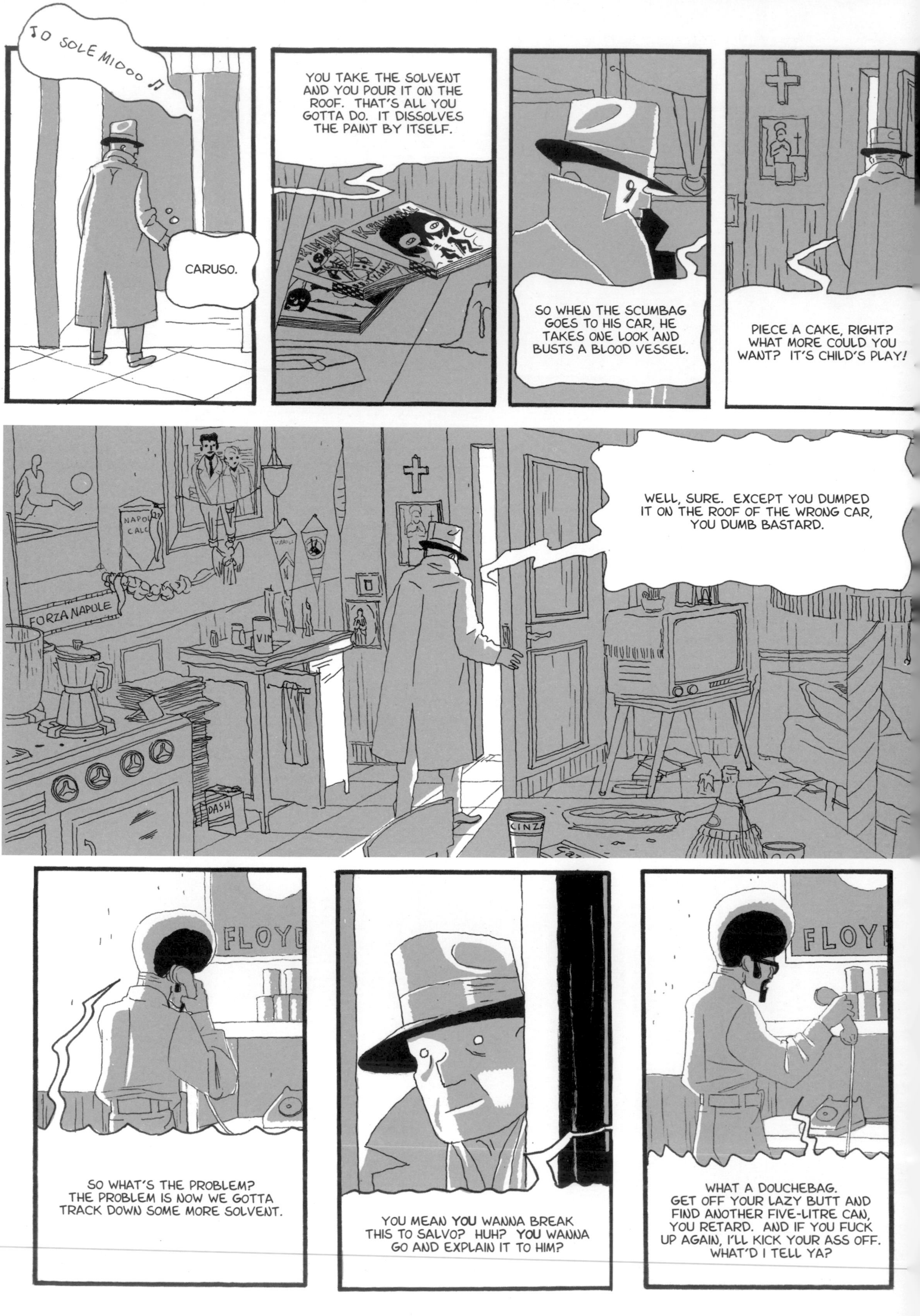
O SOLE MIOOO
CARUSO.
YOU TAKE THE SOLVENT AND YOU POUR IT ON THE ROOF. THAT'S ALL YOU GOTTA DO. IT DISSOLVES THE PAINT BY ITSELF.
SO WHEN THE SCUMBAG GOES TO HIS CAR, HE TAKES ONE LOOK AND BUSTS A BLOOD VESSEL.
PIECE A CAKE, RIGHT? WHAT MORE COULD YOU WANT? IT'S CHILD'S PLAY!
FORZA NAPULE
WELL, SURE. EXCEPT YOU DUMPED IT ON THE ROOF OF THE WRONG CAR, YOU DUMB BASTARD.
DASH
FLOYD
SO WHAT'S THE PROBLEM? THE PROBLEM IS NOW WE GOTTA TRACK DOWN SOME MORE SOLVENT.
YOU MEAN YOU WANNA BREAK THIS TO SALVO? HUH? YOU WANNA GO AND EXPLAIN IT TO HIM?
WHAT A DOUCHEBAG. GET OFF YOUR LAZY BUTT AND FIND ANOTHER FIVE-LITRE CAN, YOU RETARD. AND IF YOU FUCK UP AGAIN, I'LL KICK YOUR ASS OFF. WHAT'D I TELL YA?

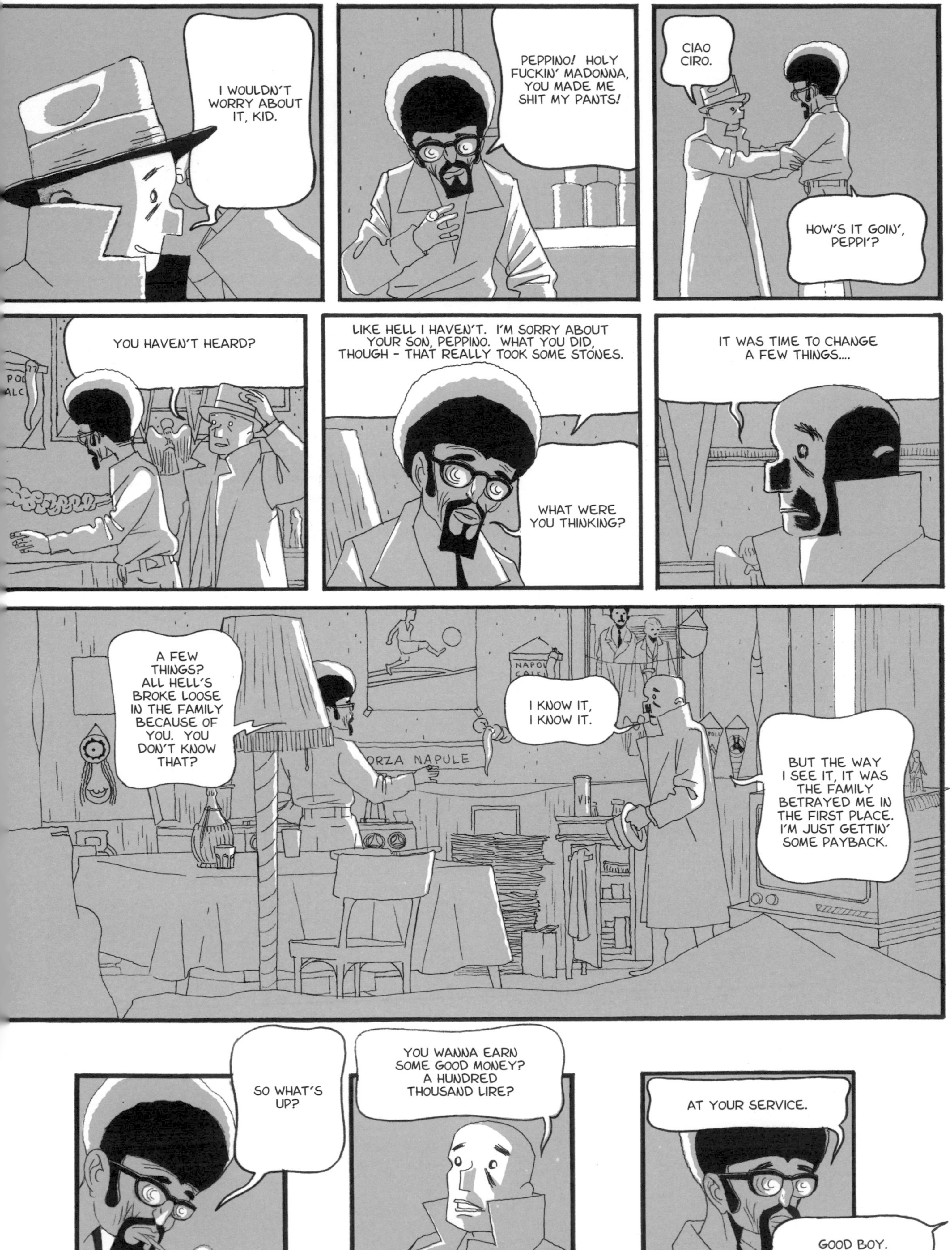
I WOULDN'T WORRY ABOUT IT, KID.
PEPPINO! HOLY FUCKIN' MADONNA, YOU MADE ME SHIT MY PANTS!
CIAO CIRO.
HOW'S IT GOIN', PEPPI'?
YOU HAVEN'T HEARD?
LIKE HELL I HAVEN'T. I'M SORRY ABOUT YOUR SON, PEPPINO. WHAT YOU DID, THOUGH - THAT REALLY TOOK SOME STONES.
WHAT WERE YOU THINKING?
IT WAS TIME TO CHANGE A FEW THINGS....
A FEW THINGS? ALL HELL'S BROKE LOOSE IN THE FAMILY BECAUSE OF YOU. YOU DON'T KNOW THAT?
I KNOW IT, I KNOW IT.
BUT THE WAY I SEE IT, IT WAS THE FAMILY BETRAYED ME IN THE FIRST PLACE. I'M JUST GETTIN' SOME PAYBACK.
ORZA NAPULE
SO WHAT'S UP?
YOU WANNA EARN SOME GOOD MONEY? A HUNDRED THOUSAND LIRE?
AT YOUR SERVICE.
GOOD BOY.

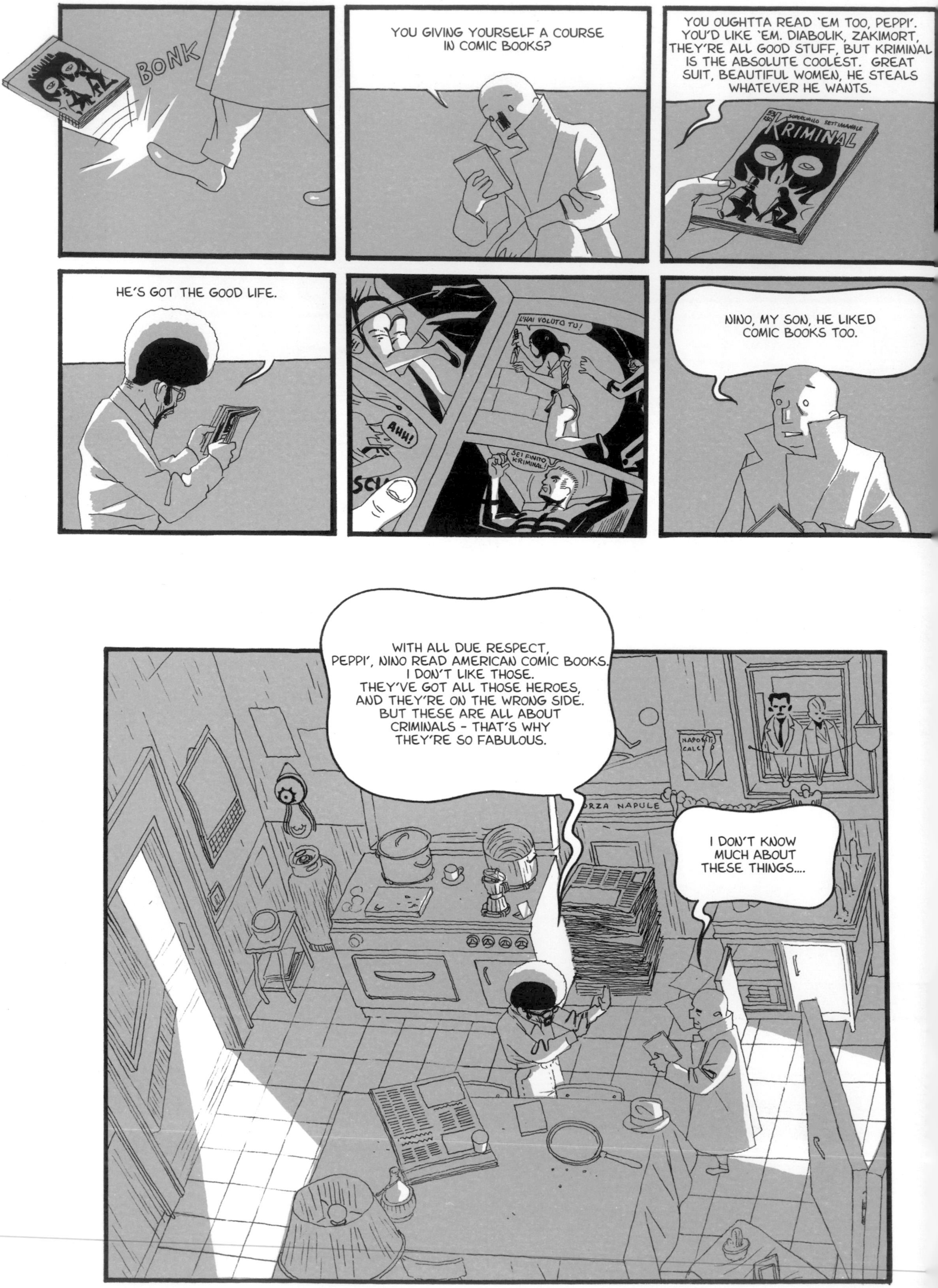
BONK
YOU GIVING YOURSELF A COURSE IN COMIC BOOKS?
YOU OUGHTTA READ 'EM TOO, PEPPI'. YOU'D LIKE 'EM. DIABOLIK, ZAKIMORT, THEY'RE ALL GOOD STUFF, BUT KRIMINAL IS THE ABSOLUTE COOLEST. GREAT SUIT, BEAUTIFUL WOMEN, HE STEALS WHATEVER HE WANTS.
KRIMINAL
HE'S GOT THE GOOD LIFE.
L'HAI VOLUTO TU!
AHH!
SEI FINITO KRIMINAL!
NINO, MY SON, HE LIKED COMIC BOOKS TOO.
WITH ALL DUE RESPECT, PEPPI', NINO READ AMERICAN COMIC BOOKS. I DON'T LIKE THOSE. THEY'VE GOT ALL THOSE HEROES, AND THEY'RE ON THE WRONG SIDE. BUT THESE ARE ALL ABOUT CRIMINALS - THAT'S WHY THEY'RE SO FABULOUS.
I DON'T KNOW MUCH ABOUT THESE THINGS....

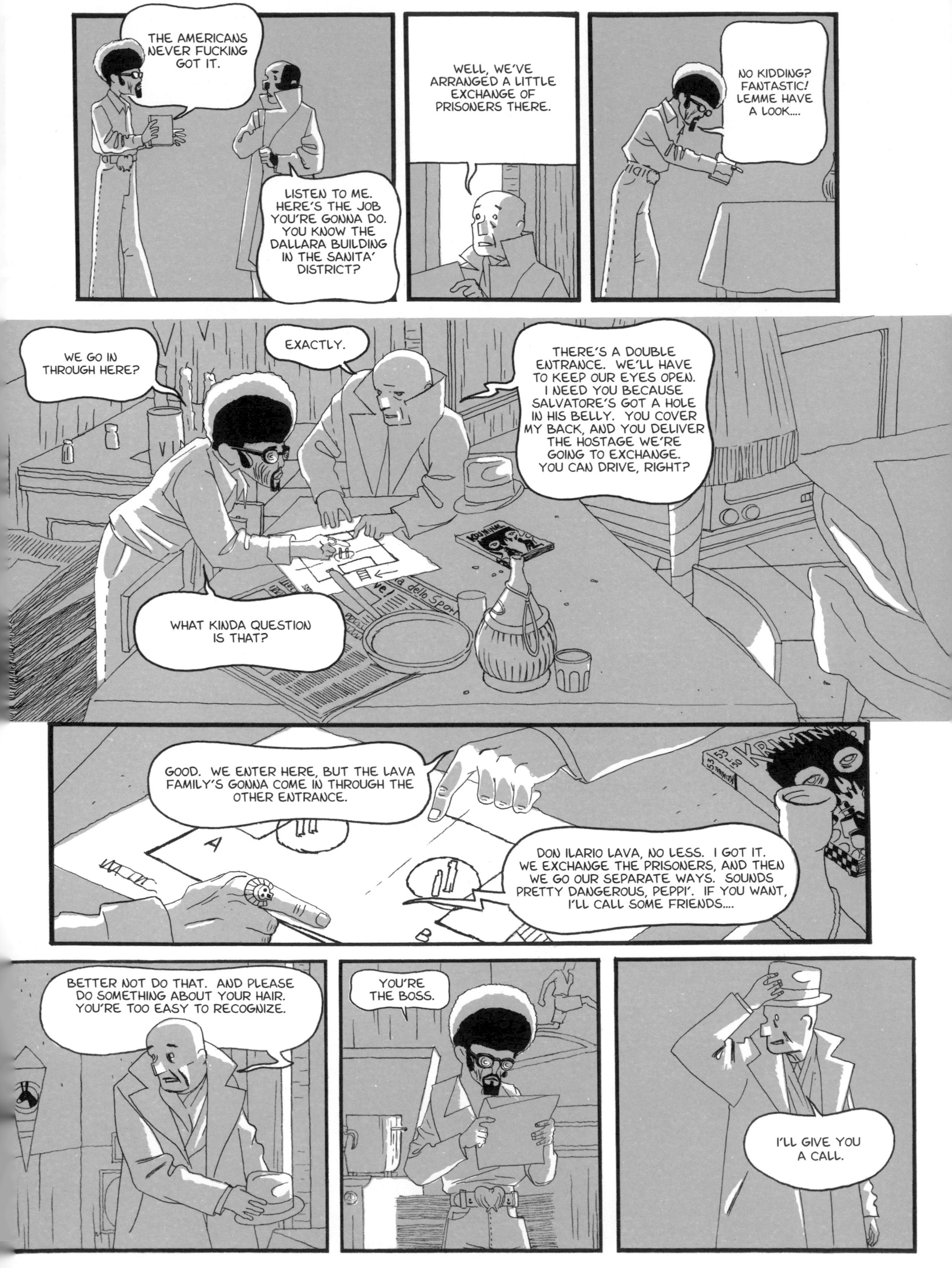
THE AMERICANS NEVER FUCKING GOT IT.
LISTEN TO ME. HERE'S THE JOB YOU'RE GONNA DO. YOU KNOW THE DALLARA BUILDING IN THE SANITA' DISTRICT?
WELL, WE'VE ARRANGED A LITTLE EXCHANGE OF PRISONERS THERE.
NO KIDDING? FANTASTIC! LEMME HAVE A LOOK....
WE GO IN THROUGH HERE?
EXACTLY.
THERE'S A DOUBLE ENTRANCE. WE'LL HAVE TO KEEP OUR EYES OPEN. I NEED YOU BECAUSE SALVATORE'S GOT A HOLE IN HIS BELLY. YOU COVER MY BACK, AND YOU DELIVER THE HOSTAGE WE'RE GOING TO EXCHANGE. YOU CAN DRIVE, RIGHT?
WHAT KINDA QUESTION IS THAT?
GOOD. WE ENTER HERE, BUT THE LAVA FAMILY'S GONNA COME IN THROUGH THE OTHER ENTRANCE.
DON ILARIO LAVA, NO LESS. I GOT IT. WE EXCHANGE THE PRISONERS, AND THEN WE GO OUR SEPARATE WAYS. SOUNDS PRETTY DANGEROUS, PEPPI'. IF YOU WANT, I'LL CALL SOME FRIENDS....
BETTER NOT DO THAT. AND PLEASE DO SOMETHING ABOUT YOUR HAIR. YOU'RE TOO EASY TO RECOGNIZE.
YOU'RE THE BOSS.
I'LL GIVE YOU A CALL.

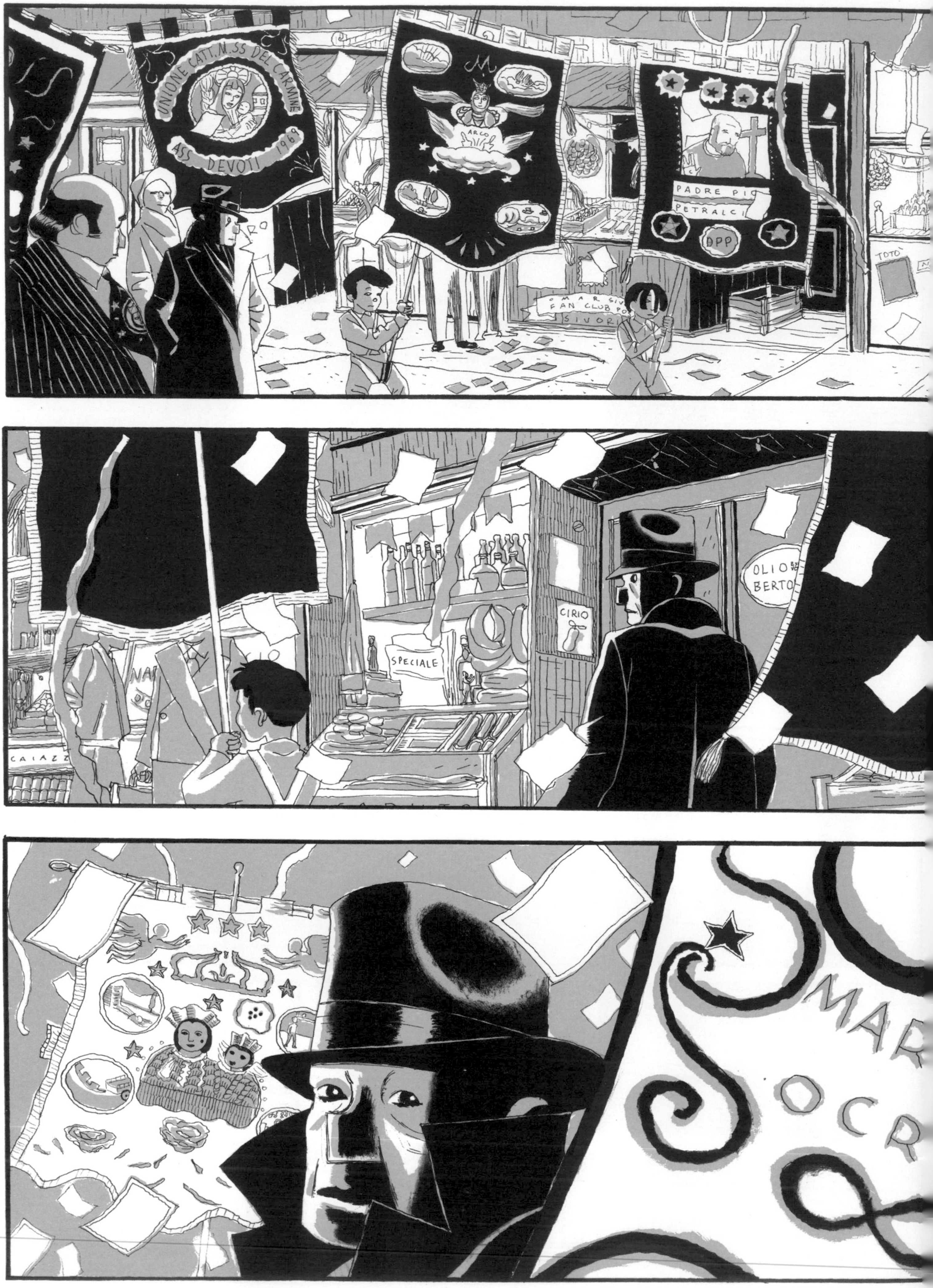
UNIONE CATT. M. SS DEL CARMINE
ASS DEVOTI 1969
ARCO
PADRE PIO
DPP
TOTO'
FAN CLUB
CIRIO
SPECIALE

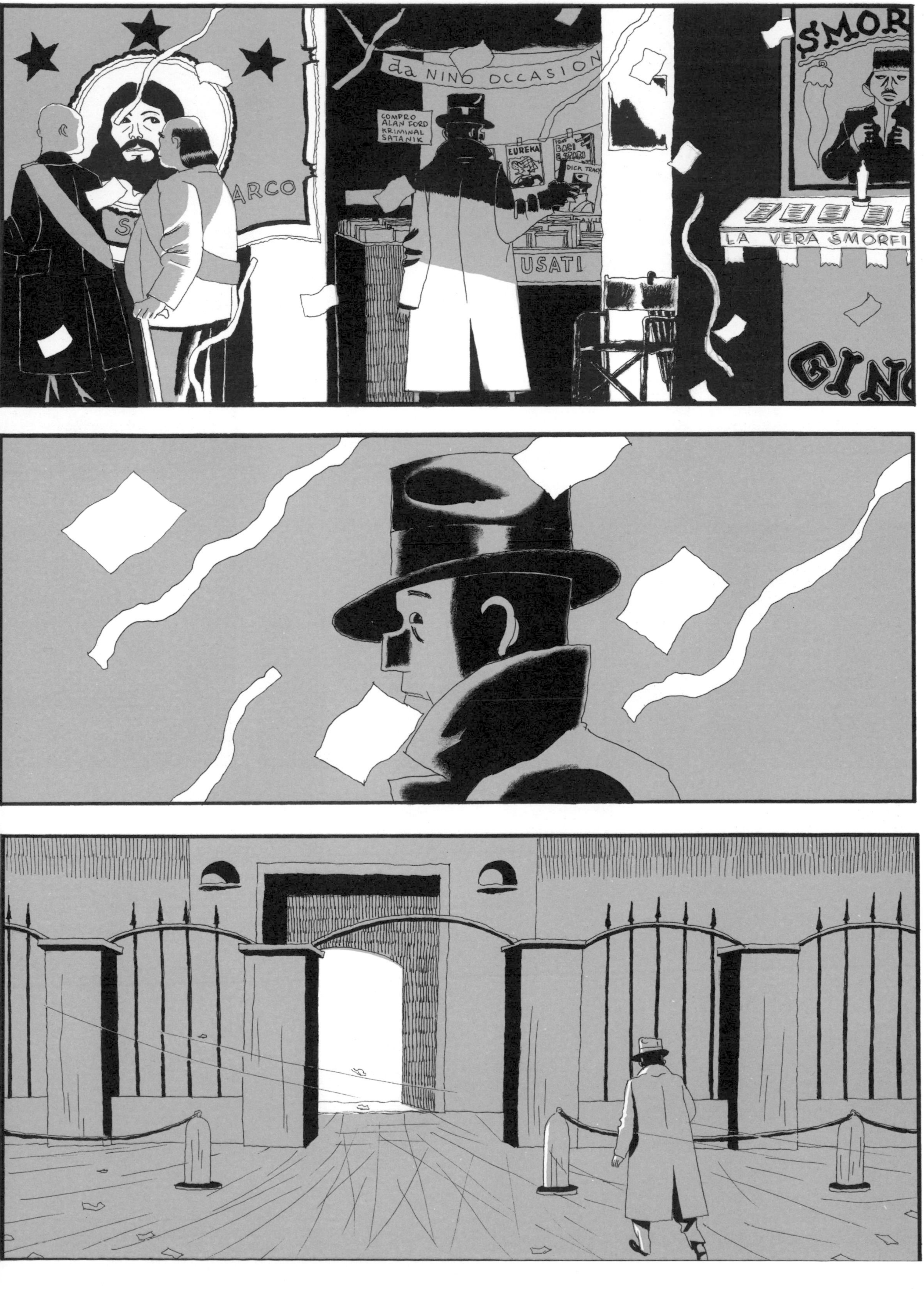
ARCO
da NINO OCCASION
COMPRO
ALAN FORD
KRIMINAL
SATANIK
EUREKA
BACI E SPARI
DICK TRACY
USATI
SMOR
LA VERA SMORFI
GINO

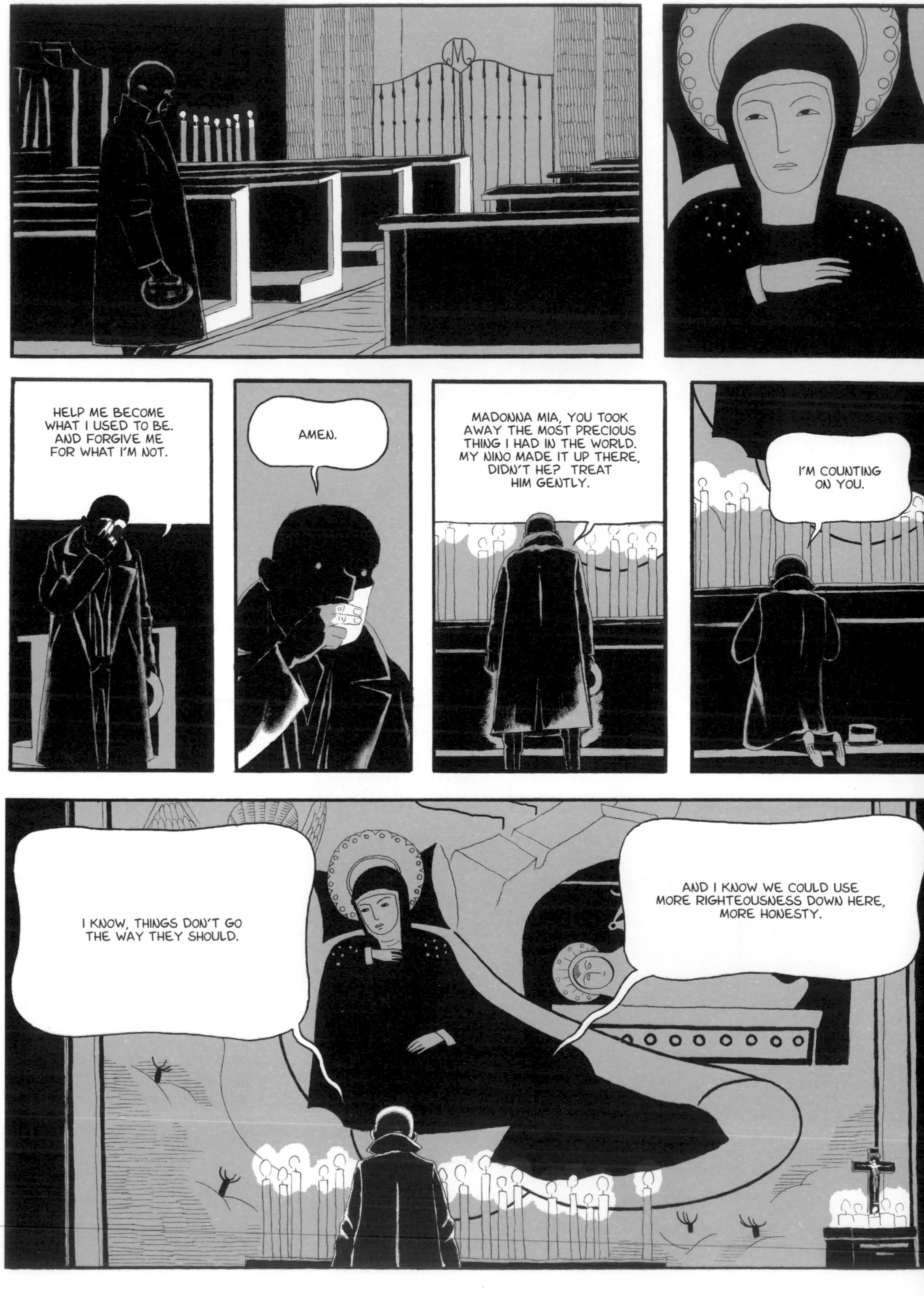

HELP ME BECOME WHAT I USED TO BE. AND FORGIVE ME FOR WHAT I'M NOT.
AMEN.
MADONNA MIA, YOU TOOK AWAY THE MOST PRECIOUS THING I HAD IN THE WORLD. MY NINO MADE IT UP THERE, DIDN'T HE? TREAT HIM GENTLY.
I'M COUNTING ON YOU.
I KNOW, THINGS DON'T GO THE WAY THEY SHOULD.
AND I KNOW WE COULD USE MORE RIGHTEOUSNESS DOWN HERE, MORE HONESTY.

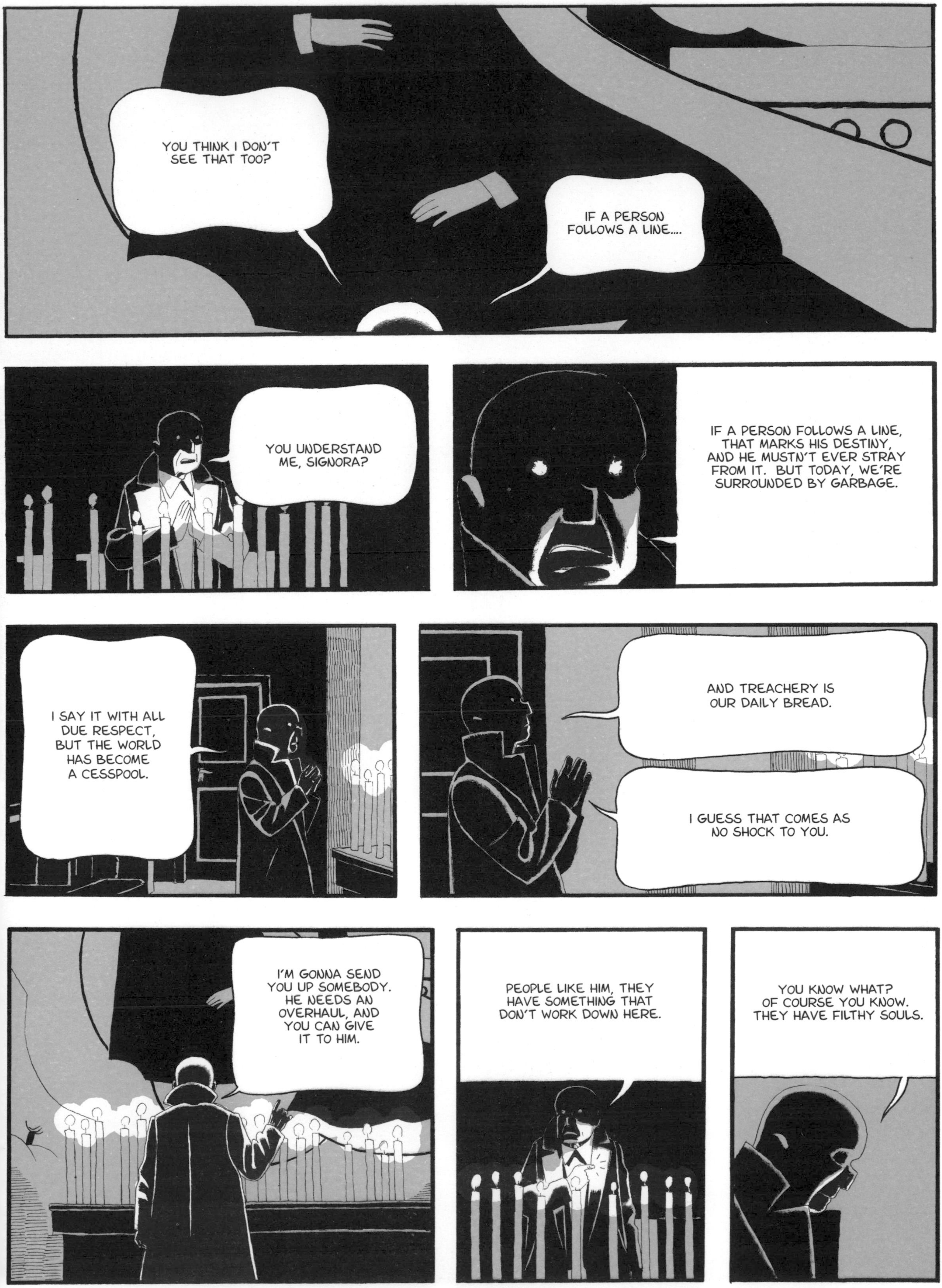
YOU THINK I DON'T SEE THAT TOO?
IF A PERSON FOLLOWS A LINE....
YOU UNDERSTAND ME, SIGNORA?
IF A PERSON FOLLOWS A LINE, THAT MARKS HIS DESTINY, AND HE MUSTN'T EVER STRAY FROM IT. BUT TODAY, WE'RE SURROUNDED BY GARBAGE.
I SAY IT WITH ALL DUE RESPECT, BUT THE WORLD HAS BECOME A CESSPOOL.
AND TREACHERY IS OUR DAILY BREAD.
I GUESS THAT COMES AS NO SHOCK TO YOU.
I'M GONNA SEND YOU UP SOMEBODY. HE NEEDS AN OVERHAUL, AND YOU CAN GIVE IT TO HIM.
PEOPLE LIKE HIM, THEY HAVE SOMETHING THAT DON'T WORK DOWN HERE.
YOU KNOW WHAT? OF COURSE YOU KNOW. THEY HAVE FILTHY SOULS.

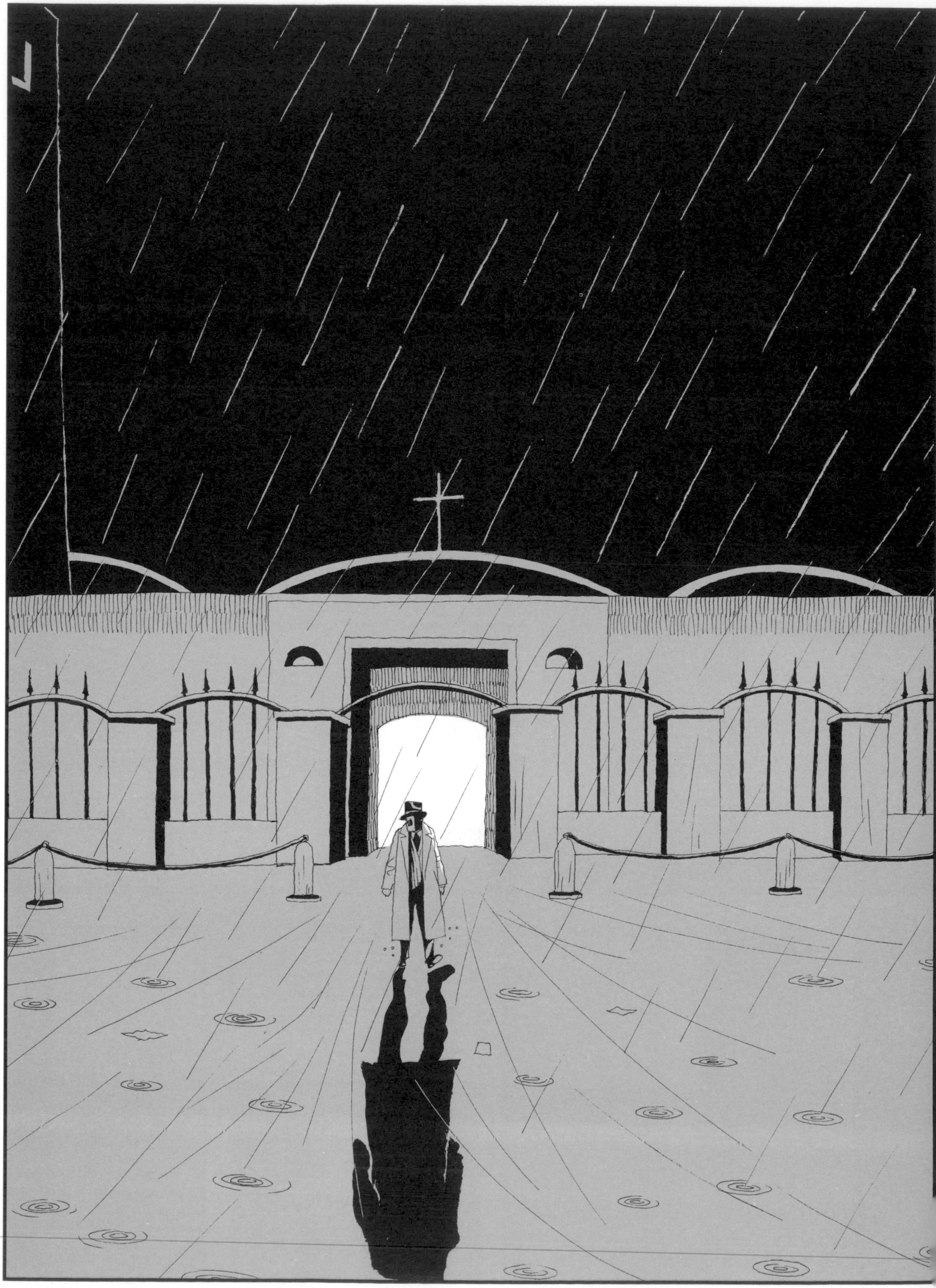

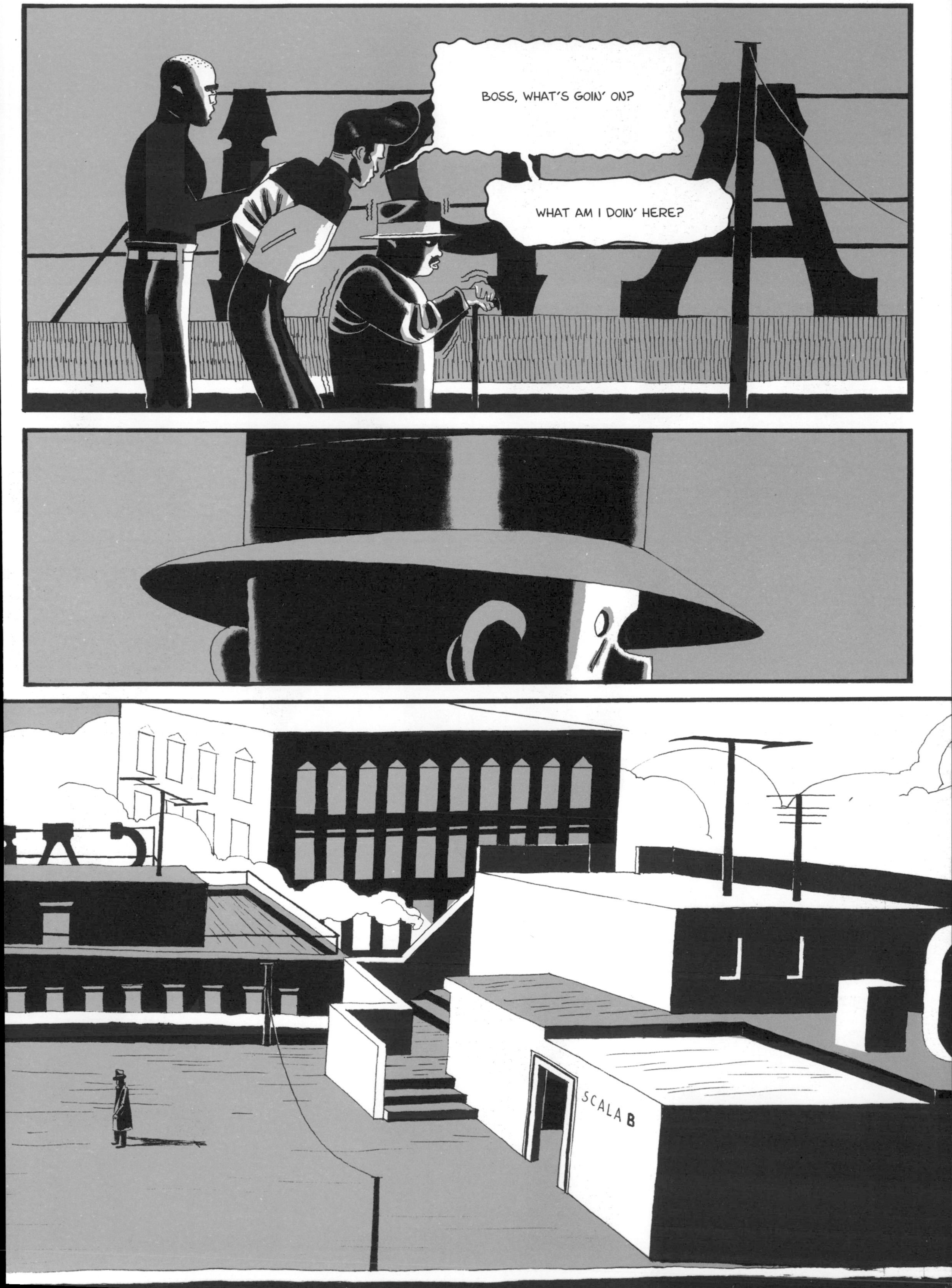
BOSS, WHAT'S GOIN' ON?
WHAT AM I DOIN' HERE?
SCALA B

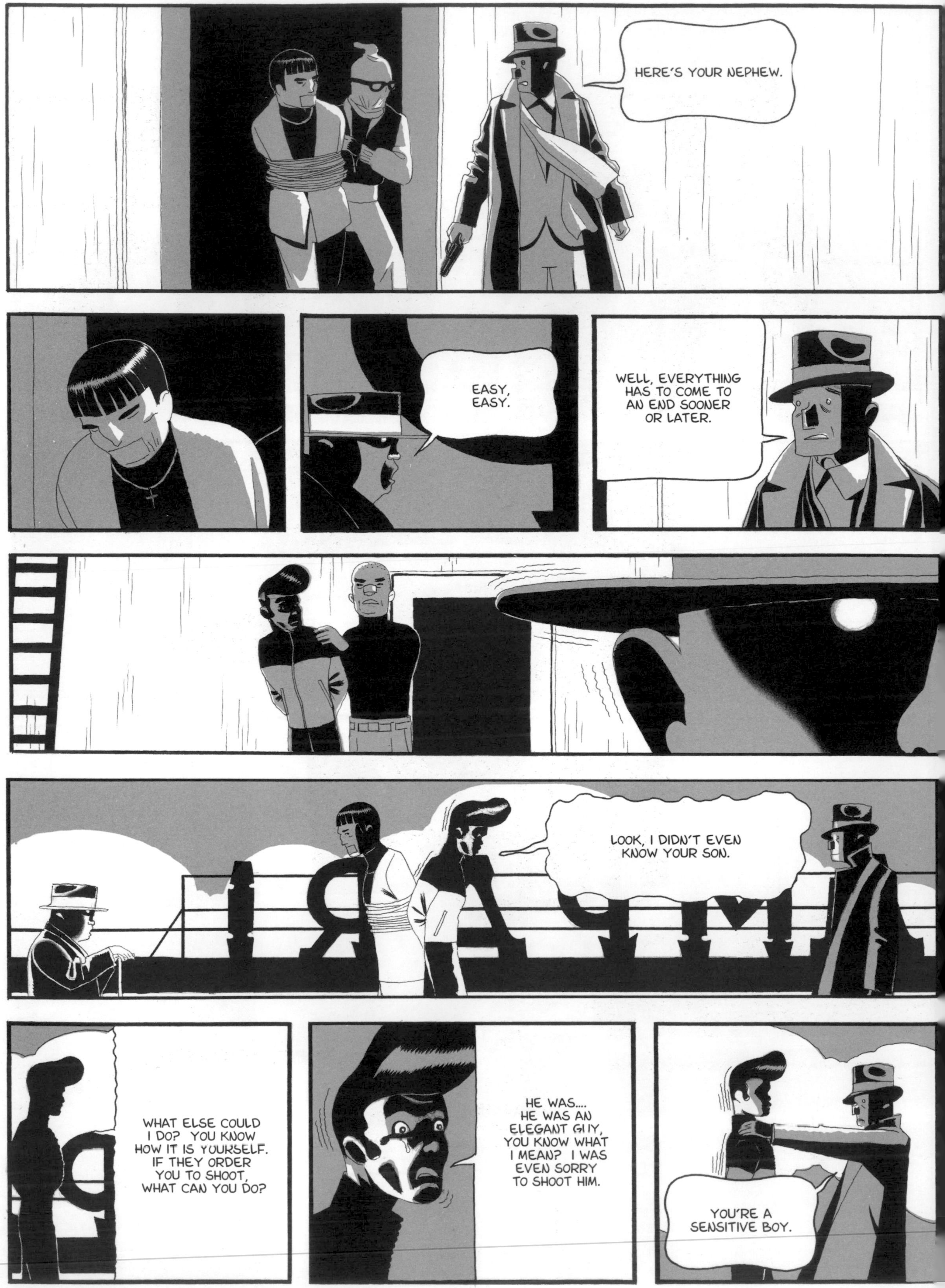
HERE'S YOUR NEPHEW.
EASY, EASY.
WELL, EVERYTHING HAS TO COME TO AN END SOONER OR LATER.
LOOK, I DIDN'T EVEN KNOW YOUR SON.
WHAT ELSE COULD I DO? YOU KNOW HOW IT IS YOURSELF. IF THEY ORDER YOU TO SHOOT, WHAT CAN YOU DO?
HE WAS.... HE WAS AN ELEGANT GUY, YOU KNOW WHAT I MEAN? I WAS EVEN SORRY TO SHOOT HIM.
YOU'RE A SENSITIVE BOY.

chapter five
5 is the perfect number

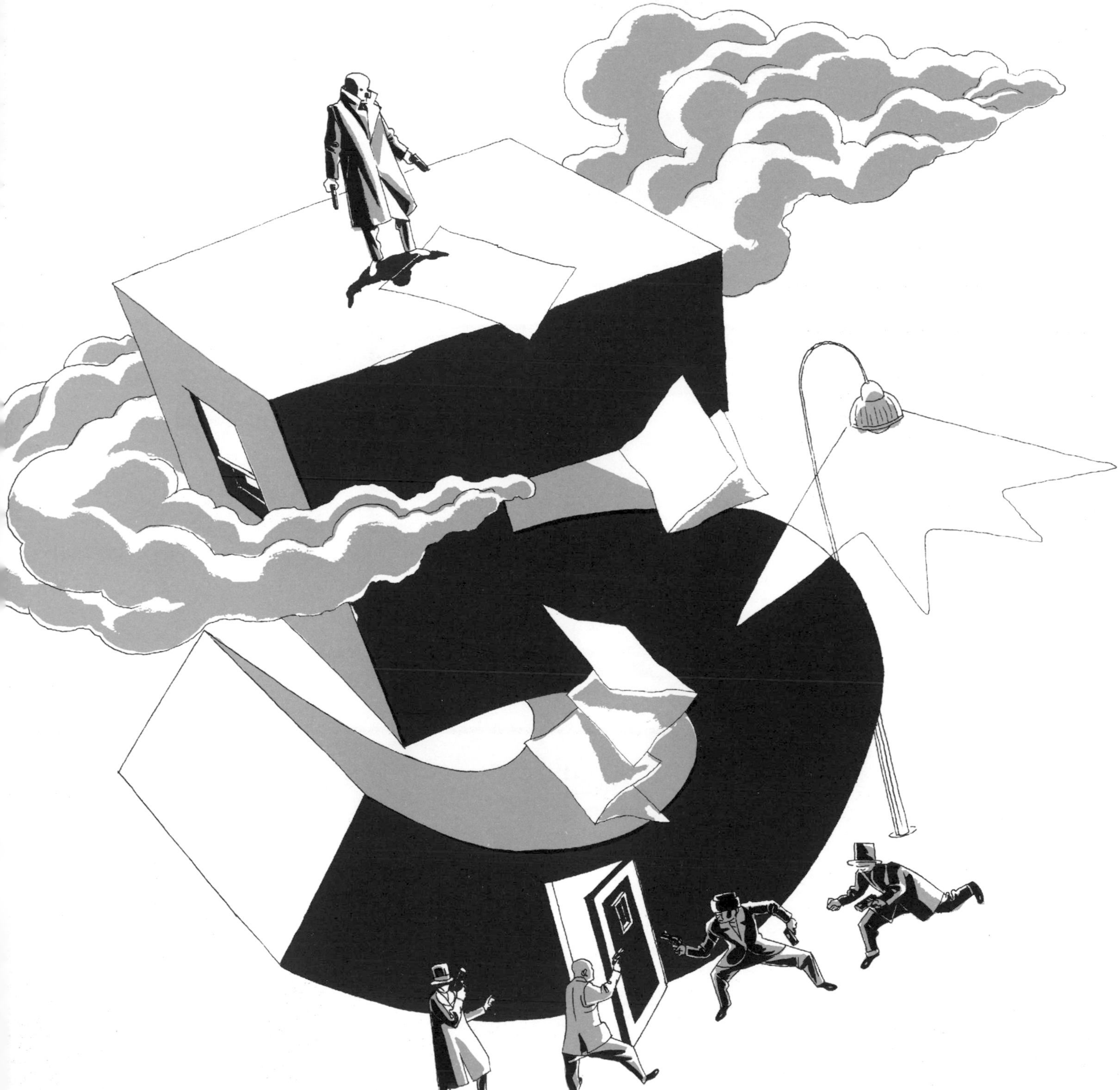

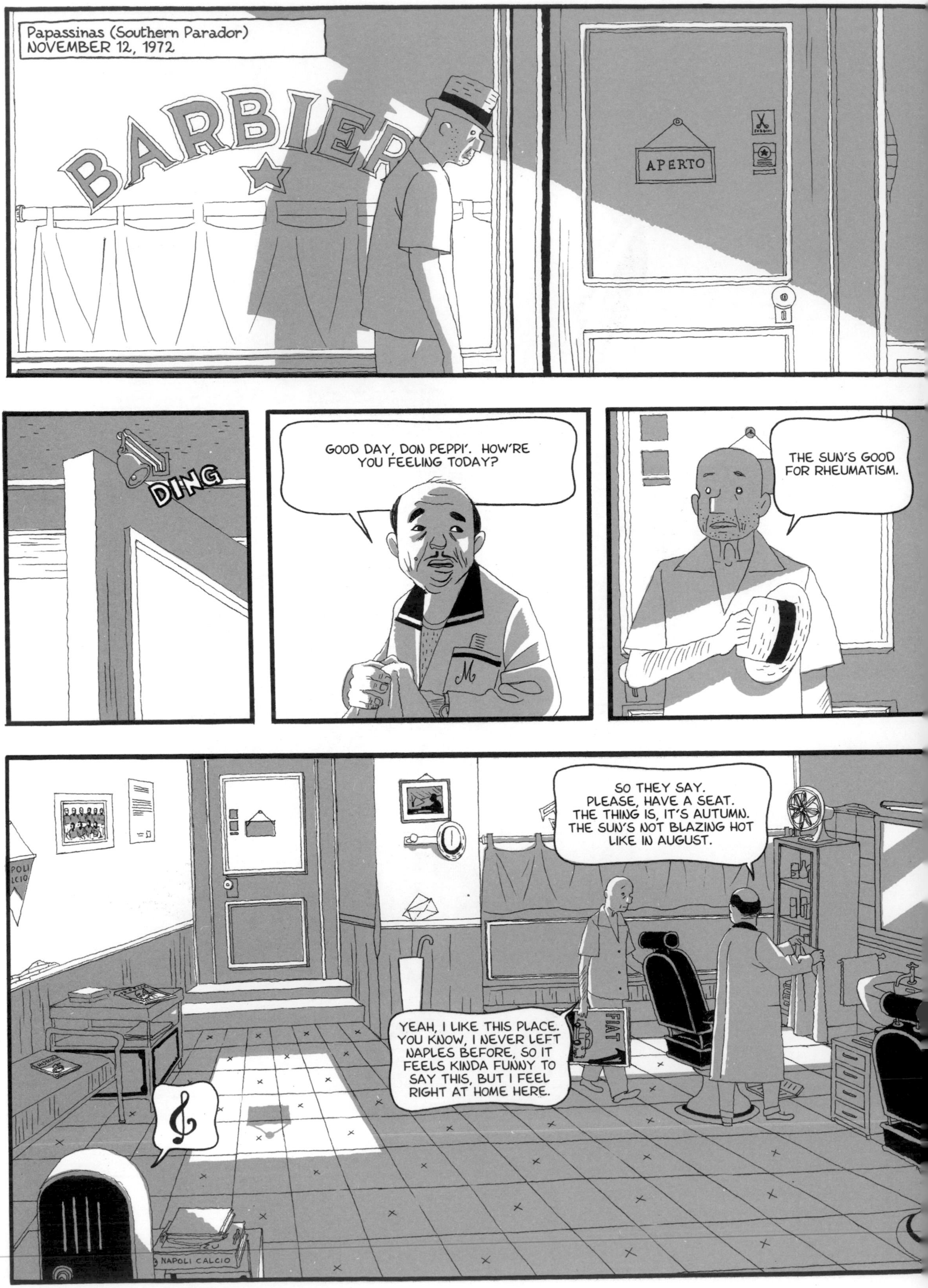
Papassinas (Southern Parador)
NOVEMBER 12, 1972
BARBIERE
APERTO
DING
GOOD DAY, DON PEPPI'. HOW'RE YOU FEELING TODAY?
THE SUN'S GOOD FOR RHEUMATISM.
SO THEY SAY. PLEASE, HAVE A SEAT. THE THING IS, IT'S AUTUMN. THE SUN'S NOT BLAZING HOT LIKE IN AUGUST.
YEAH, I LIKE THIS PLACE. YOU KNOW, I NEVER LEFT NAPLES BEFORE, SO IT FEELS KINDA FUNNY TO SAY THIS, BUT I FEEL RIGHT AT HOME HERE.
FIAT
NAPOLI CALCIO

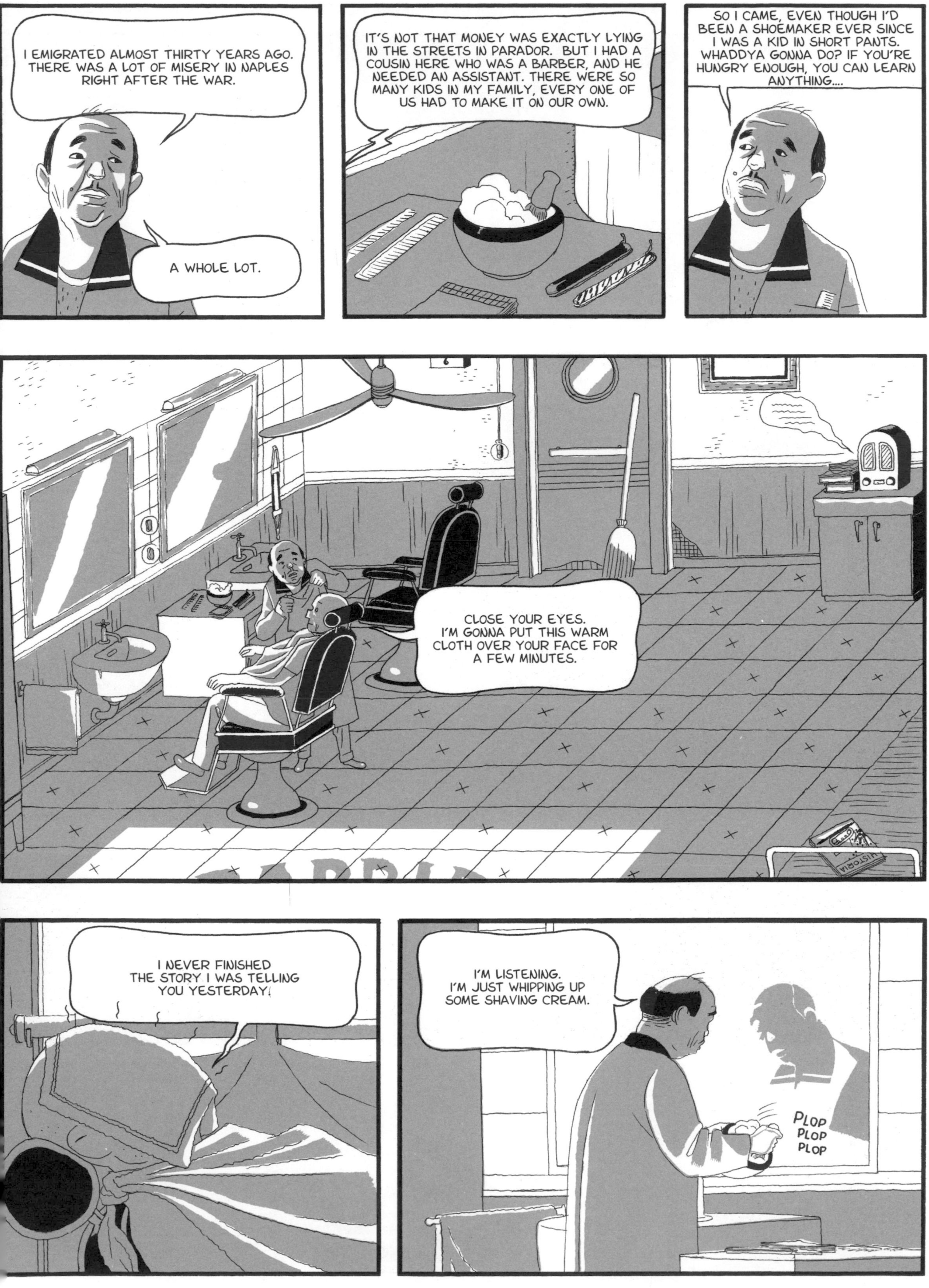
I EMIGRATED ALMOST THIRTY YEARS AGO. THERE WAS A LOT OF MISERY IN NAPLES RIGHT AFTER THE WAR.
A WHOLE LOT.
IT'S NOT THAT MONEY WAS EXACTLY LYING IN THE STREETS IN PARADOR. BUT I HAD A COUSIN HERE WHO WAS A BARBER, AND HE NEEDED AN ASSISTANT. THERE WERE SO MANY KIDS IN MY FAMILY, EVERY ONE OF US HAD TO MAKE IT ON OUR OWN.
SO I CAME, EVEN THOUGH I'D BEEN A SHOEMAKER EVER SINCE I WAS A KID IN SHORT PANTS. WHADDYA GONNA DO? IF YOU'RE HUNGRY ENOUGH, YOU CAN LEARN ANYTHING....
CLOSE YOUR EYES. I'M GONNA PUT THIS WARM CLOTH OVER YOUR FACE FOR A FEW MINUTES.
HISTORIA
I NEVER FINISHED THE STORY I WAS TELLING YOU YESTERDAY.
I'M LISTENING. I'M JUST WHIPPING UP SOME SHAVING CREAM.
PLOP PLOP PLOP

Like I was saying, I was willing to go to any lengths to get my hands on the guy who killed my son. It was a pretty delicate moment. Two times outta three, a prisoner exchange winds up in a bloodbath.

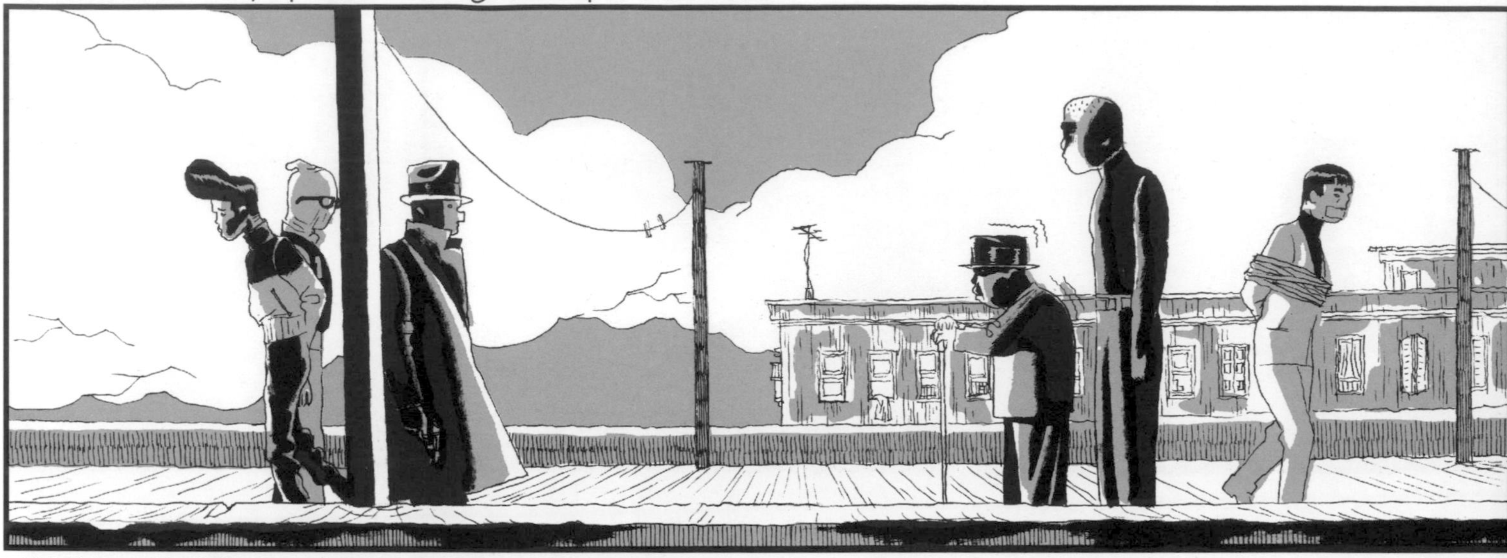

I didn't know it at the time, but the whole thing was a set-up. There were guys in the building across the street, waiting to ambush us. Did I tell you who turned my man over to me? Don Lava himself, the boss of all that part of town.

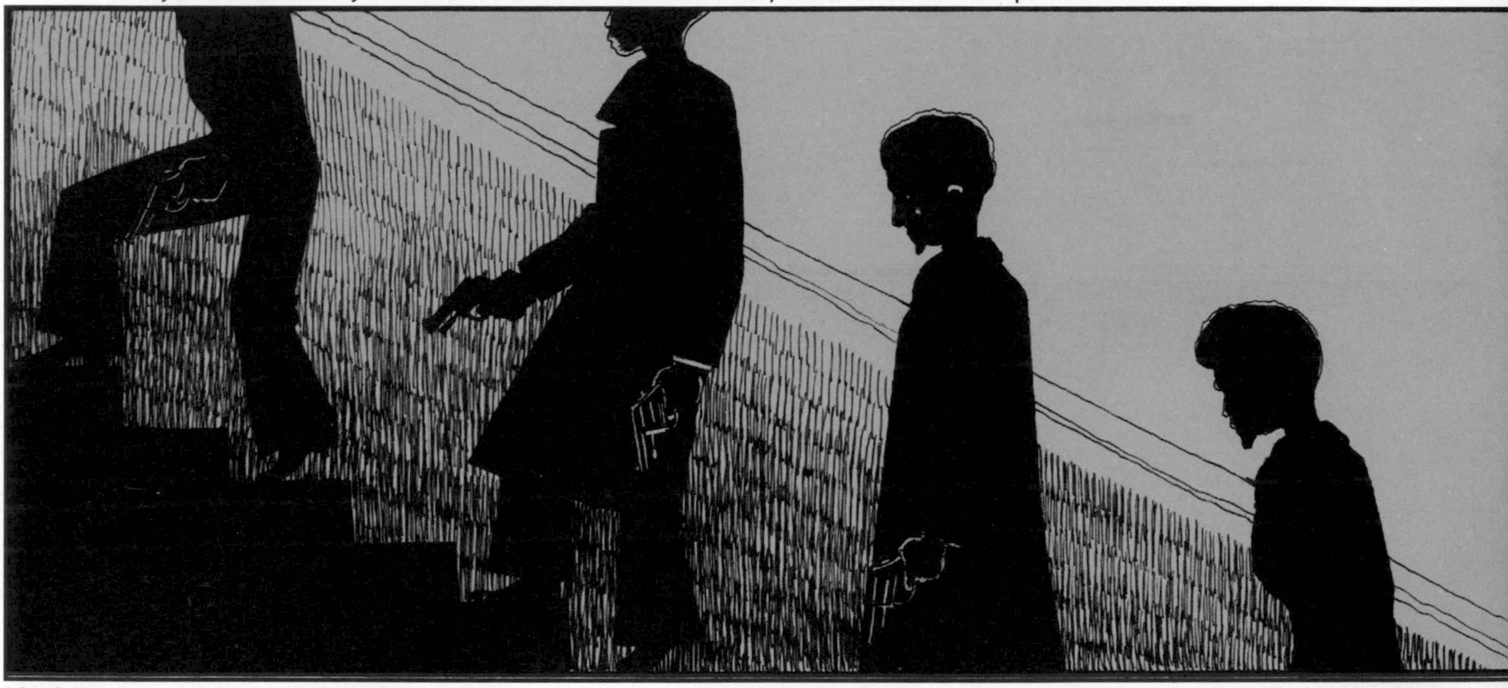

I had Ciro, one of my son's friends, covering my back. Don Lava had some fuckin' colossus. We were standing there, scowling at one another. We were all fully exposed, an easy target.

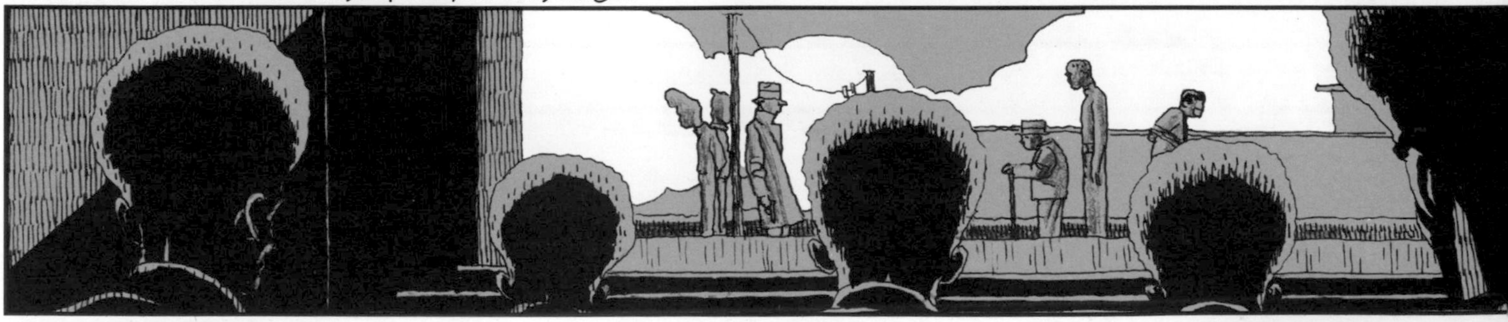

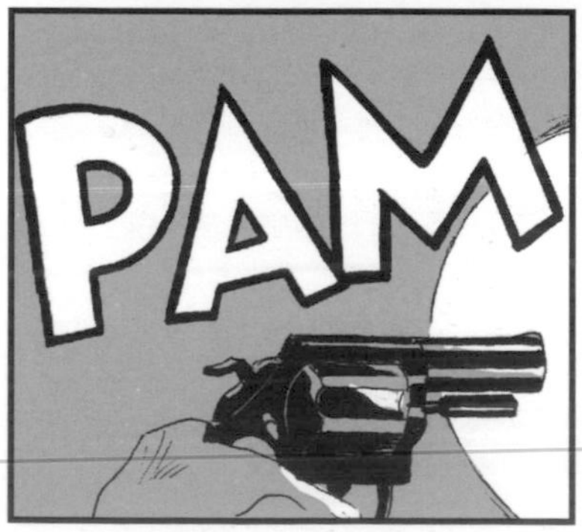
PAM

Then the shooting started from the building across the street. It was so close they used their handguns. But their main target was Don Lava! I was an insignificant detail.

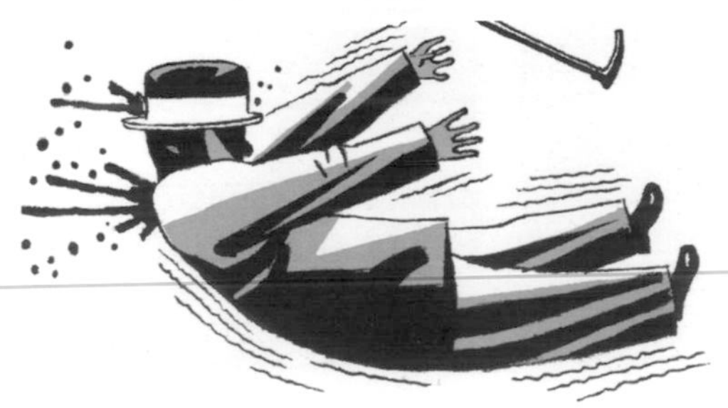

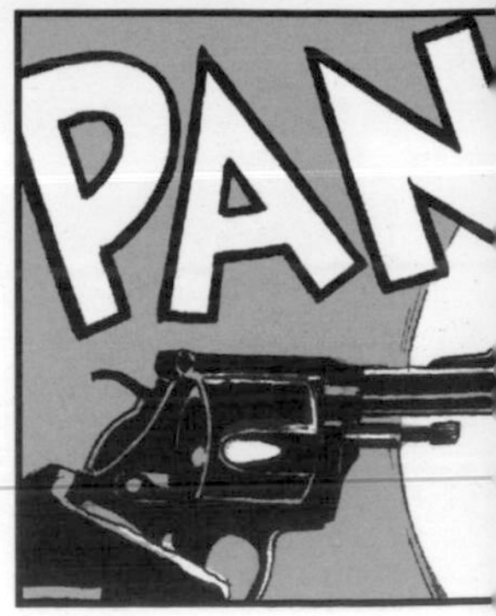
PAN

To make a long story short, I hit the deck. Aside from a tear in my raincoat, nothing even grazed me. Nothing at all. We charged down the stairs like madmen.

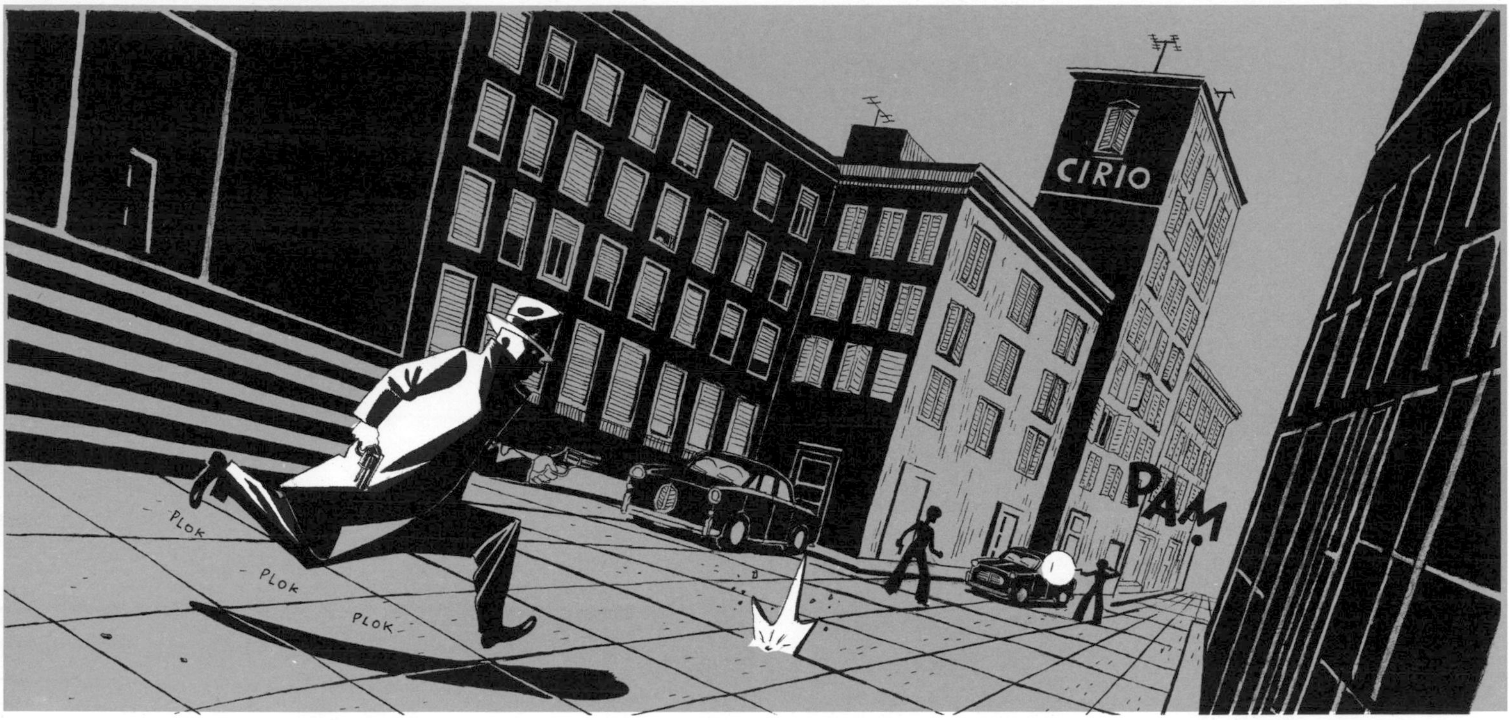
CIRIO
PLOK
PLOK
PLOK
PAM

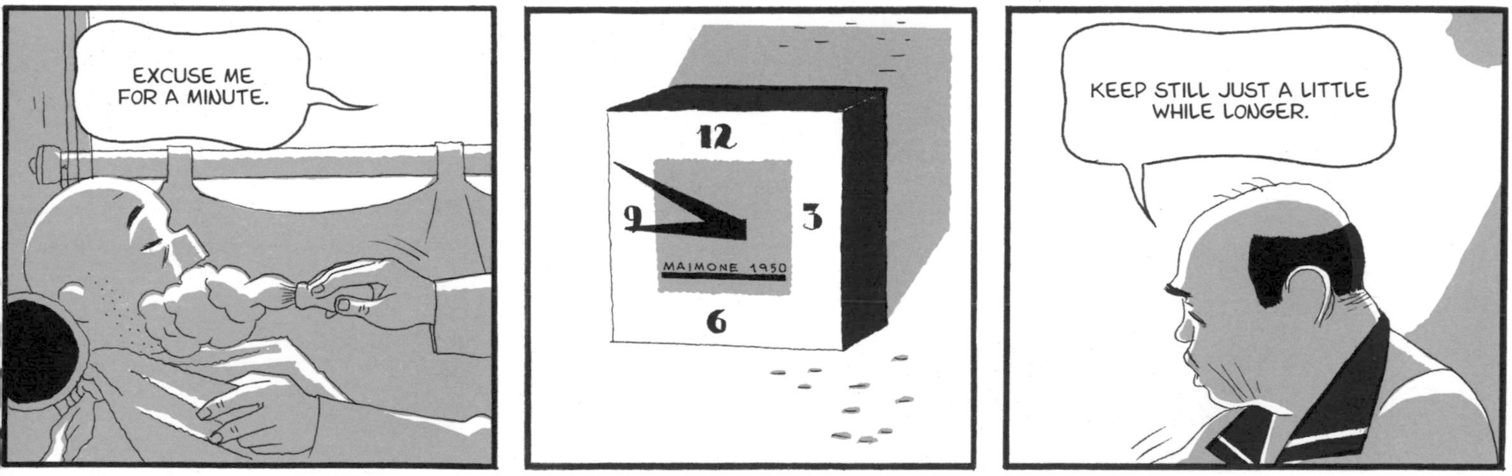
EXCUSE ME FOR A MINUTE.
12
9
3
MAIMONE 1950
6
KEEP STILL JUST A LITTLE WHILE LONGER.

Once we were outside, we decided to go in different directions. I made a bad choice and got trapped. There were guys with guns everywhere. I thought....

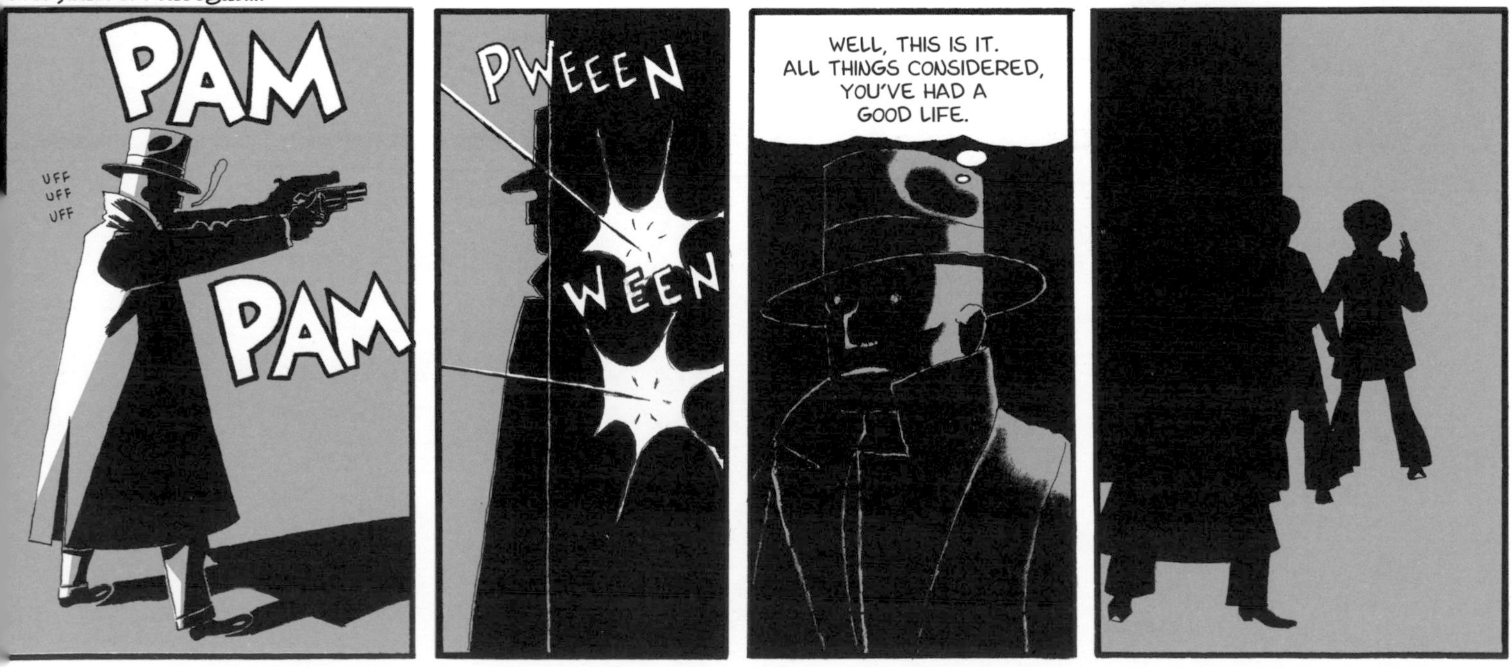
PAM
UFF
UFF
UFF
PAM
PWEEEN
WEEN
WELL, THIS IS IT. ALL THINGS CONSIDERED, YOU'VE HAD A GOOD LIFE.

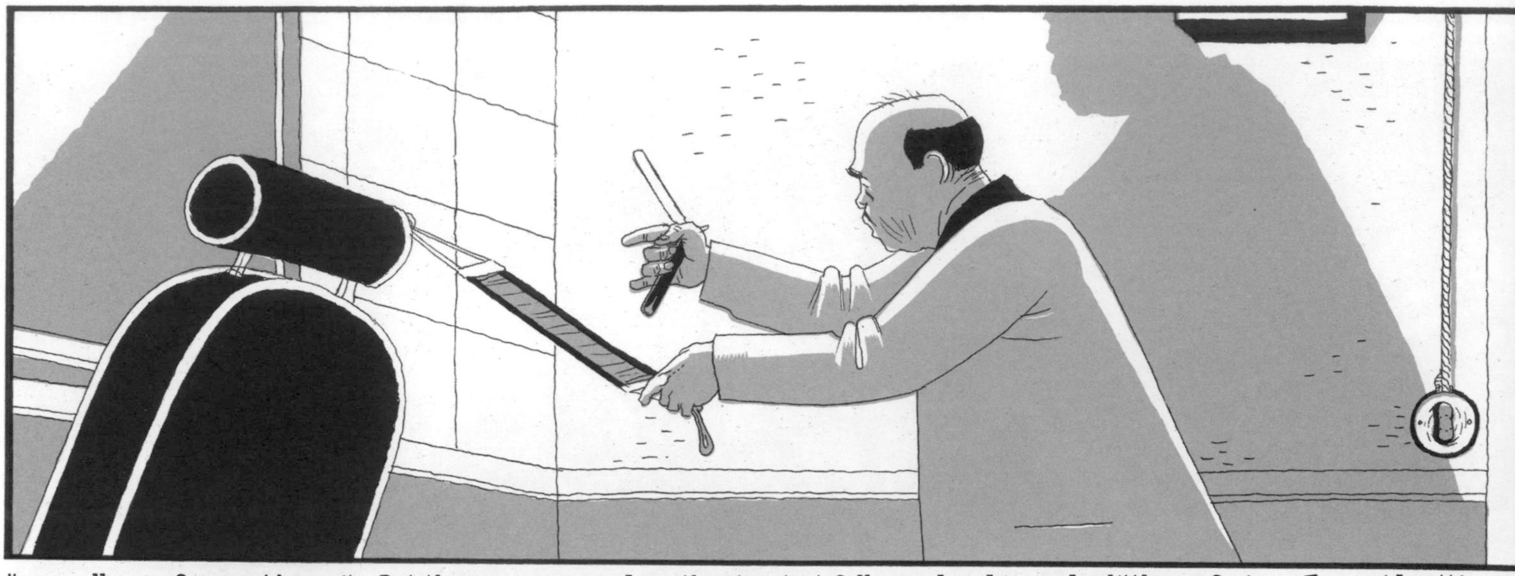

It was all over for me, I knew it. But then a car came down the street at full speed and caused a little confusion. To avoid getting run over, the killers threw themselves out of the way. I recognized the car - it was my son Nino's Fiat Bianchina. But I knew it couldn't be him at the wheel. It's a known fact: the dead don't drive.

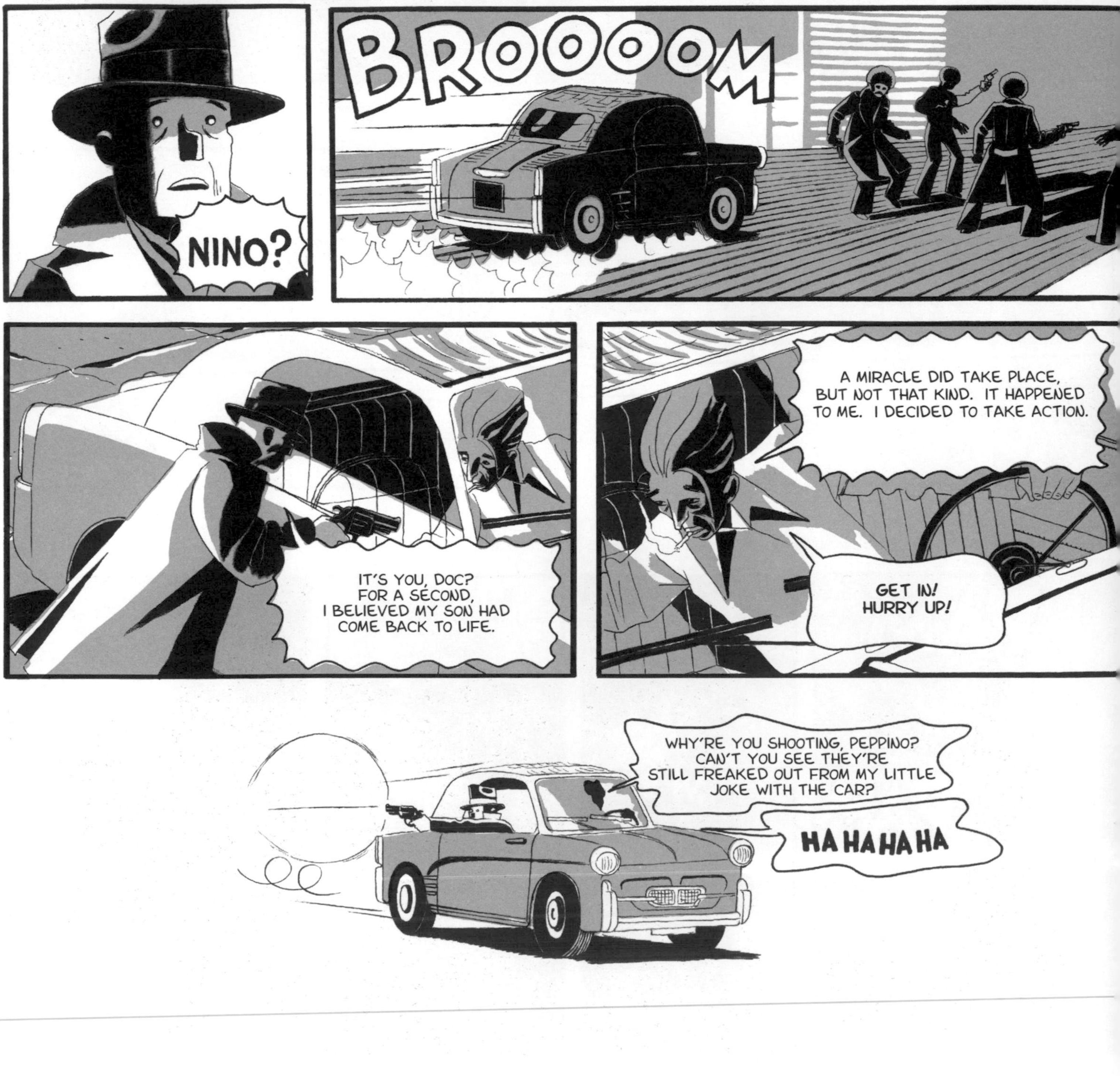
NINO?
BROOOOM
IT'S YOU, DOC? FOR A SECOND, I BELIEVED MY SON HAD COME BACK TO LIFE.
A MIRACLE DID TAKE PLACE, BUT NOT THAT KIND. IT HAPPENED TO ME. I DECIDED TO TAKE ACTION.
GET IN! HURRY UP!
WHY'RE YOU SHOOTING, PEPPINO? CAN'T YOU SEE THEY'RE STILL FREAKED OUT FROM MY LITTLE JOKE WITH THE CAR?
HA HA HA HA

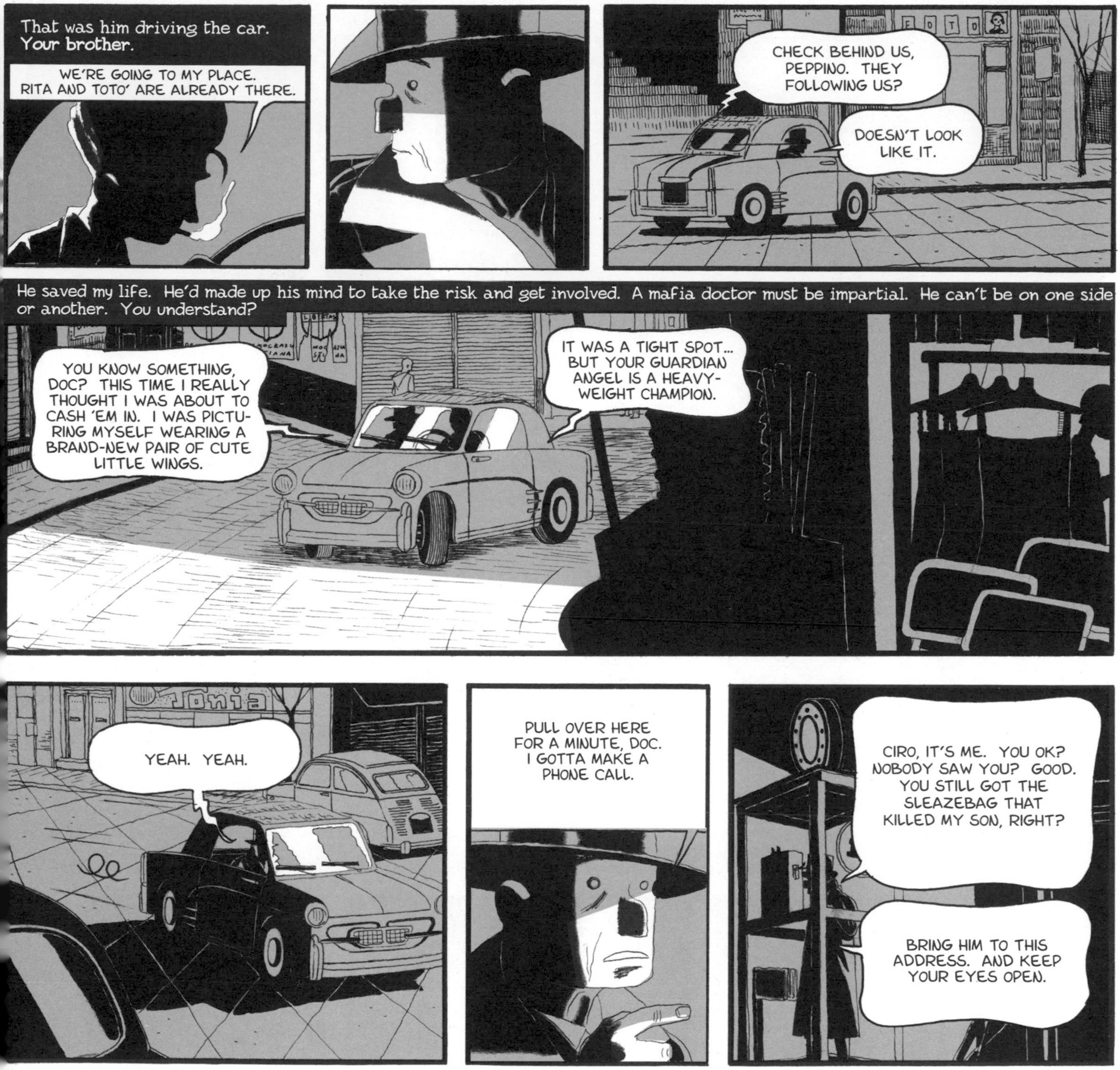
That was him driving the car. Your brother.
WE'RE GOING TO MY PLACE. RITA AND TOTO' ARE ALREADY THERE.
CHECK BEHIND US, PEPPINO. THEY FOLLOWING US?
DOESN'T LOOK LIKE IT.
He saved my life. He'd made up his mind to take the risk and get involved. A mafia doctor must be impartial. He can't be on one side or another. You understand?
YOU KNOW SOMETHING, DOC? THIS TIME I REALLY THOUGHT I WAS ABOUT TO CASH 'EM IN. I WAS PICTURING MYSELF WEARING A BRAND-NEW PAIR OF CUTE LITTLE WINGS.
IT WAS A TIGHT SPOT... BUT YOUR GUARDIAN ANGEL IS A HEAVYWEIGHT CHAMPION.
Jonia
YEAH. YEAH.
PULL OVER HERE FOR A MINUTE, DOC. I GOTTA MAKE A PHONE CALL.
CIRO, IT'S ME. YOU OK? NOBODY SAW YOU? GOOD. YOU STILL GOT THE SLEAZEBAG THAT KILLED MY SON, RIGHT?
BRING HIM TO THIS ADDRESS. AND KEEP YOUR EYES OPEN.

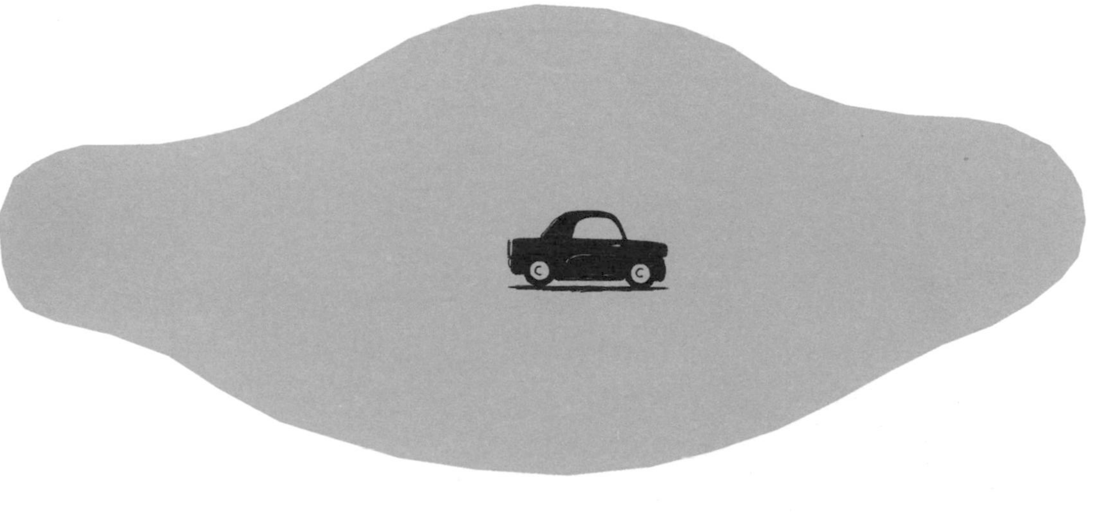

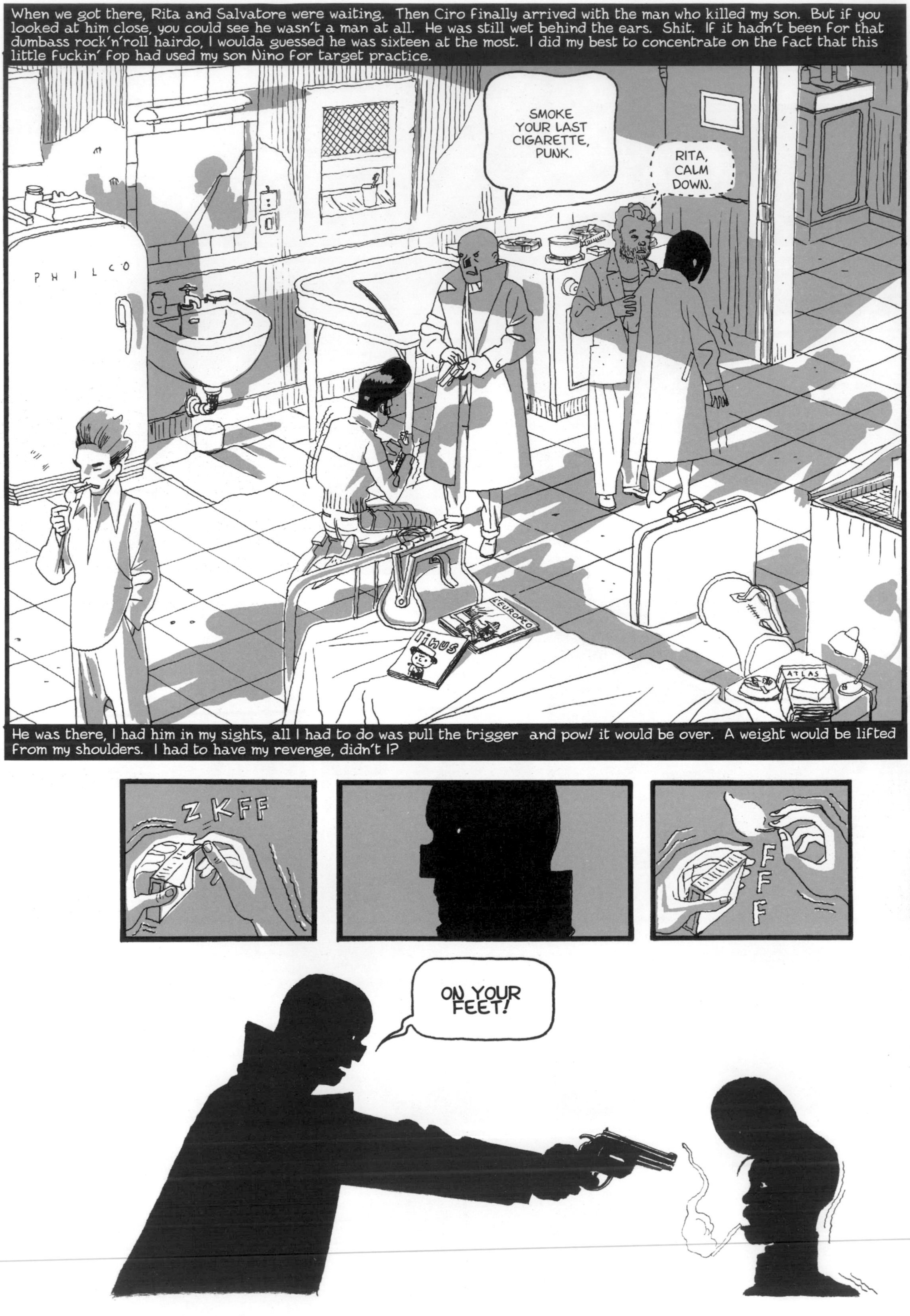
When we got there, Rita and Salvatore were waiting. Then Ciro finally arrived with the man who killed my son. But if you looked at him close, you could see he wasn't a man at all. He was still wet behind the ears. Shit. If it hadn't been for that dumbass rock'n'roll hairdo, I woulda guessed he was sixteen at the most. I did my best to concentrate on the fact that this little fuckin' fop had used my son Nino for target practice.
SMOKE YOUR LAST CIGARETTE, PUNK.
RITA, CALM DOWN.
PHILCO
linus
ATLAS
He was there, I had him in my sights, all I had to do was pull the trigger and pow! it would be over. A weight would be lifted from my shoulders. I had to have my revenge, didn't I?
ZKFF
FFF
ON YOUR FEET!

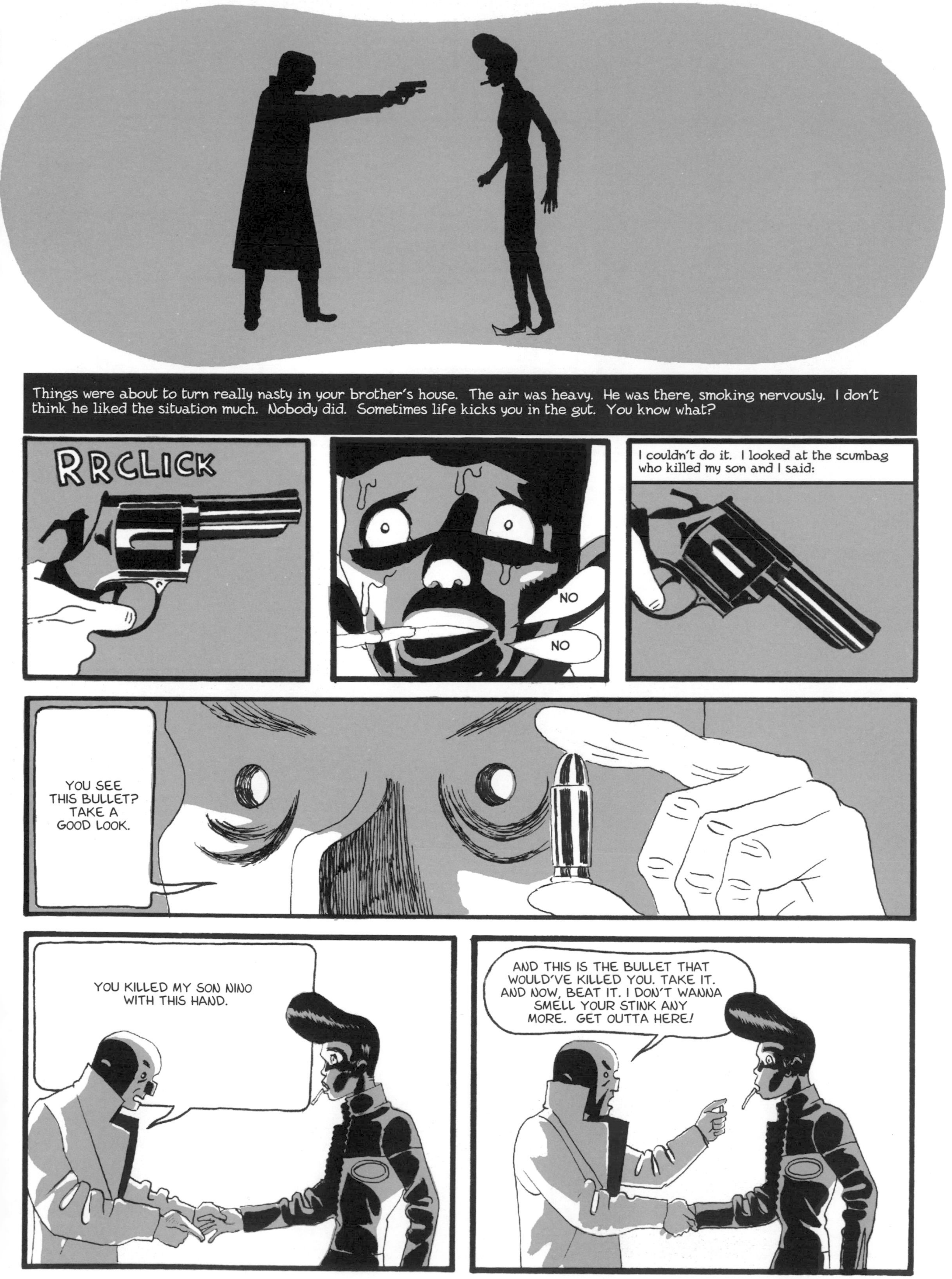
Things were about to turn really nasty in your brother's house. The air was heavy. He was there, smoking nervously. I don't think he liked the situation much. Nobody did. Sometimes life kicks you in the gut. You know what?
RRCLICK
NO
NO
I couldn't do it. I looked at the scumbag who killed my son and I said:
YOU SEE THIS BULLET? TAKE A GOOD LOOK.
YOU KILLED MY SON NINO WITH THIS HAND.
AND THIS IS THE BULLET THAT WOULD'VE KILLED YOU. TAKE IT. AND NOW, BEAT IT. I DON'T WANNA SMELL YOUR STINK ANY MORE. GET OUTTA HERE!

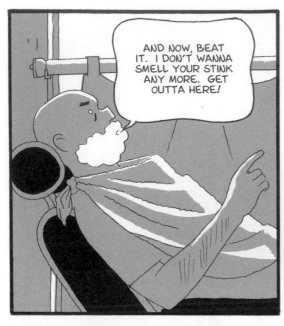

AND NOW, BEAT IT. I DON'T WANNA SMELL YOUR STINK ANY MORE. GET OUTTA HERE!

I CAN STILL HEAR THOSE WORDS. IT'S AS IF IT WASN'T ME WHO SAID THEM.

BUT HE DIDN'T MOVE. HE JUST STOOD THERE, SAYING OVER AND OVER, 'WHAT? WHAT?'

I LITERALLY HAD TO KICK HIS ASS OUTTA THERE.

WAIT. KEEP STILL A SECOND. YOU'VE GOT A LITTLE CUT. I'LL USE THE STYPTIC STICK ON IT.

MAYBE IT WAS A TRAGIC MISTAKE, I DON'T KNOW. BUT SOMETHING HAD SNAPPED. YOU KNOW, MICHELE, I THINK IT WAS A BIG RELIEF FOR EVERYONE AT THE MOMENT.

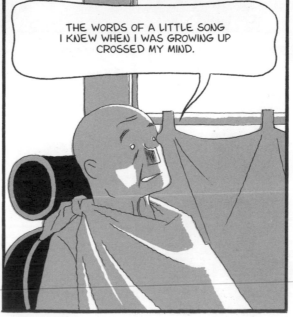

THE WORDS OF A LITTLE SONG I KNEW WHEN I WAS GROWING UP CROSSED MY MIND.

AND I BELIEVE I HAD A STUPID GRIN ON MY FACE.

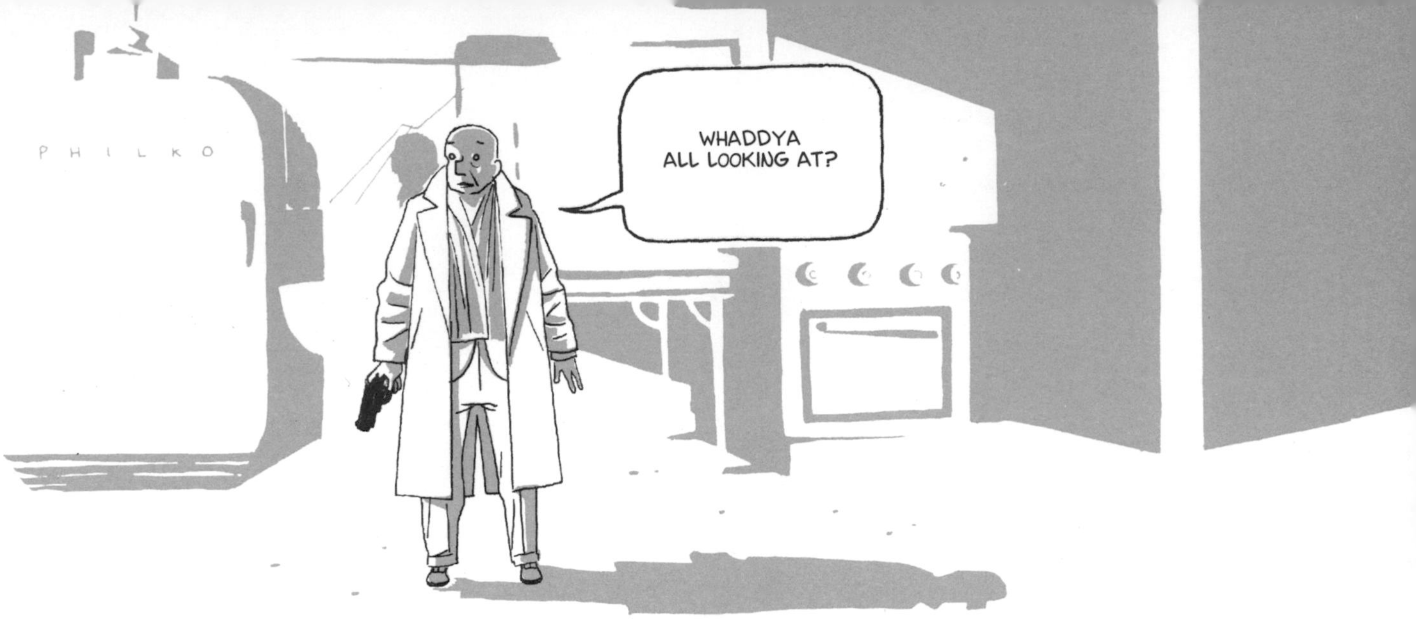
PHILKO
WHADDYA ALL LOOKING AT?

They were staring at me without a word. Ha, ha! I can understand why. We all looked at the door my son's murderer had just closed behind him. I had started a war to find this guy, and now, POOF! There was a great silence in the room. Rita was still pretty upset.

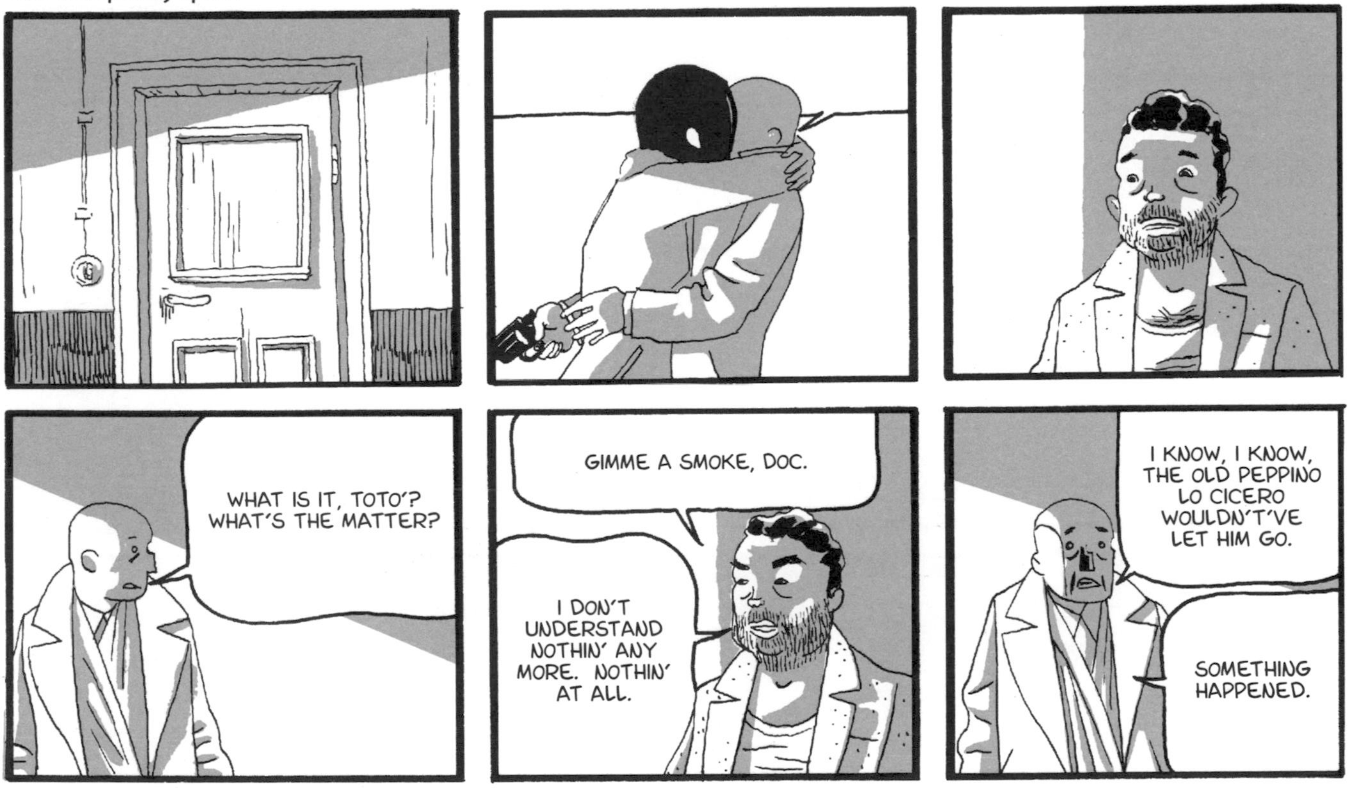
WHAT IS IT, TOTO'? WHAT'S THE MATTER?
GIMME A SMOKE, DOC.
I DON'T UNDERSTAND NOTHIN' ANY MORE. NOTHIN' AT ALL.
I KNOW, I KNOW, THE OLD PEPPINO LO CICERO WOULDN'T'VE LET HIM GO.
SOMETHING HAPPENED.

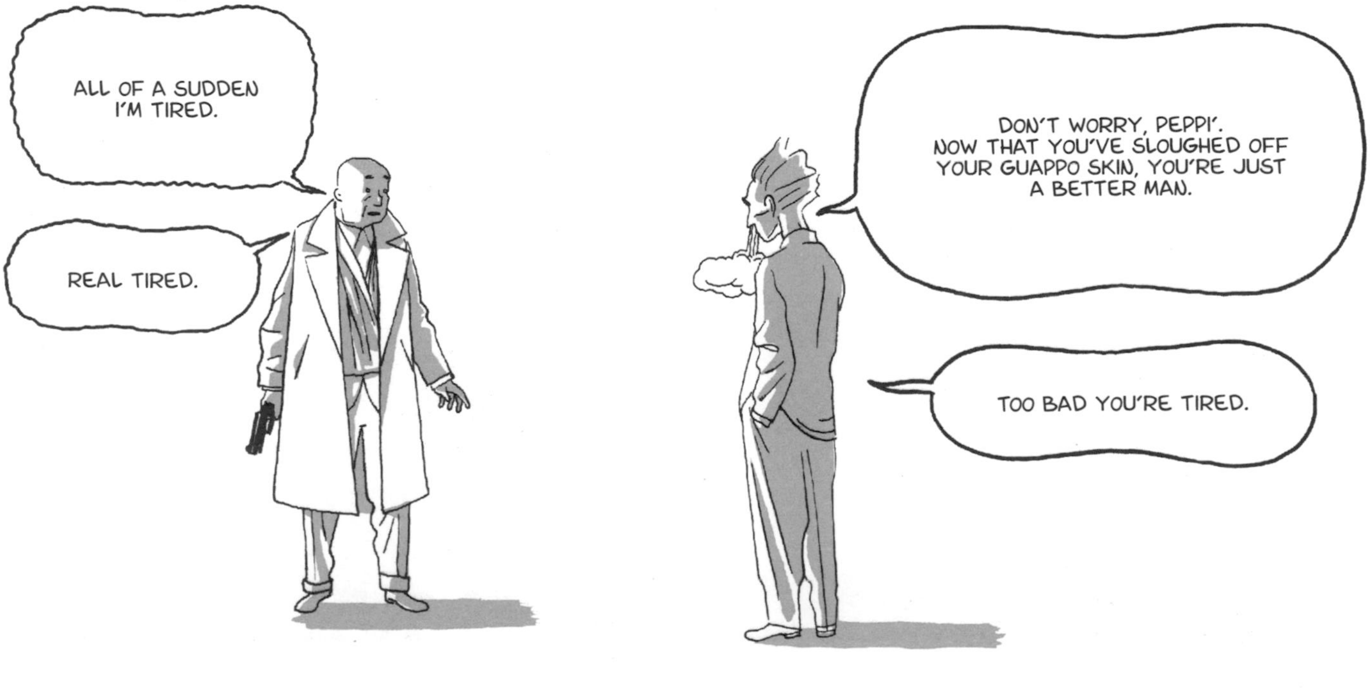
ALL OF A SUDDEN I'M TIRED.
REAL TIRED.
DON'T WORRY, PEPPI'. NOW THAT YOU'VE SLOUGHED OFF YOUR GUAPPO SKIN, YOU'RE JUST A BETTER MAN.
TOO BAD YOU'RE TIRED.

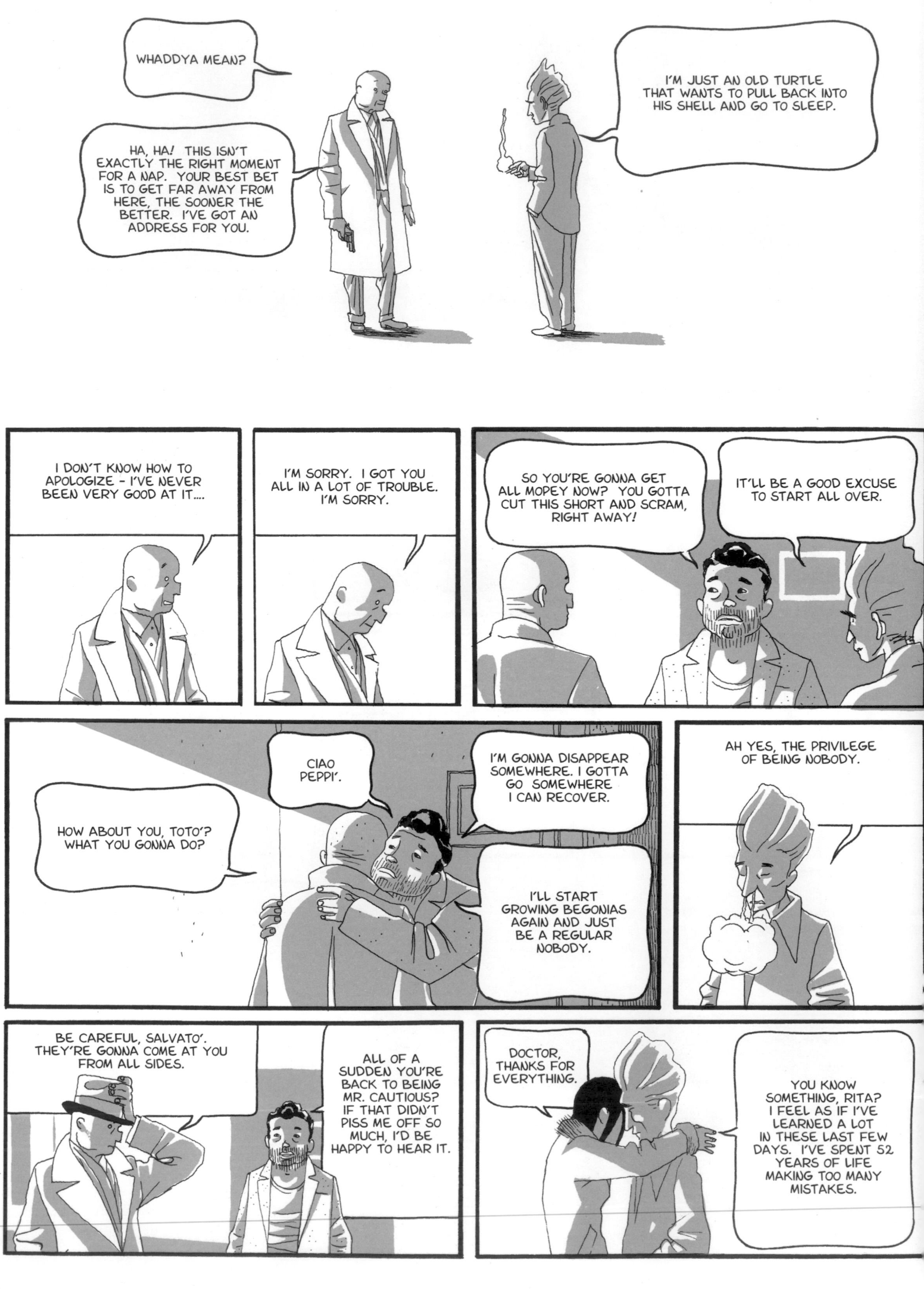
WHADDYA MEAN?
I'M JUST AN OLD TURTLE THAT WANTS TO PULL BACK INTO HIS SHELL AND GO TO SLEEP.
HA, HA! THIS ISN'T EXACTLY THE RIGHT MOMENT FOR A NAP. YOUR BEST BET IS TO GET FAR AWAY FROM HERE, THE SOONER THE BETTER. I'VE GOT AN ADDRESS FOR YOU.
I DON'T KNOW HOW TO APOLOGIZE - I'VE NEVER BEEN VERY GOOD AT IT....
I'M SORRY. I GOT YOU ALL IN A LOT OF TROUBLE. I'M SORRY.
SO YOU'RE GONNA GET ALL MOPEY NOW? YOU GOTTA CUT THIS SHORT AND SCRAM, RIGHT AWAY!
IT'LL BE A GOOD EXCUSE TO START ALL OVER.
HOW ABOUT YOU, TOTO'? WHAT YOU GONNA DO?
CIAO PEPPI'.
I'M GONNA DISAPPEAR SOMEWHERE. I GOTTA GO SOMEWHERE I CAN RECOVER.
I'LL START GROWING BEGONIAS AGAIN AND JUST BE A REGULAR NOBODY.
AH YES, THE PRIVILEGE OF BEING NOBODY.
BE CAREFUL, SALVATO'. THEY'RE GONNA COME AT YOU FROM ALL SIDES.
ALL OF A SUDDEN YOU'RE BACK TO BEING MR. CAUTIOUS? IF THAT DIDN'T PISS ME OFF SO MUCH, I'D BE HAPPY TO HEAR IT.
DOCTOR, THANKS FOR EVERYTHING.
YOU KNOW SOMETHING, RITA? I FEEL AS IF I'VE LEARNED A LOT IN THESE LAST FEW DAYS. I'VE SPENT 52 YEARS OF LIFE MAKING TOO MANY MISTAKES.

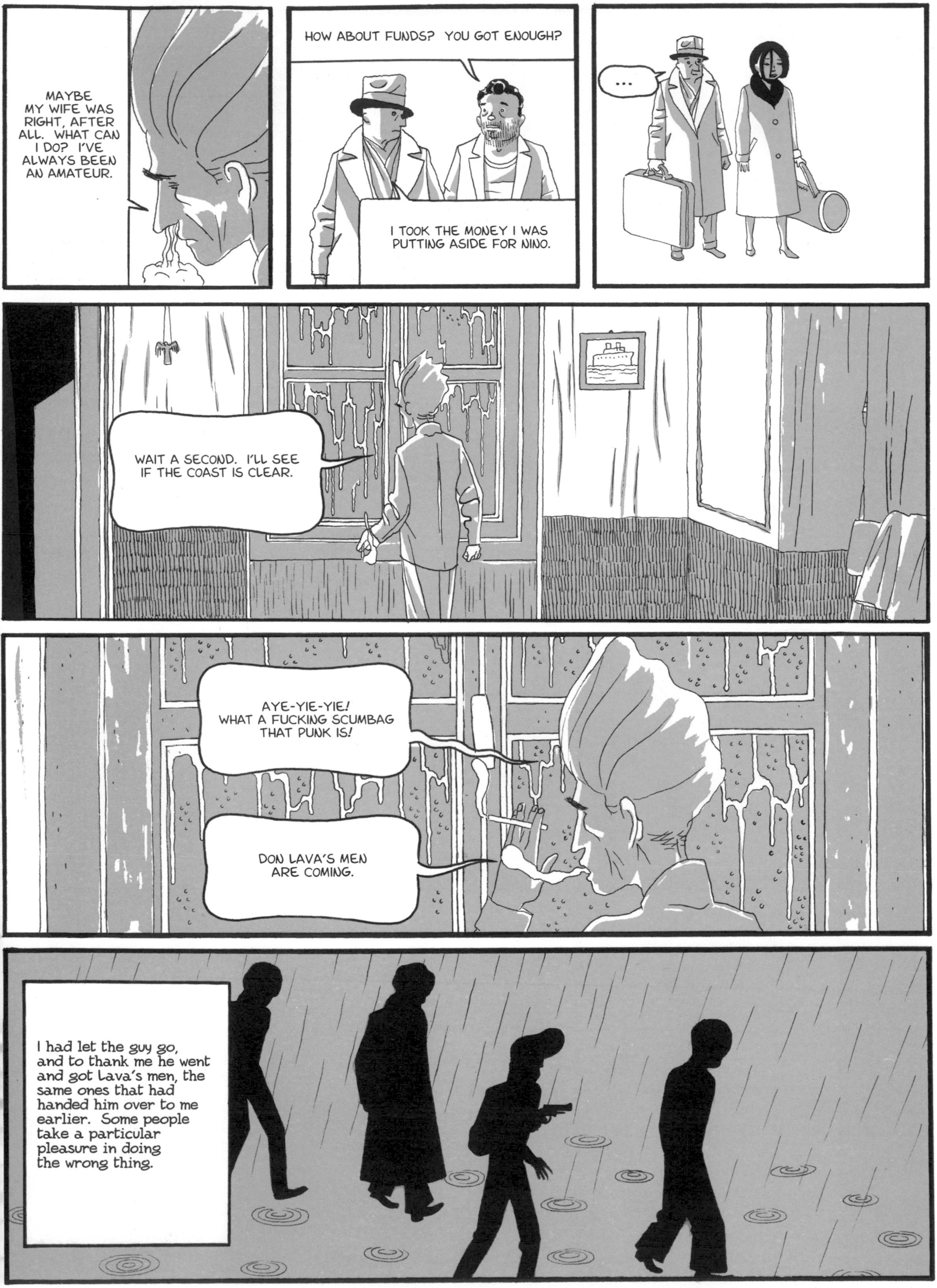
MAYBE MY WIFE WAS RIGHT, AFTER ALL. WHAT CAN I DO? I'VE ALWAYS BEEN AN AMATEUR.
HOW ABOUT FUNDS? YOU GOT ENOUGH?
I TOOK THE MONEY I WAS PUTTING ASIDE FOR NINO.
...
WAIT A SECOND. I'LL SEE IF THE COAST IS CLEAR.
AYE-YIE-YIE! WHAT A FUCKING SCUMBAG THAT PUNK IS!
DON LAVA'S MEN ARE COMING.
I had let the guy go, and to thank me he went and got Lava's men, the same ones that had handed him over to me earlier. Some people take a particular pleasure in doing the wrong thing.

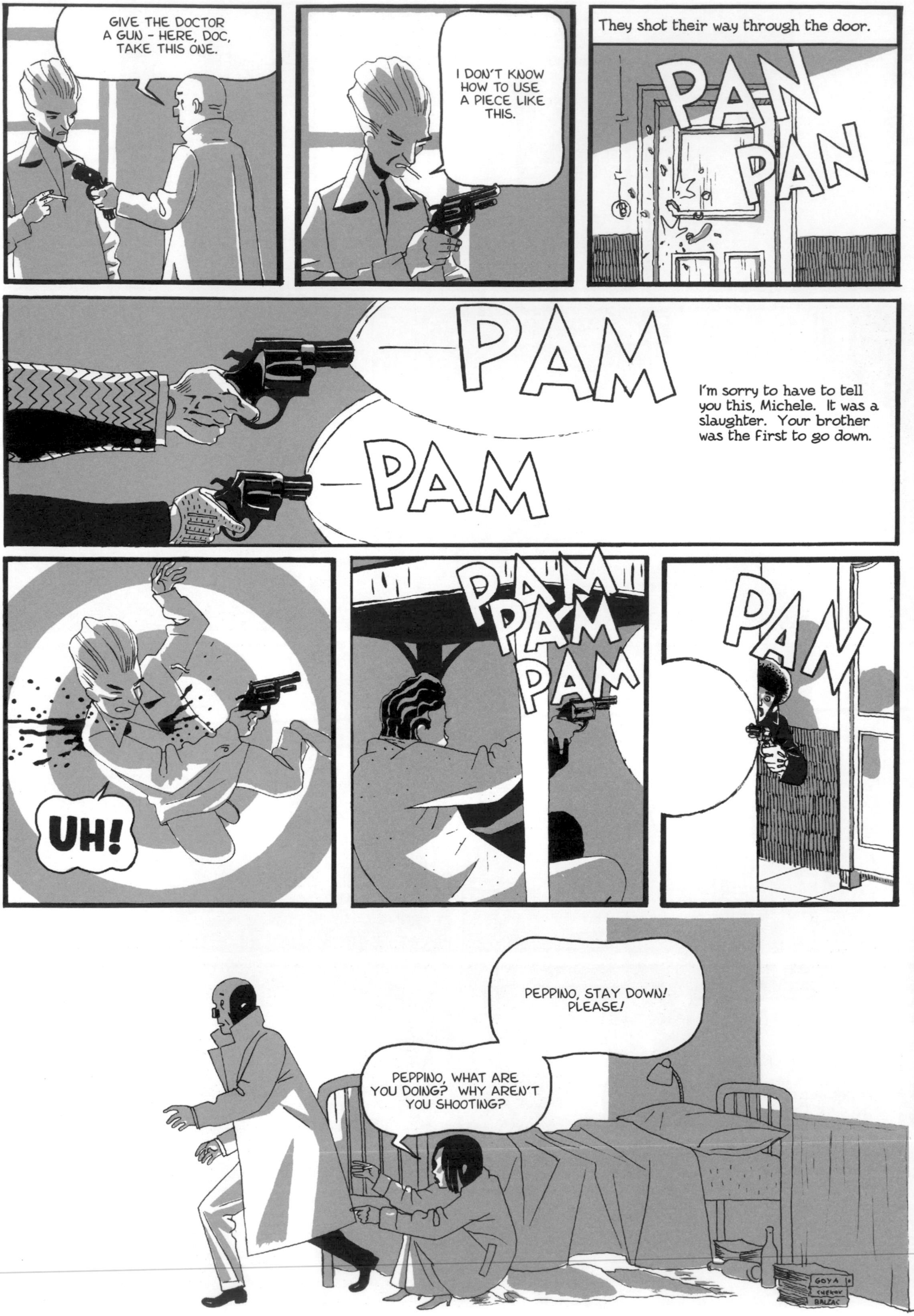
GIVE THE DOCTOR A GUN - HERE, DOC, TAKE THIS ONE.
I DON'T KNOW HOW TO USE A PIECE LIKE THIS.
They shot their way through the door.
PAN PAN
PAM
PAM
I'm sorry to have to tell you this, Michele. It was a slaughter. Your brother was the first to go down.
UH!
PAM PAM PAM
PAN
PEPPINO, STAY DOWN! PLEASE!
PEPPINO, WHAT ARE YOU DOING? WHY AREN'T YOU SHOOTING?

Like a halfwit, I walked across the room with bullets whistling all around me. Like a sleepwalker. I was lost, Michele. You see what I mean? Sometimes I think I shoulda died, then at least I wouldn't have to carry the weight of the things I did. Anyway, suddenly everything seemed like nonsense. All I knew was there was a man lying on the floor, wounded. I had to know if he was still alive. Don't misunderstand me. There wasn't nothing heroic in what I did. Just the ego of an old man who knows he's caused a lotta grief.

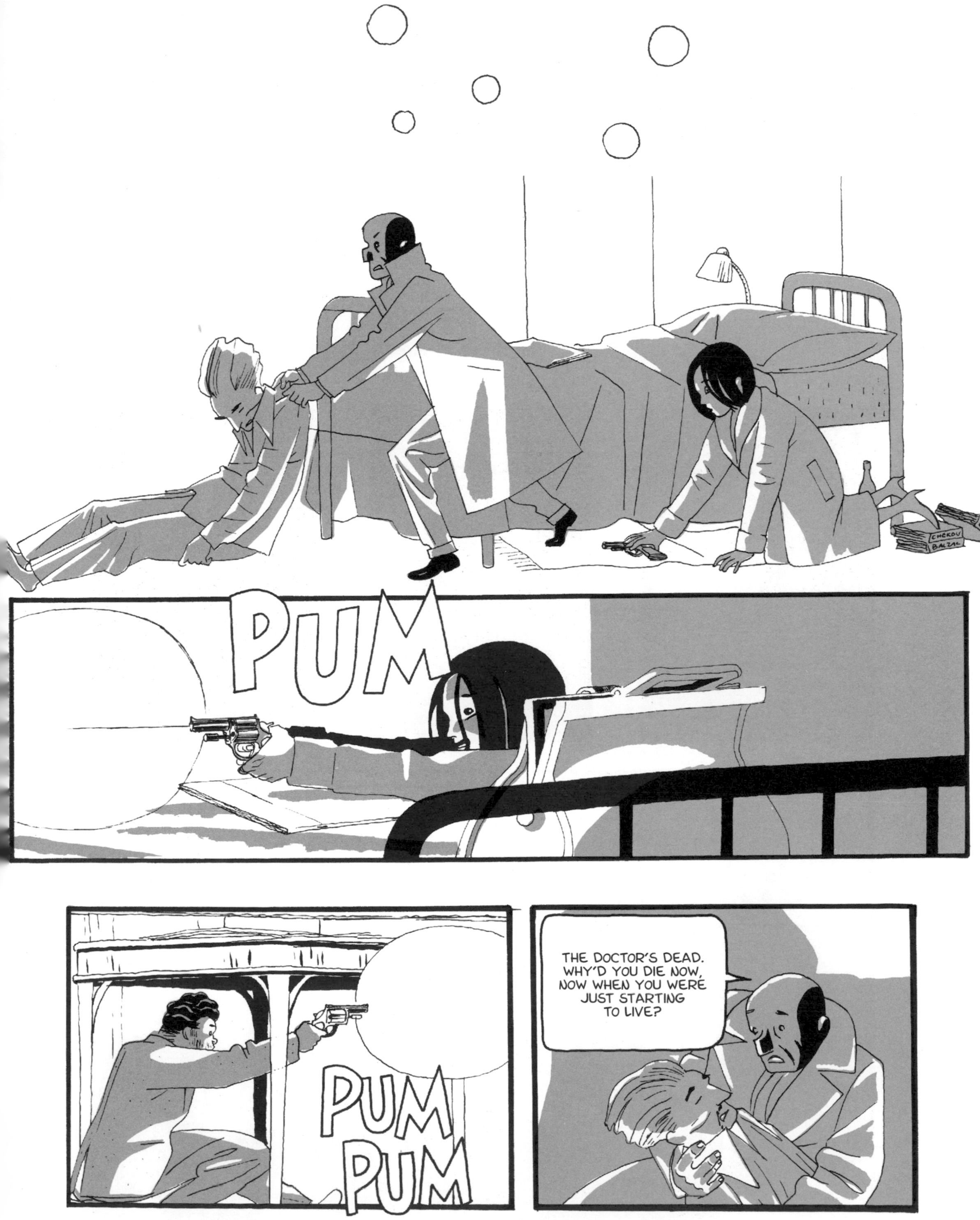
PUM
PUM PUM
THE DOCTOR'S DEAD. WHY'D YOU DIE NOW, NOW WHEN YOU WERE JUST STARTING TO LIVE?

Salvatore was shooting and howling like a maniac. He killed almost all of them and helped us get to our car. As for me, I felt as fragile as a baby. I had completely withdrawn from what was going on. Whenever I thought about the way I'd behaved recently, I got nauseated. What a waste of energy...and how horrible it is to realize you've been wrong about everything.

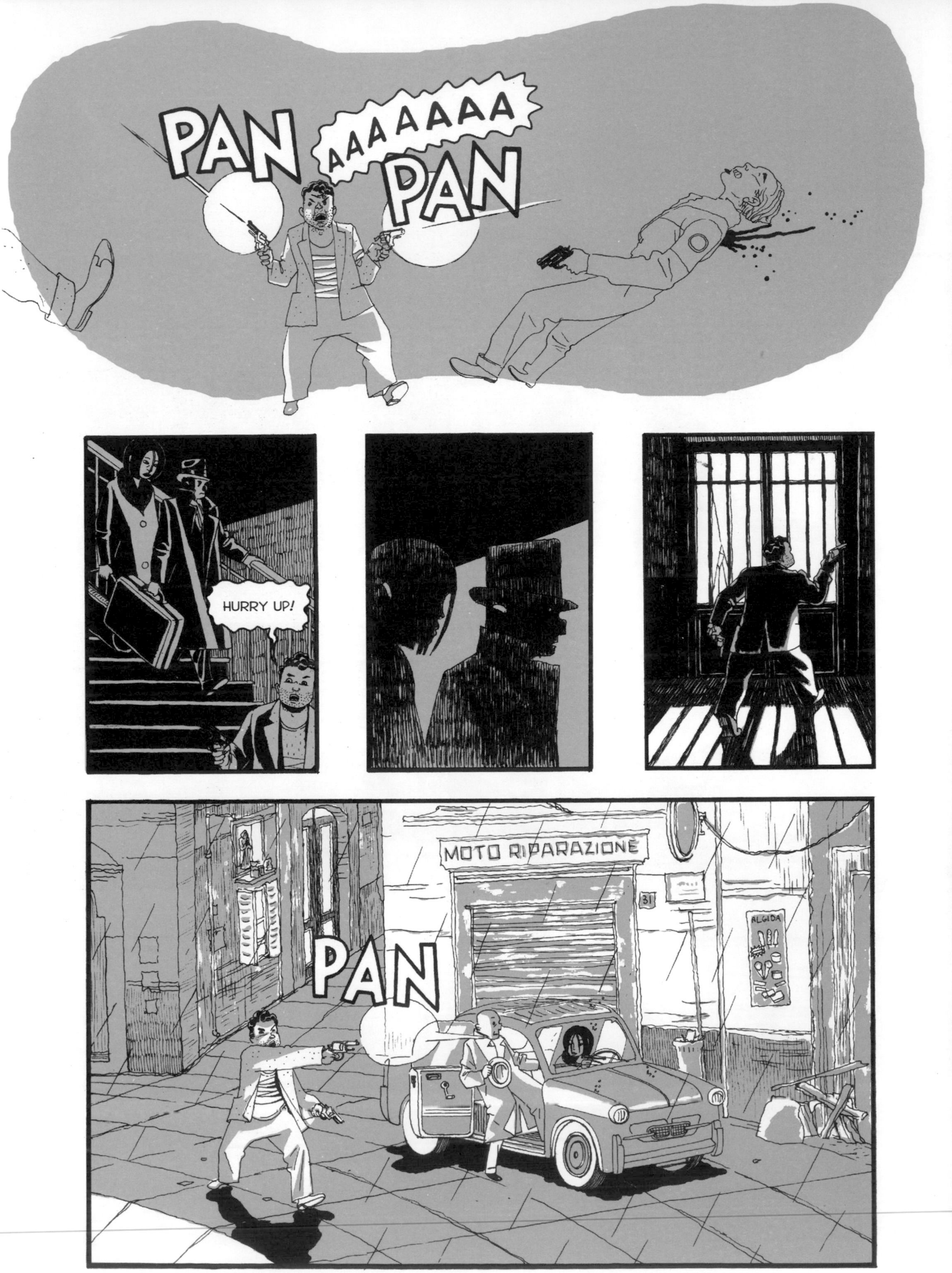
PAN
AAAAAAA
PAN
HURRY UP!
MOTO RIPARAZIONE
31
ALGIDA
PAN

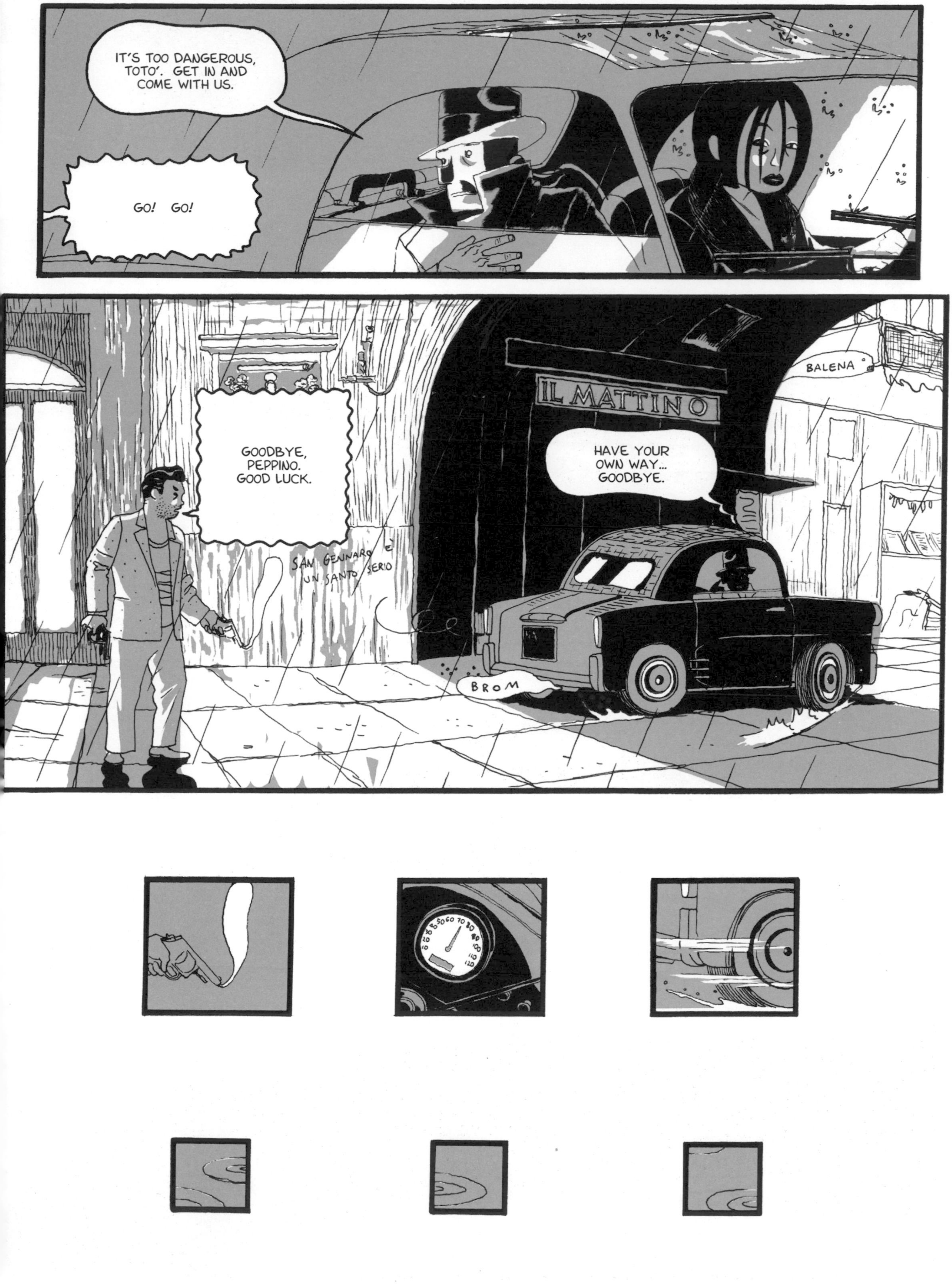
IT'S TOO DANGEROUS, TOTO'. GET IN AND COME WITH US.
GO! GO!
IL MATTINO
BALENA
GOODBYE, PEPPINO. GOOD LUCK.
HAVE YOUR OWN WAY... GOODBYE.
SAN GENNARO E' UN SANTO SERIO
BROM

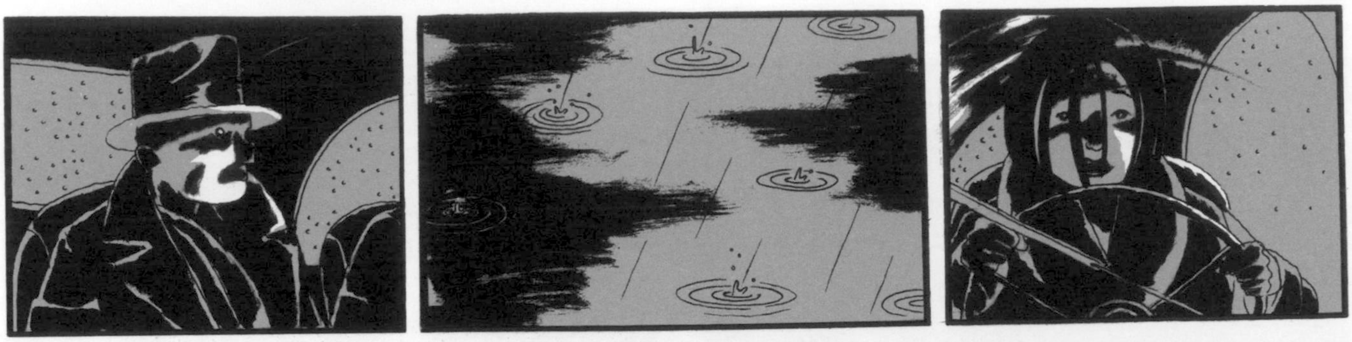

Toto' stayed behind to cover our escape, risking his life one more time, and I was ... it was like I was in shock. I remember it was raining. So much water. I'd never realized that I liked rain.

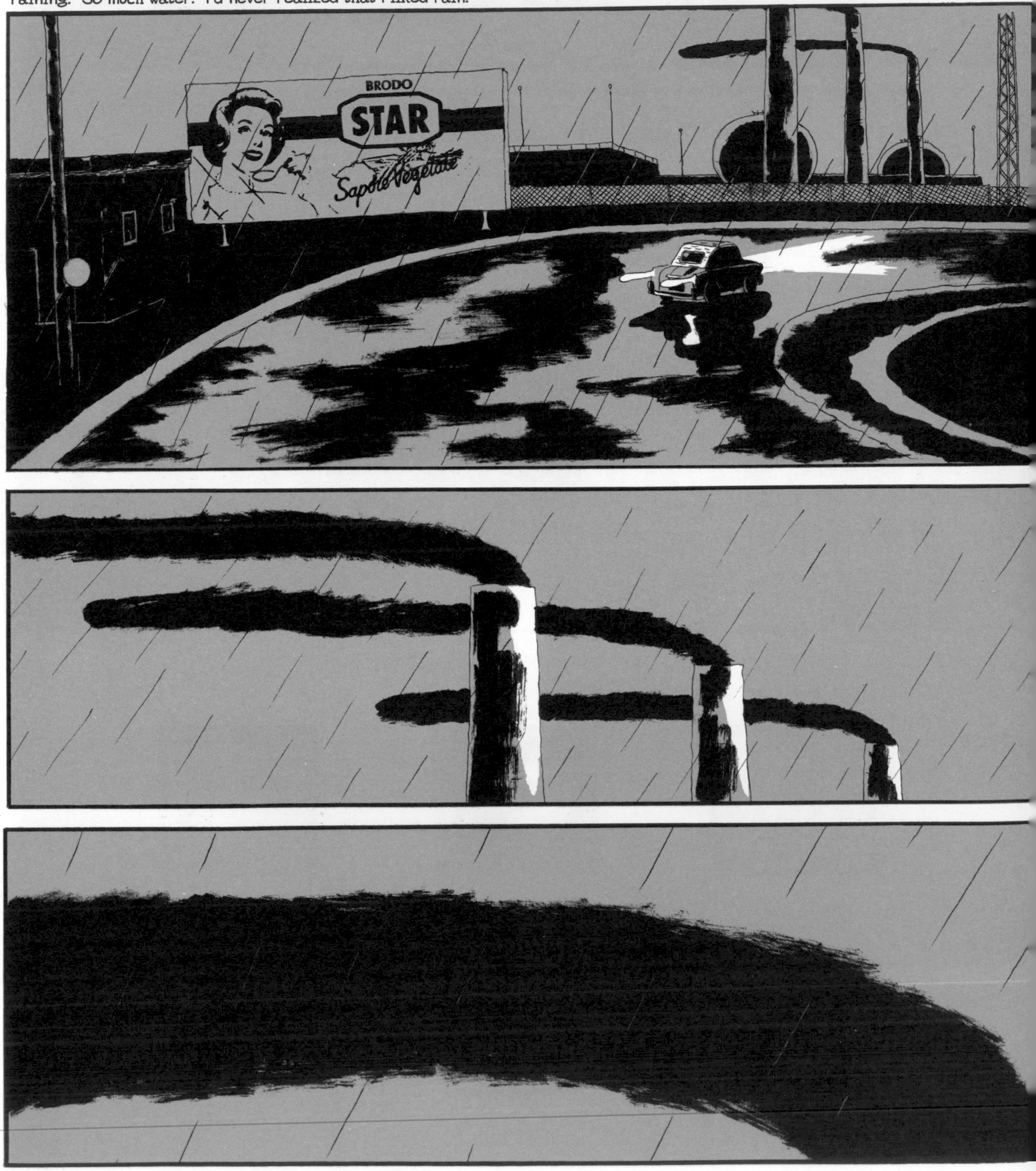
BRODO
STAR
Sapore Vegetale

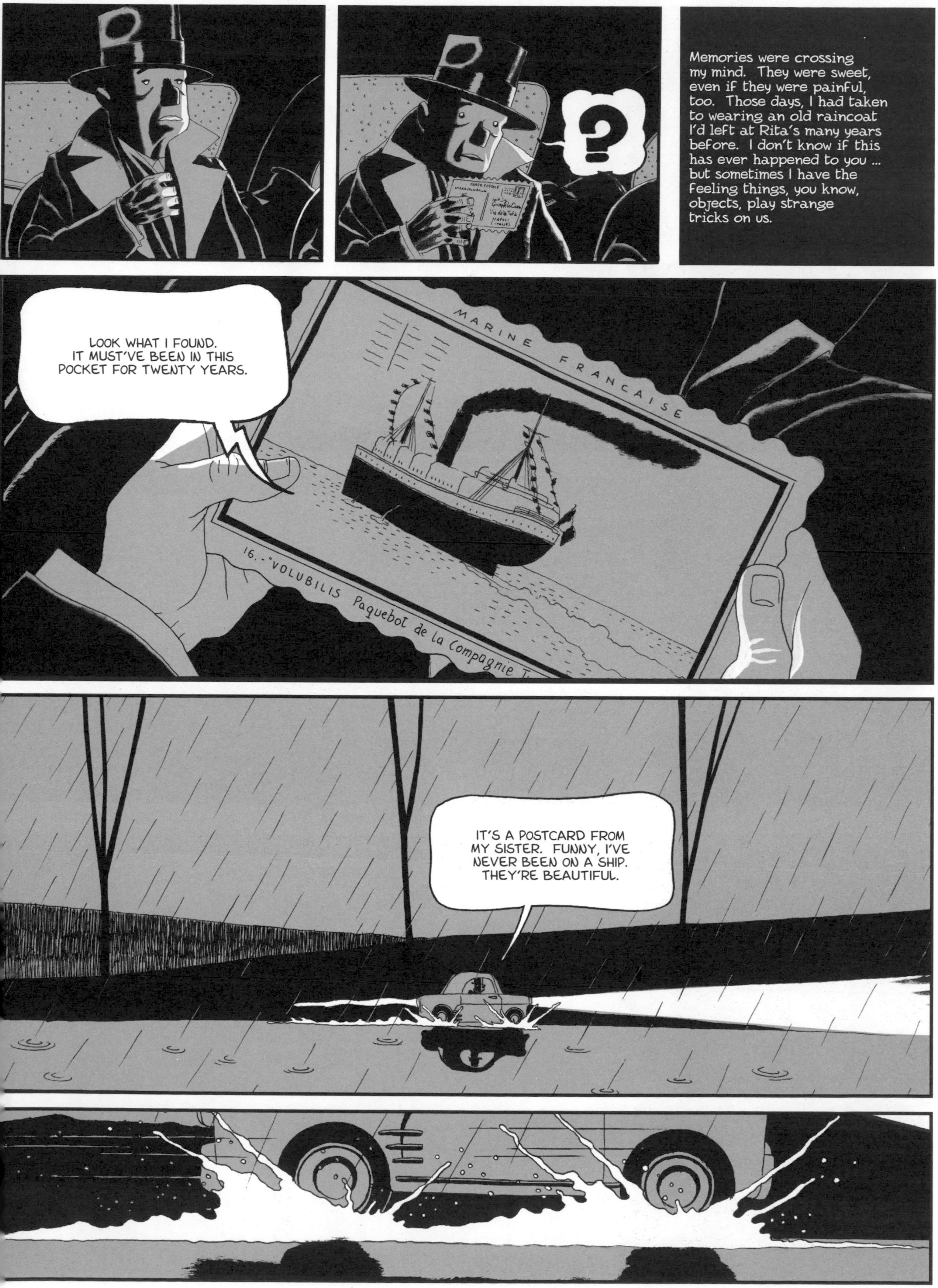

?
Memories were crossing my mind. They were sweet, even if they were painful, too. Those days, I had taken to wearing an old raincoat I'd left at Rita's many years before. I don't know if this has ever happened to you ... but sometimes I have the feeling things, you know, objects, play strange tricks on us.
LOOK WHAT I FOUND. IT MUST'VE BEEN IN THIS POCKET FOR TWENTY YEARS.
MARINE FRANCAISE
16.-"VOLUBILIS Paquebot de la Compagnie
IT'S A POSTCARD FROM MY SISTER. FUNNY, I'VE NEVER BEEN ON A SHIP. THEY'RE BEAUTIFUL.

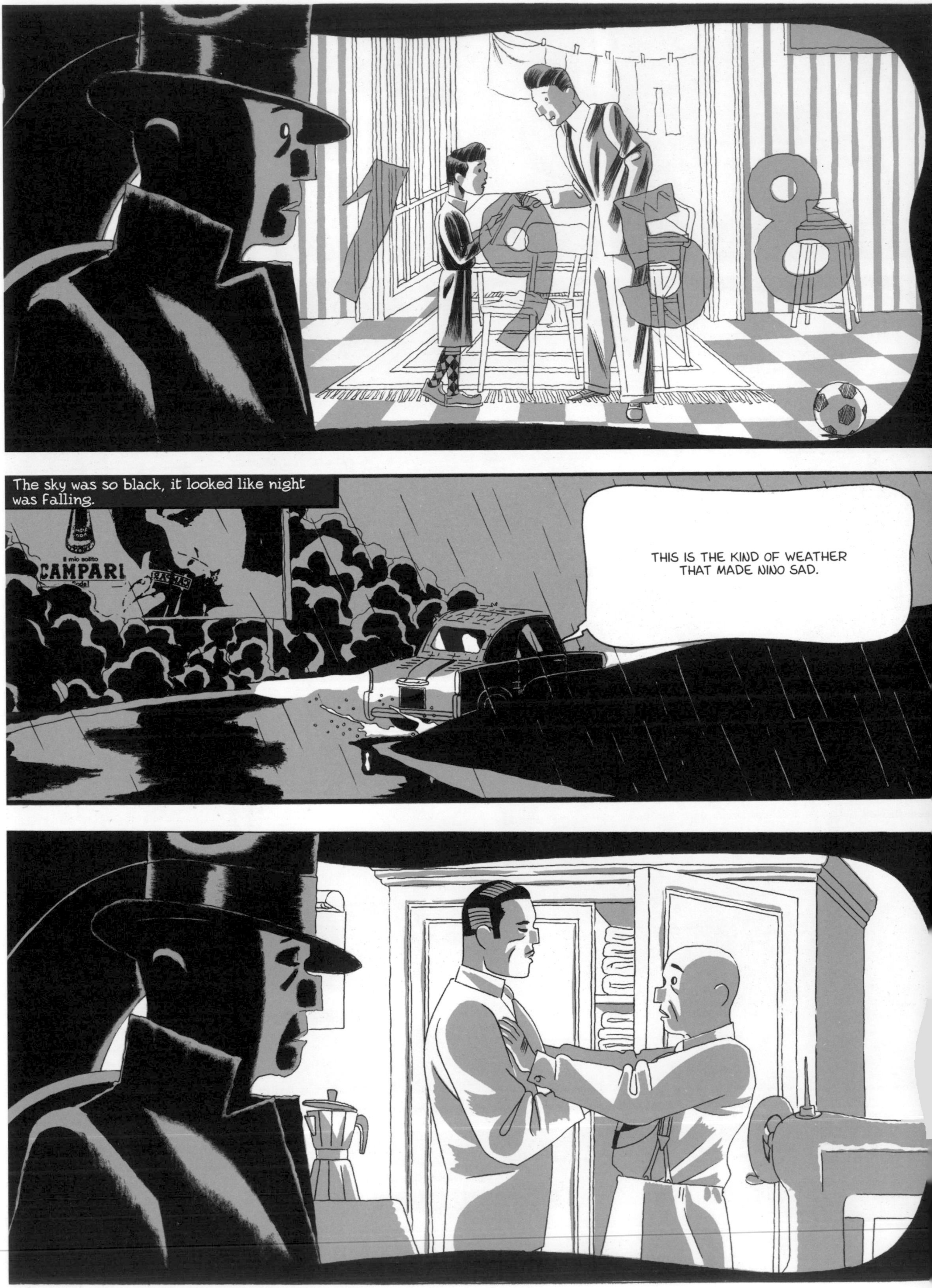
The sky was so black, it looked like night was falling.
Il mio solito
CAMPARI
THIS IS THE KIND OF WEATHER THAT MADE NINO SAD.

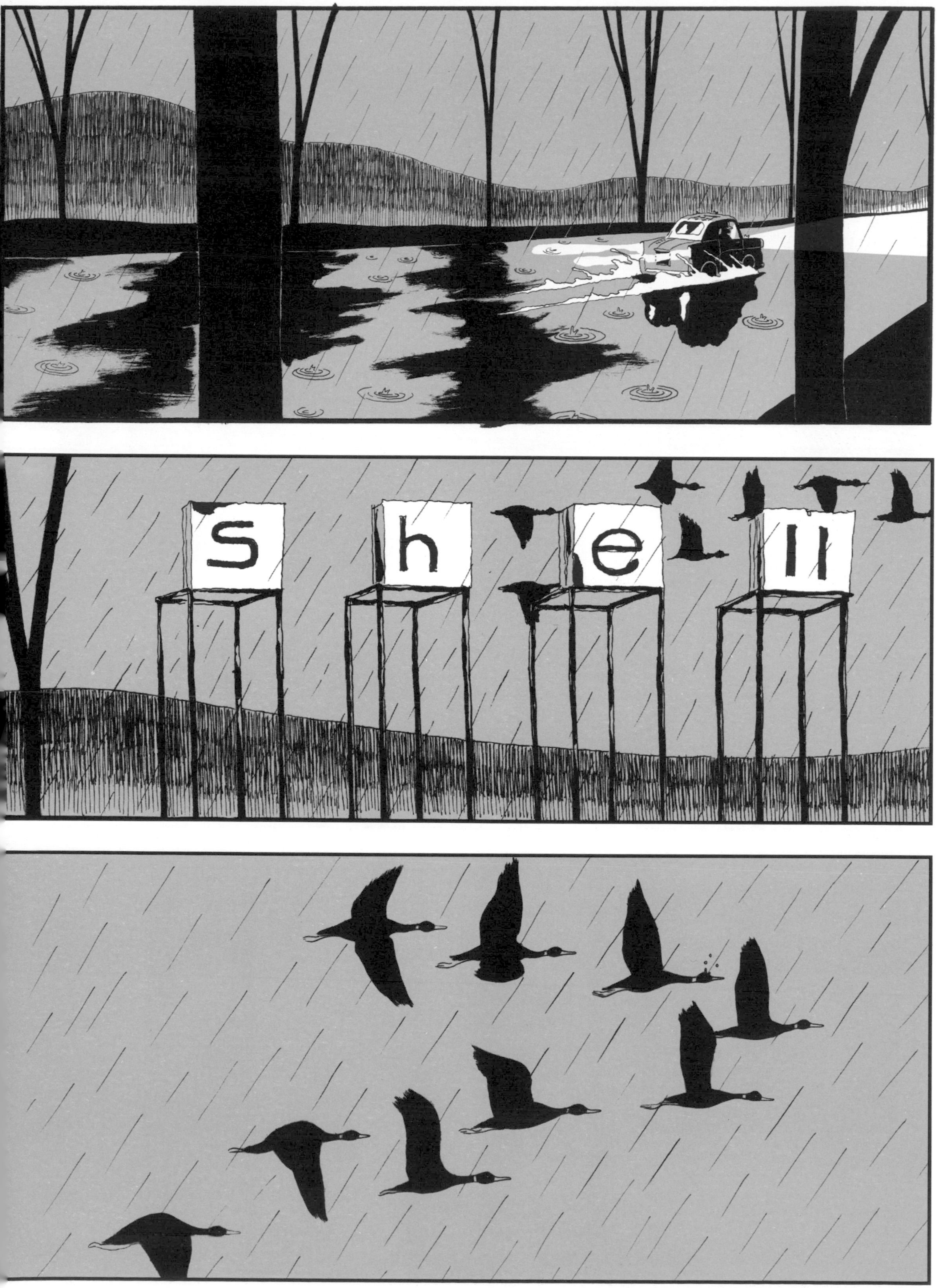
s h e ll

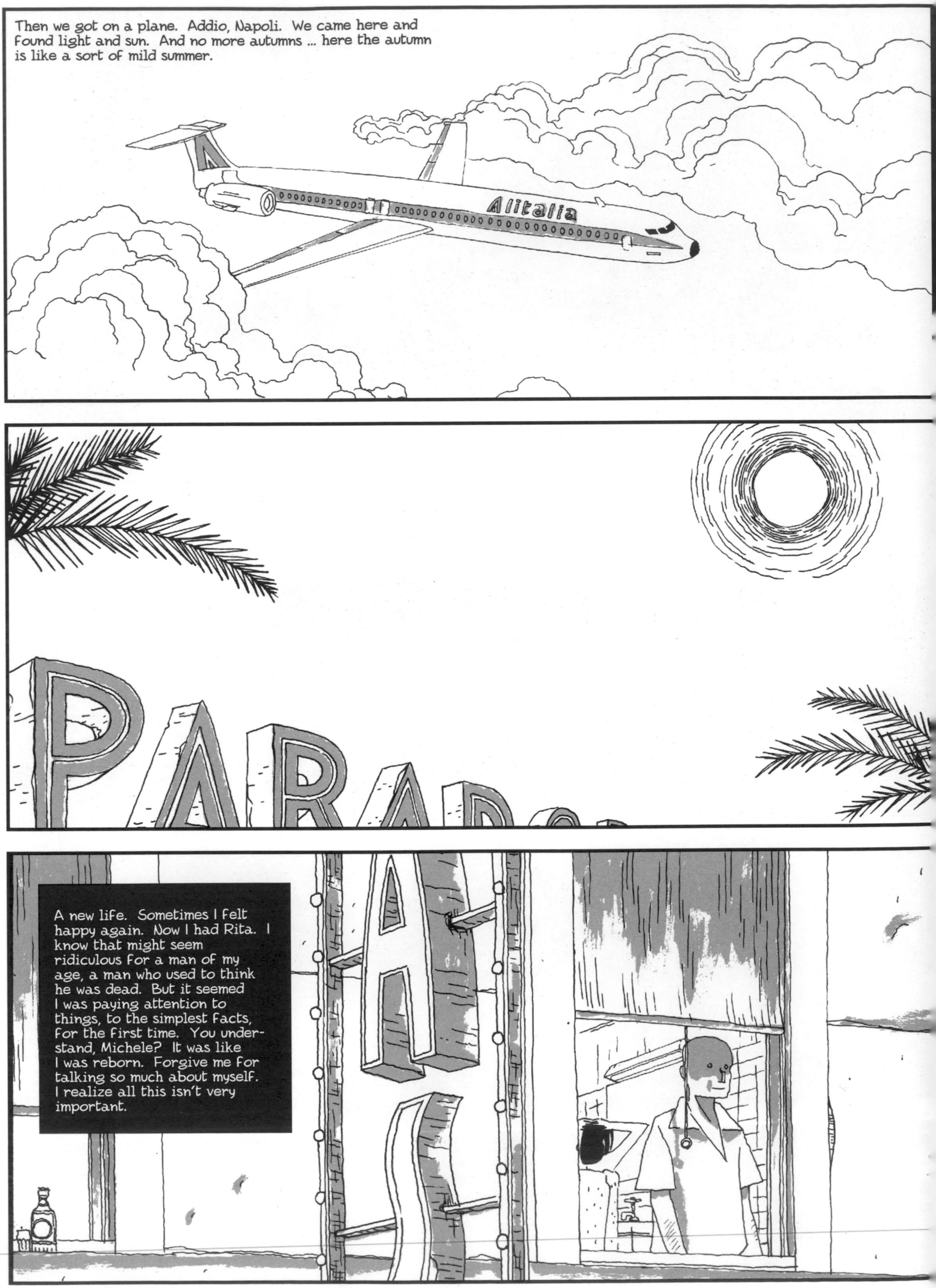
Then we got on a plane. Addio, Napoli. We came here and found light and sun. And no more autumns ... here the autumn is like a sort of mild summer.
Alitalia
A new life. Sometimes I felt happy again. Now I had Rita. I know that might seem ridiculous for a man of my age, a man who used to think he was dead. But it seemed I was paying attention to things, to the simplest facts, for the first time. You understand, Michele? It was like I was reborn. Forgive me for talking so much about myself. I realize all this isn't very important.

Time passed, and I tried to forget. I didn't have the courage to look you up. What could I say to you? Hello, I'm Peppino Lo Cicero. Your brother died because of me.

So I hesitated for a month....

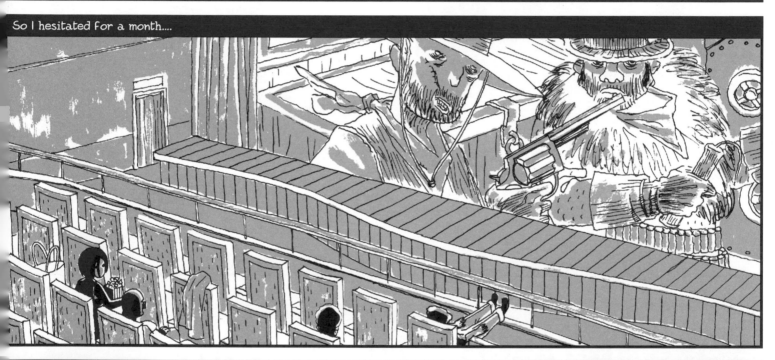

But then I thought that the doctor would've wanted us to meet. I didn't know you and he had been out of touch for so long....

MORE THAN TWENTY-FIVE YEARS. FOR A STUPID REASON. IT WAS OVER A WOMAN... WHAT IDIOTS...

I GOTTA TELL YOU, YOUR BROTHER WAS A GOOD MAN, MICHELE. PEOPLE LIKE HIM ARE RARE.

I'M SORRY. I DIDN'T WANNA RUIN YOUR DAY.

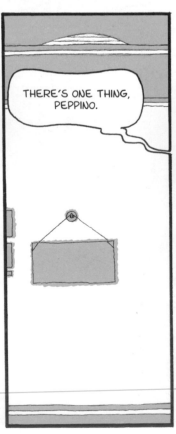

THERE'S ONE THING, PEPPINO.

SAY IT.

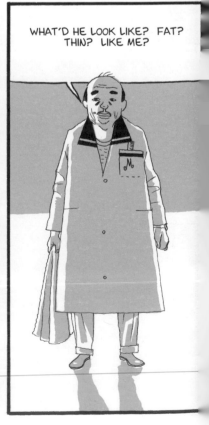

WHAT'D HE LOOK LIKE? FAT? THIN? LIKE ME?

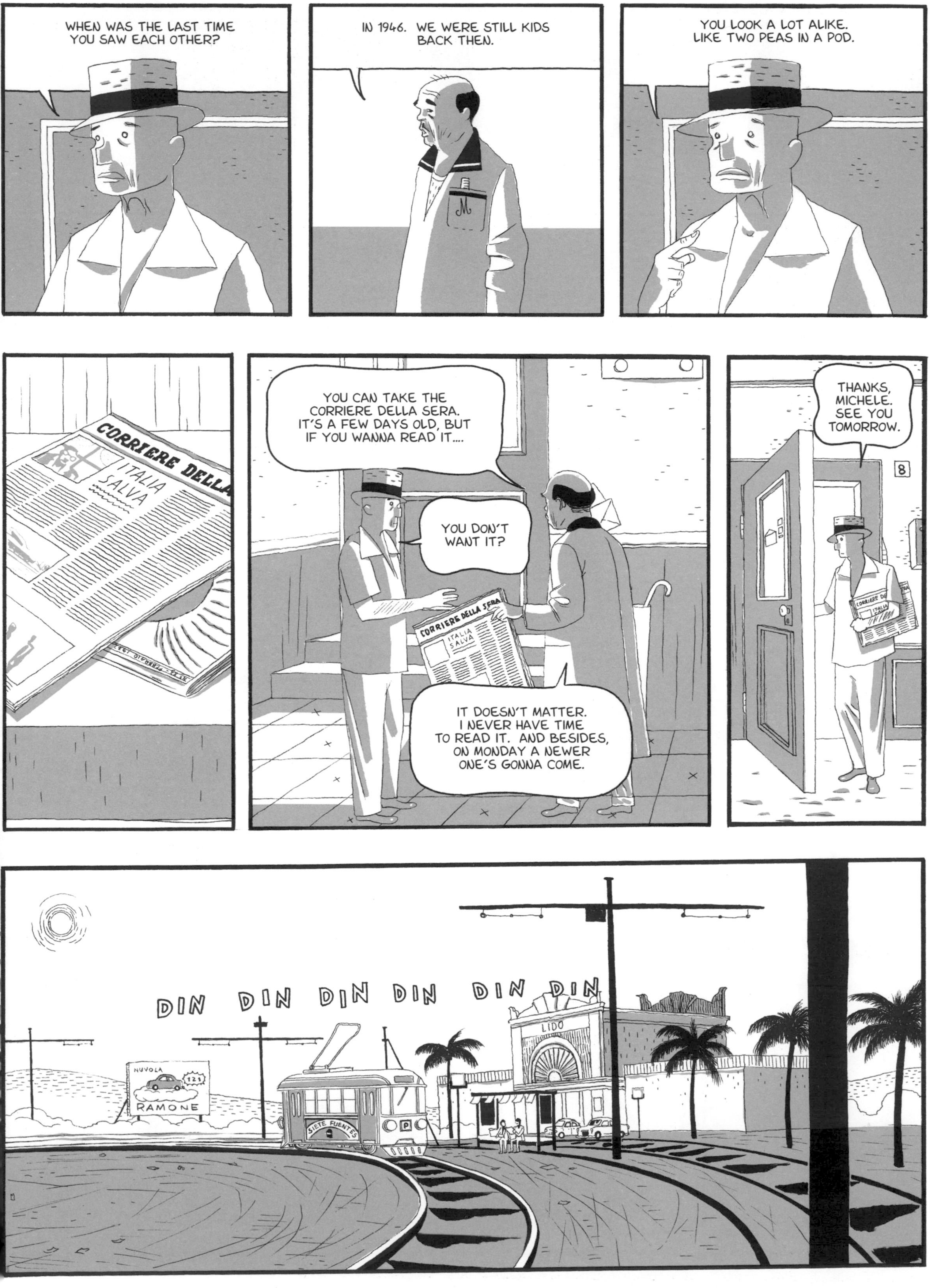
WHEN WAS THE LAST TIME YOU SAW EACH OTHER?
IN 1946. WE WERE STILL KIDS BACK THEN.
YOU LOOK A LOT ALIKE. LIKE TWO PEAS IN A POD.
CORRIERE DELLA
ITALIA SALVA
YOU CAN TAKE THE CORRIERE DELLA SERA. IT'S A FEW DAYS OLD, BUT IF YOU WANNA READ IT....
YOU DON'T WANT IT?
CORRIERE DELLA SERA
IT DOESN'T MATTER. I NEVER HAVE TIME TO READ IT. AND BESIDES, ON MONDAY A NEWER ONE'S GONNA COME.
THANKS, MICHELE. SEE YOU TOMORROW.
8
DIN DIN DIN DIN DIN DIN
NUVOLA
RAMONE
LIDO
SIETE FUENTES

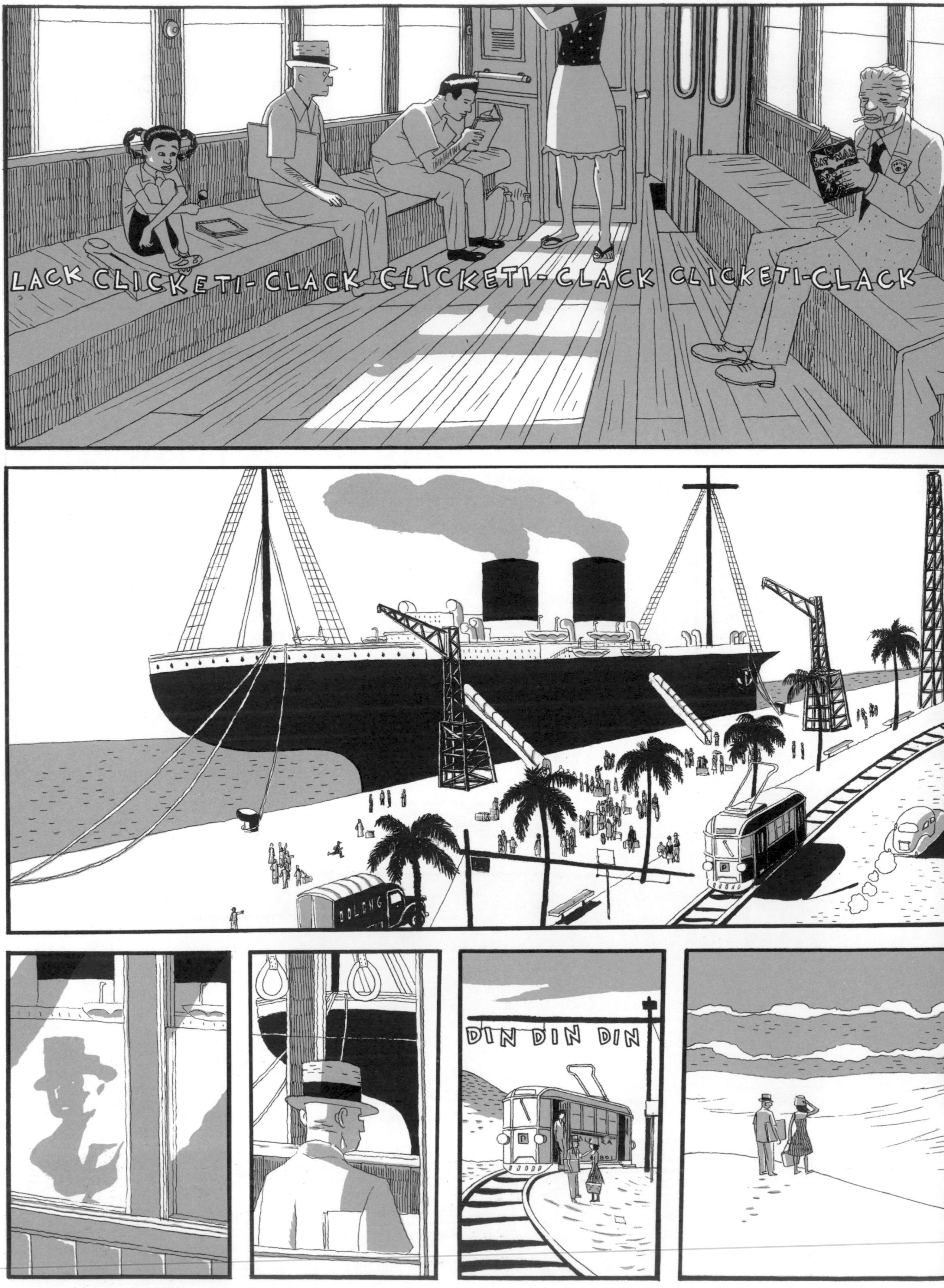
LACK CLICKETI-CLACK CLICKETI-CLACK CLICKETI-CLACK
DIN DIN DIN

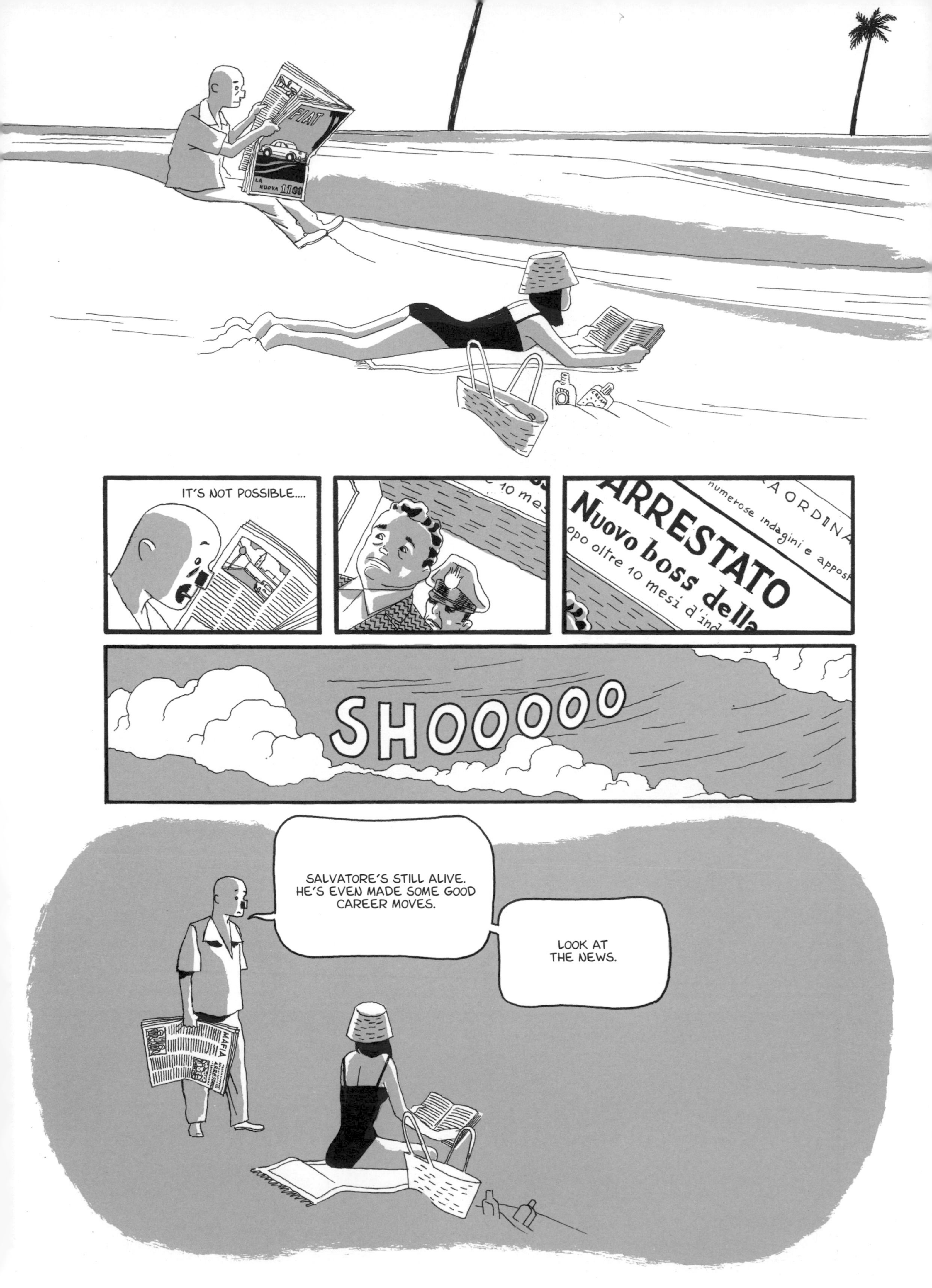
FIAT
LA NUOVA 1100
IT'S NOT POSSIBLE....
ARRESTATO
Nuovo boss della
SHOOOOO
SALVATORE'S STILL ALIVE. HE'S EVEN MADE SOME GOOD CAREER MOVES.
LOOK AT THE NEWS.
MAFIA

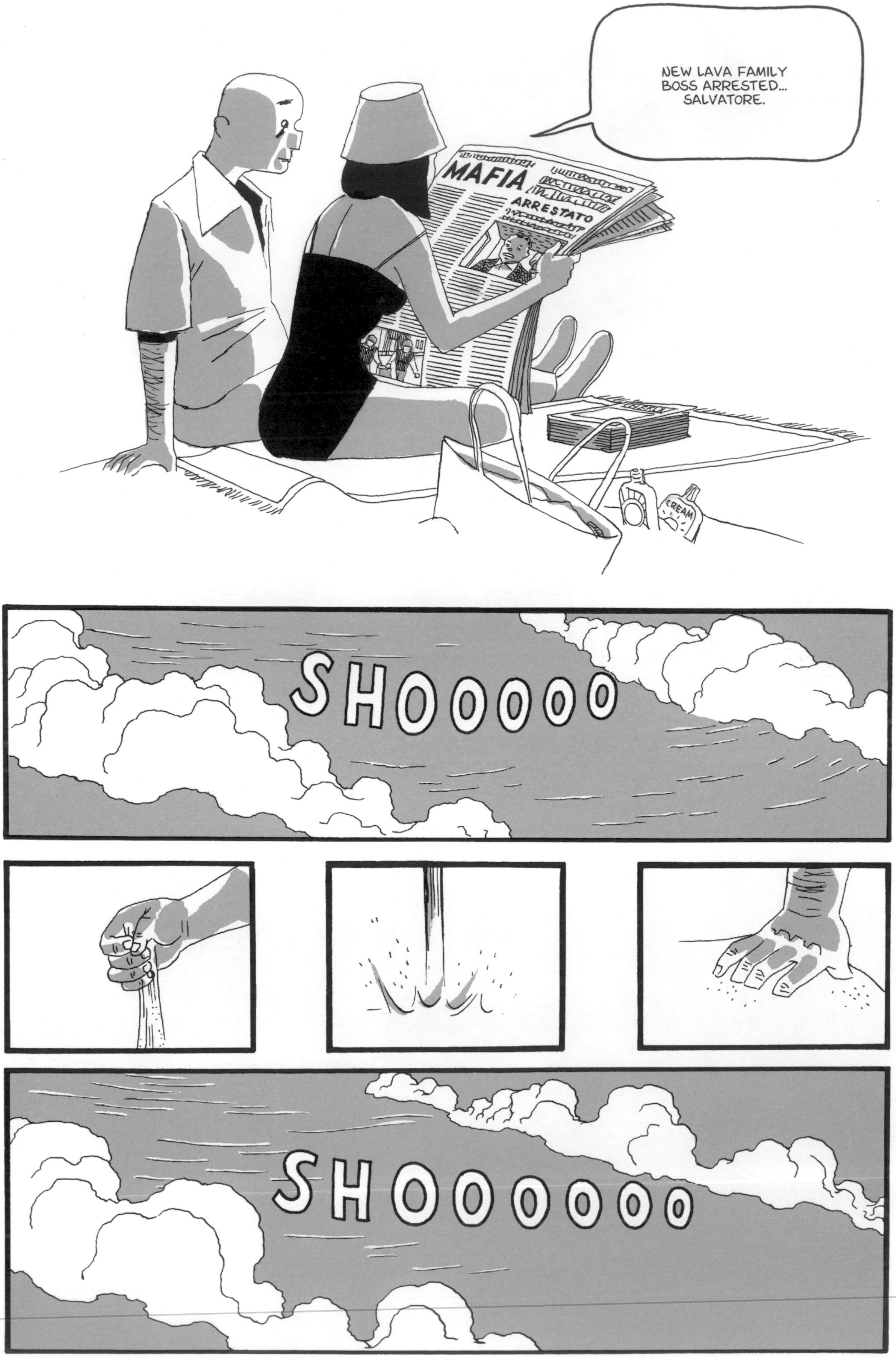
NEW LAVA FAMILY BOSS ARRESTED... SALVATORE.
MAFIA
ARRESTATO
CREAM
SHOOOOO
SHOOOOOO

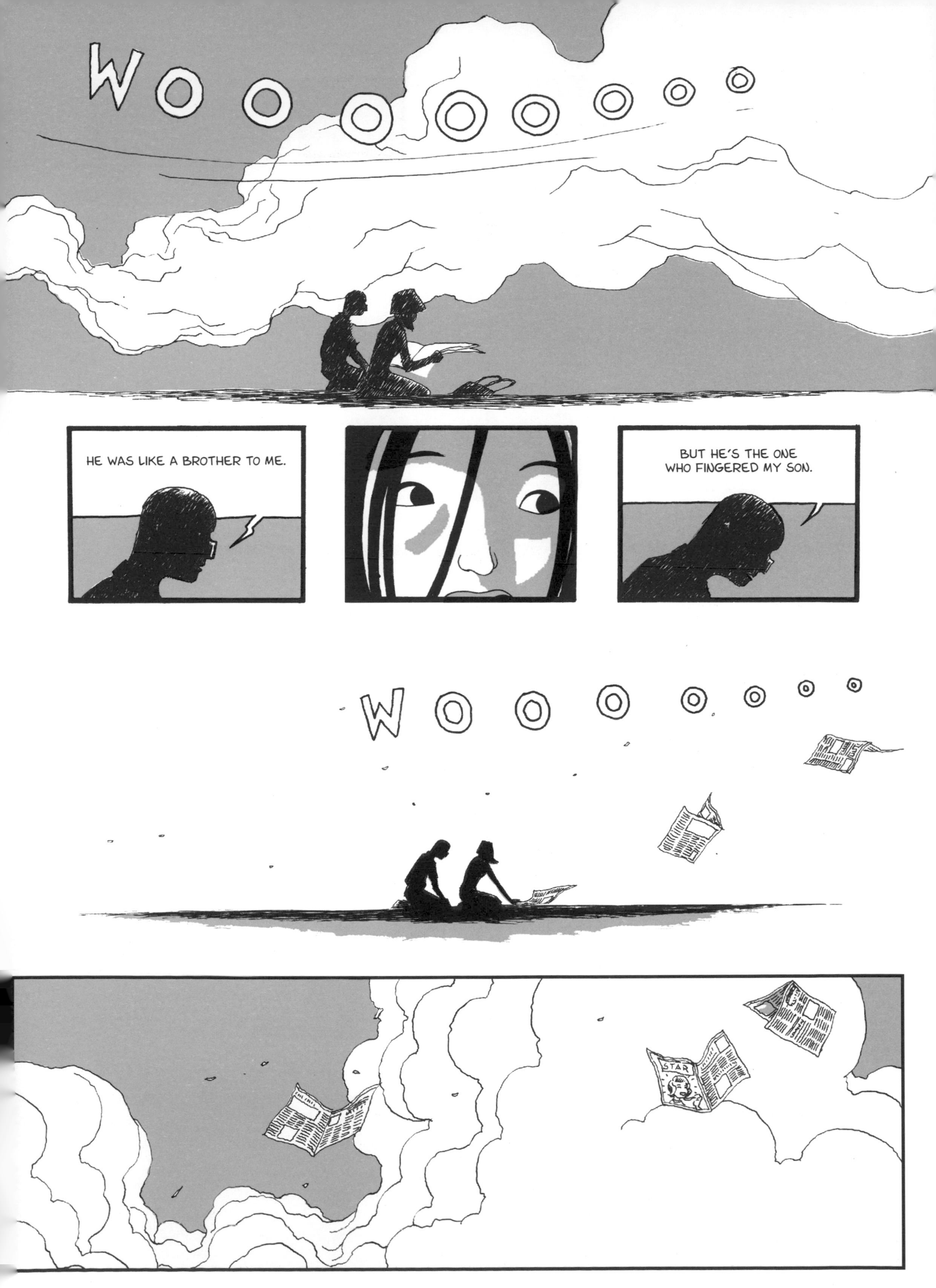
WOOOOOOOO
HE WAS LIKE A BROTHER TO ME.
BUT HE'S THE ONE WHO FINGERED MY SON.
WOOOOOOO
STAR

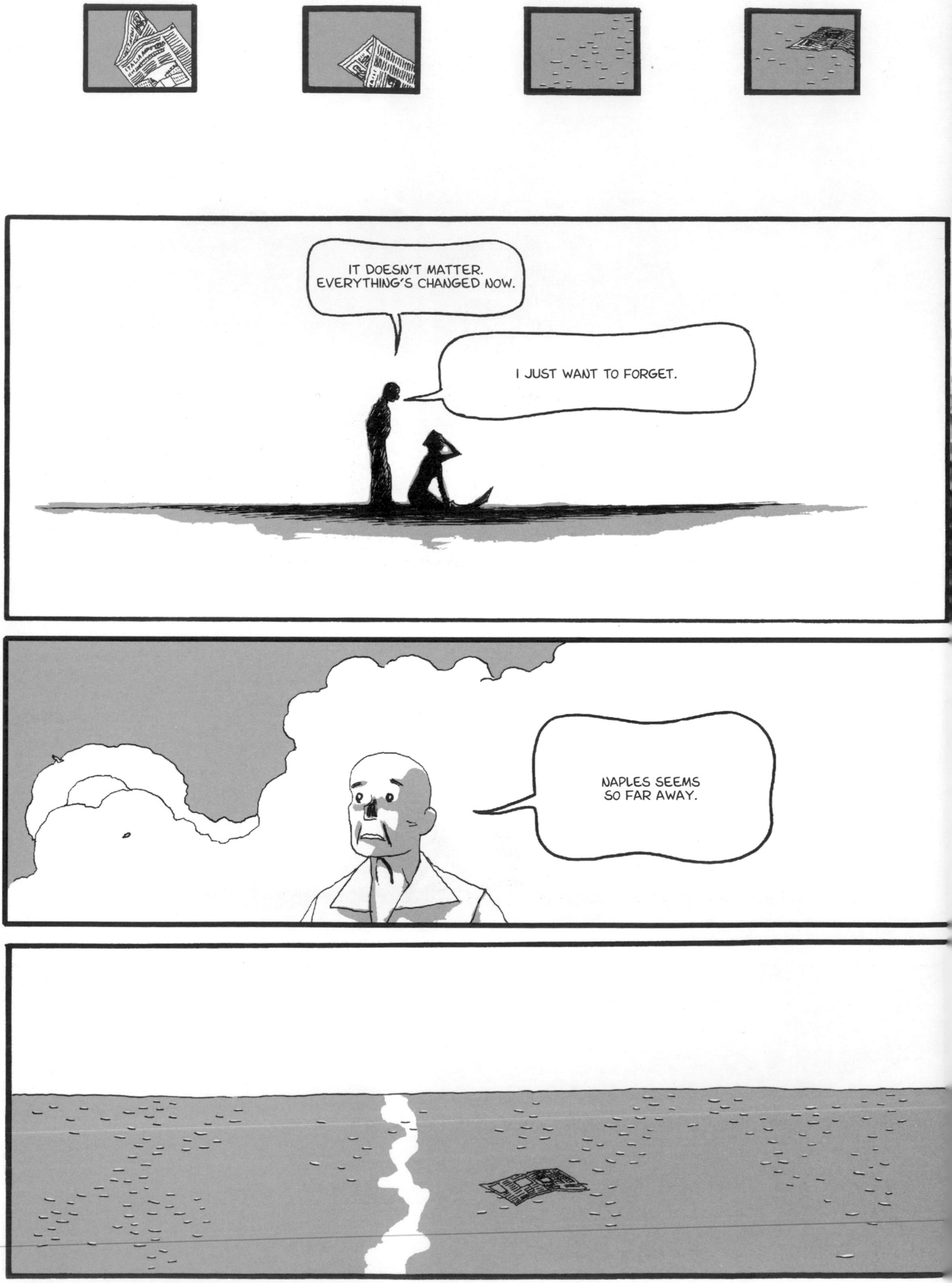
IT DOESN'T MATTER. EVERYTHING'S CHANGED NOW.
I JUST WANT TO FORGET.
NAPLES SEEMS SO FAR AWAY.

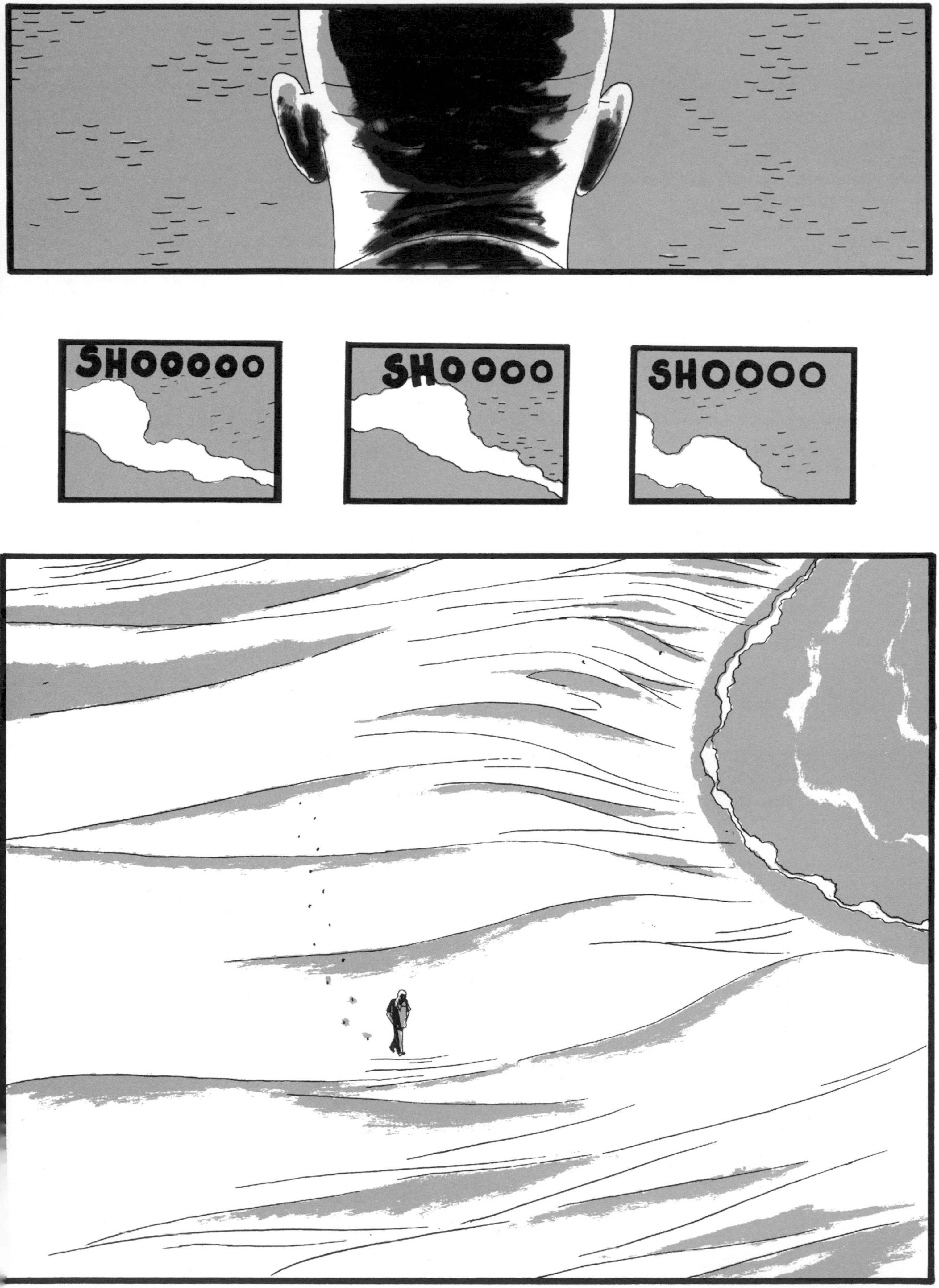
SHOOOOO
SHOOOO
SHOOOO

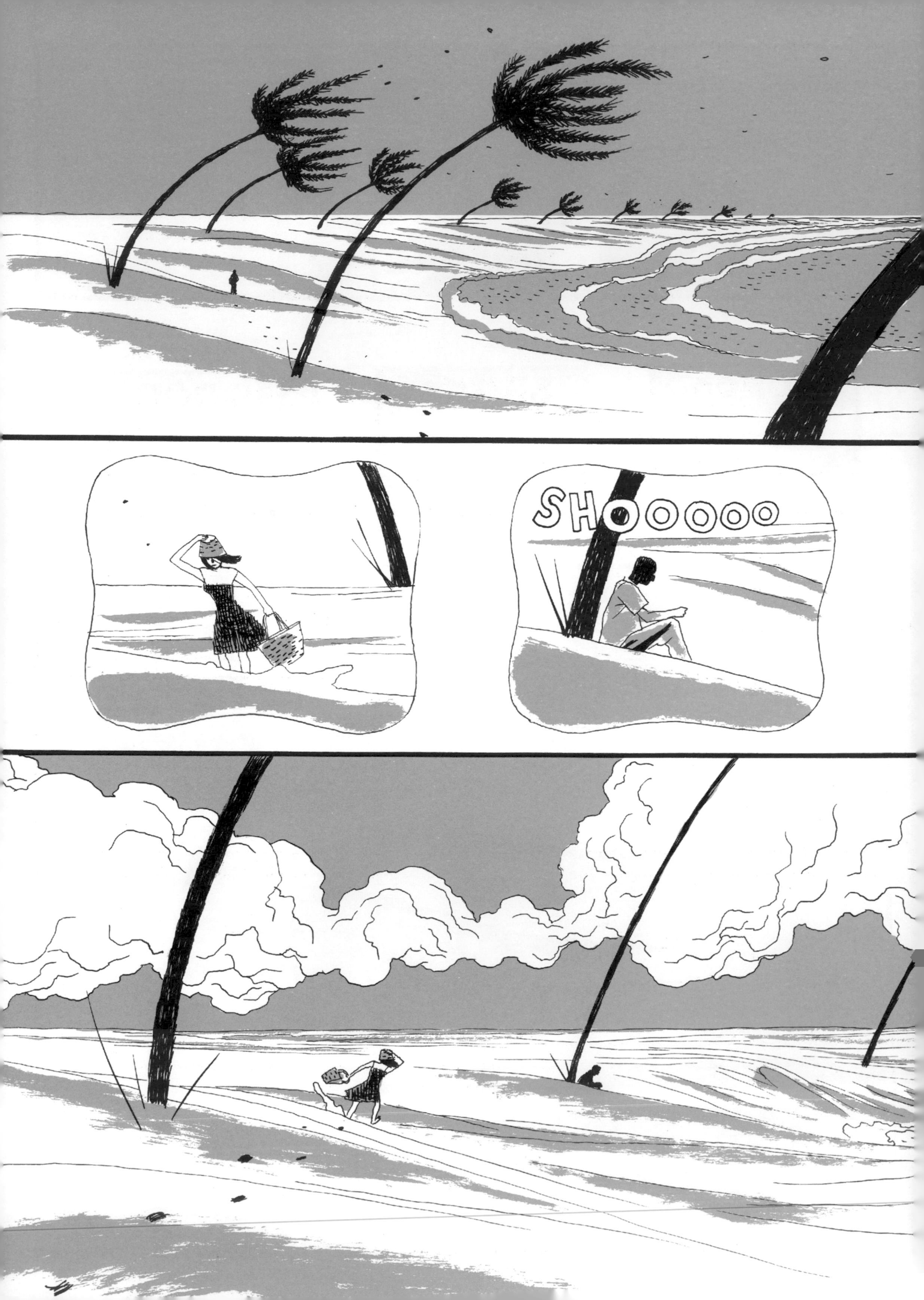
SHOOOOO

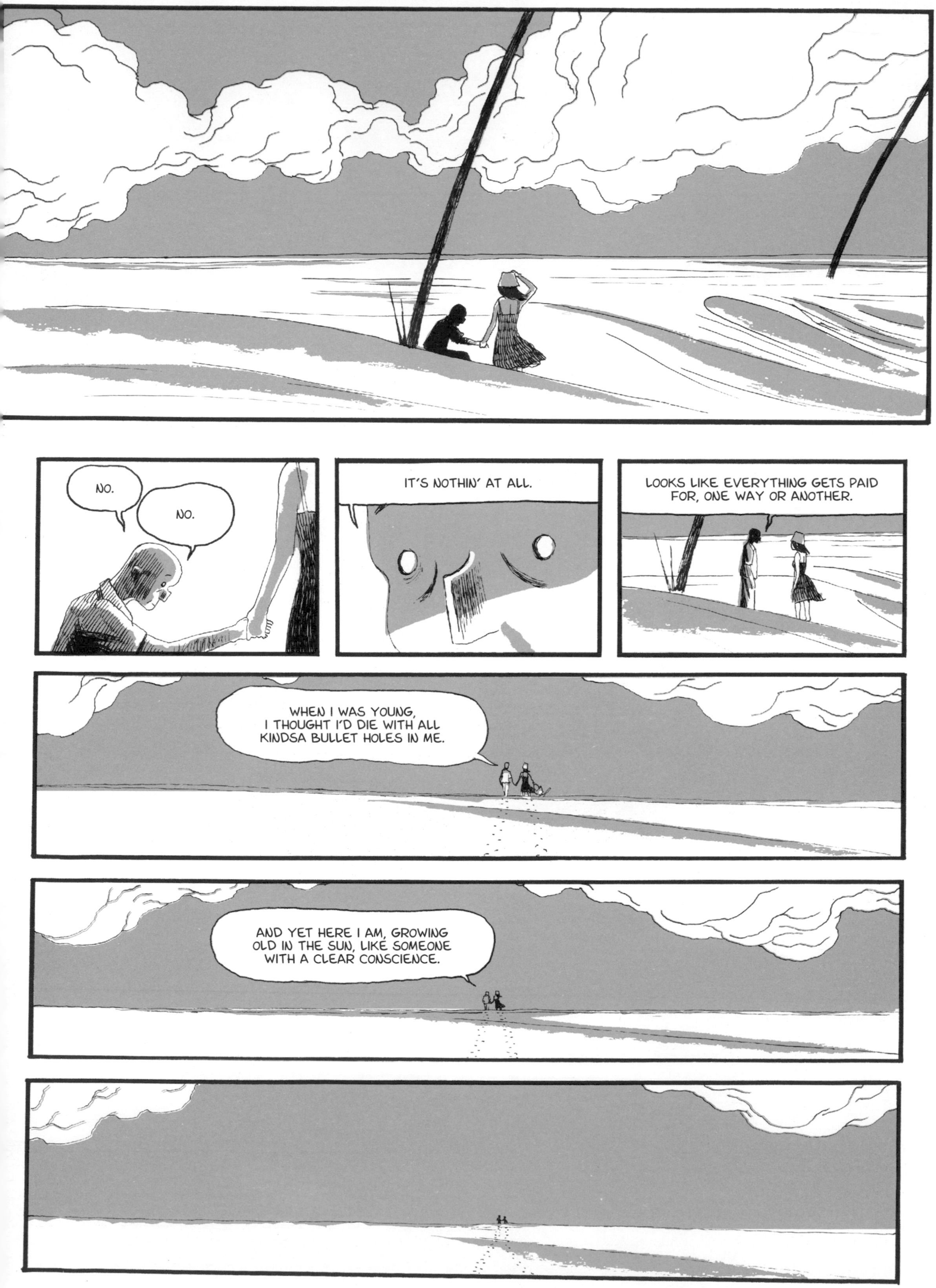
NO.
NO.
IT'S NOTHIN' AT ALL.
LOOKS LIKE EVERYTHING GETS PAID FOR, ONE WAY OR ANOTHER.
WHEN I WAS YOUNG, I THOUGHT I'D DIE WITH ALL KINDSA BULLET HOLES IN ME.
AND YET HERE I AM, GROWING OLD IN THE SUN, LIKE SOMEONE WITH A CLEAR CONSCIENCE.

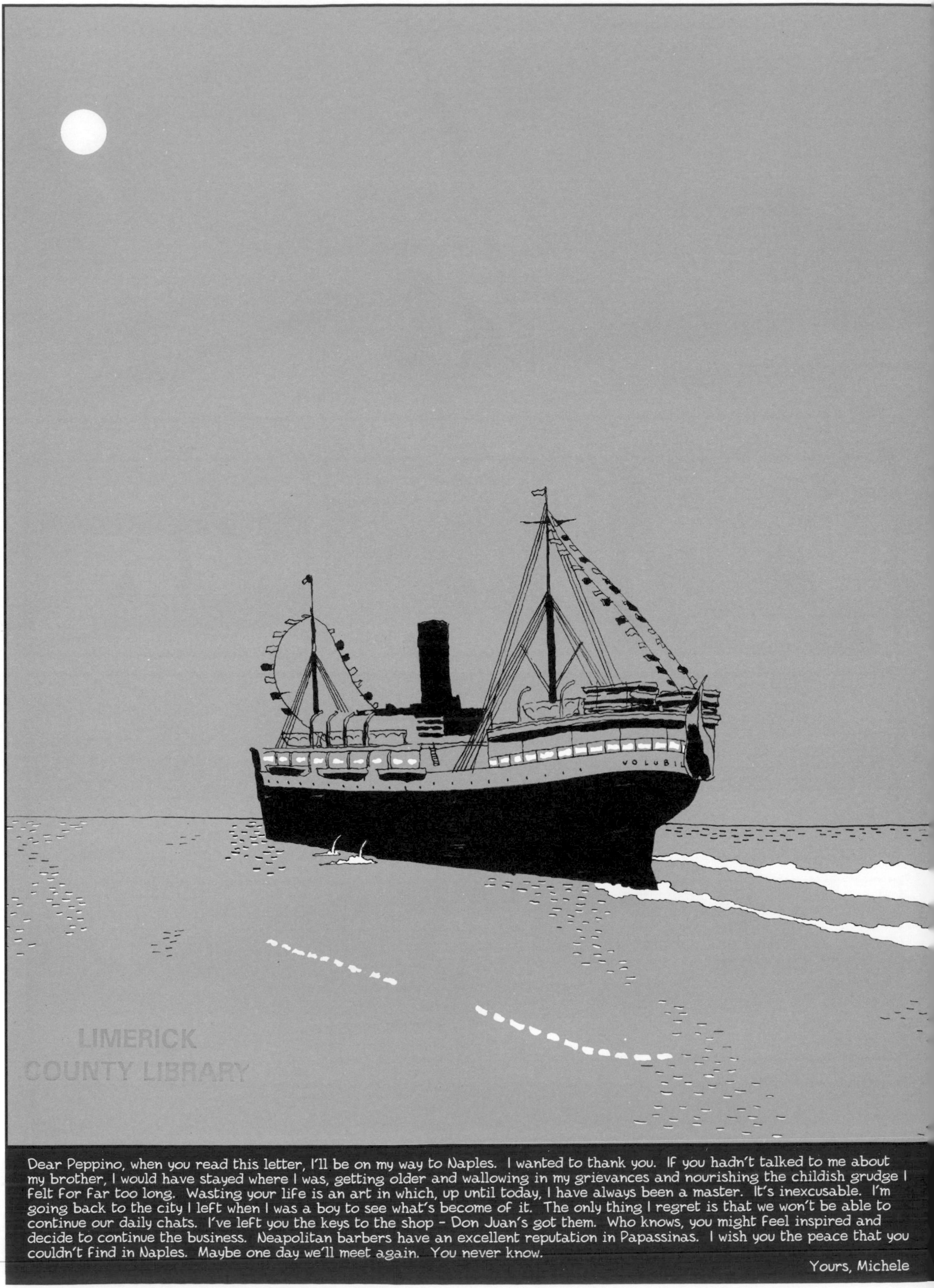
VOLUBIL
Dear Peppino, when you read this letter, I'll be on my way to Naples. I wanted to thank you. If you hadn't talked to me about my brother, I would have stayed where I was, getting older and wallowing in my grievances and nourishing the childish grudge I felt for far too long. Wasting your life is an art in which, up until today, I have always been a master. It's inexcusable. I'm going back to the city I left when I was a boy to see what's become of it. The only thing I regret is that we won't be able to continue our daily chats. I've left you the keys to the shop - Don Juan's got them. Who knows, you might feel inspired and decide to continue the business. Neapolitan barbers have an excellent reputation in Papassinas. I wish you the peace that you couldn't find in Naples. Maybe one day we'll meet again. You never know.
Yours, Michele